THE HEROIC GANGSTER

ALSO BY NEIL HANSON

The Confident Hope of a Miracle

Unknown Soldiers

THE HEROIC GANGSTER

THE STORY OF MONK EASTMAN, FROM THE STREETS OF NEW YORK TO THE BATTLEFIELDS OF EUROPE AND BACK

NEIL HANSON

Skyhorse Publishing

For the members of my gang:
Lynn, Jack, and Drew

Skyhorse Publishing books may be purchased in bulk at special discounts for sales promotion, corporate gifts, fund-raising, or educational purposes. Special editions can also be created to specifications. For details, contact the Special Sales Department, Skyhorse Publishing, 307 West 36th Street, 11th Floor, New York, NY 10018 or info@skyhorsepublishing.com.

Skyhorse® and Skyhorse Publishing® are registered trademarks of Skyhorse Publishing, Inc.®, a Delaware corporation.

Visit our website at www.skyhorsepublishing.com.

10 9 8 7 6 5 4 3 2 1

Library of Congress Cataloging-in-Publication Data is available on file.
ISBN: 978-1-62087-815-6

Printed in the United States of America

CONTENTS

MAPS

PART 1

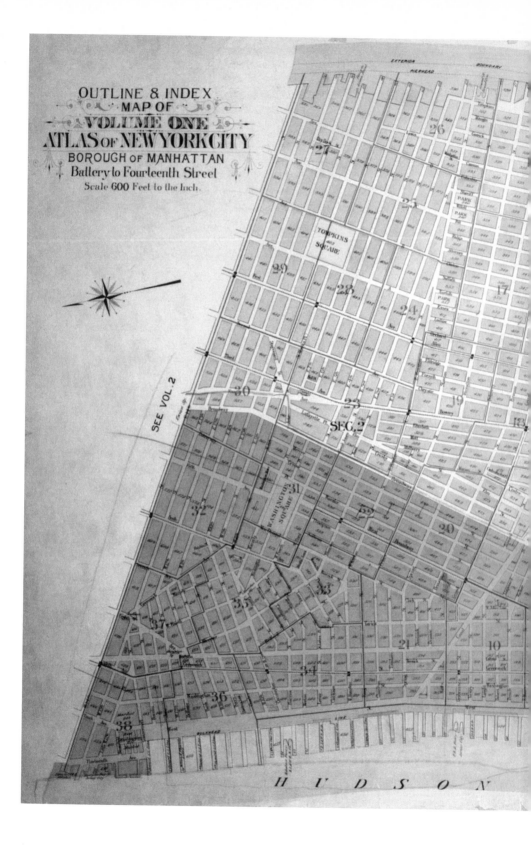

OUTLINE & INDEX
MAP OF
VOLUME ONE
ATLAS OF NEW YORK CITY
BOROUGH OF MANHATTAN
Battery to Fourteenth Street
Scale 600 Feet to the Inch.

Monk Eastman's Domain: The Lower East Side in 1902

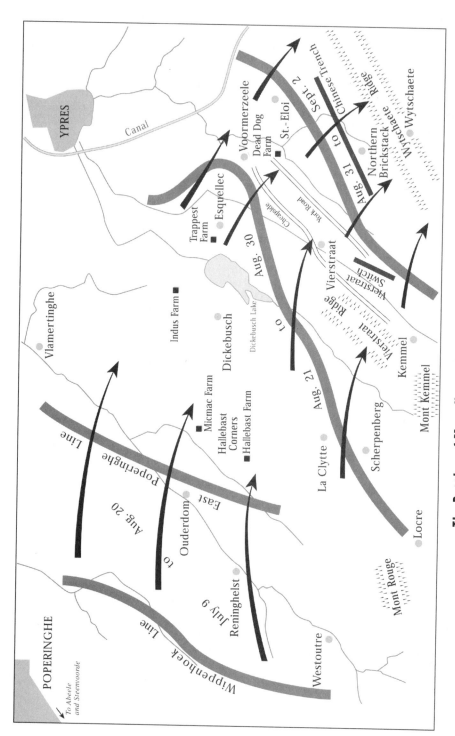

The Battles of Mont Kemmel and Vierstraat Ridge

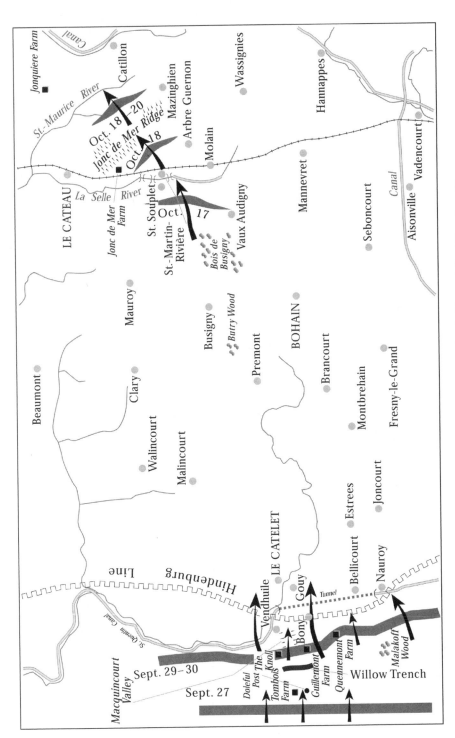

The Battles of the Hindenburg Line and the Selle and St.-Maurice Rivers

Prologue

A LOT OF LITTLE WARS

SEPTEMBER 21, 1917

When the sergeant manning the recruiting desk in the Brooklyn Armory glanced at the next man in the line of potential recruits, he did a double take. Since the U.S. declaration of war on April 6 of that year, he had processed an endless stream of volunteers and conscripts. Most were young and fresh-faced, excited but more than a little frightened at the prospect of going to war on a continent from which most of their forefathers had sprung, but to which they owed no present allegiance, and of which they often displayed the most profound ignorance and indifference.

The man now standing, impassive, before him, was unlike any of those who had come before him. He was much older—thirty-nine, he said, though in that, as in much else in his life, he lied, since he was actually forty-three—but his age was not the only thing that held the recruiting sergeant's gaze. Just five foot seven inches tall, the man was as solid as a tenement block, with powerful, simian arms and fists like clubs. His knuckles were crosshatched with faint white scars. His neck and face also bore scar tissue: both the rough, ragged marks left by brass knuckles, clubs, and bottles, and the clean white lines of razor and knife cuts.

Even in his prime he was never a handsome man, but he now redefined ugliness. He was coarse and fleshy-featured, his skin pockmarked, his dark-brown, almost black, eyes hooded and close-set. "The aftermath of smallpox and brawls, his face looked like a stretch of Carolina landscape after a hurricane has blown over, with boats in the middle of town, cars overturned, cows hooked on flagpoles . . . Coming down a dark downtown street, he must have looked like death itself." His hair was parted neatly—"an odd dandified touch, like a hat on a horse"—but his ears were cauliflowered and mangled, and his broken, flattened nose gave his thick East Side accent an even more nasal quality. His front teeth, broken in fistfights, had been capped with gold, the precious metal in this bruiser's face as incongruous as a diamond in a dung heap.

As he stripped to the waist for his medical examination, he revealed more scars on his back and torso, and the ugly marks left by two bullet wounds in his stomach. With the air of a man retelling a favorite anecdote, he told the sergeant that after he was shot, he'd plugged the holes with his fingers and walked to the hospital. As he stood on the scale, he added that he'd been shot so often that they should allow a little extra for the weight of the bullets still embedded in his body.

"So what battles have you been in?" the sergeant asked.

"Oh, a lot of little wars around New York."

The path that had led the man to this armory in Brooklyn was a long and tortuous one. He had tasted wealth and fame—or at least infamy— that few had ever known, and he had sunk to depths that few others had reached. Now, in a moment that marked a personal epiphany, he stood on the brink of a final disgrace, or redemption, or perhaps even death. For the first time in his life, the man's undoubted personal courage and his skill with his fists, knives, clubs, and firearms were to be used not in criminal pursuits, but in the legitimate service of the state.

This year of 1917 was also an epochal moment for New York and the United States. Neither this gangster and the criminal world he inhabited nor the city in which he had lived and built his fearsome reputation would emerge from the war unchanged. Over the past century, the nation born largely of European immigrants had turned its back on the Old World and set its face resolutely to the West. Now it found itself being drawn out of its insularity to take its place in the wider world. Not all were happy with this development. For many Americans, the war raging beyond the Atlantic was just another of the endless disputes and conflicts between the decaying European powers, as meaningless and irrelevant to the United States as some Ruritanian melodrama. However, if that feeling was strongest in the American heartlands of the Midwest, it was far less keenly felt on the East Coast, and particularly in New York, where old-world ties of blood, heritage, and trade were strongest. The hordes of recent immigrants from Russia, Germany, Italy, Britain, and other European countries had left friends and family behind who were now enmeshed in the bloody conflict and, whether soldiers or civilians, were paying a heavy price. Even the Irish, locked in an increasingly bloody struggle for independence from English rule, had sent thousands of men to fight and bleed alongside their English comrades.

The U.S. declaration of war had also forced many foreign-born Americans, perhaps for the first time in their lives, to confront the question of their core identity: Did they define themselves by the land of their birth, or by that of their adopted country? Hundreds of thousands of foreign-born men gave a categorical answer to the question. Before serving with the American Expeditionary Force, they adopted American citizenship under the "naturalization tree" in Louisville, Kentucky, or at similar ceremonies the length and breadth of the United States.

German-Americans, the largest single group of foreign origin within the United States, whose patriotism was now under scrutiny and whose ancestry, language, and culture were often vilified, rarely equated their roots with sympathy for the Kaiser and German militarism. Many of the Germans who arrived in the United States in the 1870s and 1880s had emigrated for political reasons or to avoid conscription, and few of them or their descendants showed much enthusiasm for supporting, let alone enlisting in, the German armies now. In fact, after a meeting in Chicago in May 1915, a group of German-Americans formed the Deutsche-Amerikaner Freikorps—a volunteer unit to fight on the Allied side.

Even before the U.S. declaration of war, Americans with ties of blood or friendship or who felt a psychological kinship with the Old World, impatient of their nation's reluctance to fight, had already found ways to serve the Allied cause. Many, including a number of distinguished writers, served with volunteer American ambulance companies ferrying the wounded from the battlefields. Those wanting more direct involvement in the fighting either crossed the border and joined the Canadian forces—thirty-five thousand Americans did so, and the 97th Battalion of the Canadian army was even christened "The American Legion"—or enlisted in the British Army or the French Foreign Legion. Pilots joined British squadrons or flew with the Lafayette Escadrille, an entirely American wing under overall French command.

Right from the outbreak of war in August 1914, daily reports on the fighting were carried in the New York newspapers and avidly read, while *The New York Times* devoted at least two pages of its weekly rotogravure section to photographs from the battlefields. British propaganda about "poor little Belgium" and "Hun" atrocities, the sinking of the *Lusitania* by a German U-boat, and the execution of Nurse Edith Cavell had also played a significant role in increasing hostility toward Germany and public sympathy for the Allies. But for American politicians, the most powerful engine for the eventual U.S. declaration of war was perhaps less moral or strategic than financial. Since the war had broken out, Britain and the other Allies had become major trading partners of the United States, and when the Allies' stocks of gold became depleted, large parts of their purchases of food and equipment were financed by American credit—loans totaling $9.5 billion were made to the Allies—giving the United States an ever more compelling vested interest in ensuring an Allied victory.

With all these factors already in operation, the German resumption of unrestricted U-boat warfare against merchant shipping in February 1917, coupled with the near-simultaneous decoding of the Zimmermann telegram, offering Mexico the return of her lost territories of Texas, Arizona, and New Mexico in return for an alliance with Germany against the United States, provided the impetus—or the excuse for the already committed—for the U.S. declaration of war.

Since then, men had been flocking to enlist at armories all over New York. Their motives were as varied as their origins, some fired by a sense of duty and patriotism, others by a thirst for adventure and excitement, while still others committed out of mere curiosity to see what this "World War" was really like. If he had been asked his reasons for enlisting, the man standing before the recruiting sergeant on that September morning might genuinely have replied that he felt he had no other choice. He gave his name as William Delaney, but he had been born Edward Eastman. At various times he had also been known as John, Jack, and "Big Jack" Eastman; Edward "Eddie" Delaney; John or Joe Marvin; John or William Murray; William Smith; and Joseph "Joe" Morris, though he was far better known—infamous, in fact—as the gang leader "Monk" Eastman, once the terror of the Lower East Side and commander of a private army of well over twelve hundred men.

A decade earlier, it would have been inconceivable that the recruiting sergeant would have failed to recognize him. In New York City he was as famous as Harry Houdini, though far less admired. Day after day, Monk's distinctive, scowling visage stared out from the pages of the newspapers, as his gang committed another outrage or he made another court appearance.

His story was also deeply entwined with the parallel tale of the place in which he rose to power. He was a criminal colossus bestriding the Lower East Side, the dark underbelly of the greatest city in the world. New York was the industrial and financial powerhouse of the nation, its political and cultural wellspring and the bridgehead between the Old World and the New. But it was also a city steeped in crime and corruption, a rat's nest where the most ruthless and predatory clawed their way to the top, and none had been more predatory than Monk Eastman.

Yet Monk was a man of puzzling contradictions. He was a brutal thug, but was often seen on the streets with a kitten tucked under his arm and a tame blue pigeon on his shoulder. He possessed iron fists but also a kind heart, and he inspired affection as well as fear. To the poor of the Lower East Side, the reasons for his charity were probably as irrelevant as the origins of his money, but if he used money as well as the threat of violence to ensure their silence about his crimes, he was also capable of acts that had no discernible ulterior motive. One naval officer who encountered Monk on the Bowery around the turn of the century still recalled his kindness and wise advice twenty years later.

In police stations, criminal courts, and newspaper interviews, Monk lied so instinctively and so consistently that even he himself must have had trouble distinguishing truth from falsehood, and on the rare occasions when he actually *did* tell the truth, he found himself disbelieved. Depending on which newspaper, police, or underworld source you referred to, Monk was either "not a moll guy" or he was a lothario, never without a woman, usually a prostitute, on his arm. He had never married; married once; married twice. He had no children; two children; four children, two of whom had died in infancy. Some said that he was illiterate, though that was contradicted by several accounts of him reading newspapers and claims that he demanded written reports from his henchmen on the crimes they committed on his behalf. Monk was an enigma to all who encountered him, and every supposed fact about him was open to question; many still remain so, nine decades after his death.

I

THE HALL OF TEARS

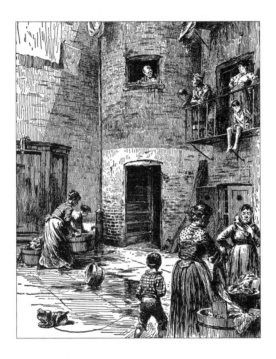

Monk Eastman's origins were as opaque as every other facet of his life. Some thought he was Irish, a dog-fancier or a drifter from Corlears Hook at the bend of the East River. There was a vestige of truth in that, for when he was a boy, his family had lived awhile in nearby Lewis Street, off Delancey, and it would certainly have been a fertile habitat for a man of Monk's dubious character. A poverty-stricken area ever since the Revolution, it remained one of the most lawless parts of the city. Others thought he was Jewish, like the majority of gang members who flocked to his colors. It was claimed that he was the son of a respectable Jewish restaurant owner from the Williamsburg district of Brooklyn, and that his name had originally been Osterman. Yet this was merely another example of the smoke and mirrors with which Monk concealed his origins and covered his tracks. Although he has featured in many lists of "tough Jews" through the years—and never was there a man better suited to demolishing the insulting stereotype of the meek, inoffensive Jew—Monk was neither Jewish nor Irish.

Unlike most gangsters, Monk was the product of a relatively affluent upbringing, and he descended into the underworld by choice. The son of respectable people—Samuel Eastman, a Manhattan wallpaper hanger, and Mary Ellen Parks—Monk was born in December 1873, though various official documents would later give the year of his birth as 1874, 1875, and 1876. He had two older sisters, Lizzie—born in California three years before Monk's birth—and Ida, and a younger sister, Francine. An older brother, Willie, had died of smallpox in infancy before Monk was born.

Although the Eastmans' surname could have been an anglicization of the Germanic "Osterman"—man from the east—Samuel had been born in New Hampshire, of American-born parents whose own births long predated the great waves of Jewish immigration to the United States. Samuel's wife, Mary, was born in New York, and her maiden name, Parks, suggested Anglo-Saxon origins, a supposition confirmed by the origins of her mother, Esther. An immigrant, Esther came to the United States not from Germany, eastern Europe, or Russia, where the vast majority of Jewish immigrants to New York originated, but from England. Neither the Eastmans nor the Parkses left any discernible record of their religion, other than one telling fact: when Monk eventually died, the committal service was read by a Methodist pastor.

Monk's early family history throws up one more revelation. In 1860, Monk's father, Samuel, was living on Seventy-third Street in the house of Thomas McSpedon. Ten years later, although Samuel had moved out and was living with his wife on Cannon Street, between Rivington and Delancey streets, deep in the Lower East Side territory his son would one day rule, Samuel's elderly mother was living at Seventy-third Street under the care of the McSpedons. The most plausible explanation is that she was a blood relative, possibly the aunt, of Thomas McSpedon, whose household seems to have been a violent one: Hester McSpedon sued her husband for divorce in 1877, citing his violence, cruelty, adultery, and obscene language; she in turn was accused of foul temper and arrogance. McSpedon was a prominent and influential Tammany politician, an alderman for the Nineteenth Ward during the "Boss" Tweed era, and his connections to Tammany Hall—the headquarters, housed in a square brownstone building just off Union Square, of the notoriously corrupt "machine" that dominated New York's political life—would prove beneficial, perhaps even crucial, to Monk when he began his criminal career.

Those who knew Monk well spoke of his devotion to his father and mother, but he most likely spent little time with his father. Although they lived as a family for a while on Lewis Street, by the time of the 1880 census, when Monk was still only six, Mary and her four children were living with her father, George Parks, on East Seventy-fifth Street, whereas Samuel had been living downtown at 10 Forsyth Street since 1878. Samuel and Mary never reunited, and he died of consumption in the House of Rest for Consumptives at Anthony Avenue in the Bronx on September 14, 1888, when Monk was just fourteen years old. Mary had already been describing herself as a widow for three years before Samuel's death, but that was probably either to avoid the shame of being a divorcée or an "abandoned wife," or because she had lost touch or severed all contact with Samuel and had no idea whether he was alive or dead.

In 1887 or 1888 Mary Eastman moved to Brooklyn with her children, eventually settling at 93 South Third Street, and by 1890 Monk was running a bird and animal store on Penn Street in Brooklyn. The writer of *The Gangs of New York,* Herbert Asbury, alleged that Monk's parents set him up in the store, but there is no evidence of that. Samuel had died two years before and, even if he had lived, his modest earnings as a paperhanger could not have afforded him the resources to bankroll his son.

The most likely source of Monk's funds was a successful businessman, Timothy Eastman, who had lived next door to the Eastmans and McSpedons on Seventy-third Street in the 1870s and was almost certainly Monk's uncle. Although originating in New Hampshire, Timothy Eastman was described in 1859 as a drover from the West, and he grew rich from his interests in the meat trade, owning three or four hundred butcher shops and an export business that shipped beef carcasses to England. He was one of the "Committee of 100" prominent New York citizens, formed to coordinate the four hundredth anniversary celebrations of the discovery of America, and at his death his estate was valued at several million dollars. Rather than Samuel, Timothy Eastman must have been the wealthy relative who set Monk up in a Brooklyn pet store at the age of seventeen, either in an attempt to keep him on the straight and narrow or merely to give his nephew a start in his working life.

The pet store was a useful "front" for the sale of stolen pigeons; like many Lower East Side and Williamsburg youths, Monk was a pigeon chaser, making money from catching or stealing the birds. He kept a few of his own, housed in a crude loft on the roof of his building; he used them as coaxers to lure strange pigeons, driving off his birds without feeding them so that when they returned, accompanied by a few other pigeons, he could quickly lure them down by showing some grain. A skilled pigeon chaser like Monk could trap thirty or forty birds a week in this way. He kept the best as breeding stock and sold the rest for from ten to twenty-five cents each. At a time when the average wage for a factory worker was only $1.50 a day, it was a useful income.

Monk retained a lifetime affection for pigeons and small animals— anyone accused of cruelty to animals could expect a severe beating if Monk got word of it—but he soon quit the pet trade for less reputable and more profitable occupations. Monk's uncle's wealth meant that he could have had a good education and upbringing, but instead he "chose for his school the sidewalks and the education to be had for the asking there." The lack of a father's restraining influence may have helped to shape his character—there was no one to call him to account if he settled an argument with blows from his fists—but if so, he was hardly unique in that. In the New York of that era there were tens of thousands of children lacking one or both parents, and many of them were living wild on the streets.

While still a teenager, Monk was already thieving, breaking and entering, and brawling with anyone who crossed his path. Always a powerful figure, he had an instinctive aptitude for street-fighting: Monk was a hard-punching, club-swinging, ear-biting, eye-gouging brawler who could flatten anyone foolish enough to oppose him. His mother, solid, hardworking, and God-fearing, had pleaded with Monk to reform, but he already appeared beyond control, perhaps even beyond redemption. In the comradeship and shared secrets of street gangs that had their own codes of dress and behavior and even their own patois, he had found his milieu.

The road to gang membership led on in easy stages. Young toughs who could keep their mouths shut and hold their own in a fight were always useful to criminal gangs, whether as "lighthouses"—lookouts—keeping watch for police or rival gangs, or as pickpockets, sneak thieves, or holders of weapons for senior gang members. If they looked old enough—and Monk was certainly never the angelic-featured choirboy type—they could earn a few dollars a day at election times, "repeating" at the polls: voting several times under different names, wearing different disguises. If a youth was caught by the police while committing a crime and held his tongue and served his time without complaint, he emerged with his gang reputation enhanced.

As a young boy in the early 1880s, Monk had watched the Brooklyn Bridge—"the big bridge"—slowly rising above the East River. The great towers were already a familiar landmark, but steel erectors and riggers still strode, sure-footed as cats, along the girders and suspension cables above the dizzying drop to the river, and the clamor of jackhammers and steam shovels echoed through the streets. When he moved to Williamsburg with his mother and sisters in 1887 or 1888, the newly opened bridge was a tangible link to the neighborhoods he had left behind. For a young man of his singular talents—brawling, theft, intimidation—there were riches to be grasped across the East River, beyond the jetties of the Manhattan waterfront, where the black, oily waters slapped against the timber piles with a sound like a fist on flesh. In 1892, at age eighteen, Monk turned his back on Brooklyn and on the name that his father had bequeathed to him. The young tough striding toward Manhattan would henceforth be known by any one of a dozen aliases, but to his criminal peers, he was simply known as "Monk."

As Monk crossed the bridge with the rolling, bandy-legged gait of a seaman pacing the deck of a ship, the river below him would have been dense with ships of every description: ferryboats; great sailing vessels from foreign ports; tugs; coasters; tramp steamers; fishing boats; and garbage scows. On the far bank were the ranks of close-packed tenements, warehouses, and sweatshops of the Lower East Side, and beyond them the spires and towers of Manhattan, where the term *skyscraper* was just coming into widespread use. By day sunlight was reflected from myriad windows; after dark, the warm glow of gaslights and the brighter, bluer glare of the new electric lighting lit up the night, leaving many newcomers to the city breathless with wonder. New York City, a British visitor observed, half in admiration and half in fright, was a "triumph of mechanics, of iron, steel, bricks and electricity, built by the titans, laid out by Euclid, and furnished by Edison." Others took a less lyrical view. New York, said one, was "a sparkling gem set in a pile of garbage."

When Monk reached the Manhattan side of the bridge, he was entering familiar territory. Beneath a sky stained mud-brown by the smoke from coal fires and the stacks of locomotives and factories, the Lower East Side spread northward from the foot of the bridge, a sprawling, dun-colored warren of tenements pierced by narrow, claustrophobic alleys that were shadowed and dark even in the midday sun. Names like Bandit's Roost, Ragpickers' Row, and Thieves' Alley were an accurate evocation of their character.

The tenements lining every street had rusting iron balconies and fire escapes festooned with bedding, "clinging to the street fronts like some form of creeper unknown to horticulture elsewhere," and "the flags of the tenements" fluttered from washlines strung between buildings. Monk knew these streets well from his childhood, but even in the few years he had lived across the river in Brooklyn, the Lower East Side had been undergoing one of its periodic transformations. The old Irish neighborhoods he had known were now teeming with newer immigrants, the sidewalks awash with streams of ragged humanity. Many faces were ravaged by smallpox scars and there were many people, hobbling on crutches and jostled by mustachioed street toughs in derby hats. Orthodox Jews with long beards and earlocks; women in shawls or headscarves with long skirts trailing in the dust; grimy, barefoot children; stooped old men; and shambling beggars all pushed their way between stalls set up on pushcarts, planks propped on oyster or ash barrels or improvised from boxes, prams, and baskets. They lined the roadside and the sidewalks and filled the tenement doorways.

The stalls were piled with "Jew bread"—black as tar, and carrying the faintly sour smell of new-baked rye—meat, fish, and other foodstuffs; household utensils; clothing; and shoes. People haggled and bought in Yiddish and a Babel of other tongues, and "an English word [fell] upon the ear almost with a sense of shock." As many as fifteen hundred peddlers operated around Hester Street alone, a market given the derisive name of "The Pig Market" by the Irish, "for pork is the one ware that is not on sale." Many of the peddlers, who hired their pushcarts for ten cents a day, sold the cheapest gleanings from Canal Street's wholesale stores, from articles of clothing down to remnants and scraps of cloth and ribbon.

In some spots the canvas awnings of more formal stores shaded the sidewalk. Cigar stores announced themselves by carved wooden figures of Indians, baseball players, Uncle Sam, and even a Scotsman in a kilt. Rival saloons offered meals for a few cents, "hot spiced rum," "sherry with an egg in it," and "oysters in every style." Coffee could be had for two cents, and a stale roll for one. There was at least one saloon on every block, the air thick with cigar smoke and the smell of stale beer; prostitutes patrolled the neighboring alleys.

The street noise was deafening, the shrill voices of newsboys yelling from every corner merging with the tramp of feet, the endless rattle of horses' hooves and iron-shod wheels, the jingle of the bells of the streetcars, and the peremptory clang of a fire engine's gong. The streets were jammed with carts, wagons, and white-painted omnibuses. Horse cars rested between the pillars of the elevated railway on Second Avenue—there were three others: at Third Avenue on the East Side, and at Sixth and Ninth avenues on the West—and the horses seemed oblivious to the thunder of trains overhead, so loud it made the whole street tremble. Almost three stories above street level, trains stopping with a screech of steel sent steam swirling around the gable-roofed stations, while fat black smut drifted down like snowflakes into the street below. Chicago had long since converted to electric power, but in New York the trains still burned soft coal and dropped live ash into the streets, distributing soot and cinders "with rare impartiality." Respectable women often wore veils and, when they emerged from a journey on the "El," the pattern was sometimes stenciled upon their faces with soot.

Largely a lower-middle-class neighborhood during the first wave of Irish immigration, when two million Irish people fled "The Great Famine" between 1846 and 1860, the Lower East Side's streets were now awash with German and Russian Jews. One and a half million arrived in America between 1880 and 1910, as pogroms in Russia provoked an exodus of biblical proportions. There were also floods of Italians, Sicilians, Greeks, Bohemians, Rumanians, Hungarians, Slovaks, and Poles, "the kind of dirty people that you find today on the sidewalks of New York." The influx provoked ever more extreme xenophobia, with one New York newspaper editorializing that "the scum of immigration is viscerating upon our shores. The horde of $9.60 [the price of the cheapest transatlantic ticket] steerage slime is being siphoned upon us."

In the twenty years between 1880 and the turn of the century, almost ten million immigrants, the majority with little more than the clothes they wore, poured off transatlantic steamers and passed through

Castle Garden in Battery Park or, after 1891, the "Hall of Tears" on Ellis Island. Many of them traveled onward no farther than the Lower East Side, where most found that the American "Promised Land" offered them only more misery and deprivation. Such were the numbers of immigrants that in 1897, only one in seven East Side children had even one American-born parent. What work there was for these tidal waves of people was paid at subsistence rates, but for many the only means of survival was to live on their wits, picking rags and sifting garbage; others turned to crime or prostitution.

The northern boundary of the Lower East Side was marked by Fourteenth Street, the frontier between two worlds, coexisting cheek by jowl, yet as remote from each other as the shores of the Atlantic. The notorious slum of the "Great Bend" on Mulberry Street, where "one finds the blackest and most abject human misery," was only two minutes from Broadway. Yet most wealthy New Yorkers lived in a state of ignorance or denial about this and the other slums that scarred their city. They knew that the Lower East Side existed, rather in the same way that they knew that Mexico existed, but few of them were ever likely to travel there.

Cosseted by servants, New York's wealthy lived in luxury in spacious uptown houses and apartments, and dined on the delicacies of the Old World and the New. They rode out through Central Park in gleaming phaetons, landaus, barouches, and rockaways, pulled by high-stepping carriage horses, with liveried drivers and footmen sitting up behind. They attended the Metropolitan Opera and fled the heat of the city for their summer residences on Long Island. Most never ventured downtown into the neighborhoods below Fourteenth Street where, penned in by invisible fence lines, the poor lived and died in crowded, festering tenements and the most basic human needs—fresh air, clean water, even daylight—were hard to come by.

At the end of the Civil War, one hundred thousand inhabitants of New York lived in slum cellars, twelve thousand women worked in brothels to keep from starving, and the garbage, alive with rats, lay two feet deep in the streets. Throughout the remainder of the nineteenth century, civic corruption, indifference, and incompetence prevented these ills from being addressed. The city of New York, the Imperial City, was already the standard-bearer of the American century that was about to be born, yet its institutions, its public servants, its housing, its services—water, roads, sewage, public health, and police—were a national disgrace. Nowhere were those conditions worse than on the Lower East Side.

A miasma of corruption hung over the Lower East Side like the winter fogs drifting in from the East River, and every measure of human despair—poverty, overcrowding, crime, filth, disease, and premature death—was found there. The Tenth Ward, at the heart of the district, was known as "The Suicide Ward" or "The Typhus Ward," and infant mortality rates there were so appalling that on one notorious street one in seven children under five years old died during the year of 1888. Typhus, cholera, and tuberculosis were endemic, and whenever epidemics erupted, just as in plague-ridden London two centuries earlier, "the rich fled the city; the poor stayed and died." Epidemics were devastating to the children of the poor because in those overcrowded tenements it was virtually impossible to isolate the sick. The death rate in the notorious Cherry Street tenement of Gotham Court during New York's regular cholera epidemics was the worst in the entire city; in one outbreak that barely touched the more affluent districts, one in five of the tenants of Gotham Court died.

Even the measles, a relatively innocuous disease among the better off, was often fatal to the poor. "Tread it ever so lightly on the avenues, in the tenements it kills right and left." When an epidemic ravaged three crowded blocks of Elizabeth Street just to the west of the Bowery, the path of the disease through those teeming districts was as clearly defined as "the track of a tornado through a forest." Children's coffins were stacked mast high on the charity commissioners' boat for the biweekly crossing to Potter's Field on Hart Island in Long Island Sound, the cemetery for the city's indigent and unknown, where the deprivation of their lives pursued them even to the grave. "In the common trench of the Poor Burying Ground, they lie packed three stories deep, shoulder to shoulder, crowded in death as they were in life."

Meanwhile, every year forty thousand still-living casualties of the fight for survival were shipped on a boat known as "the tub of misery" to the asylums and workhouses of "The Island": Blackwell's Island (now Roosevelt Island), in the middle of the East River. Once an oasis of flowers and orchards of apple, cherry, peach, and plum, it was now home to some of New York's grimmest establishments: a penitentiary; a reformatory; a workhouse; almshouses for men and women; the echoing, soulless wards of the charity hospital for incurables; a blind asylum; a lunatic asylum; and, half-hidden among the trees at the downstream end of the island, the isolation hospitals for contagious diseases.

The buildings on the island were turreted and battlemented like medieval castles, and the treatment meted out within their stone walls could be equally feudal. Clad in their dirt-brown uniforms, the occupants of the workhouse, many of them "old hags long given to drink, who began life in low dance-houses and are ending it in the gutter," were forced to carry out the most menial tasks. The penitentiary included punishment cells known as "dark cells," sited on the lower floor, from which even the faintest trace of light was excluded. Prisoners who lost their minds were transferred to the lunatic asylum, where, behind its high fence, stood three separate buildings: the asylum, the retreat, and the lodge, or madhouse, where the most violent cases were confined and visitors were never allowed.

Unable to survive in New York, many other immigrants headed west in pursuit of the American dream that had lured them from their homelands. Others returned home broken by poverty and failure. But the tides of new immigrants always far outnumbered those who left. They created a permanent housing shortage and a labor surplus that together drove the treadmill of poverty, forcing down wages while rents rose ever higher.

Periodic economic crashes increased the sum of human misery. In the year after Monk returned from Brooklyn to the streets of Manhattan came the Great Crash of 1893—the worst economic crisis in the history of the United States, heralding a depression that lasted four years. Within twelve months two and a half million men were out of work; when an army of the unemployed marched on Washington in protest, they were arrested for walking on the grass of the Capitol lawn.

There were soup kitchens on the streets and make-work schemes mending roads or working in parks, but many people simply starved. Joseph Pulitzer's *World* newspaper set up a "Free Bread" fund, leading its rivals, the *Herald* and the *Tribune,* to establish "Free Clothing" and "Coal and Food" funds, while Fleischmann's bakery, next to Grace Church on Broadway, began distributing a third of a loaf of bread to all comers at midnight every night, inadvertently spawning the term *breadline,* but such palliatives were few and far between. As in every crash, thousands of recent immigrants besieged the ports and steamer companies, hoping to return to Europe.

Those who remained fought for whatever work they could find, but even those in full-time employment struggled to pay their bills and feed their families, with hourly wages often measured in cents. Laws protecting factory workers were weak enough—in a single year, 1904, there were fifty thousand industrial accidents in New York City alone, and twenty-seven thousand workers across the United States lost their lives as a result of their jobs—but work contracted out to tenement sweatshops bypassed even those feeble safeguards. The legal maximum working day in factories was ten hours, and no child under the age of fourteen was to be employed. Yet in sweatshops, children as young as four or five worked alongside their fathers, mothers, and siblings, with a working day that started at six in the morning and could continue until midnight. Many toiled for seventy or eighty hours a week, including on Saturdays and Sundays. "A sign would go up on Saturday afternoon: 'If you don't come in on Sunday, you need not come in on Monday' . . . children's dreams of a day-off shattered. We wept, for after all, we were only children."

The already miserable wages could be cut without warning, and many poor families existed on little more than tea and bread, the tea boiled and reboiled to extract the last vestige of strength and flavor from it, the bread usually bought stale for a cent or two. Others bought their food from the pushcart market on Mulberry Street, even though the produce on offer was of the lowest possible quality: stale bread sold by the sackful, "tainted meat, poultry blue with age and skinny beyond belief, vegetables in every stage of wiltedness, fruit half-rotten or moldy, butter so rancid that it poisons the air, eggs broken in transit, sold by the spoonful for omelets, fish that long ago left the water." Even worse were the "fragments of bread and other farinaceous food, decaying potatoes, cabbage, &c, interspersed with lifeless cats, rats and puppies, thus introduced to a post-mortem fellowship," that ragpickers gleaned from the rubbish and resold to those unscrupulous enough to convert even this foul mixture into sausages or lobscouse. Board of Health officers repeatedly raided the Bend and dumped the contents of the entire market into the river, but by the next day, the market was once more thronged with customers. To the poor and destitute, half-rotten food for a cent or two was better than no food at all.

For many of the inhabitants of the Lower East Side, the only employment was in ragpicking, begging, theft, or prostitution. Clouds of dust and ash billowing from cellars announced the presence of ragpickers carrying out their dismal trade, hauling in burlap sacks full of garbage and sifting it for items that could be repaired or reconditioned and for the clean paper, rags, bones, cigar stubs, bottles, and metals that, gathered together, could be sold for a few cents to junk dealers. "Paper wasn't worth much. They got only a penny for ten pounds. Rags brought two cents a pound and iron, four." Their few possessions piled to one side to allow the stinking contents of their sacks to be spread across the floor and sorted, the ragpickers were smothered from head to foot in fine dust, and moved like wraiths among the garbage they were sifting.

An estimated six thousand beggars and ten times as many homeless men and women spent their nights on the streets of Manhattan alongside the countless thousands of barefoot, dirt-encrusted homeless children, known as "street-arabs," "street-rats," or "dock-rats"— the weakest were called "guttersnipes"—who found shelter in boxes or barrels or dark holes under flights of stairs. In bitter weather hundreds huddled on top of the steel gratings, where the heating mains laid throughout Lower Manhattan in 1881 sent gouts of steam billowing upward, fogging in the still, cold air.

Almost all the newsboys were homeless. Most wore shoes only in winter, and often bought their clothes from ragpickers who had stripped them from the bodies of smallpox or typhus victims, adding yet one more hazard to the newsboys' perilous lives. Homeless boys also worked as bootblacks or peddlers of matches or "small notions," or they found work swill-gathering or ragpicking. Many more turned to petty crime—pilfering, theft, pickpocketing, stripping lead from roofs—and aped in their dress and mannerisms the adult gang members they sought to emulate.

When the social reformer Jacob Riis surveyed 278 juvenile prisoners, none more than thirteen years old, he found burglars as young as four, while the charge sheets for the others included drunkenness, theft, brawling, forgery, highway robbery, arson, and assault. Some gambling dens, saloons, and dives catered exclusively to street-rats, selling them "frightful whiskey at three cents a glass and providing small girls for their amusement."

In every slum tenement and thieves' kitchen there were children "wild as hawks and as fierce and untamable," but there were other, even younger denizens of the streets. More than two hundred foundlings and more than a hundred dead infants were found by the police every year, and these were only a few of the actual numbers abandoned by poverty-stricken or unmarried mothers. Babies were often left at night outside well-to-do uptown houses, in the hope that they would be adopted and enjoy a better life than the unfortunate mother who had abandoned them there. Rarely were such hopes justified, for even those found alive had a survival rate of just 20 percent. There was "an odd coincidence" in New York: "year by year, the lives that are begun in the gutter, the little, nameless waifs whom the police pick up and the city adopts as its wards, are balanced by the even more forlorn lives that are ended in the river. I do not know how or why it happens, or that it is more than a mere coincidence . . . But there it is. Year by year, the balance is struck—a few more, a few less—substantially the same when the record is closed."

2

BLACKER THAN A WOLF'S THROAT

These mean streets of the Lower East Side were a paradise for criminals, and Monk Eastman was soon claiming his share of the spoils. He was a hulking figure, and although only five foot seven inches tall, he still towered above most of his peers—police and prison records show that the average gang member of the era was just five foot three inches tall and weighed only 120 to 135 pounds.

In the early 1890s, a "City Missionary and Philanthropist" had an encounter on Monroe Street, Monk's home turf, with an eighteen-year-old thug, "brutal in face and form." The thug was not identified by name, but his age and physical description, and the timing and location, make it very probable that the thug was Monk. Seized by two policemen, both of who bore the look of "having come through a severe conflict," he kept swearing and throwing punches until he took a few blows from the policemen's clubs. Their sergeant described him as "the devil himself . . . Every one on the streets that he bulldozes is afraid to complain of him."

By now Monk was already a familiar figure to the police, but his true name and origins remained unknown to them—and to almost everyone else. They believed that he really was William Delaney, the name under which his first arrest was recorded in 1892, the year he returned to the Lower East Side from Brooklyn. "I gave my name Edward Eastman when I was arrested," Monk later claimed, "and the officer jumped up and said, 'I know him, his name is William Delaney.' . . . I says, 'Well, if my name is William Delaney, put it down William Delaney.' "

Monk used the same alias in September 1893, when he "handled" one of the professional prizefighters who were breaking state law by taking part in a boxing match at Coney Island. Monk's police file remained in the name of William Delaney throughout his nearly thirty-year criminal career, and that was constantly cited as "Monk Eastman's real name," in police briefings and newspaper reports. The name does not appear to have had any special significance for Monk, and may simply have been protective coloration, an Irish-sounding name adopted in his early days of brawling around Cherry Hill, when the street gangs, like the police, were still Irish-dominated and the great Jewish diaspora from Russia and Germany had yet to complete the transformation of the Lower East Side.

Monk's first arrest had been for the relatively minor offense of stealing pigeons, and his first brushes with the law resulted in nothing worse than an occasional night in the police cells and a brief appearance before the magistrates. But in January 1898 he was caught carrying burglars' tools; using another alias, William Murray, he appeared in court and was sentenced to three months on the Island. He emerged unscathed and unreformed and at once returned to "The Gap," an area of Cherry Hill around Hamilton and Market streets, where he was already known as one of a group of particularly ruthless young thugs.

Monk further honed his pugilistic talents by taking work as a bouncer at the Silver Dollar Saloon, famed throughout the Lower East

Side for its floor inlaid with a thousand silver dollars. The owner of the saloon, a Jew named Charles Solomon, who operated under the more Anglo-Saxon-sounding soubriquet of Silver Dollar Smith, had close links to Tammany bosses; such political connections were of great value not just to saloon owners but also to aspiring criminals like Monk. Opposite the Essex Market Court, the saloon was the headquarters for a gang of shyster lawyers, bail bondsmen, false witnesses, and corrupt cops, who had made the court a byword for crooked justice, a place where the innocent were often convicted while the guilty walked free, and a key focus of political influence on the Lower East Side. The night court heard three to four hundred cases every night—it was claimed that during one sitting, one hundred cases had been disposed of in one hundred minutes—and it was easy for corrupt junior court officials to mislay or fabricate evidence, or to mislead judges overwhelmed by the sheer volume of court business.

Corrupt lawyers—"fixers" and "bellowers," "the use of the first being silently to pervert the course of justice and of the other to cover this up by bawling a few inches away from a judge's nose a diatribe concerning the rights of man and the oppression of the poor"—worked with "one chief purpose: the defense of the criminal." They conspired to destroy or manufacture evidence or postpone cases until they could be heard by a corrupt or pliable judge, though interference in the machinery of justice could be even more overt than that. When a notorious hotel at 23 Bowery, the hangout of a band of thieves and prostitutes, was raided and its proprietors put on trial, the judges were constantly summoned from the bench to take telephone calls from Tammany politicians demanding the release of the prisoners.

After serving his apprenticeship at the Silver Dollar Saloon, Monk graduated to the post of "sheriff"—bouncer—of a far larger and grander establishment: the New Irving Dance Hall at 214 Broome Street, "a dive notorious for its rapes and robberies." It was said that when Monk walked in and asked for the job, the owner tried to turn him away, gesturing to the two massive figures he already employed. Monk then set upon the pair of them and, single-handed, left them in a bloodied heap on the floor. The owner was convinced: the two battered thugs were fired and Monk hired in their place.

Young working-class women, immigrants or the daughters of immigrants, were the dance halls' best customers. They ranged in age from fourteen to twenty-five, with the majority under twenty.

The men were generally older. There were some genuine "dancing academies, beckoning and calling to tired and lonesome souls sweating their flower and youth away to the time of spindles and belts and foot-powered machines," but the majority of Lower East Side dance halls were thinly disguised brothels. Women were usually admitted free and men either paid to dance or paid for drinks for themselves and their women companions, who were provided by the management for men who came alone. Those who failed to buy drinks often enough were thrown into the street by fearsome bouncers like Monk.

At the larger dances, attended by as many as seven or eight hundred people, there were always men who became "boisterously drunk after midnight, and enough of the rougher class of girls to assist the men in fixing a certain obviously immoral character upon the assemblage." Erotic "circuses" were often staged, with curtained back rooms or alcoves available for private shows and assignations. Dance halls where girls danced naked and took part in simulated or genuine sex acts with naked men were so common that in the late 1880s the price of admission to such performances dropped from five dollars to fifty cents. In the lowest places, like the Cremorne, "it was not unusual to see a drunk stretched unconscious on the floor while half a dozen women fought for the right to pick his pockets. A bouncer always stood patiently by, waiting for the ladies to conclude their explorations, after which the victim was dragged into the street."

The dances held at the New Irving were often what were known in thieves' argot—"the foulest of all human lingoes, that dialect of sin and death, known as the Cant language, or the Flash"—as "ballum-rancums": balls at which all the customers were criminals or prostitutes. The dance halls also regularly featured balls known as "tough rackets." Ostensibly sporting, cultural, or benevolent organizations, their members, known as "hard guys," were in fact invariably dubious characters: thugs, pickpockets, thieves, and pimps.

Tickets to such rackets were sold to individuals and businesses on terms that often amounted to blackmail—those who declined to buy sufficient tickets would find their windows smashed or their business stock destroyed. Rackets were often used as fund-raisers by Tammany politicians and by aspiring gang leaders like Monk, particularly if a court case was looming and cash was needed for lawyers. It was easy money. "He bulldozes the merchants in the neighborhood to advertise in his ball journal. He disposes of his tickets in the very same way.

Those who do not take tickets walk up to the box office on the night of the ball and bring with them their 'slap down,' which means two, three, five, ten, or sometimes twenty or twenty-five dollars."

Monk and his assistants, armed with clubs, presided over these gatherings and "were in the habit of quelling any disturbances . . . and sometimes started the trouble themselves just to demonstrate how expert they were in quieting it." Monk kept order with the huge bludgeon he carried, the blackjack in his pocket, and the brass knuckles on both hands. Brass knuckles were formidable weapons; "a blow behind the ear from a strong man's fist felled the victim like an ox." Monk also regularly wielded his bludgeon, and every time he used it on a recalcitrant customer, he cut another notch in it. One evening he walked up to an inoffensive man drinking beer at the bar and laid him out with a blow to the head. When asked why, he pointed to his bludgeon. "Well, I had forty-nine nicks in me stick, an' I wanted to make it an even fifty."

Monk was skilled with a revolver, and he wielded a beer bottle or a lead pipe "with an aptitude that was little short of genius," but he maintained certain moral standards. It was his proud boast that he always removed his brass knuckles before hitting obstreperous women at the dance hall, and he never used his club on them. "I only give her a little poke, just enough to put a shanty on her glimmer [black her eye], but I always takes off me knucks first."

The role of dance-hall sheriff was no more than a stepping-stone for Monk. He used it to establish his reputation as the toughest of the Lower East Side's hard men and to foster criminal and political connections that would aid his developing career as a strong-arm man and gang leader. His assistants from the dance hall became his first gang members. Monk continued to send out decoy pigeons trained to lure the flocks of the East Side to his premises, but he also operated as "a pimp, a thief, and a trainer and manager of young Jewish pickpockets. He had a staff of them, whom he sent out over the city to steal," a task made easier by the new fashion for conspicuous consumption, with gold pocket watches, jeweled tiepins, and rings on prominent display. Each recruit learned how to take watches, extract pins from neckties, and steal pokes and scratches—wallets and rolls of bills—out of a man's pocket. "He learns how to become a wire, an instrument, digging his hands into the man's clothes, working as the tool for the mob who stall and jostle for him."

The skills of the young boys were such that one old-time pickpocket complained,

> Those little boys on the East Side have got all us old guys beaten by a city block. Why, they took my watch and chain the other night like I was a simple gilly from the country, and it cost me $30 to get back my stuff . . . Formerly when a pickpocket took your watch, he was satisfied to twist it from the ring that attached it to the chain. The East Side boys now take watch, chain, charm and whatever may be attached to the other end of the chain in your opposite waistcoat pocket. They consider the ancient system coarse work.

As well as participating directly in crime, Monk's gang members could also make use of his criminal and political contacts to find easy work as lookouts, runners, touts, doormen, and bodyguards at poolrooms, racetracks, saloons, gambling dens, and brothels.

Monk's schooling had been on the streets, not in the classroom, but he was far from inarticulate, and his lack of formal education did not mean that he was unintelligent. If his rise was based on his prowess as a street fighter, skilled with his fists and a revolver and not afraid to use either, Monk also brought an unprecedented degree of business efficiency and organization to the traditional gangland rackets. Alongside the Eastman gang's own burgeoning enterprises, Monk was also soon seeking tribute from every other criminal operating on his turf, and from every legitimate and illegitimate business. His territory eventually extended from the Bowery to the East River, and the teeming tenements were a fecund source of recruits for his ever-growing gang of thugs and criminals.

Before New York's breakneck expansion, its brick or brownstone tenements had been pleasant dwellings, often occupied by a single family, with a garden at the rear sometimes ending in a small stream. Those days were long past. As pressure on Manhattan's scarce space increased— and New York's population all but quintupled, from 850,000 to 4 million, in the half century following the Civil War—property owners and speculators were not slow to realize that large profits could be made by dividing and subdividing those once fine houses, thus accommodating ten, twenty, thirty, or forty families in the space that had once held only one. Extra stories were also added, often with scant attention to what the original foundations and walls would bear, and many buildings were torn down and rebuilt by speculators as seven- to ten-story tenements, often with a further one or two stories belowground.

At the same time, "in a triumph of efficiency over humanity," rear tenements were erected in what had once been the gardens, reached either by an alley between buildings or by a passageway like a low tunnel, head-high and as little as two or three feet wide, running through the front house and opening into a yard lined with garbage barrels and privies. Construction costs were pared to the bone; when a tenement collapsed in 1885, it was discovered that, to save money, the builder had used the soil excavated from the cellar instead of sand in the mortar.

The long-established common-law doctrine of "ancient lights"—the right to unobstructed windows and access to air and light—was usually ignored. Rear tenements routinely had no windows in the rear or side walls, and were overshadowed on every side by taller, close-packed buildings. The windows and doors of one five-story tenement off Roosevelt Street were one short stride away from the featureless, blank brick wall of the neighboring building. No trace of sunlight ever penetrated the alley. Halfway up Roosevelt Street was a dark, narrow alley, ending in a blank wall—"Slaughter Alley," though no map of New York ever carried that name. It was dark even in daylight, and the stones underfoot were slimy and strewn with refuse. At the far end a low doorway opened onto a black, stinking hallway—Stephen Crane's description of a hallway "blacker than a wolf's throat" could have been coined with this place in mind. It led to unlit stairs that had rotted through in places. There were gaps in the handrails, and the walls and ceilings were black with filth. Some rooms had a little natural light; others were in permanent, stygian darkness.

Such tenements crawled with humanity, as many as four hundred people, sometimes even more, crowded into a single building. Rents were fixed high enough to cover dilapidation and damage by tenants, and to help pay the rent, almost every family found room for two to ten boarders who often slept in rotation in beds that never went cold. One room, twelve feet square with only two beds and no partitions, screens, or even a table, was found to be home to five families—twenty people of both sexes and all ages.

All the occupants of a tenement might have to share a single foul and overflowing earth closet, and children and adults alike often defecated in dark corners, alleyways, and cellars. In some tenements the only source of water was the hydrant in the yard, and the always fickle water supply often gave out altogether. Even when the water was flowing, two million New Yorkers were at risk of cholera because the supply was contaminated by sewage.

In winter the tenement roofs leaked water, and drafts whistled through walls that were little more barrier to the cold than were the thin clothes and rags their inhabitants wore. In bitter weather, when icicles dangled from every fire escape and tenement roof, and the horse cars and the trains of the elevated railway froze to the rails, some tenement dwellers simply froze to death.

In summer, the tenements sweltered. Whole buildings seemed to sweat as condensation formed on every wall, and the stench—always terrible, even in the depths of winter frosts—reached new heights of toxicity, flowing up from the sewers, privies, and yards and filling the halls, stairwells, and airshafts like a rising tide. The tenements were so baking hot that thousands of people slept out on roofs, fire escapes, sidewalks, or any level space they could find, until it was "almost impossible to pass along without stepping on a human body." People turning over in their sleep sometimes rolled off the roofs or window ledges on which they were lying and plunged to their deaths.

Winter or summer, the noise of the tenements was unending and inescapable: the wailing of hungry babies; the tramping of feet over uneven, uncarpeted wooden boards; the slamming of flimsy doors; and always the voices, often raised in rancor, drunken, pugnacious, words punctuated by the sounds of punches, kicks, and screams. In the rare moments of relative quiet, the creak of timbers could be heard, as if the tenement itself was groaning under the weight of human misery it had to bear. There was "no waste in these tenements. Lives, like clothes, are worn through and out before put aside."

These anthills of humanity were more densely populated than anywhere on Earth, with 290,000 people to the square mile; the comparable figure for the worst of the London slums was 175,000. Even these figures masked still worse overcrowding; a single block on Houston Street contained 3,500 people, equivalent to 1 million to the square mile, making it "the most crowded block, in the most crowded neighborhood in the world."

While their tenants struggled to survive, slum landlords like the Astors made fortunes. Witnesses before a Senate committee declared 40 percent to be a fair average annual return on a tenement, and instances were cited of more than 100 percent being achieved. It was one of the blacker ironies of New York life that rents per square foot were from a quarter to a third higher on the Lower East Side than in the most fashionable uptown districts.

Those without the means to rent a room of their own hired lodgings that descended in stages from the relative respectability of the twenty-eight cents that secured a bed for a night in a moderately clean room shared by no more than a handful of others, and perhaps with a curtain or flimsy screen to give a little privacy. At the lower end of the range, the seven-cent lodging gave the right to sleep "packed in like herrings" in a filthy cellar on bare wooden benches or strips of dirty canvas strung between wooden rails arranged in two or three tiers. If seven cents was too much, "one may sleep on the floor for five cents a spot, or squat in a sheltered hallway for three." Those unable to pay even that amount could seek shelter in police "lodging rooms": basements where the bed was "the soft side of a plank." In the bitter winter of 1896, sixty thousand homeless people—known as "revolvers" because they were forbidden to sleep more than one or two nights a month in any one police station and had to keep moving on night after night—used these police basements.

Even worse, at the very bottom of the abyss were the two-cents-a-night "stale beer dives": roach-infested, dank, stinking cellars with a floor of hardened mud. Sometimes a single gas jet gave a flickering light, casting black, malevolent shadows into the corners where sleeping bodies were littered. A faint, leathery rustle in the rare moments of silence showed that the walls and ceilings were alive with cockroaches. In other cellars there was no light at all, and no air, just a reek so foul that it had an almost physical presence. When they crept into the light of day, the denizens of such dwellings were as white and noisome as maggots emerging from a carcass.

The proprietors of these foul establishments sold beer slops drained from the bottoms of barrels left out on the sidewalk for the brewers' drays. The stolen slops were then "touched up with drugs to put a froth on it" and "needled"—adulterated—with barely palatable and often poisonous ingredients like grain alcohol, camphor, benzene, or metal polish, to give them an extra "kick." Some dives were known as "block and fall joints" because those who drank their rotgut booze wouldn't get more than a block before falling in the gutter, and on Bayard Street there was a notorious "tumbler" dive where stale beer was sold cut with a spirit—allegedly whiskey—so potent that men would often collapse before they'd finished their drink. In many dives, the dregs of drinks, together with "the washings of the bar and the rinsings of the cloths with which it is wiped," were thrown into a tub and sold as "dog's-nose," "all-sorts," or "swipes." Two cents bought a mug of this filthy brew and the opportunity to slump with your head on a table as rank as its surroundings. Boards placed on the tops of beer kegs served as seats. Underneath were those too drunk to sit or stand. Few people ever hauled themselves back from such depths as these.

Along with the dirt went depravity, and nowhere more so than on the most notorious thoroughfare in America: the Bowery. Broadway and the Bowery offered similar entertainments—dancing, drinking, gambling, and sex—but while Broadway was "the theater of the bourgeoisie," catering to wealthier patrons in discreet, opulent surroundings, the Bowery was "the circus of the masses . . . the street of amusement for all of the Lower East Side." Well-to-do "slummers" from uptown also "explored the Bowery, as those of a later fashion went into the South Seas," and street-arabs would accost passengers arriving at Grand Central and offer to "show you the Bowery for a dollar, mister."

In the Bowery, everything was on display, everything was on sale—cheap—and everyone from the rubbernecking tourist to the bum with a few cents in his pocket was equally welcome, and equally vulnerable to the bottom-feeders who prowled sidewalks and alleys in search of prey. Even newsboys often doubled as pickpockets, brandishing a paper in a streetcar passenger's face and using the distraction to pick his pocket or steal his watch and chain. One bragged that "if you will stand for a newspaper under your chin, I can even get your socks." By 1905 even the Grand Street streetcar conductors were rifling passengers' pockets.

Packed with humanity at all hours, the Bowery came into its own after dark, when it was ablaze with light from end to end, "the most brilliantly lighted thoroughfare on this planet." In the glare of the lights, newsboys and shoeblacks jostled with street peddlers hawking everything from hair oil, trinkets, and fake cologne to the sheet music of the latest popular tunes and paper cups full of ice cream. Children dodged around them, earning pennies or candy for distributing the cards of prostitutes. Making their way among them all, almost unnoticed, were the sandwich-board men, usually alcoholic or otherwise destitute men bearing advertising boards that often emphasized their own dereliction: "An anemic, hollow-eyed, gaunt-bodied man carrying the announcement of a good dinner," or a man dressed in rags advertising a warm winter overcoat.

Fourteenth Street was the haunt of a number of fortune-tellers, attractive young women with caged songbirds trained to pick up in their beaks one of a score of envelopes containing horoscopes. Nearby, street organ players ground out popular songs and snatches of opera, and silhouette artists, ragmen, and beggars also added their voices to the clamor and bustle of the streets. Overhead, forests of pictorial signs offered New York's polyglot inhabitants wordless advertisements for a multitude of goods and trades.

The crowds filling the sidewalks also had a stream of handbills thrust at them and were continually accosted by ropers-in, barkers, cappers, and steerers, whose pitches "combined elements of the carny barker's routine and the preacher's harangue, the confidence man's patter and a sort of stream-of-consciousness poetry." They tried to lure passersby into fake auction rooms, shooting galleries, tattoo parlors, gambling dens, "free and easys"—confusingly, a term for both a whorehouse and a place where boxing bouts were staged—and dance halls, where a dime bought a dance and almost anything else was available for the right amount.

The dime museums were emblazoned with richly painted signs promising exotic wonders to delight the most jaded palate: mermaids, giants, pygmies, wild men, cannibals, and tattooed ladies—a thinly veiled pretext for the display of semi-naked female flesh. Tourists were warned to avoid such places, as the illustrated advertisements were always far more lavish than the dismal reality that confronted the patron who had parted with his cash. "Palming" and shortchanging were routine; hulking figures—often Monk's gang members—with scarred knuckles and clubs or weighted lengths of pipe protruding from their pockets ensured that few asked for a refund and fewer still got one. Those who pressed their complaints too far might have had need of the services of the "black-eye fixers," whose self-explanatory trade was itself testament to the rough-and-ready habits of the Bowery's vast, transient population.

The gin palaces and saloons of the Bowery itself, the bucket shops, dives, and opium dens in the side streets, and "Cocaine Row"—Third Avenue from Twelfth to Sixteenth streets—offered intoxication to patrons of all means and circumstances. In the Eleventh Precinct there was not a block that was not lined with "dives and houses of assignation without number," and cigar stores and cider mills that were also thinly disguised brothels. There were gaming clubs guarded by locked doors with sliding panels for the inspection of potential patrons, low gambling dens and on-street card games played in the shadow of the elevated railways. Few people left the lower-grade gambling den to which ropers-in had brought them without leaving most or all of their money behind. Those reluctant to gamble heavily were plied with drink until their inhibitions faded, and any still resistant would be rendered insensible with drink, drugs—chloral hydrate "knockout drops" were particularly popular—or a blunt implement, and their pockets emptied. A carriage was then summoned to a nearby street and the unconscious victim dumped in an uptown doorway. If he was doubly unlucky he was taken in by the police, charged with drunkenness, and, without the money to pay a fine, might end up in jail on Blackwell's Island for a ten-day stretch. Other men, less fortunate even than these, might simply disappear, their bloated bodies hauled from the East River some days later.

The bright lights of the Bowery merely served to throw the surrounding side streets into even deeper shade, and there, where the glow of the lights faded into darkness, began the sprawl of lodging houses and tenements. There was a New York saying, "The nearer the river, the nearer to hell," and the dismal districts bordering the East River showed that there was some justification for it, especially after night had fallen. Pearl Street had once been the riverfront and the home of rich merchants, but over the decades, as New York's restless, relentless expansion continued, piers were pushed out farther and farther and the docks were filled in and built over, giving birth in turn to Water Street, Front Street, and, finally, South Street.

Between Water Street and the East River, from the Brooklyn Bridge as far as James Street, was all reclaimed land, damp, inhospitable, and prone to flooding at high tides. The floors of sixteen basements and cellars, home to nineteen families—110 people—were below the high-water mark; as well as the damp, the contents of neighboring privies frequently oozed through the walls. Rats swarmed everywhere; then as now, there were more rats than people in New York.

Along the waterfront, the air of purpose and industry did not spread far beyond Water Street even by day, and at dusk the riverside districts were abandoned to the denizens of the night. Iron gates clanged shut as dockworkers, longshoremen, porters, and factory workers made for home or for the saloons, and only the distant rumble of the elevated trains broke the silence of the deserted streets. On the Lower East Side, however, the end of the working day merely marked a transition point; as some left, others emerged to take their places, people whose natural habitat was the night-darkened street. On every corner, standing around the saloons and lurking in the side streets, were whores and their pimps, drunks, nook-and-corner men, robbers, hustlers and con men, pickpockets and street toughs, predatory as rats, all seeking marks.

The East River, lined by the rows of black hulls and the forest of masts piercing the river mist, was the scene of a constant losing battle fought by night watchmen to guard their cargoes against the endless depredations of thieves and smugglers. The riverbank was lined by warehouses and machine shops, but behind them lay a network of narrow lanes and squalid tenements where the gangs of river thieves based themselves. The streets were unlit, and the occasional yellow glow of light from a saloon only stained the surrounding darkness a deeper black.

In the side streets, cock-pits vied for trade with rat-pits, dog-pits, and yards where bare-knuckle fights were staged. Rat-baiting and dog- and cockfighting were so popular that the price of admission was usually greater than for an illegal prizefight. A typical rat-pit, often housed in a basement, was lit by a single dim bulb above a dirt ring, with five-foot wooden walls, the lower part clad in zinc. Surrounding it were rough wooden bleachers. Bets were placed on the speed with which a terrier could dispose of a set number of rats, and there was never any shortage of the raw material for the patrons' sport. The stench that filled such rooms suggested that the bodies of dead rats and dogs were routinely disposed of in the dirt beneath the bleachers.

Few strangers ever strayed into these districts, safe havens for criminals and vagrants and clapped-out whores, far gone in alcoholism or addiction, for whom this riverside district was often the last step on a downward spiral that would end in the river itself. The speed of their decline was shocking. One policeman, speaking in 1909, talked of "generations" of prostitutes; by a generation he meant just two years.

3

AS A POOL REFLECTS
THE SKY

This "modern Gomorrah," a crime-ridden sink of crumbling tenements, brothels, and dives, worse than the meanest old-world slums, was the Lower East Side kingdom Monk Eastman had set himself to conquer. His rise to power depended on no single incident, but more on a long, slow process of attrition. Monk's gang warfare began with genuine or manufactured provocations and incidents on the frontiers separating his territory from that of rival gangs. Disputes, small fights, and regular incursions would follow in a steady escalation that eventually led either to a series of humiliating retreats by his rivals or an all-out gang war and their complete elimination. Monk was also enough of a skilled diplomat to build alliances with some potential rivals and isolate others.

Some of his former adversaries were co-opted into Monk's "army," but he also recruited more and more gang members from among the dirt-poor Jewish immigrants flooding into New York, for whom crime under the protection of a gang was often the only means to put food on the table. Orthodox Jews from Poland and Russia, whose way of life had been virtually unaltered for centuries, watched in helpless horror as their children turned their backs on their beliefs and traditions. Their daughters often became prostitutes, while their sons embraced a life of drinking, gambling, womanizing, and crime. "It was an abyss of many generations; it was between parents out of the Middle Ages . . . and the children of the streets of New York today." Some Jewish fathers disowned their errant daughters and "formally cast them off as dead; among the very orthodox, there were cases where the family went through the ancient ceremonial for the dead—slashing the lapels of their clothing and sitting out the seven days of mourning in their houses."

Yet Monk's gang also provided what might be described as a public service by protecting the Jewish population of the East Side from the depredations and attacks of Italian and Irish New Yorkers, often operating with the tacit consent, encouragement, and sometimes active participation of New York's predominantly Irish police. In an area virtually devoid of the rule of law, Monk's gang offered the possibility of protection, restitution, and retribution to those who felt themselves threatened or wronged, and who had no one else—least of all the police—to whom they could turn. Such aid almost always came at a price, of course, but it was one that many were prepared to pay, and the Eastman gang went out "every afternoon, just like mechanics going to work." In a society where the law "exactly reflected, as a pool reflects the sky, the demands and self-interest of the growing propertied classes," even some upright citizens regarded gang activities—including theft and murder—as little worse than the wrongs daily inflicted on the poor.

Monk had married in 1896, at the age of twenty-two. His wife, Margaret, was twenty-one, and had been born in New York, though her parents came to America from Germany. Beyond that, little is known about her. It would be surprising, though, if Monk had not picked her from among the prostitutes whom he both exploited and befriended. Neither of their first two children survived infancy, but two others were born just after the turn of the century. The 1900 U.S. census, the only one in which the adult Monk ever appeared, recorded him as living with Margaret at 101 East First Street and gave his occupation as "Salesman, birds." A year or so earlier he had indeed set up a pet store on Broome Street, though the animal-loving Monk reportedly refused to sell any of the five hundred animals and birds in the shop, and the large profits generated by the business came from activities entirely unconnected with pets.

Monk's Broome Street premises were opposite Public School No. 110 at Cannon and Broome streets. It was a tough school, and when a new headmistress, Miss Adeline E. Simpson, took charge, she was inclined to be discouraged by the problems she faced. Not the least of those problems was Monk. One day he chose the school windows as "objects for target practice with his revolver. Bullets rained through the schoolrooms, and the children were in panic. Without stopping to think that he might transfer his attentions to me," Miss Simpson later recalled, "I ran out and remonstrated with him, telling him that his own children were being endangered. He looked at me a moment, pistol in hand, and then said, 'Yer all right. Yer a good sport f'r not callin' th' cops.' And he did as I asked him."

Few other law-abiding citizens would have dared to emulate Miss Simpson's bravery when facing Monk and his gang of "hard-fisted, tough-faced young bullies." It was an era when gangsters not only were tough, but also were expected to look and act tough. When cartoonists drew caricatures of gangsters with broken noses, cauliflower ears, and caps pulled low over narrowed eyes, they might well have been drawn from living models. Monk was the archetype, and other gangsters strove to imitate his walk, his mannerisms, the slang words, and his "Toity-toid Street and Toid Avenue" speech. Like virtually all gang members and criminals, Monk was known only by his nickname, making the job of identification and arrest doubly difficult.

Although one observer attributed Monk's nickname to his "monkey-like face," he had acquired it not because of his features or a monastic vow of silence under interrogation by the police, but in tribute to the housebreaking skills he showed in clambering up and down the sides of buildings. "Monk" was an abbreviation of "monkey"; despite his bulk, he was a remarkably agile and fearless climber, scaling drainpipes and walls and swinging like an ape through windows and from ledge to ledge of upper stories and lofts to carry out burglaries.

Even if surprised by the householders, men as skilled in brawling as Monk and his street toughs had little trouble in making their escape. His gang included specialists of every type: hotel thieves, boardinghouse thieves, house thieves, and sneak thieves. "Second-story" burglars would go to work when a family was on a lower floor of the house, rifling the bedrooms and then either dropping the loot out the window to accomplices in the street or brazenly descending the stairs and letting themselves out the front door. Sneak thieves pillaged houses by picking the front-door lock and sneaking through the house in rubber-soled or woolen shoes. In other houses, a servant might be bribed to produce a key, or the bolts slid from outside using a loop of wire. There were other, even more specialized thieves, like "Long John" Garvey, whose chosen field was to rob newlyweds of their wedding presents and jewels. He studied the wedding announcements in the newspapers, then broke into his victims' houses while they were away on their honeymoon. Eventually he died on the job after falling through a skylight, trying to burgle a house while drunk.

Stolen goods were disposed of through a receiver, who rarely paid more than a quarter of the value and ran few risks because he never paid out until the goods had been removed to a place unknown to the thieves. The receiver thereby avoided any risk of being double-crossed and, if the thieves were later arrested, they could not betray him by leading the police to the stolen property. Many receivers doubled as the owners of pawnshops and were often known euphemistically as "my uncle." The typical pawnshop had a long counter and shelves overflowing with pledged goods: clocks, guns, ornaments, pictures, musical instruments, and the tools of carpenters and mechanics. More valuable and easily portable items like watches, jewelry, and silverware were stored in a vault built entirely of iron, and usually accessible only through the "office": an iron-barred enclosure where the pawnbroker pronounced valuations and dispensed hard cash. Bulkier items were transferred to storage on an upper or lower floor by means of a chute or dumbwaiter known as "the spout," from which developed the expression "up the spout," meaning lost, dead, or useless.

As Monk's gang grew in size, wealth, and power, he was able to delegate more and more of his crimes to his lieutenants, though he admitted that he still liked to "beat up a guy once in a while. It keeps my hand in." Other New York gangs hid behind soubriquets—the

Five Pointers, the Whyos, the Yakey Yakes, the Gophers—but Monk's gang members, unafraid to show their allegiance, were universally known as "the Eastmans." Monk and his henchmen put so many people in the hospital that ambulance drivers started calling the accident ward at Bellevue "The Eastman Pavilion." With its forbidding gray façade on the East River waterfront at Twenty-sixth Street, Bellevue was "the poor man's hospital" and, along with Gouverneur near Grand Street and East Broadway, served the population of the Lower East Side.

Monk's growing gangland reputation—and his increasing notoriety with the police—led him to become ever more wary. He hid his identity and his true address, moving house frequently and operating his gang from a constantly shifting series of saloons and poolrooms, and even a disused graveyard. The Eastmans also hung out in two stores on Rivington Street near the East River, one at Goerck Street and one at Mangin Street. Monk's expanding army of toughs were almost all young Jews from the Lower East Side territories he ruled; few members of the Eastmans or any of the rival gangs were older than twenty-five. Their readiness to use violence and intimidation made Monk a powerful figure in gambling, extortion, and prostitution.

The protection rackets that Monk set up, initially to extort money from street vendors, were the prototypes for the kinds of extortion and rackets used by later generations of gangsters, like the mafia. The East Side streets were jammed with pushcart peddlers selling the staples of life: food, clothing, crockery, and furniture. An upset cart was a disaster for its owner, and a couple of thugs could do it in seconds, one wrecking the cart while the other held back or beat up the hapless owner. A pushcart vendor had to pay the gangsters twice: first to stop the destruction of his cart and goods, and second to buy protection from the other gangs in the same line of work. Many of the most vicious gang fights grew out of disputes over this trade.

The profits from this kind of protection racket were not vast—pushcart vendors were not wealthy individuals, and even the most ruthless gangster could not extort money when there was no more to be extorted—but they were easily obtained. Even though protection rackets were soon extended to stores, restaurants, and factories—a failure to pay was met by attacks on employees, the destruction of stock and buildings, and the wrecking of delivery vehicles—one estimate suggested that the New York gangs were exacting no more than $75,000 annually from protection. Nonetheless, Monk took the lion's share of that, and also extorted money from less legitimate trades. He was "a sort of licensed bandit on the East Side," forcing other thieves, gamblers, and the owners of whorehouses and gambling dens to pay him a share of their profits. Protection rackets gave Monk a useful addition to his four main sources of profit: robbery; violence on commission from individuals, organizations, and politicians; gambling; and prostitution. In return Monk could always "be appealed to by the criminal for political influence with the police or courts."

The operators of the stuss and crap games scattered throughout the East Side and Mulberry Bend districts also had to pay the Eastmans for protection. Kid Twist, one of Monk's lieutenants, used to walk into a stuss or crap joint and say, "I want fifty dollars. What, you're not going to cough up? I'll shoot up your **** place." When he got his fifty, he would say, "I'll see you again in about a month." In time Monk and other gang leaders took over many of the most lucrative games, and a suitable proportion of the take always found its way to Monk's friends in the police and Tammany Hall.

Even more than gambling, prostitution was probably the most profitable of all of Monk's enterprises. At one time "a real gangman" would never have admitted to earning money as a pimp, though none ever hesitated about exacting protection money from brothel owners. In Monk's day that stigma no longer applied; prostitution was just another—very rich—source of income, and all the criminal gangs profited from it. In the 1870s there were more than twenty thousand full-time prostitutes in New York, approximately one to every forty inhabitants, and probably a similar number of part-timers. Sex was on sale for as little as fifty cents, a price that remained unaltered for decades, and there were five thousand overt brothels, together with countless others that masqueraded as cider mills, cigar stores, groggeries, dance halls, and concert saloons. There were also thousands of "blind pigs"—illegal dives concealed by innocuous-looking storefronts—and speakeasies.

The only thing that had changed in the remaining years of the century was that the number of brothels and prostitutes had increased. Brothels ranged all the way from the dismal sailors' haunts by the East River, where "half-exposed women, often far gone in age, looks and alcoholism, sat on stoops of tenements" and would render almost any service for the price of a drink. There were brothels catering to male laborers, where prostitutes serviced prodigious numbers of men at rates from fifty cents to one or two dollars a time. One "Stakhanovite of sex" claimed to have serviced fifty-eight men in three hours. Many of the prostitutes were girls aged between ten and fifteen; in New York the age of consent was raised from ten to sixteen in 1889, and to eighteen in 1895, but that was routinely ignored by policemen on the take.

Some brothels specialized in very young girls, and others catered to those who preferred "unnatural practices." The prostitutes of "Soubrette Row" offered oral sex, a service few prostitutes would render because of the stigma associated with it at the time; "as a result the other girls will not associate or eat with them." There were small places with one, two, or three women, like the places run by "Jennie the Factory" on Eighteenth Street or "Sadie the Chink" on Twenty-seventh Street, and at the top end of the scale, establishments like the extraordinary "Sister's Row" in the Tenderloin, run by seven sisters in adjoining brownstone houses, where prices ranged up to a hundred dollars and "on certain days of each month, gentlemen were only admitted if they carried bouquets of flowers and wore evening clothes." Madame Josephine Woods ran an even more exclusive brothel, where only champagne was served and the sordid topic of money was never mentioned. Her gentlemen received a monthly statement of "professional services" rendered, which they paid by check.

In less exalted establishments, prostitution was also often a cover for robbery or fraud. Some women worked with "panel-thieves" who, while the prostitute was occupying her customer, would slide open a panel or other concealed opening and rifle the man's jacket and trousers. In another variant, "the badger game," the victim would be interrupted in the act by a man posing as the prostitute's irate husband. After threatening violence and death to the victim, he would then allow himself to be pacified with cash.

By the turn of the century, Monk's gang had grown into a twelve-hundred-strong army of thieves, pickpockets, safecrackers, prostitutes, and thugs, ruling over the area between Monroe and Fourteenth streets and from the Bowery to the East River, including "the treasure-laden Red Light district." He set up his headquarters in a dive on Chrystie Street, just off the Bowery, called The Palm. It was just one of many Lower East Side dives with evocative names: others included The Flea Bag; The Bucket of Blood; The Morgue, whose owner's proud boast was that his liquor was equally efficacious as a drink or an embalming fluid; and McGurk's Suicide Hall, a place notorious for the number of young women who had thrown themselves from the balconies to their deaths on the dance floor below.

This was the heyday of the Eastmans, and Monk and his followers wore expensive clothes, drank good liquor, squired the best-looking prostitutes, and had money to burn. There were many other gangs, including the Whyos, the Gas House and Cherry Hill gangs, and the "Razor" Riley, "Mike the Bite," "Kid" Gorman, "Ike" Fadinsky, and "Humpty" Jackson gangs—the latter's acolytes met in a graveyard between Twelfth and Thirteenth streets—but they seldom went beyond brawling and petty crime. Monk's rise heralded the emergence of large-scale organized crime, and of federations of criminal gangs uniting to further their interests or defend their territories. He was the bridge between the era when the Irish gangs had been dominant and the emergence of the mafia and organized crime as we know it today.

Monk's gang was less a single entity, like one of the old Irish gangs, than a series of separate but interlinked organizations. When necessary, this "Prince of Thugs" could call not only on his own army of men, but also on the allegiance of smaller gangs. These gangs all had their independence, their own territories and sources of revenue, which they policed, but all also paid tribute to the supreme commander, Monk, who along with the right to impose "taxation" also had the right to conscript their men in time of war with other gangs.

In addition to his pet and bird store, Monk had also set up another "front": a bicycle store. One of his principal lieutenants, "Crazy Butch," established a gang of young criminals called the Squab Wheelmen, in homage to Monk's twin "legitimate" trades: squabs—pigeons—and bicycles. Crazy Butch then fully justified his nickname by staging a midnight attack on the Squab Wheelmen's own poolroom, "by way of testing their valor and settling definitely, in event of trouble, who would stick and who would duck." The results did not encourage him; there were sixty gang members in the room when he and six others ran up the stairway with pistols blazing, and almost all sixty fled in terror. "Little Kishky," who was sitting by the open window, was so startled and terrified that he fell out the window and broke his neck. Some of those who had fled for their lives were outraged that Little Kishky's life had been needlessly sacrificed, but the gangland consensus was that he was a weak link who deserved his fate: "If Little Kishky hadn't been a quitter, he would never have fallen out. Butch was not only exonerated but applauded."

Crazy Butch had once been closer to "the heart of that grim gang captain," Monk, than any other man, but, after serving four years in Sing Sing for a botched burglary, Butch played a much less active part in the Eastmans' gang activities and instead began operating as a New York Fagin, with thirty boys on the streets "all trained in pocket-picking to a feather-edge." Butch would mount a bicycle (no doubt rented from Monk's store) and knock over a woman pedestrian. As Butch and the woman exchanged recriminations and accusations, a crowd of onlookers would form around them and Butch's young pickpockets would go to work.

Butch even trained his dog Rabbi—inevitably, he had stolen it—to retrieve women's bags and purses. When Butch saw a promising purse, he drew it to "the rascal notice of Rabbi" and left the dog to seize it in its jaws, wrest it away from its owner, and race off through the streets before delivering "the touch" to Butch at the corner of Willett and Stanton streets.

As well as Butch's Squab Wheelmen, Monk could also draw on the ranks of juvenile gangs like the Junior Eastmans, boys from as young as seven or eight up to sixteen or seventeen who tried to emulate their heroes in dress, speech, and deed, in the hope of one day winning admission to the adult ranks. If all Monk's smaller affiliates and juniors were added to his strength, he could put a private army of somewhere near two thousand in the field. They were also formidably well-armed. When police—perhaps angered that their customary slice of the action had not been paid—staged a raid on Monk's headquarters at The Palm, they removed two wagonloads of brass knuckles, slungshots (a rock or other dense object in a thick, close-woven net), blackjacks, knives, pistols, and other weapons.

Despite the rough-and-ready nature of his enterprises, Monk was sufficiently businesslike—even at the risk of providing evidence that might be used against him—to require his lieutenants to compile written reports of the crimes they were commissioned to carry out; one of his most efficient blackjackers always handed in a formal, typewritten document. Monk was also "the first of the gangsters to exploit the labor field." In 1897 he accepted a commission to break up a union action in the garment industry and beat up two of the ringleaders. After that, Monk found regular work during labor disputes, and he was more than willing to take money from either side.

Profound social changes were beginning to sweep America, and the dominance of the capitalist robber barons was threatened by the emergence of organized labor. Strikes meant long hours on duty and hard work for the police. As a result, they were instinctively hostile to strikers and "not tender" in handling them. While suppressing strikes, they often found themselves in unofficial alliance with Monk. However, when not strikebreaking and intimidating or assaulting union pickets on behalf of the employers, Monk and other gang leaders were also often placed on union payrolls, earning twenty-five to fifty dollars a week as a retainer, and taking a 25 percent slice of the ten dollars a day each of their thugs was paid for threatening and blackjacking strike-breakers. During the strikes arising from attempts to unionize the garment trades on the Lower East Side, groups of Monk's *shtarkes* (sluggers) were simultaneously assaulting strikers on behalf of the Jewish manufacturers and attacking scabs for the union organizers.

As his powers grew, Monk began to do criminal business with "respectable" New Yorkers and operate beyond the confines of his Lower East Side domain. He hired out small gangs of strong-arm men to private individuals to collect debts, pursue personal vendettas, frighten off business or sexual competitors, or ensure the silence or nonattendance of court witnesses. One of the individuals who made use of Monk's services was a ruthless young criminal called Arnold Rothstein. Just eighteen at the turn of the century, Rothstein was already running his own card games, and soon branched out into loan-sharking, employing Monk's gang members to pressure or beat up his more recalcitrant clients.

Monk's terms were the same for either side in a dispute, or for any other prospective customer. One of his more fearsome lieutenants, "Big Jack" Zelig, had a comprehensive list of charges:

> Slash on cheek with knife: $1–$10
> Shot in leg: $1–$25
> Shot in arm: $5–$25
> Throwing a bomb: $5–$50
> Murder: $10–$100.

The bargain rates, even for murder, reflected not only the general poverty of the Lower East Side and the power of competition to drive down prices, but also, perhaps, the low level of risk attached to even bombing and murder in a city policed with such rampant incompetence and corruption.

Monk and his men went about their business with something close to impunity, as was illustrated when two members of his gang were charged in 1903 after Monk was hired by "a blonde of striking appearance." Seeking to be rid of her husband, a wealthy dentist, she allegedly paid Monk three hundred dollars to throw acid in his face or kill him. However, when the case came before the Essex Market Court, Magistrate Pool dismissed all charges against the wife and Monk's men, and even claimed that the witnesses' affidavits branded them as perjurers: "the conspiracy in the case was on the other side."

Police claimed to have traced a score of murders to the areas in which Monk and his fellow gangsters were operating, but no convictions ever followed. He was arrested dozens of times, often for serious assault and once for murder, but he was never brought to justice. "In the three years I was over there," a policeman said, after his transfer from the Lower East Side to the City Hall Squad, "Monk Eastman was arrested thirty times, but we never got him dead to rights, and had to let him go."

4

A MODERN ROBIN HOOD

The leader of the first primarily Jewish criminal gang, Monk had now become the dominant figure in New York's criminal underworld, and his power and influence grew with the steady expansion of his domain as the Eastmans eroded the territories of the old Irish gangs, ousted, defeated, or co-opted their gang members, and adopted their techniques. From rival gangs like the Irish Whyos and Yakey Yakes, the Eastmans learned the use of strong-arm methods, and from the Italian Five Pointers they appropriated a method of terrifying the

patrons of poolrooms by playing a game of pool using revolvers instead
of cues.

Monk's gang operated from a string of other hangouts apart from
his headquarters at The Palm, including a barbershop on Allen Street,
a place at the back of a hat store on Delancey Street, and around New
Irving Hall, on Broome Street. He was also spreading his operations
from the relatively lean pickings in the Jewish districts and into the
riches of the Sixth Avenue shopping area and the Tenderloin—Midtown from Twenty-third to Forty-second streets between Fifth and
Seventh avenues. Year by year, the Eastmans had moved westward
toward the Bowery, "that mecca of all criminals. Ten years ago they
were at Goerck Street, three years ago they had reached Allen Street
and in their migration had changed character and race."

Allen Street was lined with brothels, and the junior members of
Monk's gang soon realized that the "cadet" business—pimping and
procuring women to work as prostitutes—was easier, more profitable, and much less risky than picking pockets. Every prostitute a cadet
pimped was "a hostage to fortune always on the street" because she was
vulnerable to the depredations of other gangs, and cadets who were not
gang members themselves had to pay the gangs for protection for their
women and their beats. As a result, prostitution and gangsterism went
hand in hand. Their political connections helped cadets to control their
prostitutes, "secure their hard- and ill-earned money," and, with the
aid of professional false witnesses, send any women who stepped out of
line to the Island.

Monk's men were now thoroughly professional criminals, and the
organization of the gang had also been refined and perfected over the
years. Just like a corporation, Monk had a legal counsel on retainer
and set aside a percentage of his earnings to pay the court expenses
for himself and his gang members. He also had a regular "fence"—a
receiver of stolen goods—though much of the property the gang stole
went through the hands of another fence, "who receives propositions
on the sidewalk of Delancey Street and offers the best prices." Even
if his uncle, Thomas McSpedon, had not already introduced him to
Tammany politicians, as the de facto boss of his teeming district, Monk
would soon have come to their attention, and a symbiotic relationship
developed between them: "the gang needed the politician, and the politician must have the gang," because politicians profited from graft and
corruption on an epic scale.

Thomas F. "Big Tom" Foley of the Second Assembly District was bull-necked and bald as a billiard ball, with a boozer's flush to his features, and looked like what he was: a bruiser. Like Monk, he had been a bouncer in saloons and dance halls, and was the owner of a Brooklyn dive before he fell afoul of the law and found it prudent to move across the East River to Manhattan. There he established a string of bars and dives, including his headquarters, a saloon on Franklin Street near the Tombs prison. "The swellest ginmill below the line [Fourteenth Street]," it became one of the most famous saloons in New York, patronized by politicians, prizefighters, prosecutors, and defense lawyers.

Timothy D. "Big Tim" Sullivan was an even more powerful figure. A former bootblack and newsboy who "never tastes tobacco, never touches liquor, never breaks his word," he became a saloonkeeper, theater and nickelodeon owner, and Tammany boss of the Bowery. As wide as a door, over six feet tall and weighing 250 pounds, with a piercing stare from his pale blue eyes, Big Tim was a controversial figure, but hugely popular in the slum districts that composed his power base. "The political boss of downtown New York" and "The King of the Underworld," Sullivan epitomized the "Tammany Man": "Politically he is corrupt; personally he is good—richly good."

Big Tim's first headquarters was a saloon on Doyers Street, just off the Bowery, a narrow, filthy thoroughfare that even by day was "repulsive enough to keep anybody from trying to penetrate its mysteries," and was "the scene of more murders than any other place in New York." Later he moved his chief base of operations to another saloon, the Occidental, with a famed erotic fresco on the ceiling. Opposite the Tombs police court, it was well patronized by police and court officials.

Big Tim had Irish roots, but as the ethnic makeup of the Lower East Side changed, he took care to cultivate both the Italian and Jewish immigrant populations, becoming an honorary member of the Paul Kelly Association. Purporting to be a sports and social club, it was the front for Kelly's largely Italian Five Points Gang. Big Tim was also vice president of the Max Hochstim Association—"the society of politicians, pimps and thieves," named in honor of a Tammany ward heeler—the leading social and political organization in the Jewish districts.

Big Tim was always content to allow others the appearance and trappings of power. He saw few people and did business only by word of mouth, but though Charles F. Murphy was the ostensible leader of Tammany Hall, no one in Tammany—or in New York—could be in any doubt where the real power lay in the city: Big Tim's "word is law to thousands." He dispensed largesse like a medieval monarch, but also used intimidation and thuggery at the ballot box to build the most cynical and effective political organization in the country. Tammany supporters on the Lower East Side would tie brooms to their railings the night before an election, in a public show of support for a Tammany sweep the next day, though such demonstrations were scarcely necessary since in Big Tim's kingdom, nothing was left to chance. In the 1892 presidential election, Sullivan's Lower East Side assembly district voted 395 to 4 for the Tammany-backed candidate, Grover Cleveland, but Big Tim felt compelled to apologize to "Boss" Croker: "Harrison got one more vote than I expected, but I'll find that feller."

The extent of Big Tim's wealth was artfully concealed. He had sixteen paid employees, whose duties included disbursing cash in response to the scores of begging letters Big Tim received daily; he counted those dollars well spent if they bought him the loyalty—and the votes—of a few more electors. He also made frequent flamboyant charitable gestures, giving away forty-five hundred pairs of shoes and socks to shoeless constituents during one harsh winter, and every year he provided a free Christmas dinner with turkey and plum duff, limitless beer and tobacco, and a pair of buckskin gloves for each of the six thousand people who turned up, at a cost estimated at ten thousand dollars. There were also glittering ballum-rancums at the New Irving Dance Hall, where, in "the great dancing hall, stuffed to the doors with painted women and lean-faced men," Big Tim held court from a box "in the name of a young Jewish friend"—possibly Monk, whom many believed to be Jewish. A judge of the general sessions court sat at the rear of Big Tim's box, and another city judge "leads through the happy mazes of the grand march a thousand pimps and thieves and prostitutes, to the blatant crying of the band: 'Sullivan, Sullivan, a damned fine Irishman!' "

Big Tim also staged an annual chowder at which a horde of his constituents and associates were treated to a daylong festival of music, sports, entertainment, food, and drink, capped off with a fireworks display at night. Heralded by as many as three brass bands, Big Tim led his army of supporters down to the South Street waterfront, where chartered paddle steamers were waiting. Lubricated by free beer, whiskey, and cigars for the men, and ice creams, candies, and entertainment for the women and children, the throngs spent the day at College Point or Coney Island, where at least some of the costs of the day were recouped from the stuss games and the gambling on boxing bouts and sports that the inebriated East Siders took to with enthusiasm. They returned late at night in a drunken, brawling cavalcade through the Lower East Side.

Sullivan supported a score of indigent families, donated money to hospitals and orphanages, and, wherever he went, he paid the bills of all who shared his company. The cost of all this largesse was stupendous, but despite all the money he gave away—"Not a splinter under three hundred thousand dollars a year"—by the time he was in his forties, his worth was estimated at more than two million dollars.

Big Tim had business interests, particularly in the field of popular entertainment, promoting boxing, horse racing, and operating chains of burlesque houses, vaudeville theaters, and nickelodeons, but even his most fervent admirers would have struggled to claim that all his wealth came by such legitimate or semi-legitimate means. Big Tim barely troubled to deny the huge income he enjoyed from gambling dens, though he fervently denied profiting from prostitution.

Like Big Tim, Tammany's other power brokers made only cursory attempts to conceal the source of their wealth, though "Boss" Croker offered an ingenious justification of the Tammany system:

> Think of the hundreds of thousands of foreigners dumped into our city . . . Not a Mugwump [do-gooder] in the city would shake hands with them . . . Tammany looks after them for the sake of their vote, grafts them upon the Republic, makes citizens of them, in short; and although you may not like our motives or our methods, what other agency is there by which so long a row could have been hoed so quickly or so well? If we go down into the gutter it is because there are men in the gutter, and you have got to go down where they are if you are to do anything with them.

One estimate put the cost of this Tammany "citizenship" program of graft at two fifths of New York's annual budget. Controller Metz, in an appendix to a 1909 report on New York's chaotic public finances, claimed that from a quarter to half of the city's annual payroll of $80 million was useless—skimmed off in supposed wages to names padding the city payroll—and in that year, New York's actual debt topped $800 million. Other skimmings, scams, bribes, and kickbacks took the total figure lost by graft even higher; one estimate put it at $80 million a year. Thousands shared in the proceeds, but there was no doubt that Sullivan took the lion's share.

State Senator and Tammany sachem George Washington Plunkitt also found his elected position no obstacle to accruing substantial wealth. Despite being a millionaire contractor and real-estate operator, his HQ and only office was his shoeshine stand in the New York County Courthouse. The first man—publicly at least—to draw the distinction between the honest graft that he practiced and the dishonest graft practiced by others, Plunkitt's motto was said to have been "I seen my opportunities and I took them."

Politicians like these stood to profit both from Monk's criminal enterprises and from his ability to get out the vote—both genuine and bogus—on primary and election days, using his army of gang members. Deals were done, and henceforth Monk's gang members spent election days working as "guerillas" (or "gorillas") stealing ballot boxes, and acting as repeaters who voted early and often and "sluggers," persuading others of the wisdom of voting the Tammany ticket, while frightening off those intent on voting for a rival candidate. "Any political wavering to Monk's philosophy meant a busted head," and his gang was particularly effective at intimidating "the nervous Hebrews, who could not be depended upon to 'vote right.' "

In return, Tammany could offer Monk the one thing a gangster craved above all others: Monk's gorillas had effective immunity from the law not just on election days but on every other day of the year as well. That immunity made the gangs even more daring, so that "youths who, alone and unaided, would run from the blue uniform of the greenest and rawest policeman, carry pistols, hold up decent citizens, and defy the law and the police in conjunction."

Tammany politicians displayed great skill in publicly denouncing organized crime while actually profiting from and building alliances with it. This was particularly true in the area of prostitution; many of the cadets who procured and pimped young women also formed a significant part of the army of repeaters and sluggers during voter registration and elections.

The shifting balance of power in the Lower East Side gangland was vividly demonstrated in the elections in the fall of 1901, when "word was sent out to all the criminal population of the East Side that 'Monk' Eastman was the sole leader of the election 'repeaters,' that every criminal was expected to be out early on election day and do his part, and that in return the politicians would stand for 'anything but murder' from the criminals."

In addition to the repeaters provided by Monk's gang, the poorer lodging houses in the Lower East Side were used for the "colonization" of voters, with prodigious numbers of tramps and other homeless derelicts registered at each address. In return for booze money, or sometimes their freedom from jail, these lodging-house voters duly came out "strong on the side of the political boss" at election times, and especially in presidential elections. After a raid on stale beer dives had rounded up 275 tramps who were routinely sentenced to six months on the Island for vagrancy, one policeman noted with an air more of resignation than outrage that at election times he had "more than once seen the same tramp sent to Blackwell's Island twice in twenty-four hours for six months at a time." Protected by Big Tim and the other Tammany bosses, few lodging-house owners were ever prosecuted for voter fraud, no matter how implausible the numbers purportedly living in their premises. The graveyards were another fruitful source of votes; the names of the deceased were registered, and large numbers rose from the grave to vote on election day.

Governor Odell and the state superintendent of elections, John McCullagh, issued threats and appeals to the police, naming the leaders of the gangs of repeaters and citing the poolrooms and "disorderly resorts" that were the centers of colonization operations in the city. They claimed that a vast number of names were illegally registered; one gang member boasted that he not only intended to vote under each of the eight names he himself had successfully registered, but also under the seven names fraudulently registered by another member of the gang who had been forced to flee the city. However, Odell's and McCullagh's appeals to the police went largely unanswered. Policemen knew where their loyalties lay; like the gangs, they also benefited from political protection and from the police graft that Tammany tolerated, or even put their way.

When reform candidates and their supporters vowed to flood the East Side with outside poll-watchers, Big Tim Sullivan ridiculed the threat and issued the ominous warning that if attempts were made to "bring down a lot of football-playing, hair-mattressed college athletes to run the polls by force, I will say now that there won't be enough ambulances in New York to carry them away." Despite the best efforts of Odell and McCullagh, the election was widely regarded as one of the least honest in New York's tarnished history. The polls did not open until the afternoon, but by six o'clock on election morning, there were ten to fifteen Jewish and Italian repeaters in line at every election booth in the district. They were "thoroughly drilled" and "a regular commissary department furnished them with breakfast and luncheon, whiskey, cigars, and even benches to sit on."

Sluggers routinely intimidated supporters of rival candidates, and even election officials. When an election inspector claimed to have been kicked, beaten, and struck on the head with a bottle by a member of the Eastman gang, his demands that the police arrest the man were "met with indifference"; Magistrate Hogan at the Essex Market Court refused to issue a warrant.

Big Tim was convincingly elected in his district, but an even more dramatic illustration of the changing face of Lower Manhattan occurred in the Second Assembly District, where Big Tom Foley was standing against another Tammany politician, Paddy Divver. Divver, an old-style Irish politician in what used to be an Irish immigrant stronghold, was routed by Monk's confederation of Jewish and Italian gangs. The "old-time Irish residents and 'repeaters' howled with impotent rage. They were outnumbered, held back from the polls, and in many instances calmly blackjacked. The police did not interfere." When the vote was counted, Foley had won with a two-thirds majority. His later election as sheriff of New York "probably exceeded all previous records for 'repeating' at election time."

Monk could furnish a minimum of four or five hundred sluggers and repeaters on election days, each one worth five to ten votes at election time and ten to twenty at primaries, when scrutiny by election officials was even more lax. One group of gang members did the repeating, while others formed strong-arm gangs, beating up any deputies or policemen who tried to arrest any of the repeaters. If the polls were carefully watched, "guys with whiskers"—bearded men—were preferred:

When they vote with their whiskers on, you take 'em to a barber and scrape off the chin fringe. Then you vote them again with side lilacs and mustache. Then to a barber again, off comes the sides and you vote 'em a third time with the mustache. If that ain't enough and the box can stand a few more ballots, clean off the mustache and vote 'em plain face. That makes every one of them good for four votes.

Scores of repeaters were even issued deputy sheriffs' badges. Having beaten all previous records for stuffing ballot boxes, by way of celebration they began firing revolvers in the street, "like a crowd of cowboys in a Western mining town." When police patrolmen arrested any of the men, their accomplices, whose badges outranked those of the patrolmen, insisted on taking charge of the prisoners, then led them around the corner and released them again.

The election day was reported by *The New York Times* under the headline quiet day at the polls: only 282 arrests. Despite prima facie cases against them, 90 percent of those arrested for electoral fraud, including the chairman of a district board of election inspectors and a state senator, were discharged. The state superintendent of elections picked his words with care in describing this as "a riddle."

When Monk or one of his toughs was arrested, word would come down to release him, or a Tammany Hall bondsman would arrive to secure bail. Big Tim Sullivan personally provided lawyers and thousands of dollars of sureties as bail for men accused of election fraud. The bail was usually forfeited and the case deleted from the records, because the gang members gave false names and addresses and then melted away when released, but politicians like Big Tim regarded the loss of bail money as simply a necessary election expense.

Whenever Monk or his men did appear in court, Tammany-appointed lawyers were there to defend them. On one occasion Monk and a couple of "stalls" were caught red-handed attempting to rob a man in a streetcar—"working the rattler," as it was known in the underworld. They beat up the conductor and a policeman who tried to interfere, surrendering only when confronted by a squad of bluecoats. Despite overwhelming evidence against them, they were all acquitted when the case went to court. "The politicians always sprung him," one New York detective complained. "He was the best man they ever had at the polls."

The only authority Monk was answerable to was Tammany Hall. When Congressman Goldfogle, a staunch ally of Big Tim Sullivan, had his "kettle" (Bowery slang for a watch) stolen in a crowded streetcar, the enraged congressman appealed to Sullivan for his help. "Instantly the word was passed out that the 'Big Fellow' was sore, and that the watch must be returned or there would be trouble." There were no witnesses to the theft, no evidence of who was responsible, yet within twenty-four hours the congressman had his watch back, without any intervention by the police. "The word of Timothy D got to the 'Eastmans,' and they gave it up."

Monk's chief rival, Paul Kelly, was also under the protection and control of Tammany Hall and Big Tim. "Over them his power is absolute; for them his word is law. To whisper 'it's the Big Fellow's order' closes the most captious mouth." Even when Kelly committed an assault and robbery so blatant that it could not be ignored, his case was "so manipulated by the police before it came to sentence that for an offense that should have cost him ten to twenty years, Kelly got nine months." As Recorder Goff complained, "The conduct of the police in this case was shameful."

The cozy arrangement by which crooked politicians, corrupt policemen, and gangsters rigged elections, fixed court cases, and shared the proceeds of crime was only occasionally threatened. Anticorruption candidates were sometimes successful in gaining election despite blatant Tammany gerrymandering and vote-rigging, but the appetite of New York's citizens for reform rarely lasted more than a single mayoral term. As "Boss" Croker remarked after Tammany lost an election, "Our people could not stand the rotten police corruption. They'll be back at the next election; they can't stand reform either."

When Asa Bird Gardiner, Tammany's nominee for district attorney at a subsequent election, shouted "To hell with reform!" at a campaign meeting, it was promptly adopted as the Tammany slogan. After the votes, genuine and bogus, were counted, "the Wigwam" had duly reestablished its control—"Tammany is not a wave, it's the sea itself"—and the Tammany politicians at once set about constructing "a new, perfected system of blackmail and bribery . . . New York is New York again."

For Tammany, the mathematics of voter fraud were straightforward. The two thirds of a million registered votes of the city were divided so closely along conventional party lines that only a slight balance was needed to secure control of the government. The crucial votes were supplied by Monk's federation of criminal sluggers and repeaters, giving Tammany bosses an iron control of both their own party organization and the city. "The government of the second largest city in the world . . . depends at bottom upon the will of the criminal population—principally thieves and pimps." Yet Tammany's "corruption with consent" also relied on the corruption of the city's wider population. "The people are not innocent . . . no doubt that was not new to many observers. It was new to me . . . The people themselves get very little; they come cheap, but they are interested."

5

THE ROGUES' GALLERY

For Monk—who grew wealthy from the corrupt and immoral earnings generated by his ever-growing gang—New York City proved a rich criminal territory. Home to several million citizens, more than any other American city, New York was the epicenter of manufacturing, finance, and the wholesale and retail trades. By the end of the nineteenth century, the value of American industrial production had already surpassed that of Britain, France, and Germany combined, and eighty of the one hundred largest U.S. companies were headquartered in New

York. Yet even in the era in which New York was surpassing London as the richest and most powerful city in the richest and most powerful nation on the planet, it still retained much of the feel of a Wild West town.

The U.S. murder rate was from ten to twenty times the murder rate of the British Empire. Other crime was rife as well, and law enforcement was virtually nonexistent, though, as one senior police officer pointed out, in some parts of the city they had "perfect devils to deal with. Within the last week, half a dozen of my men have come into the stations with their clothes actually torn off them."

The police met force with force, using clubs—"billys" and "nightsticks"—made of locust wood, which was less prone to splitting than hickory or oak. Billys were short clubs, whereas nightsticks were twenty-two inches long and one and three-eighths inches thick. They were used by the predominantly Irish-American police with such vigor and brutality on poor New Yorkers, especially those of eastern and southern European origin, that police stations were colloquially known as "slaughterhouses." Apart from cracking heads, police clubs also had another use; while London policemen blew whistles to call for assistance, New York cops beat on the sidewalks and the iron manhole covers with their nightsticks, producing an unnerving drumming sound that was audible even above the relentless noise of the city streets.

On a triangular site bounded by Broome, Grand, and Centre streets, police headquarters was a four-story building, surrounded by iron railings and approached by a steep flight of stone steps. The granite exterior carried a minimum of decoration; the only touches of color in its drab gray façade were the striped awnings screening the windows from the fierce glare of the summer sun. The records of every arrest, charge, conviction, place, and term of imprisonment entered in the leather-bound police blotter kept at each station house were consolidated at headquarters, and portraits of thousands of known criminals were kept in the "Rogue's Gallery" in a room on the first floor. Monk's likeness was among them, Number 5,844. Arrested men made strenuous attempts to distort their features as the photograph was taken in the hope of escaping future detection, often in vain.

The museum of crime on the first floor of police headquarters displayed pictures of the most notorious of these criminals, alongside examples of the tools of their trade: lock picks, sledgehammers, drags, drills, jimmies, blowpipes, jackscrews, dark lanterns, powder flasks, "no end of dirks, knives and pistols, and a good assortment of black caps and ropes of murderers that make one shudder to look upon." The first floor also housed the criminal record room, the night captains' room, and the detectives' main assembly room, where the daily lineup of criminals took place. In order to pick up the first news of crimes and arrests, every newspaper kept a reporter permanently stationed at police headquarters, and they reported the crimes and wars of the Eastman gang with "a sensational minuteness of detail that does its share toward keeping up its evil traditions and inflaming the ambition of its members to be as bad as the worst."

For police purposes, the city was divided into three inspection districts, each under the control of an inspector, and subdivided into twelve precincts, controlled by a captain. In turn the precincts were divided into patrol beats or posts, with roundsmen maintaining a watch on individual patrolmen. With rare exceptions, those who wished to join the police had to pay a bribe to do so, and Tammany influence ensured that loyal supporters of the Wigwam were disproportionately represented among those new recruits—one of the reasons why the New York City Police Department had always contained so many Irishmen. Policemen then bought their promotions from their superiors—in the 1890s the going rate for promotion from patrolman to roundsman was $300, and from roundsman to sergeant $1,600—and then set about reclaiming the money in bribes, kickbacks, and the proceeds from the gambling, prostitution, and robberies to which they routinely turned a blind eye. The only policemen potentially exempt from the normal system of purchases, bribes, and kickbacks were the handsome, powerful-looking men recruited for the Broadway Squad, whose main role was to patrol the eponymous thoroughfare, keeping petty criminals at bay so that New York's more respectable and affluent citizens could continue to cherish the illusion that the city as a whole was similarly well policed.

The system was virtually self-perpetuating; the only way to recoup the money paid to join the force in the first place, and for every promotion thereafter, was to partake of the graft on offer. As one policeman remarked, "Of course there are cops who have never taken a dollar, at least I've heard about them, but I never saw one." Those principled policemen who somehow slipped through the net, refusing to pay or accept graft, or insisting on arresting "connected" criminals, were banished to "the Goats." Once the nickname for the shantytown on the marshy ground that would become Central Park, where squatters lived with their goats and foraging pigs, the Goats had come to mean any district remote from the rewards and opportunities of downtown and midtown Manhattan.

Even when policemen had not been bribed to look the other way, criminals routinely escaped the law, often making use of the parallel universe of the rooftops, crowded with pigeon coops, that acted as a secondary sidewalk linking the tenements high above the city streets. Criminals could make their way from building to building along the rooftops as quickly as the pedestrians on the sidewalk moved several stories below. There was a gap of only three feet between the rear tenements on Cherry and Hamilton streets, and criminals being chased by the police ran up to the roof, jumped the gap, and were through a skylight, down the stairs, and off up the street before the police had even rounded the corner.

The criminal gangs operated with virtual impunity within the areas they controlled, but their territories were rigidly defined. The Lower West Side was the last stronghold of the Irish, and the Lower East Side was divided between the Italian and Jewish gangs—and they rarely strayed into the respectable uptown or downtown districts, where the solid citizens went about their daily business largely untroubled by crime.

The financial district had not always been so crime-free. Wall Street had once been plagued by gangs of bank thieves, forgers, and pickpockets, and thefts of cash and securities from bank messengers and bank tellers, and even from counting rooms, banks, and vaults, were commonplace. When Inspector Thomas Byrnes took charge of the detective department, he tackled the problem of crime in the financial district by discreetly renting an office on Wall Street at his own expense and installing nine of his detectives there. He then established "dead-lines" at Fulton Street and Fourteenth Street. Any known pickpocket, thief, or other blue-collar criminal found south of Fulton Street or north of Fourteenth Street was picked up and, unless he could provide a valid reason for being there, was clubbed with police nightsticks and sent to Blackwell's Island as a habitual criminal. Later a special room in the stock exchange was set aside for the detectives.

The system worked so well that robberies around Wall Street declined dramatically. On occasion Byrnes even arranged the return of goods that had been stolen; in separate incidents, diamonds and valuable papers were returned by thieves, with the compliments of the inspector. Byrnes was rewarded by the grateful members of the stock exchange with stock tips, "good things," and gratuities—the source, so he claimed, of $350,000 worth of real estate and $292,000 in cash, held in his wife's name, that he accumulated. He was also given a handsome $500 gold watch at a presentation that was only slightly marred by the theft of the president of the exchange's splendid new fur-lined overcoat during the ceremony.

Although Byrnes's dead-line system curtailed the extramural activities of Lower East Side criminals to some extent, there were also other slum areas with their attendant gangs above the Fourteenth Street dead-line, which was supposed to "fence off the good from the bad." Hell's Kitchen on the West Side, the Rag Gang's territory on the East River at Thirty-ninth Street, "Battle Row" on East Sixty-third Street, and "the Village" at Twenty-ninth Street and First Avenue—where the roof of almost every tenement was piled with bricks and missiles for bombarding police—were as tough and lawless as Monk's Lower East Side heartlands. Nor did the dead-line system do anything to restrain the white-collar criminals who robbed savers and investors through frauds and share scams. While crime was reduced south of Fulton Street and north of Fourteenth Street, between those dead-lines, Monk and the other crooks of the Lower East Side enjoyed a virtual free rein, provided they paid the police protection money or gave them a slice of the action.

Occasionally the public would be roused to outrage by some particularly flagrant abuse of the law and the police would flex their muscles and raid brothels, gambling dens, and thieves' kitchens . . . which almost invariably proved to be models of decorum because the owners were tipped off in advance. A few token criminals were arrested, convicted, and jailed, but in the main they were loners, those without political connections or who had tried to cheat the police of their share. Meanwhile, street gangs operated with the tacit consent of police and politicians, and institutionalized corruption permeated every aspect of the life of the city.

An investigation into corruption by the Lexow Committee in 1894, albeit highly selective and partisan, had concluded, "We see the powers of government prostituted to protect criminals, to demoralize the police, to debauch the public conscience and to turn governmental functions into channels for private gain." Evidence of such corruption was not hard to uncover. A representative of the committee sent to serve a bench warrant upon a brothel owner, Madame Hastings, retired in confusion without serving the warrant when he found her entertaining several city officials and a judge of the criminal court, and the commissioner of police ordered a policeman who raided a brothel owned by Madame Sadie West to go back and apologize to her.

The Reverend Charles Parkhurst, minister of the Madison Square Church and president of the Society for the Prevention of Crime, became one of the most fervent campaigners against crime and corruption. In his "rustic innocence," Parkhurst thought the police were there to repress crime, but it now began to dawn on him that, like Tammany Hall, their principal object was "to protect and foster crime and make capital out of it." Tammany was not so much a political party as a business that fostered the crime and vice from which it profited, and protected criminals from the law.

On February 14, 1892, Parkhurst used his Sunday sermon to launch a blistering attack on the vice and corruption that riddled New York. "While we fight iniquity, the mayor and his whole gang of drunken and lecherous subordinates shield and patronize it; while we try to convert criminals, they manufacture them." The "polluted harpies" of Tammany Hall were "a lying, perjured, rum-soaked and libidinous lot," and New York had become "an industrialized Sodom" from which even the established Church sometimes profited; Trinity Church was the city's largest single owner of slum and whorehouse properties.

Accompanied by Charles Gardner, a private detective who later published a pamphlet describing their experiences, and John Langdon Erving, the son of well-to-do parents of unimpeachable social standing, Parkhurst took to visiting the most sordid parts of the city so he could himself bear witness to New York's degradation. In order to pass incognito, Gardner first had to adjust the clergyman's outfit: "the coat was cut in ministerial fashion, the trousers had the very aroma of the pulpit about them." After supplying him with a more suitable outfit, Gardner also greased down Parkhurst's flowing locks, though he left the muttonchop whiskers untouched.

In one low dive on Cherry Street, Parkhurst watched little boys and girls not more than ten years old buy whiskey and beer in bottles, pans, tin cans, and pitchers, and he also visited an opium den on Mott Street, but it was in the brothels and bordellos that the reverend's fortitude was tested to its limits. In one he was greeted by a young woman asking, "Hey, whiskers, going to ball me off?"; on Water Street he saw half a dozen prostitutes "soliciting men to enter the resort with the same air that a Grand Central Station hackman asks you to 'have a cab' "; and on Elizabeth Street a naked woman smoked a cigarette standing on her head and then asked the good doctor if he'd like to see her other acrobatic feats for three dollars. He witnessed a naked "dance of nature" at the bordello of Hattie Adams, where he also played "leap-frog" with the dancers, an exploit that earned him a great deal of public derision when it was revealed, though it was afterward made clear that he had not removed any of his clothing, apart from his hat, and "would not permit any of the customary variations."

Parkhurst also witnessed a "French Circus" in the house of Marie Andrea, "one of the most infamous resorts in New York City." Gardner could not bring himself to describe "the unspeakable horror of it," but Parkhurst, whose constant refrain was "Show me something worse!" peered through his glasses at the whole "circus" without a murmur of complaint. However, in Scotch Ann's "Golden Rule Pleasure Club" in a dingy basement in Greenwich Village, the doctor's nerve finally cracked. In each room was a young man "whose face was painted, eye-brows blackened, and whose airs were those of a young girl. Each person talked in a high falsetto voice and called the others by women's names." When the nature of the establishment was explained to Parkhurst, he fled from the house at top speed. "Why, I wouldn't stay in that house," he gasped, "for all the money in the world."

When Parkhurst preached about what he had seen, he forced police into a temporary show of enforcement of the law. Inspector Byrnes's men descended on several brothels, including Hattie Adams's, and, telling them they were acting on Parkhurst's orders, forced the prostitutes out into the snow without even allowing them to get their coats. As a result, the living room of Parkhurst's Madison Square vicarage was invaded by irate whores, but he managed to convince them of his good intentions while his wife served them tea and cookies.

Despite Parkhurst's campaigning and a horrific crime rate, politicians and police continued to conspire in corruption, protecting Monk and his fellow criminals and sharing their spoils. Men who profited from crime and vice held power in most large American cities at the time. That was "true in no other civilized country in the world," and it was true of New York above all other American cities. Corruption extended from the top to the bottom of the city government. The salary of every single city officeholder was subject to an assessment of 5 to 10 percent, paid to the "wiskinskie" of Tammany Hall, and, despite a lack of testimony from "Boss" Croker, "urgent business demanding his presence in England throughout the investigation," the Lexow Committee had succeeded in demonstrating that virtually every member of the police department paid bribes and "subscriptions" to Tammany. There were rich rewards for those who did so. The wardman in each police precinct collected payments from brothels, illegal saloons, and gambling dens. The money was passed from the wardman to the captain and then made its way up the police hierarchy, "with appropriate subtractions at each step."

When Theodore Roosevelt became president of the police board in May 1895, following the election of a reform administration after the Lexow Committee's revelations, one of his first acts was to cancel the annual police parade, saying, "We will parade when we need not be ashamed to show ourselves." Roosevelt also introduced new physical standards and a series of compulsory examinations for policemen, but his attempts to enforce liquor legislation drafted by rural conservatives and prohibitionists made him deeply unpopular in the city. He was swept from office and the old system of bribery and corruption restored at the 1898 election, the first held following the enlargement of New York to the five boroughs, incorporating the formerly independent city of Brooklyn, Queens, the Bronx, and Staten Island.

The incoming administration of Mayor Van Wyck was corrupt even by New York's dismal standards. His victory meant control of sixty thousand employees—with all the power of patronage that implied—and an annual budget of over $90 million, plus tens of millions more from rents, fees, fines, interest, bond sales, premiums, and the other scams and skimmings by which Tammany politicians enriched themselves. Van Wyck's supporters jubilantly celebrated the fact that the town was once more to be "wide open" (i.e., wide open to corruption). If proof were required, an inquiry into the American Ice Company's monopoly, which had allowed it to double its prices, later revealed that, on an official salary of $15,000 a year, Mayor Van Wyck had somehow acquired $680,000 of Ice Company stock. Just like the Lexow Committee five years earlier, the Mazet Committee of 1899 found evidence of wholesale corruption in New York, but had little more long-term impact than its predecessor.

In return for their bribes, owners of brothels, bars, and gaming dens were shielded from new competition; "operators encroaching upon a territorial franchise were very promptly closed down by the police." However, police protection was an expensive commodity. One madam of a string of brothels revealed that she paid thirty thousand dollars a year, and the wealth of police chief Alexander S. "Clubber" Williams offered even more glaring proof. Nicknamed in tribute to his brutality as a patrolman when he famously claimed "there's more law in the end of a policeman's nightstick than in a decision of the Supreme Court," Williams had announced himself as a young policeman by selecting two of the toughest thugs in his district, flattening them with his nightstick, and then pitching them through the window of the saloon that was their preferred hangout. Toward the end of his long and lucrative police career, he admitted that, despite his modest official salary, he had accumulated enough wealth to have acquired a substantial estate in Cos Cob, Connecticut, with a purpose-built $39,000 dock for his yacht; a large house and several other properties in Manhattan; and a dozen bank accounts, all awash with cash. All this, he told the investigating committees with disarming sincerity, was the product of property speculation in Japan. In addition to his bribes and takings from the crime on his turf, Williams also received a substantial commission on the sale of a brand of whiskey called Hollywood Whiskey. Any saloonkeepers or brothel owners who didn't push it were liable to police raids and revocation of their licenses.

Another police chief, William S. "Big Bill" Devery, a huge man, rarely without a big cigar, conceded that in a single year, police graft was something over three million dollars, but even that was a considerable underestimate of the sums annually grafted, swindled, and extorted. In 1900, *The New York Times* published a detailed account claiming that in the previous year, the owners of gambling houses alone had paid a total of $3,095,000 to the "Gambling House Commission"—an entirely unofficial body consisting of two state senators, a representative of the poolroom proprietors, and the head of a city department. The commission also illustrated a curious anomaly: when there was an honest chief of police and no central downtown "fix," the small fry of the police got most of the graft, but when corrupt politicians were in control, they took the bulk of the graft and the police had to be content with what was left.

Whichever hands the cash stuck to most readily, New York was "a graft-ridden town." Given the scale of the corruption, it was one of the wonders of the age that New York finally emerged from this blighted era so well endowed with great public buildings, libraries, museums, parks, and open spaces, but it "paid dear tribute for every forward step . . . Imagination fails at picturing the metropolis that might have been, could the city throughout the [nineteenth] century have been guided and controlled in the light of present-day civic ideals."

6

THE GANGLAND CODE

Monk's share of the graft and criminal activity on offer had already been substantial enough to allow him to purchase a large detached house for his mother, Mary, in the upmarket suburb of Richmond Hill on Long Island. It stood on a large plot of land and included a barn where Monk kept his pigeons. The house also accommodated his married sisters, Lizzie Reynolds and Francine Wouters, their husbands, and Lizzie's three children. Later, Monk may also have bought separate houses for Lizzie and Francine; by 1910, both were living in properties near Flatbush Avenue in Brooklyn.

Monk also treated himself to one of the first automobiles in New York, a grandiose and luxurious machine that looked like "the by-blow of a Venetian gondola." He had now become something of a lowlife celebrity, an attraction in his own right for the elegant slummers coming from uptown for the vicarious thrill of an evening in the Bowery. His fame even reached the ears of a visiting English writer, P. G. Wodehouse, who subsequently used a thinly disguised Monk as the basis for a fictional character he christened Bat Jarvis:

> Mr. Jarvis's reputation was far from being purely local. Broadway knew him, and the Tenderloin. Tammany Hall knew him. Long Island City knew him. In the underworld of New York his name was a by-word. For Bat Jarvis was the leader of the famous Groome Street Gang, the most noted of all New York's collections of Apaches. More, he was the founder and originator of it . . . Off-shoots of the main gang sprang up here and there about the East Side. Small thieves, pickpockets and the like, flocked to Mr. Jarvis as their tribal leader and protector and he protected them. For he, with his followers, were of use to the politicians. The New York gangs, and especially the Groome Street Gang, have brought to a fine art the gentle practice of "repeating"; which, broadly speaking, is the art of voting a number of different times at different polling-stations on election days. A man who can vote, say, ten times in a single day for you, and who controls a great number of followers who are also prepared, if they like you, to vote ten times in a single day for you, is worth cultivating. So the politicians passed the word to the police, and the police left the Groome Street Gang unmolested and they waxed fat and flourished. Such was Bat Jarvis.

As his fictional portrait suggests, Monk had become a very prominent figure in the underworld, but his largely Jewish gang also had "a feud code like that of the Kentucky Mountains" with their nearest and fiercest rivals in both size and influence, the Five Points Social Club, better known as the Five Pointers. This "great Italian band of cut-throats and pimps" was led by Paul Kelly from his headquarters in a room over a dive on Great Jones Street, near Third Avenue, across the street from the green lamps of the police station. The windows carried a crudely lettered sign: paul kelly association. A series of boot marks on the splintered door bore witness to past police raids, and the room was as filthy as the staircase leading to it, and furnished only with a ramshackle table and a few battered stools. The walls were decorated with cheap lithographs and woodcuts of prizefighters and East Side politicians, including a prominent portrait of "The Big Feller"—Big Tim Sullivan—which hung "like a bland heathen divinity on the walls of all the Bowery dives." "An odor of stale beer and cigarettes, combined with many indescribably more evil smells, filled the place. Half a dozen youths, several of them obviously not yet of voting age and all somehow conveying the impression that their chief aim in life was to look tougher than they really were, sat quarrelling over a greasy pack of cards."

Despite his Irish-sounding name, Kelly was an Italian immigrant, born in 1876 and christened Paolo Antonini Vaccarelli (or Paolo Corelli, according to one New York newspaper). Since the Irish were still the dominant, though fading, ethnic group on the East Side, Kelly took an Irish name, just as Monk had adopted the name Delaney, "after the common custom of both the Italian and Jew of his class." When Kelly first appeared in the Bowery in the mid-1890s, he worked as a lowly clerk in an Italian bank. In the evenings he entertained himself in the Bowery, where his charm won him "the favor of the tired women who frequented McGurk's and the other dives," but also earned him "not a few thrashings from bigger and stronger competitors." Kelly learned quickly; he became a professional boxer, "acquired some reputation as a lightweight scrapper," and formed alliances with other young toughs.

From those beginnings had grown Kelly's Five Points gang, named for the intersections of the five streets that defined their territory, an area once ruled by the Irish "Dead Rabbits." Kelly, however, drew adherents from all over the city. Among them was Salvatore Luciana—better known as Charles "Lucky" Luciano—who grew up in Monk's territory near First Avenue and Fourteenth Street, but began his criminal career selling heroin and morphine under Kelly's protection around Mulberry Bend. Ciro Terranova, the future "Artichoke King," was another Kelly gang member; so, briefly, was Alphonse "Scarface" Capone.

Monk and Kelly were polar opposites. Despite the slightly flattened nose that spoke of his former career as a professional boxer, "Dapper" Paul Kelly was a handsome dandy with olive skin and brilliantined dark hair. He fit well the description of the New York gunman coined by one writer: "exquisitely scented, wearing silk socks, silk ties to his tan shoes, with rings on his well-kept fingers and a gold-watch on his well-kept clothes." Another newspaper description of him dripped condescension, describing Kelly's clothes,

> which the Bowery accepts as the pink of fashion and gentility, pointed patent leather shoes of the type still stylish in that region, some flashy jewelry, and a watch, which by right of possession at least, is his own . . . It is darkly hinted that in Italy before the East Side got him, he belonged to the aristocracy, but was forced into exile by an unfortunate affair of the heart with a beautiful lady, also moving in the highest circles of society. There are some members of the gang who have told this so often in the Bowery that they almost believe it themselves.

Whatever some uptown sophisticates may have thought of him, it was undeniable that Kelly was far from a typical denizen of the Bowery. He spoke four languages, could hold his own in a conversation about fine art, had a ready wit and an engaging smile, and was rarely without a woman on his arm. His New Brighton Dance Hall, "one of the flashiest palaces of sin in the city," was often frequented by New York's upper-class socialites, who went slumming for the vicarious thrill of experiencing a little of the wicked, seamy side of life—and meeting a real gangster like Monk or Kelly only added to the excitement.

In comparison to the dapper Kelly, Monk was a crude, clumsy-looking figure and, even before his face was scarred and battered in street brawls, his own mother would have struggled to describe him as handsome. His suits were expensive and hand-tailored, but looked ill-fitting on his ungainly frame. He often went shirtless or collarless, and his looks were not improved by his habit of wearing a narrow-brimmed derby hat several sizes too small for him, perched on top of his shock of bristling, unruly hair. The effect must have been comical, but few would have risked laughter. Yet it was the bruising, scowling Monk, not the flashy Kelly or "the flabby and epicene Capone," who was the model for the typical gunman depicted in Hollywood movies, and it was said that the actor Louis Wolheim regularly portrayed gangsters mainly because his coarse, fleshy features reminded people of "the deplorable Monk Eastman."

Yet if outsiders saw him as a daunting, even terrifying, figure, Monk inspired great loyalty and affection in his gang members. "Monk hadn't a real personal enemy that I knew of," one contemporary said. "Most of his acquaintance with the police was due to troubles of others that he took up because he was leader of the gang." Even his greatest rival, Paul Kelly, had only good words for Monk, calling him "a soft easy-going fellow," but with "a gang of cowards behind him, second-story men, yeggs, flat-robbers and moll-buzzers."

Like other leading gangsters, Monk and Kelly delighted in squiring the most beautiful or feisty prostitutes, and battles—sometimes to the death—were fought over their affections. Monk was far from handsome, but he possessed two potent aphrodisiac properties: he was famous, and he had money to burn. In addition to his two wives—the second one possibly acquired without the formality of a divorce from the first—there would have been no shortage of brief couplings with the prostitutes he controlled, but his life, as far as women are concerned, was something of a mystery, even to his friends.

Monk and Kelly were by far the most powerful gang leaders in New York and were bitter rivals, apart from during elections, when their followers worked alongside one another to turn out the Tammany vote. There had already been trouble between the gangs when at midnight on April 13, 1901, two members of the Five Points Gang—the brothers "Peggy" and James Donovan, a Bowery saloonkeeper and an ex-convict—walked into a saloon where Monk was drinking. According to Monk's later account, "Peggy Donovan, without warning, pulled his revolver and fired at me." The bullet missed Monk and struck eighteen-year-old Samuel Frankel in the guts, but it was stopped by his watch and he was only slightly wounded. Monk ran into the street, but the Donovans pursued him, shouting "Stop, thief!"

Monk ran to Grand and Orchard streets, where, he later said, "Two men grabbed me, thinking I was a thief. Peggy Donovan reached me first. He pulled his revolver, pressed it against my stomach and fired [twice] into my abdomen. I fell to the sidewalk. Then the other brother shot me behind the ear as I lay on the walk." James Donovan was cornered by police and fired twice at Policeman Hogan of the Eldridge Street station before he was overpowered, but Peggy Donovan escaped.

The Donovans had left Monk for dead but, as he was often later to boast, he got to his feet, dazed and badly bloodied, plugged the bullet holes in his stomach with his fingers, and staggered to Gouverneur Hospital. He was taken first to the receiving room, where the examining surgeon made a swift inspection of the wounds and assigned Monk to one of the surgical wards. The orderlies sponged him with warm water, then laid him in bed and reported him ready. After he underwent an operation in the surgical amphitheater to remove the bullets and staunch the bleeding, a nurse in a starched white cap and apron brought him a liquid opiate in a glass, carried on a wooden tray.

Monk had lost pints of blood. Told that he was not expected to survive, he made an antemortem statement to the coroner, naming his attackers and offering a motive for the shooting: "The Donovans were heard to say they intended to kill the gang that hung out in Silver Dollar's place, as it was made up of 'stool pigeons.' " Two days later, *The New York Times* reported that Edward Eastman of 101 First Street had "died in the Gouverneur Hospital yesterday." The report was wrong. Although he remained on the critical list for several weeks, Monk survived. When he realized that he would live, he reverted to the gangland code, withdrew his earlier deathbed statement, and refused to testify against his assailants, preferring to bide his time and exact his own brand of justice. Within a week of Monk being discharged from the hospital, a Five Pointer was decoyed out of a bar by a woman and then shot dead at the corner of Grand and Chrystie streets. No one was ever arrested for the crime, but the police said "Monk got his man."

In later years the incident in which Monk was gut-shot became mythologized by Herbert Asbury. He described Monk in the summer of 1901, venturing alone into Chatham Square—"a jagged confluence of streets over which clatter two old elevated lines," which converged at the square and briefly ran double-decked. There, said Asbury, Monk was set upon by half a dozen Five Pointers, but laid out three of his assailants with his brass knuckles and slungshot before another of them shot him twice in the guts. However, the chances of Monk having been hospitalized with two gunshot wounds to the stomach twice within three or four months are slim, and Asbury's version and timing of events are unsupported by any independent evidence. Much of *The Gangs of New York* drew on Asbury's conversations with reporters and police contacts, years and sometimes decades after the events in question, and his account of the shooting is one of several stories in the book that perhaps have more of the flavor of half-remembered hearsay and police department gossip than of hard fact.

However, it was indisputable that there was constant fighting between the Eastmans and the Five Pointers. In the previous era, the street fights for supremacy had been between the Cherry Hill and Five Point gangs, but those ancient foes were now united, as Kelly's gang and the Old Irish Yakey Yakes and their allies fought against the might of the Eastmans. It was a vicious fight for supremacy, "a veritable Wild West reign of terror . . . the greatest and most bloody of a generation in the three lowest wards of the city." Cherry Hill, Chinatown, and the old red-light district around Chrystie, Allen, Stanton, and Forsyth streets were the battlegrounds, and several lives had already been sacrificed in the blood feud.

Since the turn of the century, the Eastmans and Five Pointers had been fighting a brutal turf war for control of a strip of disputed territory between the Bowery and a dive called Nigger Mike's on Pell Street, a dismal thoroughfare lined with opium dens, in an area colonized by Chinese immigrants. Chinese criminal gangs had yet to establish themselves in New York, and Monk and Kelly both sent regular patrols of their men into this disputed territory with instructions to beat, blackjack, or shoot any member of the rival gang they encountered. This turf war may have been behind a killing in April 1902, when Thomas Cominsky shot and killed Isidor Zucker in Silver Dollar Smith's saloon. He then fled to a place owned by Monk on Ninth Street, where he hoped to hide out, but armed police went to the third-floor room and, though Cominsky made a run for it, he was cornered in the cellar and arrested.

In late September 1902 the small-scale killings erupted into a full-scale battle. The trouble began when a Five Points gang member, the son of a Mulberry Street saloonkeeper, was robbed and beaten senseless in Doyers Street. The following night Isidore Foster, "said to be of the Eastman crowd," was beaten so badly in Broome Street that he died in Gouverneur Hospital. The next night Chinatown echoed with the sound of shots. The rioting started about nine o'clock, when the Eastmans, about sixty strong, invaded Chinatown. They divided into two groups, one going through Doyers Street and the other along Walker Street, "looking for the enemy. Pistols were the general weapons, but some of the men carried long knives and murderous 'slung-shots.'" The first confrontation took place on the corner of White and Walker streets. As the Chinese inhabitants and bystanders dove for cover, bullets and bricks filled the air. The gangs fought their way along Walker Street to Broadway, where police armed with clubs and revolvers quelled the riot and took four prisoners. Fighting then flared up again at Centre and White streets, where another thirteen prisoners, thirteen revolvers, six knives, and three blackjacks were seized. Police reserves patrolling in squads of five men eventually quelled the riot, "pouncing on the knots of fighters at every opportunity and sending them to prison in groups."

Five days later, hostilities broke out again when thirty-five members of the Five Points Gang, heavily armed and looking for revenge, burst into one of the Eastmans' hangouts, a poolroom on Suffolk Street. Taken by surprise, the Eastmans were rallied by Monk, who was in the room at the time, and for ten minutes there was a ferocious battle during which three men jumped or were pushed out of windows. One of them, Samuel Levinson, an Eastman gang member, fractured his skull and died at Gouverneur Hospital. A loaded revolver was found in his clothing.

Once more the police had to summon reserves before confronting the gangs. Twenty-nine arrests were made, and a dozen loaded and half-loaded revolvers were found on the floor of the poolroom. All twenty-nine men, most of them Eastmans and including Monk himself, were arraigned the following morning before the Essex Market Court, where they heard their gang described as "a disgrace to the city" but, ably defended by ex-assemblyman Isidor Cohn, who countered that they were all just "innocent boys . . . arrested without cause," all were discharged.

Ignoring the classic military dictum of never waging war simultaneously on two fronts, Monk was also trying to achieve the final elimination of Yakey Yake Brady's gang and the small gang led by "Big Dave" Bernstein. The declining Irish Yakey Yakes had once ruled the area around Water, Roosevelt, and Cherry streets, but their territory was now a dying ward. The fighting went on throughout the winter of 1902–1903, and by March the hostility between the two gangs grew so strong that there was almost a nightly pitched battle and an exchange of shots. Police were powerless to stem the fighting or bring the culprits to justice, as shooters and victims alike remained closemouthed. An Eastman gang member, Louis Karp, refused to reveal who had shot him in the leg, but not long afterward, Big Dave Bernstein was severely wounded. A familiar figure in the Bowery, he was shot a few minutes after he had been seen talking to Monk. When taken to the hospital, he swore that Monk was not the man who had shot him, but then added, "Anyway, I'll settle my own scores."

However, the Eastmans learned of his intentions and, shortly after midnight, four of them went to Houston Street. Standing on the sidewalk, they poured a fusillade of shots into Bernstein's saloon, though "no one knows how many revolvers were used and who used them." John "Mugsy" Bayard, a member of Bernstein's gang, was one of two seriously wounded men and was unable to fulfill his threat to "get even," as he died that night in Gouverneur Hospital. A thin, hatchet-faced member of Monk's gang, the nineteen-year-old Max Zwerbach, also known as Kid Twist or Joe Fox, was arrested for the killing, but claimed he had acted in self-defense after Bayard began shooting up the place. With no witnesses coming forward to dispute his version of events, Twist was eventually released.

As the feuding continued, Patrick Shea, "a friend of Monk Eastman . . . known among his peculiar following as 'Paddy the Snake,'" was badly beaten by the members of a gang headed by a small-time gangster called William "Billy Argument" McMahon, and taken to Gouverneur Hospital. Once more, Shea would say only, "I ain't no squealer, not me. When I get out of the hospital, I will attend to this matter myself and maybe I won't do a little six-shooting." Released from the hospital two days later, Shea went straight to McMahon's house in Hamilton Street—"the wickedest street in New York"—and lay in wait. When McMahon emerged, Shea "pressed a revolver to the base of his skull and blew the top of his head off."

According to one report, the conflict began over a woman, but reporters looking to add color or glamour to their accounts of gang warfare often overstated the role of an East Side femme fatale. Fights over women were by no means unknown, but they were often not crimes of passion but feuds over the control of prostitutes, gangland turf, or rackets. The subject of this dispute was said to be an Italian girl, originally employed by a paper-box manufacturer but more recently a prostitute in a Chinatown dive, who had been the girlfriend of one of the Yakey Yakes until one of the Eastmans took her over. That night, he was leading a waltz with her at the New Irving Hall, surrounded by some of his admiring comrades, when a dozen Yakey Yakes burst in with drawn revolvers, "laid violent hands on the maiden and departed in triumph to Cherry Hill, leaving behind them sore hearts and sorer heads." In revenge for this humiliation in their own stronghold, the Eastmans shot a Yakey Yake a few nights later; a week after that an Eastman was in turn left dying on a Cherry Street sidewalk.

In an attempt to control, or at least moderate, the intergang violence, police made a series of ax and sledgehammer raids on poolrooms used as gang hangouts. Thirty-three men in various stages of fright were rounded up after police smashed their way into "Biff" Ellison's poolroom at 231 East Fourteenth Street; so many were arrested that the patrol wagon had to make seven trips to transport them all to the police station.

Another force, led by Inspector George McClusky, raided a poolroom in a cellar on West Third Street. After arresting the lookouts and smashing their way through armored doors and steel bars, they were confronted by "a labyrinth so cunningly arranged" that they could not tell whether they were moving toward or away from the poolroom. They found themselves in a small anteroom with three doors, and when a detective smashed through the first of those with an ax, he only entered another anteroom with three more doors. He retraced his steps and attacked the second of the doors in the original anteroom but again found himself in another anteroom, faced with three more doors. When he attacked the oak partition next to the doors with his ax he merely broke through into yet another anteroom with yet another set of three doors. A detective eventually "cut the Gordian knot" by retreating to a room that he knew to be over the poolroom. He smashed through the floor with his ax and dropped down almost on the heads of a startled crowd of men.

The police raids had little effect on the levels of gang violence, but Tammany politicians now intervened. The one factor that they feared was that the often bloody rivalry between the gangs would spill into open war, rousing even New York's soporific or indifferent electorate, and the fighting had now reached the point where Tammany bosses felt compelled to take action. Kelly and Monk were summoned to separate meetings with Big Tom Foley, who laid down the law to them individually and then arranged a conference between delegations from the two clubs at the downtown Tammany headquarters, with Foley acting as chairman and arbitrator of disputes. There he again warned them that while an occasional beating or murder might be just part of doing business, open warfare that terrorized whole city blocks was counterproductive for everyone. Foley then delivered an ultimatum, phrased in the starkest possible terms: either the fighting ceased or Tammany would withdraw its protection and the gangs and their leaders would be hounded to extinction. It is not clear whether he could actually have delivered on the threat, or even whether he would have wanted to, given the gangs' central role in ensuring his reelection, but it was enough to persuade Monk and Kelly to at least make a show of settling their differences.

In language more appropriate to a schoolteacher separating fighting infants than a Tammany boss dealing with two warring gangs, Foley then felt able to tell reporters that "the representatives of these rival factions have given their words that they will never more be bad, thus obviating the necessity of calling out the police reserves to quell riots and disperse gangs armed with pistols, clubs and other weapons." Foley sealed the peace treaty with a chowder at New Dorp, Staten Island, attended by Monk, Kelly, and almost all of their followers. Food and drink flowed freely, and if the day passed peacefully, it ended in predictable fashion. Returning to New York by ferry at midnight, and led through the streets from South Ferry by a brass band also supplied by Foley, six hundred Five Pointers began firing revolvers in the air as they marched up Broadway. Turning onto Franklin Street, "the gang reached the old Five Points stamping ground, and awoke the echoes vociferously." Fifteen policemen attempting to restore order were badly beaten and were "able to bring but two of their assailants to the Tombs Police Court" the next morning.

7

THE WOLF OF WALL STREET

Even while the gang feuds and police raids were taking place, Monk's normal gangland activity continued. His fame had spread far beyond the Lower East Side; accompanied by one of his men, Joseph Brown, he now accepted a lucrative mission in Long Branch, New Jersey, where "The Wolf of Wall Street," financier and fraudster David Lamar, was about to face trial, charged with assault. The charges arose from an altercation between Lamar and his coachman, Joseph McMahon, who while taking Lamar's wife for a drive refused to chase after her pet dog when it jumped from the carriage and ran off. When Mrs. Lamar ordered McMahon to bring the dog back, he said, "I'm paid for driving horses, not for catching dogs. If you want the dog, get him yourself." After Lamar was told of this, he allegedly struck McMahon in the face with his cane. Lamar also stood accused of attacking McMahon's wife and driving her out of her home with an iron bar.

Lamar was anxious that the coachman should not testify against him and recruited Monk to ensure McMahon's silence, though Lamar claimed that he had merely hired Monk to guard his house. He said that Monk had not even wanted money but had taken the job as a favor to a friend, in return for nothing more than the promise of a few drinks. Intimidating witnesses was the sort of job that was meat and drink to a gangster, but Monk's rival, Paul Kelly, would have delegated the job to a couple of his men. Whether out of hubris or his desire to "keep his hand in" by beating up a guy once in a while, Monk elected to carry out the job himself.

Several times Lamar and his hired thugs tried to lure McMahon away from his home in Long Branch. On one occasion, McMahon's sister, Minnie, received a call from someone purporting to be his bail bondsman, who asked her to tell her brother to go to List's Hotel. However, she recognized Lamar's voice and called the bondsman, who knew nothing about the meeting. As a result, McMahon did not go to the hotel, where witnesses claimed that four burly men had waited for him for some time.

On July 9, 1903, all subterfuge having failed, Monk and Brown simply set upon McMahon in broad daylight in front of the Long Branch police court, where he was due to give evidence. McMahon said he was in a bootblack's chair at the foot of the stairs leading to the justice's office when he saw Monk, Brown, and another man walk by. The next moment he was struck on the jaw, the blow knocking him off the chair. The last he remembered, he said, was Monk's voice shouting, "Soak him! Soak him!" His injuries included two black eyes, two cuts on the mouth, and several teeth knocked out. He was left unconscious while his assailants escaped in a waiting carriage. It was claimed that the assault took place right in front of a policeman, who made no effort to arrest the thugs.

When McMahon recovered, he was taken to New York and took less than two minutes to identify Monk and Brown from their pictures in the police Rogues' Gallery. The two men were arrested on the cor-

ner of Rivington and Forsyth streets on the East Side, by detectives
with drawn revolvers. Monk, said to be an out-of-work printer whose
face bore "the scars of two or three knife wounds," was reported to
have said, "Arrest me, will yer? Say, yer wants ter look out where yer
going. I cut some ice in this town. Why, I make half the big politicians in New York." McMahon subsequently picked Monk and Brown
out in a police lineup, though the value of his identification was later
called into question in court when it was revealed that McMahon, who
claimed to have seen the two men around Forty-first Street in New
York on some unspecified previous occasion, had been shown only
two photos in the Rogues' Gallery—those of Monk and Brown. In the
lineup that followed, the suspects Monk and Brown were the only men
wearing collarless shirts.

Monk, "whose real name is William Delaney according to the
police," was described as "the leader of a band of Cherry Hill ruffi-
ans accused of many crimes." He gave his address as 93 South Third
Street, Williamsburg—as usual, a false address, though his mother had
lived nearby, at 96 South Third Street, for several years. Held overnight, Monk and Brown appeared before the Tombs police court the
next morning, in a room crowded with their friends and gang members. When Detective Sergeant McCafferty stood near him, Monk was
unable to contain his fury at the sight of a man who had arrested him on
several previous occasions. He shouted, "Take that fellow away from
me," and took a few steps toward him before detectives pushed him
back.

In answer to the charges, Monk affected his customary air of injured
innocence. "Who is this man Lamar?" he said. "I wouldn't know him if
he came up and struck me in the face. As for McMahon, why, I never saw
him until he identified me at headquarters." Monk claimed it was a case
of mistaken identity and said he had an alibi—he said he was fishing in
Connecticut with Brown at the time of the assault. His brother-in-law,
Lizzie's husband, Patrick Reynolds, backed him up and "spoke bitterly
about his brother-in-law's picture being in the Rogues' Gallery. 'It aint
right, Eastman comes from as good a family as there is in the city. Those
detectives have been pursuing The Monk for years but he's never done
time yet. Inspector McClusky is trying to get even with Lamar because
it was Lamar who got him fired out of the Detective Bureau.' "

However, Monk's alibi was contradicted by a barman from a Long
Branch hotel, who said that the day before McMahon was beaten and

stabbed the barman was introduced to Monk and Brown by Lamar and told to give them whatever refreshments they wanted and send the bill to him; Lamar later admitted paying their bills at that hotel and another one. The barman claimed to have overheard Monk and his companions plotting to attack someone and hide the body in the rear of the gashouse in Long Branch. It was also revealed that six days before the assault, Monk, Brown, and two other Eastman gang members had been arrested as suspicious persons on one of the steamboats bound for the Jersey Coast just before it sailed from Rector Street. A West Side gambler had found them a lawyer, who secured their prompt discharge at the Jefferson Market police court.

New York Police Inspector McClusky then testified that Lamar had first gone to Herbert Thompson's saloon on Seventh Avenue to hire a prizefighter to beat up McMahon, but the fighter turned the job down, so Lamar hired Monk. The inspector also claimed that, while at police headquarters, Monk had described Lamar as "a four-flusher and if he don't stand by me he'll get a taste of Jersey justice." Arrested in New York, Monk and Brown would face the official form of Jersey justice only when extradition proceedings to Monmouth County, New Jersey, had been completed. The lawyer who entered writs of habeas corpus and certiorari on their behalf was a state senator, Thomas F. Grady, a Tammany "lickspittle"—a vivid demonstration of Monk's importance to Tammany Hall.

Senator Grady launched a sustained attack on McMahon's character, repeatedly accusing him of being an ex-convict. When McMahon's brother-in-law took the stand, Grady again shouted, "Are you not an ex-convict?" and when the man made no reply, Grady rounded on the prosecuting counsel and said, "So this is the kind of witness you are going to have testify against my clients?" At the end of the day's proceedings, Grady also informed the press that there were "influences behind the case" that had not been disclosed to the public. When reporters asked if he was referring to a Wall Street clique reportedly trying to destroy David Lamar, he told them to draw their own conclusions.

That night Monk and Brown were transferred from the Tombs to cells at police headquarters. When a sergeant there was asked why the transfer had been made, he refused to give an answer other than to say "it was thought better to have the prisoners locked up there." The implication was either that police feared an attempted breakout from the Tombs or, more plausibly, that they wanted to prevent Monk from communicating with his gang members via other prisoners in the Tombs and—if the appeal against extradition to New Jersey was lost—arranging an escape on the journey to New Jersey or from the much less formidable jail in Monmouth County.

At the extradition hearing before the state supreme court, both prisoners seemed to enjoy the attention they received from the crowds of spectators. Monk in particular appeared to be "much elated over the notoriety he had achieved." By their next appearance, the crowd, most of them Lower East Siders, had grown so large and menacing that officials had the court cleared before continuing. The two accused could not produce a single witness to back up their alibi that they were on a fishing excursion on the day McMahon was attacked, whereas the prosecuting counsel was flanked by a dozen witnesses, all prepared to swear that they had seen Monk and Brown at the scene of the assault.

In an acid commentary on the case, *The New York Times* linked Grady's "strenuous efforts" to free Monk and Brown to the elections that coming fall. "At primary elections and district fights, the Eastmans have been important aids in disposing of those who did not 'vote right' as well as influencing the doubtful by methods of their own." The New Jersey police also expressed astonishment at the ways in which the case had been delayed, but in the end Grady could not prevent the men's extradition to New Jersey.

On August 6, Monk and Joseph Brown were finally taken to New Jersey and incarcerated in the Monmouth County Jail in Freehold. Their route was changed at the last minute after reports that an attempt would be made to free them during a staged fight on the ferry. A hundred of Monk's gang members had been in and around the courthouse and, after making signals to the prisoners, they hurried to Pier No. 8, North River, where they expected to find Monk and Brown guarded by only two New Jersey officers. However, after announcing that they would be put on the boat to Long Branch at eleven o'clock, police took their prisoners in a patrol wagon to the Liberty Street ferry and then put them on a train in Jersey City. They claimed that Monk could not hide his disappointment when he realized his men had been outwitted. "When I get out of this," he was said to have growled, "I'll kill some of that crowd."

Despite Inspector McClusky's claims that the prisoners would "squeal" and implicate Lamar, both men remained tight-lipped. Wearing good clothes, smoking cigarettes, and with their pockets full of cash, Monk and Brown were handcuffed together and, with Monk's scarred face and their uneasy behavior, attracted considerable attention from the other passengers throughout the journey from New York. Constable George Van Winkle of the Long Branch police had already told reporters he was confident of obtaining a guilty verdict. "They are the fellows, all right," he said, "and I saw them make the assault. I can produce other witnesses too, who saw the scuffle, including a woman who heard Delaney say 'Give it to him good! Put him out!' I nabbed Delaney all right, but he got in a quick jab . . . a vicious blow in the stomach that knocked the wind out of me, and then he jumped into a carriage which was waiting . . . and made his escape."

Monk and Brown were put in cell number 1 and cell number 4 on the second tier of the Monmouth County Jail—kept apart to prevent them from conspiring to escape together—and, save for an hour's daily exercise in the barred corridors, were confined to their cells. One of Monk's principal lieutenants, Kid Twist, backed by fifty heavily armed gang members, was then alleged to be on his way to attempt to free his leader by force. Security at the Monmouth jail was at once greatly increased. New locks and chain bolts were fitted on all the exterior doors of the jail and on the warden's house, and a panic button was connected to the alarm bell in the courthouse, alongside the jail, to summon help in an emergency. The previously feeble jail now had the look of a fortress, and hastily sworn-in deputies maintained an all-night vigil, patrolling the outer prison yard, surrounded by a high, spiked wall. Guards armed with revolvers had instructions to shoot anybody scaling the wall or throwing anything through the prison windows.

After it was revealed that Monk had corrupted a prisoner who was about to be discharged and slipped him a letter that he had concealed in his clothing, Monk and Brown were isolated from the rest of the prisoners, for fear that Monk would reveal the weak points of the prison's defenses to his gang. The warden's anxieties increased when he discovered that the prisoner had already thrown the letter out his jail window. A search by the guards proved fruitless, and it was suspected that it had been picked up by one of Monk's gang. All new short-term prisoners who were brought in were carefully searched, since some of the Eastmans were believed to be planning to get themselves committed to jail on trivial charges in order to help Monk and Brown break out.

A fresh alarm was raised when a turnkey saw Monk giving a signal to Brown, just as five or six mysterious figures appeared outside the jail. At the same time, a white bull terrier that roamed the prison yard at night began barking furiously as one of the mysterious figures tried to climb the wall at the back of the yard. Amid the increasingly wild speculation about a possible jailbreak, the *Monmouth Democrat* offered a welcome note of reason: "The cases are bailable ones and if the accused men have so many friends, it would seem more likely that they would rather go about the easier and more orderly method of releasing their friends, by putting up money as security."

The "great Monk Eastman rescue plot" ended in anticlimax. Lamar, who was in such financial difficulties that his mortgage was foreclosed and his house put up for sale, had sold his entire stable of horses, including the champion Speedway trotter of 1903 and the pacing champion of the Speedway, to the Fiss, Doerr & Carroll Horse Company. As a result, three stablemen and five stable boys were sent to Freehold to arrange the transport of the horses to New York. Their immediate visit to Lamar's house, near Sea Bright, aroused suspicions that they were members of Monk's gang. The jail was further barricaded against an attack from outside and a mob of police and heavily armed volunteer citizens followed the stablehands everywhere until they left town with Lamar's horses.

In New York, Inspector McClusky had heard the rumors about an attempt to storm the Monmouth County jail and at once ordered a roundup of alleged thieves that netted thirty-three East Side thugs, including twenty-five members of Monk's gang. They were "packed in the cells to the point of suffocation, but that didn't matter." Among them were "Big Shinsky," "Kid" Carter, "Sheeny Sam," "Whitey," and "Little Frank," though Inspector McClusky noted that "Eastman is the only real tough one in the lot."

When they appeared in court the next morning, the extent to which corrupt politicians and police colluded in the protection of the gangs was blatantly displayed. Inspector McClusky claimed that all but three of the men were professional thieves, and "I guess it didn't hurt the other three to be in keep for the night." Yet Inspector Max Schmittberger urged the discharge of all the prisoners, and Deputy Police Commissioner Davis added that he did not think there were any gangs "organized specifically for the purposes of plunder." He explained away the existence of "the so-called 'Monk' Eastman gang" as merely being part of "the gregariousness of young toughs." Inspector McClusky's attempts to keep the Eastmans away from Freehold, New

Jersey, came to nothing. When the thirty-three men appeared before the Tombs police court, Magistrate Hogan duly discharged every one of them, adding that "the arrest of these men was a nice piece of nonsense on the part of the police."

If Kid Twist and the Eastman gang *did* go to New Jersey, no rescue attempt was made, and Monk himself laughed off such talk, declaring, "I would not have walked out of jail without bail, even if the doors had been opened for me." Even without a posse of rescuers to break him out, his freedom was not to be long delayed. Flush with cash, he and Brown at first spared no expense on their comfort, spurning the jail food and having Freehold "scoured for luxuries." The newspapers printed the supper brought in for Monk and Brown: "Tenderloin steak, hot buns, pears, cakes, jelly, tea and ice cream soda. He sent out for two boxes of the best cigars obtainable, and grumbled over the quality." Two sets of all the editions of the New York morning and evening newspapers were also delivered to their cells and, after complaining that the light filtering into his cell was so dim that it hurt his eyes to read, Monk also sent out for some candles.

Such was their rate of spending that within a few days their money was running out, but a letter from Monk's wife, Margaret, who had written in an attempt to cheer him up, telling him he would soon be freed, proved correct. After ten days' incarceration in the Monmouth County jailhouse, the two men were released on bail following a visit by Margaret and Monk's brother-in-law Patrick Reynolds. Reynolds told reporters that Monk's mother was very ill on Long Island and was anxious to see her son before undergoing an operation the following day. Reynolds said he was prepared to stand bail, but the five-thousand-dollar bond was probably beyond his means, so a Navesink businessman eventually put up the money, stating that it was "merely a business transaction with him." There were claims that Monk's gang paid him well for the favor. As soon as he was released, Monk caught the first available train for New York and went straight to see his mother for what would prove to be almost the last time; she died later that year, the day before Thanksgiving.

When Monk and Brown reappeared before the court to answer to their bail, they arrived so late that it was suspected that they had taken "leg bail" (absconded). Justice Fort, in the course of instructing the jury, laid out the state's damning case and concluded that "it is difficult to bring oneself to believe that in this age any person can be so steeped in moral depravity as to willfully premeditate a scheme to assault another person . . . engaging persons to carry it out. It shocks human credulity still more to believe it possible that any person would accept such an iniquitous commission."

A further lengthy delay then ensued, during which Monk and Brown were again bailed, before the trial proper eventually got under way in Freehold before County Judge Heisley. A number of Monk's gang members were in the public seating, watched closely by the court officers. Judge Heisley ordered the jury to be kept under guard together at lunchtime and at night, "a precaution unusual in New Jersey except at murder trials." Monk and Brown again appeared to be reveling in their notoriety and were dressed in new clothes, with their hair "newly clipped in the distinctive Bowery fashion." Monk wore a well-tailored black suit, and his normally unruly shock of hair was parted in the middle and smoothed down flat on his forehead. However, he appeared "nervous, this man who has seen as many battles as an ancient gladiator. Eastman crossed his legs, shifted them, rubbed his hands . . . He chewed gum with his front teeth, the teeth which are capped with gold."

The powerful influence of Tammany Hall was once more very much in evidence, as State Senator Riordan appeared as a witness for the defense. Called to the stand, he said that Monk and Brown were intimate friends of himself, Senator Grady, and Tom Foley. Riordan stated that he had met Constable Van Winkle of the New Jersey police and told him that Monk and Brown were not guilty and were "valuable friends" of Big Tom Foley. According to Riordan, Van Winkle had expressed his regrets but said that he "had to get the boys" as part of a Wall Street conspiracy to discredit or bankrupt Lamar.

When the prosecuting counsel asked him why he was interested in the case, Riordan said, "I am always interested in my friends when they are in trouble."

"Are you being paid to come here?"

"No."

"You are neglecting your business then for nothing?"

"I'll neglect my business every day in the year for politics in the interest of my leader, Senator Grady."

One of Tammany's most persuasive lawyers, former senator Henry S. Terhune, represented Monk, armed with affidavits placing him and his associates miles from the crime scene at the time the attack was carried out. Terhune said that he would prove the innocence of the defendants beyond all doubt and claimed that McMahon had been put up to his story by his lawyer, Thomas P. Fay, who wanted a rich man to sue. When James McMahon was assaulted, Terhune said, he was taken not to the Monmouth Memorial Hospital, "where poor men usually go," but to Fay's office, where his wounds were dressed by Fay's own family physician. Terhune claimed that the missing link in the case—the alleged attackers—was then supplied by Police Inspector George McClusky. " 'Leave it all to me,' said 'Chesty George,' as they call the Inspector in New York, 'and I'll furnish the crooks.' "

McMahon was forced to deny claims that he had told an acquaintance that he expected to get enough money out of Lamar to last him the rest of his life and had hired the smartest lawyer in the state to do so. Terhune also pointed to a number of inconsistencies in McMahon's testimony and called Justice Walter Brinley of Long Branch to the stand, who testified that he had witnessed the attack on McMahon from a distance of eight feet and claimed that neither Brown nor Monk had been the assailants.

It was a surprise to many when Monk took the stand, exposing himself to cross-examination. However, when asked if he'd ever been convicted of any crime, Monk replied "Never," his lips parting in a grin that showed the two gold front teeth by which one of the witnesses said he had identified him. Monk said that he'd been asked by a saloon owner to go to New Jersey and help Lamar, whose wife was living in fear of attack by McMahon. After going to New Jersey, he and Brown had a few drinks, then went to McMahon's house "just to scare him . . . so he would not bother Mr. Lamar any more." Monk claimed that when they sobered up, they went back to New York and, on the day of the assault on McMahon, they were at Coney Island, where they rode the merry-go-round, had some drinks, and stayed at a hotel overnight. When asked if he'd registered at the hotel, Monk claimed that he never registered because he couldn't read or write. It was a surprising assertion from someone who had the morning and evening newspapers delivered to his cell and complained that the light was too dim to read.

Asked if he had pulled a gun when he was later arrested, Monk said, "No, I never carry a gun," at which point there was loud laughter in the court. Monk said that after his arrest, Inspector McClusky had pushed him down stairs to make him confess, and when he and Brown were put on an identity parade, they were lined up alongside a row of detectives. "Anyone can tell a detective, you know," he said, turning to the jury, "and I asked McClusky to put a bootblack in the line and to give us a fair show. He would not do it."

Cross-examination failed to shake Monk's testimony, and his claim to have been on Coney Island on the day that McMahon was attacked was corroborated by statements from the two proprietors of the American Hotel there. Lamar also took the stand, and his testimony, delivered in an undertone, with his head sunk between his shoulders, "dovetailed with considerable accuracy into that of his associates."

However, despite Terhune's best efforts, the evidence for the prosecution appeared overwhelming, and in his closing address, Judge Heisley issued a warning to the jurors: "If you have no reasonable doubt of guilt and yet bring in a verdict of acquittal, that will mean the enactment in this court of a greater scandal than the crime at Long Branch. I trust there will be nothing in your connection with this case which you will have cause to regret . . . If the perpetrators of the assault which happened in this county go unpunished, it will be an awful disgrace."

Earlier in the trial, District Attorney Foster had bemoaned political interference and warned that "there may be one black sheep in the jury box, but if we can keep the Lamar money away from him, I am sure of a conviction." The chances of that began to recede when the jurors' deliberations became unusually protracted. At midnight, the judge gave up and went home, leaving the court clerk to accept the verdict.

The jury was later said to have decided on its verdict soon after midnight, but a crowd of "honest Monmouth County men" were still waiting in the courtroom, which was visible from the jury room on the far side of the courtyard. Perhaps fearing retribution if the "wrong" verdict was returned, the jurors remained in their room until four in the morning, when the crowd had dispersed and only the court officials remained. The jury foreman then announced that they had reached a verdict—not guilty—and the jurors left the building with considerable haste.

So, too, did Monk and Brown. They were in the cells when Warden Fitzgerald told them they were free men. Incredulous, they "manifested childish delight," and Monk said they wouldn't "lose any time in getting out of this town." Lamar showed no emotion when he was informed of the verdict and left town on the same 8:15 a.m. train as Monk and Brown.

Informed of the verdict, Judge Heisley would say only, "Well, persons who have had experience with juries are often disappointed but never surprised." One local newspaper used heavy irony when claiming that the verdict was "not necessarily a confession that the administration of justice in Monmouth is a failure; that the county may be invaded at pleasure by lawless people for the purpose of committing crime, and, if influential enough, expect protection in its commission; or that the average intelligence of the citizens is not above that of the people in the Southern states where lynching is justified and deliberate murder goes unpunished."

Criticism of the verdict was almost universal. There were sinister rumors of attempts to bribe or otherwise influence jurors, and suggestions that they had not carried out their duties in the customary solemn manner. Noises had emanated from the jury room "as if a game were in progress. Much evidence of hilarity continued" until a few minutes before they delivered their verdict.

Monk had returned to his Lower East Side territory in triumph but, as he entered James Donovan's saloon in the Bowery for a celebratory drinking bout with five of his followers, Donovan, whose brother Peggy had wounded Monk in gunplay so badly two years earlier that he almost died, whipped out a revolver. Monk showed him his empty hands and said, "No more guns for me. I'm through. I've got money enough now to go into business and it's 'to the woods for mine.' So put up your irons, Donovan, and forget it."

Monk paid all the bills for the party, which continued for most of the day at several saloons and restaurants and at a theater, where Monk took a box. Everywhere he went, he was shadowed by Inspector Schmittberger and eight of his men, emphasizing Schmittberger's warning that New York would be made too warm for Monk. "The reign of terror of this crowd down here is at an end," Schmittberger said. "We have sent 121 of them to the Island and we'll send as many more if they show their heads. We have a big bunch of them now employed digging graves in Potter's Field. I don't expect to have much more trouble with Eastman. He was given to understand today by my men that he must get out of this city and I think you will have difficulty in finding him here tomorrow." The police had stopped and searched Monk and his companions as they left Donovan's but failed to find any weapons. "When I say I am through with gunwork, I mean it," Monk said to them. "Youse fellers go and eat peanuts on the corner and save your shoes."

The next day, Monk duly "took to the woods" and was absent from his usual haunts for several weeks, but, contrary to Schmittberger's boasts, Monk's absence proved to be purely temporary. He remained away from the East Side only while his Tammany allies were issuing the necessary reminders to the police department about who paid their wages and the importance of Monk Eastman at election times. Schmittberger's crusade against the gangs then came to an abrupt halt, and Monk at once returned to his old districts, where, with Monk surrounded by his gang members, business as usual resumed.

8

THE BATTLE OF RIVINGTON STREET

During Monk's lengthy court case in New Jersey, the conflict between his gang and the Five Pointers had been rumbling on, with both staging raids on their rivals' turf; disrupting their gambling, protection, and prostitution rackets; and carrying out random assaults as well as New York's first ever drive-by shootings. There was a cease-fire on September 15, 1903, when the Eastmans and the Five Pointers spent the day repeating at the West Side primaries. It was Tammany's first return on its investment in securing Monk's freedom, but open warfare broke out again between the gangs over the division of the spoils. That same night, a steamy Manhattan evening, the Eastmans fought their bloodiest pitched battle yet.

Monk and his friends had been missing from their usual haunts all day, but at about nine o'clock, forty men—typical Bowery toughs, according to one witness—boarded a crosstown car at Stanton Street. They got off at Chrystie Street, walked into Livingston's saloon at the northwest corner of First Avenue and First Street, and began fighting with eight men standing at the bar. They then made for the Bowery, where fighting and gunplay again broke out, and the furious last fusillade did not come until five hours later.

The worst fighting occurred when half a dozen of Monk's men chanced upon a similar number of Five Pointers who were about to raid one of the Eastman gang's stuss games on Rivington Street, under the Allen Street arch of the Second Avenue elevated railroad. A "fifty foot crevasse between two rows of tenements," Allen Street was known as the street of perpetual shadow, both for the constant darkness beneath the railroad and because it was a notorious haunt of prostitutes; one newspaper made the hyperbolic claim that there were a hundred women on every corner on Allen Street. Even on the brightest day, sunlight barely lightened the gloom under the arches, where the steel streetcar tracks laid in the granite cobbles shone like slug trails in the darkness.

When the Eastmans and the Five Pointers caught sight of one another, they pulled out their revolvers and began firing indiscriminately. Monk's gang shot and killed one of the raiders, and the remaining men on both sides took cover behind the iron pillars of the railway, from where they kept up a barrage of shots. More men from both gangs soon came running to join the fight, and by the time two policemen attempted to intervene, they found about fifty men already involved and bullets striking sparks from the ironwork. The gangs had turned out the streetlamps, further hampering the policemen, who fled for their lives as they came under fire from both sides. As gang reinforcements poured into the area, it became a fevered battle. Monk arrived hotfoot from his Chrystie Street headquarters and, contrary to his pledge that he was through with gunwork, directed the shooting like an army forward-fire controller from a position behind the pillar closest to the enemy. Paul Kelly's presence was not recorded, but it is unlikely that the leader of the Five Pointers would have failed to join fighting on such a scale. By midnight, around a hundred gang members were blazing away from "behind their parapets of iron and the night." Half a dozen members of the Gophers gang from Hell's Kitchen had also arrived on the scene and joined in, firing indiscriminately at both sides. "A lot of the guys was poppin' at each other," one later explained, "so why shouldn't we do a little poppin' ourselves?"

Bullets flew in all directions, smashing windows in the neighboring tenements, ricocheting from the pylons of the El, and rattling against the undersides of trains overhead. Many windows were broken. A further half dozen policemen made a brief appearance but, greeted by a fresh hail of bullets, they also fled, and it was only when the reserves from several police stations banded together that they were able to storm Rivington Street, firing as they came. For about fifteen minutes the air was full of the sound of shooting while men on the rooftops rained bricks on the heads of the fighting policemen.

The battle had raged along two miles of streets in defiance of the police, until a square mile of territory was panic-stricken. When the gangs finally melted away into the night, they left a swath of destruction and many casualties in their wake. The walking wounded went with them, but the dead and some of the more seriously wounded had to be left behind. Once the police had reclaimed the streets, calls for ambulances were made to Gouverneur and Bellevue hospitals, and for once "the Eastman Pavilion" was treating Monk's men as well as their victims.

The ambulances were hearse-black, even to the beds, the pillows, the stretchers, and the curtains that screened the occupants from the curious stares of passersby. The drivers sounded their gongs as they lashed their horses on with whips, their hooves thundering on the cobbles and their flanks streaked with sweat as they tore through the traffic.

Michael Donovan, twenty-seven years old and possibly a cousin of the saloonkeeper James Donovan, had been shot in the mouth at Stanton and Forsyth streets, and died in Bellevue an hour later from hemorrhage and strangulation. John Carroll, or John Smith, which he later said was his real name, thirty-seven years old, was shot in the stomach and left arm in the final battle, and was taken to Gouverneur Hospital. Anton Bernhauser was shot through both cheeks and seriously wounded. The dead and wounded had lain untended in the street throughout the fighting, in some cases for hours.

The wounded gang members were held in "the Cage"—the prisoners' ward at Bellevue—cells normally used for sick prisoners from police stations, the Tombs, or Blackwell's Island. Surrounded by iron bars, watched over by warders as well as nurses, sick and wounded prisoners either recovered and were returned to custody or made the one-way journey to the morgue at the end of the lawns at Bellevue. On the bank of the river and partly built out over the water, the long, low building that housed the morgue usually contained thirty to forty unclaimed, unidentified bodies at a time, in the cheapest rough pine boxes, pending their removal to unmarked paupers' graves in Potter's Field on Hart Island. At the head of each coffin was a card held by an iron tack, giving all the information known about the body; often those cards were blank, save for the location where the body was found—commonly the East River. Some were suicides; many others were the disappeared, hapless, nameless, numberless victims of crimes.

Twenty men had been arrested at or near the scene of the Battle of Rivington Street, including Monk, who gave his name as Joseph Morris and claimed to have been a mere passerby who had stopped to see what was going on. With his wife, Margaret, and three of his henchmen and their wives, he was locked up at the Eldridge Street station. Margaret gave her address as 601 East Thirty-ninth Street, which bore no relation to any known address of Monk's. Several other gangsters were seized after police broke down the door of an Allen Street house where the gangsters had retreated and barricaded themselves inside. They were sent to the house of detention as witnesses, but the rest of the fighters had disappeared into the hallways and doorways of saloons and Raines Law hotels. (Passed in 1896, the Raines Law aimed to curb alcohol consumption by restricting its sale on Sunday to hotels, but since the law allowed any business that served sandwiches with drinks and had ten bedrooms to call itself a hotel, saloonkeepers exploited the loophole and became "Raines Law hotels." To comply with the letter, if not the spirit, of the law, they often had bedrooms no bigger than cupboards, and the only food on offer was a "sandwich" of a stone, a piece of brick, or roof slate between two slices of stale bread.)

Despite all the shooting, the only revolver recovered was one found upon the desperately wounded John Carroll/Smith. Its chambers were still warm when, along with a knife, it was taken from him. Carroll refused to implicate any gangster in his shooting, preferring instead to claim that he'd been shot by Detective McCoy.

As usual, Tammany lawyers arrived to defend Monk the following morning as he made his customary brief appearance before the courts and was then discharged. His men were detained for a further twenty-four hours and were then also given their freedom when it emerged that Inspector Schmittberger and his detectives could not find a single person "along the line of the fighting who would admit having seen the affray, although many buildings bore bullet marks or had windows broken by stray missiles."

Of all those arrested, only George "Lolly" Meyers, one of Monk's chief lieutenants, went to jail. Twenty-four hours after his arrest it was discovered that Meyers had been shot through the thigh of one leg and just above the knee of the other. He had been examined and reexamined by lawyers and police and moved from place to place, yet had remained silent about his wounds until the pain became too much to bear. No member of the Eastmans was in court when Meyers was convicted of highway robbery for holding up a man during the fighting, shooting him in the left cheek and relieving him of forty-seven dollars. Meyers was sentenced at the Tombs police court to fourteen years hard labor in Sing Sing. Everyone else walked free.

However, the Battle of Rivington Street had been so blatant and violent that even Tammany could not swallow it without comment, and Big Tom Foley now once more threatened the gang leaders with the removal of their political protection if they did not settle their differences in less damaging ways. After Kelly was given a safe conduct guaranteed by Tammany Hall, he and Monk met face-to-face in The Palm, Monk's Chrystie Street headquarters. Peace was declared, with the disputed territory henceforth a neutral zone, open to exploitation by both gangs; it was as sure a guarantee of future hostilities as the Treaty of Versailles. To celebrate the truce, Big Tom Foley organized a ball at which Monk and Kelly met in the center of the dance floor to shake hands and then shared a box as their followers got the ballum-rancum under way and "each gang danced with the best girls of the other."

Although Tammany was merely trying to moderate the gang's excesses, Police Commissioner Francis V. Greene was seeking to go much further. The morning after the Battle of Rivington Street, Greene had called a conference with Inspector Schmittberger and Assistant District Attorney Rand and announced that he would act to end the gangs' lawlessness and gunplay. He backed up his words by authorizing a series of raids on the gangs, and also fired a warning shot across the bows of corrupt or cowardly policemen by charging one sergeant and five patrolmen with neglect of duty for their inaction during the battle.

The Five Pointers were the first to suffer Commissioner Greene's wrath. They had assembled the night after the battle to raise funds to pay the hospital expenses of badly wounded John Carroll/Smith, and wore black badges, printed in silver letters with the words we mourn our loss. Inspector Schmittberger sought no warrants but simply turned up at the gang hangout with a force of twenty-five detectives a few minutes before midnight. "There was no ceremony about entering," but the detective who led the way was greeted by chairs thrown at his head, one of which felled him. As more police poured into the room, the gang members made a rush for the windows but were beaten back by police clubs. Schmittberger then jumped onto a table and shouted, "This meeting is adjourned and it is the last meeting you'll ever hold here. The Paul Kelly Association is dead from now on." Three men who had drawn pistols were arrested and the rest were told to get out, and as each man passed through the doorway, he took a punch in the face or a kick from the detectives. Any Five Pointers who tried to fight back were brutally beaten.

After the room had been cleared, the contents were wrecked. Offering a dangerous hostage to fortune, Inspector Schmittberger said afterward, "I think we have succeeded in putting the Paul Kelly Association out of business. If they ever try to hold another meeting, they will get a worse deal than they did tonight. You cannot deal too severely with these men. We will attend to the other gangs in a similar way." His words were made to look a little hollow when, in a defiant show of strength and despite a huge police presence, Paul Kelly then paraded an estimated two thousand gang members at the Brooklyn funeral of Michael Donovan, who had been shot and killed during the battle.

The Eastmans were next to be targeted in another brutal police roundup. To avoid being spotted prematurely by lookouts for the gang, a score of policemen wore disguises. Some only removed their collars, scarves, and cuffs and put on a slouch hat; others dressed as trolley conductors, motormen, butchers, bakers, printers, and street cleaners; and a few wore false mustaches and whiskers. The effectiveness of the subterfuge was questionable, but more than thirty Eastmans, including Joseph Brown, were arrested.

The arrests were accompanied by considerable police violence.

Commissioner Greene had earlier claimed that he did not believe that liberal use of the nightstick was the proper method for wiping out the East Side gangs. The police, he said, would use their nightsticks only in self-defense or in making an arrest; the fact that a man was an ex-convict or a reputed member of a gang would not justify using a club on him. However, newspaper reports quoting unnamed police sources said the East Side gangs were "to get a dose of their own medicine—they are to be beaten within an inch of their lives by the police whenever the slightest excuse is offered." Suspicions that the commissioner's statement was primarily for public consumption hardened when the Eastmans appeared in court, bearing fresh bruises and scars from police nightsticks. Despite police claims that almost all of them had been carrying concealed weapons, all but three were released without charge, and one of the three escaped with a ten-dollar fine.

The magistrate's hands were tied by the terms of the Sullivan Law, which carried a maximum penalty of a ten-dollar fine for carrying a concealed weapon. It was not without irony that the law had been promulgated by Big Tim Sullivan to mollify constituents outraged by gang gunplay on the streets, though, weak as it was, the law did enable police to plant a gun on any suspected criminal and then charge him with carrying a concealed weapon. It led some gangsters to sew up their pockets while their moll or one of the junior gang members paced alongside them, carrying their weapons for them.

The next Eastman gang member to face trial was a surprising one, a fifteen-year-old girl named Driga, aka "Bridget" or "The Bride," Colonna. Despite her Sicilian roots, Bridget had thrown in her lot with Monk's predominantly Jewish gang, rather than with Paul Kelly's Italians. She had graduated rapidly through the ranks of the Junior Eastmans and notwithstanding her youth and sex was now a much-feared—and much-admired—member of the adult gang, "as reckless and desperate as any of the young men who compose those notorious bands." Whenever the Eastman gang was out on one of its raids, "this bright faced, wild-eyed young girl was prominent in the melee and . . . could be seen flourishing a revolver and joining in the furious rushes of the gang with all the abandon of a young brigand." She was involved so often that police began to look upon her as one of the leaders in the battles that terrorized Cherry Hill.

She was arrested after her mother reported her missing, "testified that she was incorrigible," and told police that she carried a revolver concealed in her stocking or under her short skirt. Police hunted for several days before they found Driga, and it took two men to restrain her and get her to the police station. When her mother arrived, Driga "abused her in such terms that even the hardened policemen in the station house were shocked at her depravity." She then scratched and swore at her captors throughout the ride to the courthouse. Although she was a member of the Eastmans, such were her reputation and her powers of attraction among the rival gangs that members of the Kelly gang, the Yakey Yakes, and several other gangs also flocked to the courtroom to watch her trial. She stood in the dock, "barely five feet high, slender, delicately formed, with an exceedingly pretty face, from which flashed a pair of great big black eyes, hurling forth a torrent of Billingsgate that would have put a truck driver to the blush."

Her mother testified that Driga had been absolutely unmanageable since she was ten years old, and that she spent her time on the streets day and night with the most undesirable acquaintances she could have made in the entire East Side, including young men and women twice her age. She now "gloried in her wickedness . . . saluted her parents with frightful oaths whenever they met her among her evil companions" and was a central figure at the Paradise Social Club, made up of members of the Eastman gang and women of equal notoriety. The club held all-night dances, which often degenerated into orgies and sometimes brawls.

"She carries a gun, Judge," one of her captors said, "and orders Eastman and Kelly and the others about."

"That's not so," Driga said. "I don't know 'The Monk.' I'm not a Dick Turpin in petticoats. I've had a gun, maybe I've shot it off too, but that don't make me a girl bandit. I never stole or smoked cigarettes. I've stayed out nights and that's about the worst thing you can say about me." However, Judge Olmstead remained immune to her charms and sent her to the reformatory.

Driga was an archetypal tough girl who, with the Bowery boy, were caricatured on the stage in a series of wildly popular productions; they were recognizable and—by some—much-admired Lower East Side types. The tough girl was "a kind of sparrow that nobody would mistake for a blue jay. It said 'Hully gee' [an abbreviation of "Holy Jesus"], and 'dis mug' and 'chase y'self,' " and wore "a skirt to the toes, a close-bodiced jacket and a hat with a broken feather." Her consort, the Bowery boy, wore "a derby hat over one ear, a light-colored check coat pulled tight, a shirt with horizontal stripes," and practiced a walk with his elbows out, so that none could pass him on a narrow sidewalk. The Bowery dance halls sometimes gave a prize for the best "hard walk."

The toughest tough girl of them all, Driga was committed to the care of the Gerry Society until she was sixteen, and then transferred to the Bedford Reformatory for Women. What happened to her after that is unknown; if she ever again came before the courts it was not under any of her previous names.

After their success with one Junior Eastman, the police of the Madison Street station next took on a poolroom full of them a couple of days later, in a cellar at 103 East Broadway. A passing streetcar had previously been attacked in front of the place and the passengers robbed, and many other thefts had also been attributed to the gang, who used the poolroom as their headquarters. When a man strolled by with his coat open, showing his watch and double chain, he was asking for trouble and immediately got it. He was hit in the face, knocked down, and robbed of his watch. As he got groggily to his feet, he saw two men run into the poolroom. He tried to follow them but was stopped at the door by a beer glass aimed at his head and warned that if he didn't go away, he would be killed. When he summoned the police, the poolroom doors were slammed in their faces and they were also told that if they didn't go about their business, they would get hurt, and "big fellows in politics" would make their lives a misery.

The police forced the doors but were greeted with a volley of beer glasses and were then attacked with chairs, pool cues, and any other weapons that came to hand. They laid about them with their nightsticks, and the fierce battle continued for a few minutes, until the superior numbers and power of the police began to tell. The watch and chain were found under a pool table, along with several pistols dropped by their owners when they saw that they could not avoid arrest.

As he was led away, the Junior Eastmans' deputy leader "Klondyke" Abrams turned to a policeman and said, "You'se go to entirely too much trouble. The politicians'll bail us out. They don't want no-one away at registration and election time." He had to wait only a few hours for confirmation of that. The next morning, all of them, even the man identified as the one who had punched the victim and stolen his watch, were released on bail. However, Magistrate Ommen bound them all over on one thousand dollars' bail to keep the peace for six months. It was "a surprise to the group of roughs and their anger was stirred to the fighting point," their threats against Ommen becoming "so violent that the police had to stand over them, with drawn clubs."

Despite the raids and arrests, few believed Greene's public statements that the gangs were on the run. The elections were due in November, and as Klondyke had predicted, Monk, Kelly, and their gangs of sluggers and repeaters were too important to Tammany Hall. However, the truce between the gangs that Big Tom Foley had brokered was soon looking fragile. The Eastmans were still smarting over a recent fight between Paul Kelly and Jake Shimsky, "the heavyweight right bower [right-hand man] of the redoubtable King Eastman." Fistfights between individual members of the rival gangs were frequent, and huge sums in bets often changed hands on the result. Some were savage brawls where kicking, biting, gouging, and even knives were tolerated, but even those fought under a simulacrum of the Queensberry rules that regulated "respectable" boxing—with a marked-out ring, seconds, timekeepers, and a referee—had to be staged in secret to avoid police raids; at one time boxing was banned in every state except Louisiana.

At a fight between Jack Hirsh of the Eastmans and Ike Fadinsky of the Kellys, Shimsky had taken a blow on the nose from Kelly that he did not return for fear of provoking a mass brawl, preferring to bide his time before seeking revenge. Kelly was only five foot two, whereas Shimsky was more than six feet tall and 230 pounds, with a fearsome reputation as a strong-arm man. A couple of weeks later, looking to settle the score, he turned up with three other Eastmans at Tom Sharkey's bar, where Kelly was drinking.

"Hello you runt," Shimsky said. "If you were a full-grown man, I'd knock the block off you."

"Go chase yourself," Kelly said. That ended the preliminaries, and Shimsky and his three friends rushed him. Kelly's bodyguard, a heavyweight fighter who claimed to have trained Jack Fitzsimmons, ran in from the back, handed out a few punches, and then persuaded them to go down into the cellar and settle their differences "accordin' to [Queensberry] rules."

Word traveled fast, and before the two men had even stripped to their waists, a dozen East Side "sports" had turned up and started laying bets. It was a bantamweight against a heavyweight, and the odds reflected the unequal contest, with eighteen hundred dollars wagered on the outcome. A twelve-foot ring was paced out, with beer kegs to mark the corners, and the two men wore skintight gloves. "Shimsky opened with a savage rush, Kelly dodged and got in one. Then the blows came thick and fast." In the third round "Kelly shot out a left that landed, and then followed it with a right that sent Shimsky to the floor." His seconds picked up the unconscious Shimsky and carried him out of the ring. By now the policeman on post had got wind of what was going on and was pounding on the door, but the fighters, their seconds, the referee, and the spectators all got out up the airshaft, and the cellar was deserted by the time the police eventually broke in.

Swallowing his humiliation at his defeat by a much smaller man, Shimsky sought out Kelly in Tom Sharkey's bar after the fight and told him, "You done me fair, an' I wanter shake. What'll y'have?" Despite that conciliatory gesture and the Foley-imposed outbreak of peace between the gangs, the Eastmans had suffered a grievous blow to their prestige, and there was a suspicion in high places that they might only be stalling until they could take their revenge.

Monk duly kept his part of the bargain with Tammany by helping to get out the vote in the elections, but the truce between the Eastmans and the Five Pointers did not hold for long after that. In that same month, November 1903, an Eastman gang member named Hurst got into an argument with a Five Pointer named Ford in a Bowery dive. It developed into a vicious brawl in which Hurst's nose was broken in two places, and one of his ears was bitten off. Monk immediately told Kelly that if he did not exact retribution on Ford himself, Monk and his gang would come to the Five Points and "wipe up de earth wit youse guys."

Kelly replied in similarly forthright and unconciliatory terms, and a fresh outbreak of gang warfare was averted only when Tammany politicians again intervened, forcing the two leaders to hold fresh peace talks at The Palm. Monk and Kelly faced each other across a table, each with one hand holding a cigar and the other resting on the butt of a pistol. After much wrangling, they agreed to resolve their differences by a bare-knuckle fistfight between the two of them. The winner would take the disputed territory; the loser would confine himself and his gang to his own turf from then on.

The prospect of a prizefight between two of New York's most notorious gangsters electrified the Lower East Side. On the appointed night Monk and Kelly, each accompanied by fifty handpicked men, and a crowd of spectators and gamblers—"toughs in cocked derby hats and women in 'Mikado tuck-ups,' the high piled, delicate hair-dos of the day"—met in an abandoned barn on the outskirts of the Bronx. The once rural Bronx was undergoing a dramatic transformation. The areas east of the Bronx River had only been annexed to New York in 1895, but the extension of the Third Avenue El through the Bronx in 1891 had already begun a building boom that saw the population more than double, from 88,000 to 200,000 people, in the course of that decade. It was in the process of doubling again during the following ten years as more and more Bronx farmland was bought up and developed, but in the outlying districts there were still large tracts of rural land and woods, where even a prizefight between New York's two most notorious gangsters might take place without police interference.

The venue for the fight was made known by word of mouth, and more than two hundred made the journey out to the Bronx. As well as gang members, there were a number of sports who "could face the searchlight of respectability without flinching." Tickets were sold for a nominal fifty cents, but the purchasers had to produce rather more money than that before the fight. Those who had already bought tickets were told to meet at a hotel on East Fourteenth Street at nine o'clock on the night of the fight. Those without tickets were told to wait at the foot of the El station at 161st Street in the Bronx an hour later. The fighters and ticketholders boarded the El at Fourteenth Street, and at every station along the line newcomers with the tip joined them. They were at least a hundred strong by the time they reached 161st Street, where a hundred more were waiting. In order to avoid rousing police suspicions, the crowd broke up into groups of four or six and made off in different directions before heading for the next rendezvous, a roadhouse on Jerome Avenue, about two miles away. It was a bitter night with no trolley cars in sight; they had to walk.

By the time they arrived at the roadhouse, the walk had "whetted their appetites and thirst, and they got away with all the sandwiches in sight and a few other articles that they did not pay for . . . Everybody seemed to be smoking good Havana cigars, and the air seemed laden with the fumes of recently opened wine." The proprietor of the roadhouse then locked the doors and told them if they did not pay for what they had stolen, the police would be called. The crowd produced enough money between them to satisfy him, whereupon the doors were unlocked and they streamed out into the night.

The trek continued, deeper into the country, over roads covered with new-fallen snow, until about fifty of them got tired of walking and boarded a Jerome Avenue streetcar. The first thing some of them then did was to steal about $2.50 in nickels and dimes from the conductor's pockets. A sport also stole one of the trolley car's lamps, placing it beneath his overcoat and telling his friend, "We may need this later on." It was past midnight when they reached an old barn on the deserted Berkeley Oval. The only person in the barn was the watchman, who was dead drunk or had been slipped knockout drops. A guard kept watch over him, and another was posted to look out for the police. The rest of them gathered around the ring, lit by the feeble light of a lantern and the stolen lamp.

The winter wind whistling through chinks in the decrepit walls cut the smell of the moldering straw, black with damp, still piled in the corners of the barn. The ring, roughly swept clear of loose straw and animal dung, was paced out and marked by straw bales and a single strand of old rope, sagging from four fence posts driven into the dirt. There were no seats or bleachers, and the crowd stood elbow to elbow around the ring, with those at the back precariously balanced on boxes, straw bales, and rotting barrels for a better view. Armed gang members were close-packed around the ring, but they left Monk and Kelly to fight it out without interference. The referee, from a rival gang with no close affiliation to either side, brought the two men together in the center of the ring. Monk was stockier and five inches taller than Kelly, but Kelly had fought professionally and, as he had demonstrated against Shimsky, his skill as a fighter could be enough to offset the greater weight, strength, and ferocity of a bigger man.

The fight began with Monk charging at Kelly, throwing roundhouse punches, while Kelly used his speed to avoid Monk's rushes, ducking and weaving but still landing some jolting shots. The shouts and the thunder of applause and stamping feet at each blow or knockdown set dust and straw cascading from the worm-eaten rafters above. Each round continued until one of the fighters was knocked down. Both men had a cornerman with a sponge and a bucket of dingy-looking water to sponge his man's cuts and splash his face between rounds, and he had one minute to revive his fighter. If his fighter had not "come up to scratch"—the line scraped in the dirt at the center of the ring—when the timekeeper rang the bell for the next round, the other man would be awarded the fight.

Kelly and Monk both went down several times, but each time they hauled themselves back to the mark for the next round. They fought for well over an hour, without either managing to land the knockout blow, and so indomitable were their wills that even after they had both collapsed to the barn floor with exhaustion they continued to aim increasingly feeble blows at each other's heads until at last their followers pulled them apart and the fight was declared a draw. There were some who suggested that, at Tammany's insistence, the fight had been fixed from the start, an honorable draw being the only way to ensure that the loser's men would not start another war to gain their revenge, but the cuts and bruises the two fighters bore were genuine enough.

It was almost two in the morning when the crowd began to straggle back toward the city. When they came across a trolley car there was a mad rush to get aboard, though few of them showed any inclination to pay the fare. After it had traveled about a mile the motorman brought the car to a halt and the conductor hailed three patrolling policemen, who threatened to arrest all the passengers unless the fares were paid. One of the sports who had won money betting on the fight magnanimously came to the rescue, giving the conductor fifty cents, and the car resumed its journey.

They reached 161st Street and Willis Avenue at half past two in the morning and got into the El car going downtown. Most got off at Fourteenth Street and, while the sports and supporters melted away into the night, the two battered and bloodied gang leaders returned to their headquarters to lick their wounds, knowing that the turf war remained unresolved and that it would be only a matter of time before hostilities between the gangs resumed.

9

THE TOMBS

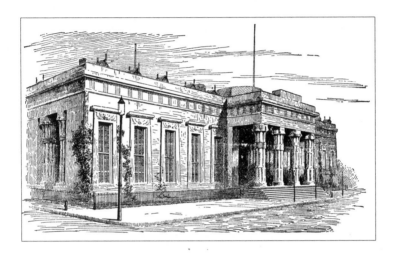

The decisive moment in the war between Monk and Paul Kelly came in the early hours of February 2, 1904. Monk, still wearing a mourning band after the death of his mother the day before Thanksgiving, was with a sidekick, Chris Wallace, and they were well north of the Fourteenth Street dead-line. They had made their way to Sixth Avenue and Forty-second Street either to blackjack a man who had crossed one of Monk's clients, as one source alleged, or just to have a few drinks, according to Monk and his cohorts. A little before three in the morning they saw a well-dressed young man, the worse for drink, staggering out of Jack's All-Night Restaurant. He lurched around the corner, then stood in a doorway, took his money out of his pocket, and started counting it.

Just behind him, lurking in the shadows, were two roughly dressed men whom Monk and Wallace took to be "lush workers" waiting to rob the drunk of his wallet. Never one to look a gift horse in the mouth, Monk and Wallace promptly held up the young man themselves. As they were relieving him of his wallet, the other men—John Rogers and George Bryan of the Pinkerton Detective Agency—emerged from the shadows. They had been hired to protect "the wayward son of a man prominent in national affairs," and as the son was "on a debauch," he was being kept under surveillance.

Following the traditional Pinkerton method of "shoot first and then ask questions," they at once began shooting at Monk and Wallace, who returned fire. After firing nearly all the shots in their guns, Monk and Wallace took to their heels and made a wild dash along Forty-second Street. The Pinkerton men kept up an intermittent fire, and their quarry paused from time to time to aim additional shots at them.

Bryan later testified that, despite the attempts of some of Monk's other companions to trip him up, he was able to overtake Wallace, whom he used as a shield, turning him from side to side to keep Wallace between them while Monk tried to get a clear shot. After firing his last shot, Monk threw his empty revolver at Bryan's head, but the Pinkerton man ducked, and it smashed through a store window, where it fell into a tea set. Despite all the shooting, the only damage done by either side was to that seventy-five-dollar plate-glass window, and to another window in a trunk store. The revolver, which police stated belonged to Monk, was found in the store window with all its chambers empty.

Police Officer Sheehan, who was standing outside the Knickerbocker Hotel at the corner of Forty-second and Broadway, had heard the shots, and as Monk sprinted around the corner, Sheehan swung his nightstick and laid him out cold. Aided by the two Pinkerton men and two detectives who had been keeping watch on nearby gambling houses, Sheehan arrested Wallace and the unconscious Monk. When his head cleared, Monk found himself on the cold stone floor of a cell in the West Forty-seventh Street police station.

At first Monk treated the police and the prospect of criminal charges with his customary indifference. He gave his address as 2060 Second Avenue and his name as William Delaney—as usual, both were false. Since his one term of imprisonment on the Island, Monk had always managed to get out of trouble, but this time the police were confident that the charges against him would stick.

Monk sat back to await the arrival of Tammany's lawyers and bail bondsmen, but the involvement of "incorruptible" Pinkerton agents in the case made Monk's position far more precarious than he at first realized. Recalcitrant policemen who tried to testify against gang leaders could be transferred to the Goats, but a Pinkerton Agency operative could reputedly be neither threatened nor bought. For once Monk had overplayed his luck and would have to suffer the consequences.

His notoriety was also making him a dubious asset to Tammany. Although he was still useful, it soon became clear that his value had strict cash limits. While Monk languished in his cell, two Tammany politicians approached Assistant District Attorney Elder and offered fifteen hundred dollars's bail, saying that they needed Monk, "one of the best men we have for registration and election day work. We cannot afford to lose his services this year." When Elder told them that he would try to have the bail fixed at twenty-five hundred dollars, they said Monk wasn't worth that much to them. Elder protested that they were effectively saying that they knew Monk would jump bail, to which they replied, "Of course. You don't suppose he'll stay to be sent to jail, do you? That's why we don't want to go as far as $2,500. Won't you let him out on $1,500 bail? That's a fair amount." The furious Elder then said that he now wouldn't even consent to ten thousand dollars' bail, and bade them good day.

Recorder Goff eventually fixed bail at seventy-five hundred dollars to cover two indictments, but no one was willing to pay that much, and Monk remained in custody. When arraigned, he described himself as a newspaper speculator and again gave his address as 2060 Second Avenue. His lawyer said his client was willing to plead guilty to a charge of disorderly conduct, but the magistrate refused the offer and Monk was eventually indicted on three counts: attempted murder, first degree, and assault, first and second degree. It was charged that he had attempted "willfully, feloniously and of his malice aforethought, and with deliberate and premeditated design to effect the death of . . . George Bryan with . . . a certain pistol then and there charged with gunpowder and one leaden bullet."

Monk also faced a further indictment after an old adversary— Inspector McClusky of the detective bureau, still smarting over the failure of the Lamar case in New Jersey—claimed that Monk had attempted to kill a young man named Harry Lewis two weeks before at First Street and Second Avenue. Lewis confirmed the story before the grand jury, and Monk was charged with that offense. Monk told reporters that the police were intent on sending him "up the river"—to Sing Sing—but with the help of a good lawyer, he was confident of beating them.

He was transferred to the Tombs to await his trial at the general sessions court. Officially known as the Manhattan House of Detention for Men, the Tombs stood on a site that had once been the Collect Pond, the source of New York's original drinking-water supply; by the early nineteenth century, it had become a dumping ground and a malarial swamp. A canal (subsequently filled in and renamed Canal Street) was then built to drain it, extending to east and west, and the site of the Collect Pond was filled and leveled with rubble and rubbish, but it remained waterlogged and mosquito-ridden.

A massive granite building, 253 feet long by 200 feet deep, was erected there, based on a steel engraving of an Egyptian tomb. A broad flight of dark stone steps led up to the entrance on Centre Street, dominated by a huge and forbidding portico, supported by four massive stone columns. The low-lying site made it barely visible from Broadway, only a hundred yards distant, and the ground was so marshy that despite the building's having much deeper foundations than normal, subsidence made it sink even lower, warping the cells and causing cracks through which water seeped, forming pools on the stone floors. Popular mythology even claimed that the building rose and fell with the tides.

Stonemasons were forever repairing and shoring up the building, which was condemned by more than one grand jury as unhealthy and unfit although it remained in use until 1902, when it was pulled down and replaced by a massive gray stone structure. The nickname was less easy to demolish and is still being used today. Conditions inside remained medieval. Although built to accommodate only two hundred prisoners, at least twice that number were routinely incarcerated there; fifty thousand prisoners passed through its portals every year.

Beyond the forbidding entrance of the Tombs was a large courtyard surrounding the male prison, which was connected with the outer building only by the "Bridge of Sighs," over which all condemned prisoners made their final walk, the gallows set up in the courtyard "meeting their eyes as they passed out into daylight." The four tiers of cells opened off a high but narrow iron-galleried hall. Prisoners were compelled to walk around the gallery for an hour every day, the only time when they were not locked in their cells. There was no running water, no heating, no mains drainage—prisoners used metal buckets, making the lack of adequate ventilation even less pleasant—and minimal natural light. The only way to measure the passing hours was by the gradual, almost imperceptible lightening and darkening of the gray-black light. No lights were allowed in the cells at night. In winter, prisoners spent two-thirds of their time shivering in darkness and silence; in summer they sweltered.

The remaining buildings of the Tombs, separated from the male prison by the courtyard, included "Bummer's Hall," housing the tramps, vagrants, and drunks pulled off the streets every day. Each morning they were taken out, tried, and convicted—few were ever discharged—and sent to the Island on a six-month sentence, but by the following night Bummer's Hall would again be full. There were separate buildings for women prisoners and juveniles. The latter, incarcerated on the Centre Street side of the jail, often completed their criminal education while imprisoned there, for prisons like the Tombs were seminaries of crime.

The Centre Street buildings also housed the warden's office and quarters, the police court, and the court of special sessions. Six large cells directly over the entrance were reserved for those able to pay for them. They did not wait long before coming to trial; more criminals daily passed before the recorder in the Tombs police court than in any other court in the world, and the justice dispensed there was brisk. Under the eyes of half a dozen policemen, the defendants were herded together in the "prison pens," surrounded by ranks of friends, witnesses, or mere curious spectators, on the wooden benches lining the room. Shyster lawyers always stood around the courtroom, looking for any defendant who might be willing or able to pay a fee of as little as fifty cents to as much as fifty dollars.

Monk had been languishing in the Tombs for a month when, in early March 1904, he was brought before Recorder Goff, a man "cold-hearted, humorless and so short as to appear stunted," who once famously asked for the shades to be drawn because there was "not enough gloom in this courtroom." The court was packed with East Side toughs who saw Monk as a hero, and for their benefit he made loud, derogatory remarks about the physique of some of the court officers, joked with his friends, and whispered to them that he was too lucky not to get out of his latest trouble.

Monk's counsel, George W. Hurlbut, had made an application to
the state supreme court for a change of venue, claiming that an attempt
was being made to railroad his client and arguing that because of Monk's
notoriety, it was impossible for him to get a fair trial in that county. He
submitted a bundle of newspaper clippings and supporting affidavits,
but the supreme court justice was unmoved and the trial went ahead in
the original venue after another month's delay. Monk had been bailed
pending the supreme court judgment—either the cost of bail had come
down or his value to Tammany had risen—but he was at once rear-
rested by police, along with five companions. Monk was discharged
by magistrates the next morning, but his chances of an acquittal in the
looming trial were not improved when *The New York Times* ran an article claiming that fifteen of his gang members had been employed to "do
up" some members of a synagogue with brass knuckles and iron bars.
Their fee was said to be ten dollars for wounding a man and fifteen dollars for killing him.

Ten days later there was further damaging publicity when police
reserves were called out to a fight involving a crowd of Eastmans. The
police could not find out what the brawl had been about, and the victim
was said to be too frightened to make a complaint against any of his
assailants.

Those latest newspaper reports could hardly have been worse
timed, appearing on the very morning, April 12, 1904, that Monk's trial
opened at the court of general sessions. Only those members of Monk's
gang under subpoena to appear were admitted to the courtroom; the
rest gathered outside in the corridors. Monk's sisters were in court, and
at the end of the day's hearing, he kissed them before returning to his
cell.

Monk was dressed better than any of the jurymen who were to pass
judgment upon him, but his relaxed and affable demeanor was tested
when the Pinkerton agent gave evidence. When he claimed that Monk
had shouted out, "Let go of him you God damned son of a bitch, or
I'll kill you," Monk half-rose from his seat, but his counsel persuaded
him to sit down again. When he was called to the stand, speaking in a
voice "like the bark of a dog," Monk told the court, "My real name is
Edward Eastman. I am twenty-eight years old, and unmarried and I live
on Ward Street, Richmond Hill. I know nothing about this holdup."
He also described himself as a dealer in pigeons. Only the first of those
six statements was true: in fact, he was thirty and still married to Margaret, and Ward Street was his mother's old house, where his sisters

Lizzie and Francine, were still living.

Assistant District Attorney William Rand's attempts under cross-examination to elicit Monk's true name, address, occupation, and marital state occupy eleven pages of the trial transcript, and at the end of it neither the prosecution, the judge, nor the jury were much, if any, the wiser. Rand began by asking Monk what address he had given to the police.

A: 2060 Second Avenue.

Q: Did you live there?

A: Well . . .

Q: Did you live there?

A: I did live there, yes.

Q: When did you move down to Richmond Hill?

A: I live up there still, and I live with private people and they sent me a letter since I have moved to Third Avenue and asking me not to disgrace them. That is why I didn't want to give that number any more.

Q: What number?

A: 2060 Second Avenue.

Q: But you did give it in the police station?

A: Yes, sir.

Q: And you said you lived in Richmond Hill, too?

A: Yes, sir.

Q: That was not true?

A: Yes, well, my sister lived there.

Q: I didn't ask if your sister lived there; don't let us drag your sister into this. Do you live there?

A: Not exactly live there. I go over there.

Q: Is that your residence?

A: Any time I want to go there, I can, and live there.

Q: Oh, I hope your sister is glad to see you. But where do you live?

A: In New York.

Q: Whereabouts? I don't know whether you live in New York or Pekin. Where do you live; what is the address?

A: Where I am living now?

Q: I know where you are living now.

A: I am living over in the Tombs.

Q: Yes, I know where you are living now. Where were you

living when you were arrested, before you were put in the
Tombs?

A: I was living in Thirteenth Street . . . or Tenth Street.

Q: What number Tenth Street?

A: I don't know the number.

Q: When did you move from Tenth Street to 2060 Second
Avenue?

A: About a couple of days before I got arrested.

Q: Did you ever live at Richmond Hill?

A: Yes, sir.

Q: When?

A: I lived there last summer.

Q: How long?

A: I raised my pigeons out there.

Q: I didn't ask that. How long did you live there?

A: I go over there and sleep there.

Q: Off and on?

A: Yes.

Q: Visit your sister?

A: Yes.

Q: When did you stop living there last summer?

A: Well, I stopped . . . I didn't stop living there. I go over
there and when I go over there, I sleep there.

Q: Let us be frank about this. Has Richmond Hill ever been
your residence?

A: Not mine exactly, no.

Q: All right, not yours exactly.

A: No, sir.

Had the police been able to establish his real address, they would
immediately have raided the building and would undoubtedly have
found his tools of trade—weapons and burglary equipment, and very
probably some of the proceeds of his crimes and rackets. Even if the
cash disappeared straight into policemen's pockets, the weapons and
robber's tools alone would have been enough to earn him another trial
and a long spell in jail.

Monk's defense rested on his claims that he and Wallace had merely
been drinking with friends, first at McDermott's gin mill in the Bowery
near Stanton Street, and then at Sig Cohen's on Forty-second Street.

By the time they left there at two or half past two in the morning, they had been drinking for six to seven hours. By then Monk had "twenty glasses of lager" in him, though he still claimed he was not drunk. He said that as they came out onto the sidewalk there was a scuffle and they "started to rumble around . . . and I says, 'There will be some trouble,' so I kept a-going and a-going; and when I got a little ways, I looked up and saw a crowd gather and heard two shots fired." He said he was walking toward Broadway when "Wallace came running past me, and I ran too. I wanted to get away in the excitement and when I went to run down [into the subway], I slipped downstairs and an officer was after me and picked me up, and I says, 'What is the matter?' and there was a lot of them there and a lot of citizens and they started to hit me there."

Monk claimed that he had run only because he did not want to be caught in a fight, as the police were always persecuting him. He denied that he ever carried, drew, fired, or threw a pistol at any time that night, or that he was ever closer than twenty feet to Bryan. He also denied shouting at Bryan, "Let go of him, you God damned son of a bitch, or I will kill you." Having already claimed not to have seen anything of the shooting until Wallace came running past him, Monk then appeared to forget his earlier testimony when trying to exonerate Wallace: he claimed that Bryan had put his gun under Wallace's arm and "held Wallace in front of him and kept shooting in the crowd."

The trial lasted three days. Summing up for the defense, George W. Hurlbut said that Monk did not want sympathy but mercy, and told the jury that they must "wonder at the nerve of the district attorney in not producing 'the wayward son of a man prominent in national affairs' who had caused all the trouble . . . Better that he should have been produced and suffer humiliation than that an innocent man should be sent to prison." Hurlbut claimed that there was a police conspiracy to send Monk to prison and that there had been no drunken youth, as the prosecution had claimed.

Rand countered that the sole reason for not producing "the wayward son" was that he had been so drunk that night he did not even know he was being robbed and would have been useless as a witness. Summing up for the prosecution, Rand declared, "Never in my experience have I known of such a scoundrel, burglar, thug and self-confessed perjurer as this Eastman." An ugly light gleamed in Monk's eyes as he listened to this, but he looked away as Rand turned and pointed at him.

The jury spent two hours deliberating over their verdict, and on the three ballots that were taken, eleven were in favor of a conviction on the more serious charge of attempted murder in the first degree. However, one juror refused to assent to the verdict, since it carried a possible sentence of twenty-five years' imprisonment. He insisted he would not change his mind no matter how long his fellow jurors argued, and after two hours, they filed back into court. Monk searched their faces for some clue to his fate; most of them avoided his gaze. The foreman then delivered their compromise verdict: guilty of assault in the first degree. Monk looked stunned; "in the language of his friends, he was 'all out.' " However, as he was being led back across the Bridge of Sighs to the prison at the Tombs, he managed a show of bravado for the police and the prison wardens. He stopped suddenly as he heard the music from an Italian funeral, pulled off his hat, and said, "Thanks gents, for this flatterin' serenade. De tune, 'Nearer My God to Thee,' is almost as 'propriate as if I was going to de chair."

At the request of Monk's counsel, Recorder Goff delayed sentencing for five days because Monk "had some property interests which he wished to settle before he went to prison"; it was as close as the famously tight-lipped Monk ever came to revealing the extent of his wealth. When Monk returned to court for sentencing on April 19, 1904, his counsel made no attempt to enter any plea in mitigation, instead telling the court, "I have ordered the defendant to serve whatever sentence your honor may impose as a warning to others . . . The defendant Eastman is not a well man. The life he has led has undermined his health but I hope he will be able to serve his sentence and when he comes out, he will be a better man."

Recorder Goff said that "the circumstances of the case and the need of conserving the public interests and deterring others of Eastman's stamp" had led him to impose the maximum punishment the law allowed: ten years in Sing Sing. This time Monk remained impassive. Whether he'd been railroaded, as his defense counsel had claimed, or was rightly convicted was no longer of any consequence; as one newspaper reporter scathingly remarked, "Nobody begrudged the Monk the ten-year sentence he received, whether he went to Sing Sing by railroad or otherwise."

Monk's prime concern was allegedly neither his property nor his business interests, nor even his own fate, but that of his beloved pigeons, and he asked the court to allow him to remain in the Tombs for another week so that he could find someone to tend his five hundred pigeons. Despite his plea, Monk was due to be sent to Sing Sing that same day, along with a convict named George Coan and four other notorious thugs. At the last moment, when he and Coan had already been hand-cuffed together, the warden of the Tombs received a telephone call from the sheriff's office, informing him that someone wanted Monk to remain a few days longer in the Tombs. It was difficult to imagine any other convicted prisoner being given such leeway; this suggests that Tammany, in its anxiety to ensure the loyalty of Monk's successor, was engaged in last-minute negotiations with Monk himself.

On the morning of April 22, 1904, with the gray stone walls above them still in deep shadow, two deputy sheriffs and three assistants led Monk and three other prisoners out of the Tombs. Smoking a big black cigar, Monk waved to the group of spectators and reporters watching as he entered the police van. "Well, I'm going now," he said. "This is the last you'll hear of Monk for a while." They were driven to Grand Central Terminal, where a crowd that police estimated at five thousand people was waiting to bid farewell to the notorious Monk Eastman. As he was led from the van handcuffed to another prisoner, twenty or thirty plainclothes policemen were sent out to mingle with the crowd, while armed police formed a cordon around Monk in case of a last des-perate attempt by the Eastmans to free their leader. By now, Monk's mood had changed and his customary bravado seemed to desert him as he realized where his life's path had led him. He glowered at the crowd, and in contrast to his earlier ebullience, refused even to acknowledge the smiles, waves, and shouts of the friends who had walked from the Lower East Side to the station just to catch his eye. As Monk stood silent, his fellow prisoner, handcuffed to him, stared at the throng of people surrounding them. "Holy smokes!" he said. "Gee, but don't they give ye an awful weighin' up when the jig's over?"

Monk and his fellow prisoners were put aboard the 2:06 train, which would take them up the Hudson Valley to Sing Sing. As a contempo-rary remarked, "That hour goin' up the river was the toughest I'd ever come to." A few reporters made the journey as well, one noting that although Monk "buried his face in a newspaper, it is said that he cannot read." When the train reached Ossining, Monk and his fellow prisoners began the slow, shackled walk along the road toward the main gate, past groups of prisoners breaking rocks on the hillside above them. At 3:15 that afternoon, beneath the watchtower like a squat lighthouse, manned by armed guards with rifles, the great gates of Sing Sing clanged shut behind Monk.

The sprawl of gray granite prison buildings was set on a promontory surrounded on three sides by the river. Clutching at any straw of distinction for the dismal institution he ran, one of Sing Sing's governors claimed the smokestack rising high above the prison was one of the highest prison smokestacks in the country. The four-story redbrick-and-steel prison hospital stood on a bluff above the prison, and "were it not for the iron bars that betray its purpose, this hospital would be the proud possession of any normal community." In its foyer was the Latin inscription *Nihil Humani Probis Alienum*—"Nothing that is human is foreign to us." From the heights around the hospital, just inside the perimeter wall, the wide sweep of the Hudson was visible for miles.

Monk handed over his money and other valuables and was assigned a prison number: 54,863. His pedigree was then taken by the prison clerk. Monk gave his parents' names, his date and place of birth, his religion, his occupation, the crime for which he was sent to Sing Sing, and the cause of it; "experienced cons answered 'bad association.' " He was described on the record of admission as a tar and tin roofer who kept a bird store. He was married, his habits were intemperate, he indulged in tobacco but not religion, and he said he could not read or write.

His next of kin was listed as his sister Lizzie Reynolds, living in the Richmond Hill house that Monk had bought for his mother. She was a puzzling choice, given that Monk was a married man, and perhaps suggests that his marriage to Margaret was already failing. His description ran to a dozen lines of the clerk's spidery copperplate handwriting, as he tried to include as many as possible of Monk's innumerable distinguishing features, scars, and bullet wounds:

> Complexion dark, Weight 167 pounds, Hair dark brown . . . good-sized head, 7 1/8 hat, 7 1/2 shoes. Several small scars on back head. An angle-shaped scar near rear of crown. Scar at crown, several small scars on left [?] side of head. Scars above right ear. Large diagonal scar, also a large scar shaped as a figure 9, back from upper rt angle of forehead. Large ears. Flat-sided head. Med. forehead. Good eyebrows. Short thick nose and broken. Two upper front middle teeth capped with gold. One tooth absent. Tough featured. Scar near left eye. Part faded cut [?] between index and forefinger each hand. Large, long ragged scar on right side of abdomen.

Even then, the clerk missed some of the most prominent marks, including the two bullet holes in Monk's stomach.

Monk then got the usual bath, haircut, and shave, and donned a suit of prison clothes—shirt and trousers and a small round cap that must have sat on his large head like a frog on a lily pad. He was then interrogated by a representative of the Department of Correction and informed of the only two legal rights enjoyed by prisoners at Sing Sing: to attend whatever religious worship accorded with his beliefs and conscience, and to receive a specific food allowance. Everything else, including fresh air and exercise in the prison yard, writing or receiving letters, having visits, smoking, and all forms of amusement were privileges that could be awarded or withheld at the whim of the wardens.

Sing Sing was the most notorious prison in America, a byword for brutality and corruption. Like the other eight hundred inmates, Monk was confined in a cell only seven feet long, three feet wide, and six feet seven inches high. Those cells, unimproved in eighty years, were "unfit for the housing of animals, much less human beings." The cell block was so damp that one head warden said that when he rubbed his hand on the first-tier walls, seven feet above the water level, it came away damp. The cells smelled horrific and were infested with rats, cockroaches, and lice. Prisoners were locked in their cells with a latrine bucket from 5:30 p.m. until the following morning. On weekends and holidays they were locked up for twenty-one hours at a time. In such a restricted and poorly ventilated space the stink from the bucket was terrible at any time, and unbearable in hot weather. When the tiny cell was occupied by two people, as was often the case, the stench was doubled. Drinking water was also kept in a bucket in the cell and was subject to contamination. The conditions caused inmates to suffer chronic rheumatism and sometimes fatal heart disease, and many of them, serving sentences of from one to twenty years, left the prison permanently crippled.

A grand jury found that the warden and head guard regularly put inmates who were "repugnant and dangerous to each other" in the same cell. Physically or mentally ill prisoners, including those with advanced tuberculosis or syphilis, were often paired with healthy men, and first offenders and young boys were condemned to share cells with habitual criminals or men who made a practice of sodomy.

Inmates were also subjected to a prison regimen of a brutality matching the worst aspects of the society beyond the prison walls. "The

whole system under which this institution is conducted . . . is pernicious . . . the prisoners are not reformed, they are merely penalized,
and in the worst way." Any breach of prison rules was punishable by
solitary confinement in "the Cooler"—one of two padded cells or one
of eight pitch-black, airless dungeons. In the Cooler, the inmate's mattress was removed by day, and he could rest only on the stone floor or
on his latrine bucket. Once every twenty-four hours he received a slice
of bread and eight ounces of water; a 150-pound man requires a minimum of fifty ounces daily. As a grand jury reported, "This situation
is as deplorable and pitiful as any we have found. So desperate is their
condition that they have been known to drink their own urine, as well
as the disinfectant placed in the cell buckets. As a result, some are driven
insane, others attempt suicide." A prison physician claimed that one of
his main duties was to knock on the doors of the dark cells every day to
discover if any of the occupants had succumbed to disease or madness.

In theory any infraction of the rules, however minor, led to a spell
in the Cooler, but the removal of men from the labor force reduced the
profits from the prison workshops, so physical punishment was often
substituted. There was no standard code of punishment, and the duration of beatings was simply left to the whim of the guards. Many went
undocumented, but the prison records still contain a staggering catalog
of whippings, "water cures," stocks, "stretchers," and "sweatboxes,"
which continued well into the twentieth century.

The water cure, also known as "the bath," was used for decades at
Sing Sing to cow and terrify the inmates. In the worst variant of the
punishment—a direct antecedent of waterboarding—the prisoner was
hung up by his arms so that he was at full stretch, standing on tiptoes.
A leather collar was placed around his neck like a noose and a torrent of
water was then unleashed onto his head. Battered, half-drowned, and
often unconscious, the man was then revived, but might face the punishment again and again, until the guards, sated, chose to cut him down.
"It's the leather collar that holds an' galls you, an' you strapped up by
the arms with your toes just touchin' the floor; an' it's the shower-bath
that leaves you in a dead faint till another dash brings you out." Prison
records showed that 170 men received this brutal punishment in 1852;
half a century later, there had been little diminution in its use.

Even in 1920, when the reforming governor, Lewis E. Lawes, took
over Sing Sing, he unearthed a catalog of brutality and abuses stretching back decades. Thirty-three male and twenty female prisoners had

simply gone missing, presumably after bribing their guards to allow them to escape, and more than thirty thousand dollars in cash had been stolen from prison bank accounts. Swindles at Sing Sing and other jails, involving the substitution of near inedible food for the meals paid for by the state, also netted the perpetrators several million dollars. Since food was scarce and of such appalling quality, inmates were often debilitated and prey to disease, and any man sent up the river to Sing Sing was aware that he might not survive.

On the Monday morning after his induction, Monk experienced the full prison regimen for the first time. At 6:30 a.m. a strident bell sounded the start of the prison day. The night staff had already made a head count of prisoners, and this tally was checked by the morning shift. At seven a second bell signaled the moment when the brakes controlling all the iron-barred cell doors on each gallery were released. The prisoners at once stepped out and marched to breakfast—cornmeal, milk, bread, and coffee, ladled into bowls as the men passed the counter.

At eight a steam whistle sounded, summoning them to work. Monk now began the grueling regimen of hard labor that made Sing Sing notorious. The first inmates had been compelled to build the jail that would confine them, shaping and laying blocks of Ossining granite. Convicts under punishment still broke rocks every day in the quarry, endlessly pounding with sledgehammers, reducing boulders to blocks, gravel, and rock dust, labor that broke men's spirits as it drained their bodies. Some "trusties" were sent outside the prison on road gangs. The other inmates worked long hours in the prison "shops," producing, among other things, highway signs, brushes, mattresses, pillows, government forms, letterheads, envelopes, socks, vests, shirts, straitjackets, pajamas, mittens, aprons, shoes, cans, and scrapers. These goods were sold to offset the costs of the prisoners' incarceration.

At ten to noon, the steam whistle blew again, summoning the prisoners to "noon mess." They formed up in pairs and, in step to loud martial music played by the prison band, marched the length of the courtyard, around the death house, through the old south gate, up the hill, through the chapel, and along a corridor to the mess hall. There they ate lunch of a small piece of gray meat of doubtful provenance, mashed potatoes, turnips and brown gravy, bread and cocoa, and corn-starch pudding. Thirty minutes' recreation was allowed in the prison courtyard after lunch, "an endless line of marchers, treading unending circles around the flower beds and the large fountain." At ten to one the steam whistle summoned them back to work, where another head count was taken.

Despite the harshness of the regimen and the totality of surveillance under which they lived, inmates at Sing Sing, as at every other prison, showed enormous ingenuity in producing rotgut alcohol, which made its "odiferous appearance" despite the most stringent regulation and supervision. Those found in possession of alcohol or under its influence had a further ninety days added to their minimum term, but this had little deterrent effect. There were also other soporifics; a Jewish chaplain, Rabbi S. Braverman, was dismissed after he confessed to smuggling opium into the prison and selling it to inmates. Three guards were also fired for smuggling money to prisoners from their friends and relatives; some of that had no doubt found its way to the rabbi.

The electric chair had been introduced to Sing Sing as early as 1891—four prisoners were executed by that method on July 7 of that year—but the legend that the lights would dim when the electric chair was switched on was apocryphal; the power for executions was generated solely for that purpose. In the gallows humor of the jail, inmates called the execution block "The Dance Hall" because the night before an execution, guards played the condemned man's choice of music on a phonograph.

Conditions at Sing Sing were so grim that after visiting the prison, Sir Arthur Conan Doyle's recommendation was brief and to the point: "Burn it down! The buildings are absolutely antiquated and it is nothing less than a disgrace for a State so great and wealthy as New York to have a prison which is a hundred years behind the times."

With Monk rotting in Sing Sing, his gang was now literally beyond his control, and at once the Eastmans began to disintegrate into rival factions fighting for dominance. Within four days of Monk's journey up the river, two aspiring young leaders of the gang, Otto Bennett and Morris Rothschild, met in a vacant lot at Second Avenue and First Street and fought what began as a street brawl but was finished under Queensberry rules. They had fought three rounds, and the succession to the powers of Monk was still in doubt, when "some alarmed and unsportsmanlike citizen" telephoned police headquarters.

Captain McDermott left the police station in such a hurry that he forgot to take his hat. Three detectives followed him, running the four blocks to the scene of the fight, with a dozen reserves chasing after them, as soon as they had grabbed their coats and nightsticks. Even this sizable force had difficulty pushing its way through the mob surrounding the combatants, and as soon as they did, the fighters and their seconds turned on them. Rothschild attacked Detective Wasserman, and in the process of subduing him, Wasserman "did some fist work himself; as Rothschild's face bore witness when he was arraigned at the station."

As well as young bloods like Bennett and Rothschild, Monk's chief lieutenants, Kid Twist and Richie "Kid" Fitzpatrick, inevitably fell out over the division of the spoils from Monk's empire. Fitzpatrick had just had an altercation that left Thomas McCauley in Gouverneur Hospital with a bullet in his hip when Kid Twist issued an invitation to a meeting to settle their differences in the back room of a Chrystie Street dive—probably The Palm. Fitzpatrick was naïve enough to accept the invitation. One of Twist's hatchetmen, Harris Stahl, was lying in wait, and Fitzpatrick was shot in the heart. He sank to the sidewalk unconscious and died before he reached Gouverneur Hospital. Twist then had five more of Fitzpatrick's men killed within a week.

As usual, hostilities were suspended while the November elections were in progress and, even without their jailed leader, the Eastmans showed they had lost none of their abilities as sluggers and repeaters. "Old-timers . . . rubbed their hands with glee," claiming that it was just like an election from the old days, as gang members intimidated and attacked voters and police who tried to intervene. "Florrie" Sullivan, Big Tim's cousin and Tammany protégé, made the breathtakingly disingenuous claim that one of the Republican district captains had hired the gang in return from a promise from Governor Odell that he would pardon Eastman after the election, which drew a withering rejoinder from Judge Otto Rosalsky: "Then how does it happen that only Republican voters and workers are assaulted?"

With the election over and his chief rivals killed or intimidated, Kid Twist set about consolidating his power. Bringing an even more ruthless efficiency to the operations and rackets that Monk had established, Twist extracted more money from the districts he controlled. One of his new scams was to force all the small refreshment and confectionery stores to buy a so-called celery tonic from him at a suitably inflated price. He wrecked the premises of anyone foolish enough to refuse to stock the tonic, and some store owners were murdered as a warning to others. Twist was also implicated in the murders of a Five Pointer, Dick Fitzgerald, and "Big Butch," a poolroom hanger-on, and at least two other murders on the East Side were widely assumed to have been carried out on his orders. He was arrested for both murders and for dozens of other offenses, but he was always discharged.

Kid Twist lasted four years as undisputed ruler of the Eastmans, but on May 14, 1908, a Five Pointer named Louie "The Lump" Pioggi shot Twist dead, along with his lieutenant Samuel Pletch, a professional wrestler and circus strongman also known as "Bat Lewis" or "Cyclone Louie," as they were dining with two women at the South Brooklyn Hotel at Coney Island. One of the women, Carroll Terry, a singer in the Imperial Music Hall in the Bowery, had been living with Pioggi but was now Twist's girl. According to one account, Twist had taunted Pioggi about her earlier that evening, then drew a gun and forced him to jump from a second-story window. Backed by a group of Five Pointers, Pioggi returned two hours later, limping on a damaged ankle, to claim his revenge.

The crowds thronging Oceanic Walk on that warm spring evening heard nine pistol shots, followed by the screams of a woman. An instant later, Kid Twist and Bat Lewis staggered through the swinging doors of the barroom and fell dead on the floor, beneath a huge floral horseshoe presented to the proprietor to commemorate the opening of the hotel the previous day. Kid Twist had been killed by a single shot behind the ear; Bat Lewis's body "held six bullets in his left arm, groin, and hand, and in his right arm and breast, as well as another behind his ear." The source of the dispute, Carroll Terry, was also shot in the arm. "I wouldn't have anything to do with him [Pioggi]," Terry told police as she recovered in the hospital, "and he got angry. I suppose he must have been following me today, for when we all left the restaurant he was standing in the doorway. He struck me with his fist and knocked me down, and then he drew the gun. He fired at the men and I saw them fall, and then he shot me."

Pioggi was arrested, convicted of the shooting, and sent to Elmira prison for at least a year, though in an era when drunkenness or vagrancy could be enough to earn a six-month stretch on Blackwell's Island, twelve months for a double murder seemed a curiously lenient sentence. After his release, Pioggi was arrested for carrying a concealed revolver. Facing another prison term, he was released on a four-thousand-dollar surety put up by a prominent Tammany alderman and promptly jumped bail. "The spectacle of a thug hurdling a four-thousand-dollar bankroll to liberty gives a true idea of the lush days in which the New York gangster now lives." An even truer idea was given when it was revealed that Kid Twist—a man who had never held an honest job in his life—had left a fortune of fifty to a hundred thousand dollars.

Although the Eastmans were in decline and riven by internecine warfare, Paul Kelly largely failed to profit from his rivals' turmoil. Kelly's Five Pointers had staged a show of force in the summer of 1905, smashing plate-glass windows, robbing a bar, a fruit stand, and a coffeehouse, and beating and intimidating passersby within fifty yards of the police headquarters on Mott Street; "evidently the gang wanted to make the police understand that it could operate right under their noses." But it was a hollow gesture, and Kelly himself was a marked man. During the course of that year there were two attempts to kill him. In the first, a man hiding in a doorway plunged a stiletto into his back. He was taken to Gouverneur Hospital and survived, unlike his bodyguard, "Jack" McManus, also known as "Eat 'Em Up" and "The Brute," who was hit on the head with an iron bar and died in Bellevue Hospital.

Kelly had barely recovered when, in November 1905, "Biff" Ellison—reputed to be able to kill a man with a single blow of his fist—"Razor" Riley, and another man, a prizefighter, raided Kelly's headquarters at Little Naples, a saloon down the street from the New Brighton Dance Hall. Kelly took three bullets, but despite his wounds, he was "last reported as running down the Bowery, hatless, in the direction of the Occidental Hotel"—Big Tim Sullivan's saloon. One of Kelly's gang members was killed in the attack, and when a patrolman passed on his rounds in the early hours, he found Kelly's bar—usually full of light and noise—dark and deserted. The mahogany bar bore the scars from large-caliber bullets, and the brass rail at the foot of the bar was bent and broken; the dead man's legs were protruding from a closet and the only signs of life were "a lurking cat, a loud ticking clock, and the usual huge portrait of The Big Feller—Big Tim Sullivan."

Kelly was hurried to the hospital, and though he again survived the attack, he came under increasing pressure from the police, who were now being forced to act against the gangs. The Great Jones Street saloon was closed down on the personal orders of Commissioner of Police William McAdoo, and the Five Pointers went into decline. Seeing the writing on the wall, Kelly's gang migrated from Five Points to the neighborhood of Seventh Avenue and Forty-first Street, and Kelly himself moved his operations even farther uptown, to a house on East 116th Street owned by Ciro Terranova and members of the Morello family. In the less actively policed districts of Harlem and Brooklyn, Kelly then established himself as a labor-union organizer. He brought together some previously ununionized workers in the Garbage Scow Trimmers' Union, and used that power base to gain the vice presidency of the International Longshoremen's Association. Although Kelly changed his name back to Vaccarelli and liked to portray himself as a reformed character and a respectable union man, he kept his underworld links and his gang methods, maintaining a link between organized crime and some branches of organized labor that continues to this day.

10

A NAPOLEON RETURNED FROM ELBA

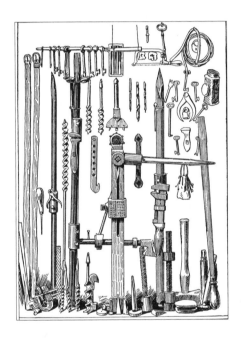

Although Monk was still behind bars, his former Tammany protectors had not given up hope of obtaining the release of the best man they ever had at the polls. They made continuing efforts to free him, but his release, when it eventually came, was not the result of Tammany influence. Instead, it was a new law that made any first-time prisoner—no matter how many offenses he might actually have committed—eligible for parole after completing half his sentence. After five years in Sing Sing, Monk was accordingly granted early release by the State

Board of Parole. He would have been granted remission of one-third of his sentence for good behavior, anyway—he was described by the prison governor as a model prisoner—but the new law brought him his liberty even quicker than that.

Announcing the decision to free him, Judge George A. Lewis, who chaired the meeting of the parole board, conceded that Monk had lived a notoriously rough life before being sent to Sing Sing, but in prison he had "conducted himself admirably. Monk is a man of intelligence and of great force for either good or bad . . . He would have got his liberty in thirteen months anyway, so why not let him earn his living outside of prison? If he makes a mis-step, back he goes to Sing Sing, and he knows that."

However, Lewis added that men of Monk's type rarely became parole violators, as "one of his intelligence and marked individuality [a polite reference to his memorable physiognomy] would find ultimate escape too improbable and difficult, and existence in the role of runaway convict intolerable." Lewis also cleared up the mystery of Monk's origins, stating that he was of Anglo–New England stock, not an Irishman as had been stated in the press, nor a Jew as many others had believed, but for whatever reason, the New York City police continued to regard Monk as an Irishman whose real name was William Delaney.

When the great gates of Sing Sing opened to release Monk into the hot, still air of a June morning in 1909, there were no wife and children waiting to greet him. What had become of Margaret Eastman is unclear. Unless she had access to at least some of the proceeds of Monk's criminal activities, her financial position would have been dire after he was sent to Sing Sing. Her husband cannot have been the easiest of marriage partners, and it is possible that she either tired of waiting for him or seized the chance offered by his incarceration to make a new start for herself and her children elsewhere, or she might even have died. Whatever happened, she left no trace of her movements, and she and her children disappeared completely from Monk's life. They were neither seen nor heard of in the Lower East Side again, and their fate remains a matter of speculation.

None of Monk's old acolytes had made the journey to Sing Sing to greet him, either, and instead he was met by his new employer, a farmer who had offered work, which Monk was willing to accept. The terms of his parole required him to report to the local police in Albany for more than a year, during which time Monk was supposed to be working on the farm in Dutchess County. However, after an abdominal operation while in prison, he was no longer very robust, and in September 1909 he walked into Harlem Hospital and asked to be operated on immediately for "some internal trouble which was causing him agony." Doctors put him on a diet to build up his strength enough to face the ordeal of an operation. The surgeon examined Monk before the operation and was astonished by his patient's forest of scars, stab and bullet wounds, and "a wound under the right eye evidently made by some blunt instrument." He asked Monk how he had come by them.

"Oh, I've been in war," Monk said.

"The Spanish war?"

"Oh, no. Half a dozen wars down on the East Side. I'm Monk Eastman."

While Monk recovered from the operation, plainclothes policemen stood guard outside the hospital, though none of them would say why they were posted there. Such round-the-clock police protection was normally given only to important witnesses or police informers, and it raised tantalizing questions about their presence. They may have been responding to a threat against him, or trying to pressure him to become an informer. If so, they were putting his life at more, not less, risk. If word reached Monk's former gangland associates that he was under police protection, the mere suspicion that he might be informing would be enough to ensure a contract on his life. In any event, the police guard ceased without explanation as soon as Monk was discharged from the hospital. He did not return to the farm and instead found less physically taxing work in Albany, living under an assumed name.

At the end of his parole period, on October 21, 1910, Monk told the chief of the Albany police that he was going to New York to see some of his old companions and then intended to go to "the wild and wooly West." Whether that was his true intention is dubious: it was hard to believe that Monk would have left his Tammany backers on the eve of an important election. The police were unsurprised when they learned a few weeks later that Monk was again active around Chrystie Street and the Bowery, "a Napoleon returned from Elba."

However, if Monk planned to resume his gang activities, he found a different New York awaiting him. Gang leaders sentenced to a long stretch in prison often emerged "stone broke, with the remnants of their little world toppling about their ears," and when Monk reached the Lower East Side there were few friends or gang members to acclaim his return or flock to his standard. As the head of the detective bureau remarked, "Most of his old mob is gone and all those gangs are under the table now."

Although there were reports that Monk had set up an opium joint, a trade he was said to have learned as a "lobbygow" in Chinatown, police took his return to the city with apparent equanimity. "He won't want to show his face around here for a while," one said, "and when he does, he'll behave—he's had his lesson. The first cop that sees him will pick him up on general principles, so the new men can take a peep at him. They'll need only one look—he's got a face you won't forget." Police also warned that if Monk went back to his old gangland ways, he wouldn't be handled with kid gloves.

Meanwhile, there were new political and gang bosses on the streets, and new gangsters like Nathan "Kid Dropper" Kaplan—who used a can opener to "carve guys up." There were new ways of doing things, too; it was reported that some members of the Eastmans and other gangs had become chauffeurs who, when off-duty, used their automobiles for quick getaways after robberies and shootings.

Many of Monk's former lieutenants were in jail or dead. Jack "Eat 'Em Up" McManus, Kid Twist, and "Red" Harrington had all died; "Humpty" Jackson was in jail; and those who remained, like "Big Jack" Zelig, no longer owed any fealty to Monk. Zelig now controlled a faction of the Eastmans, enforcing his rule through a group of killers who were vicious even by the standards of that era. "Lefty" Louis Rosenberg, "Dago" Frank Cirofici, and "Whitey" Lewis were all cold-blooded, but even they paled beside Harry "Gyp the Blood" Horowitz, whose horrific party trick, often performed for no other reason than to win a couple of dollars in bets, was to break the back of a hapless victim across his knees, leaving him flopping on the floor, gasping out his last breaths like a fish out of water.

Monk was also a less imposing figure than in his heyday. He was now almost thirty-seven, an old man in gang terms; very few gangsters, pimps, and prostitutes were in their thirties, and virtually none were in their forties. Five years of hard labor, bad food, and bad conditions in Sing Sing and the stomach complaint that had caused him to have two operations had left their mark on him. According to one report, he had also begun using opium, further weakening him, and when a gangster lost his strength and his reputation as a "hard man," he lost his principal business asset.

While Monk had been behind bars, the Lower East Side—indeed the city itself—"a seething realm of change that was virtually unrecognizable from one generation to the next," had also been undergoing one of its regular transformations. The physical look of the city was radically different, with old landmarks torn down and ever higher skyscrapers being built. When Monk went to jail, the tallest building in New York was thirty stories high; the Metropolitan Life Tower now stood fifty stories and seven hundred feet above the city streets. The Bowery, the western frontier of Monk's old domain, was deep in decline from its raucous heyday. Even in 1890 there had been an estimated nine thousand homeless men in and around the Bowery; by the year of Monk's release from Sing Sing, 1909, that number had grown to twenty-five thousand.

Just as Jewish immigrants had supplanted the Irish on the Lower East Side during the 1880s and 1890s, so the Jews were now finding themselves being displaced by newer immigrants. As their circumstances improved, the Lower East Side Jews who had furnished Monk with most of his recruits and many of his victims were migrating uptown, crossing the new Williamsburg and Manhattan bridges (completed in 1903 and 1909) or boarding the expanding subway network to make new homes in the outlying districts. Their places were taken by fresh floods of Italian and Sicilian immigrants who neither knew nor feared Monk.

Over the succeeding days and weeks, Monk failed to recruit more than a handful of followers, old or new. Yet one observer claimed that it was not the effects of the years in Sing Sing that sapped Monk's spirit and broke his power, but the knowledge that the politicians no longer regarded him as worth protecting from the law. Even if Tammany had been eager to rehabilitate its old protégé, its power to do so was no longer unquestioned. Even at its worst, the stench of the city was not worse than the stink that clung to the way the rich had made their money, but now New York City and its wealthier inhabitants were concerned about sanitizing themselves.

The politicians and police who had rooted in the gutters for kickbacks and bribes were now cloaking themselves in respectability; reform was no longer a dirty word. The capitalist robber barons who had clawed their way to the top of the heap of humanity, bribing, bullying, cheating, and beating their way to fortunes from steel, coal, railroads, mining, and oil that dwarfed those of the crowned heads of the

Old World, were now also transmuted into churchgoing paragons of respectability. They endowed charitable foundations and cleansed their family histories of the taint of rapacity and corruption as they strove to join the Astors, rack-renting landlords of the most scabrous Lower East Side slum properties, at the very pinnacle of fashionable New York society.

As the city's rich and powerful secured their positions and burnished their reputations, New York was also reinventing itself, as some of the worst slums and tenements were cleared and rebuilt, or even turned into public open spaces. The notorious Mulberry Bend tenements, between Mulberry, Worth, Baxter, and Bayard streets—the foul core of New York, according to Jacob A. Riis—had been demolished as far back as 1897, with a small park, eventually named Columbus Park, in their place. While Monk had been in Sing Sing, other open spaces had been created in the most densely populated part of the city, like Seward Park at the corner of Essex Street and East Broadway, where the demolition of the existing tenements displaced three thousand people.

The campaigns of Charles Parkhurst and the polemics of writers like Riis and Lincoln Steffens had exposed the rotten core at the heart of the Big Apple, and reforming politicians had at last begun to purge their more flagrantly corrupt officials, while a few crusading police chiefs, once as drenched in corruption as the wharves were shrouded in winter fogs, were now harassing and arresting the gangsters who had been their paymasters and partners in crime. However, it was a halting process, hampered at every step by entrenched corrupt politicians and officials.

Politicians now had to at least offer some semblance of being tough on crime, and mayors often appointed "incorruptible" police chiefs as proof of it, but if the police chiefs showed signs of too much success in their task, they found themselves removed from office. The reelection of Tammany sachem George Brinton McClellan Jr. as mayor in 1906 had been greeted by gamblers and brothel keepers gathering in front of his headquarters to acclaim his victory and celebrate the reemergence of New York as a "wide-open town." On the day his second term began, McLellan fired his reforming police chief, William McAdoo, who noted that "a combination of interests which thrive on the non-enforcement of the law or make large profits by allying themselves in a business way with criminal and vicious groups, can bring more pressure to bear for the removal of a police commissioner than an army of law-abiding honest citizens . . . An honest police commissioner must expect a perpetual conspiracy against his continuance in office."

McAdoo's replacement, General Theodore A. Bingham, also tried to wage war on the criminal gangs of the Lower East Side, but later complained that he could not even trust the men in his own department to carry out his orders, for police commissioners were frequently changed, but the politicians always remained. "I was head of the department for an indeterminate period, which might end at any time. Back of me was the mayor, who chose me, and whose office would also end at an early date. Back of him was the permanent political machine, which elected him. As the policeman is in office for life, he very logically looked past both the mayor and me and made his alliances and took his orders from the only permanent influence concerned—the politician."

In April 1907, Bingham embarked on a wholesale reform of the police department in an attempt to root out the most corrupt officers. Eight inspectors and countless detective sergeants were transferred or demoted, and "common patrolmen cluttered the earth," as Bingham reduced them in rank, transferred them to other, less lucrative districts, and sent the worst into exile "among the goats." The head of the detective bureau, William W. McLaughlin, known as a "millionaire cop" with a mansion on East Eighty-third Street, suffered the biggest fall, being banished to the Westchester precinct, where the opportunities for graft were minimal. Monk's old foe, Inspector "Chesty" George McClusky, was also "sent to do captain's work" in a district that had long been used as "a scaffold" on which uncooperative policemen were hung out to dry.

In July 1909, just like his predecessor, Bingham found that his reward for attempting to clean up the city was his abrupt removal from office by Mayor McClellan. After a two-year hiatus, the drive to clean up the police department and confront the gangs resumed in 1911 under Police Commissioner Rhinelander Waldo, a well-connected socialite with a fervent belief in police reform whose wealth made him less susceptible to bribery. An investigating committee was set up to look into allegations of a clearinghouse for police graft and claims that police officers had been forced to pay as much as ten thousand dollars for promotion. Waldo also formed special squads to break up the street gangs that had dominated Lower Manhattan. The means to do so were simple: "Permit the police to club the gangster out of existence without fear of political interference or reprisal." To achieve this, the police were said to require only three things: a blackjack, a nightstick, and their superiors' absolute and total backing under any circumstances.

Strong-arm squads of police had first been used against street gangs more than half a century before. Every policeman was given a list of known gangsters and told to beat them with a nightstick whenever he sighted any of them, and warn that if they did not leave the district, they would get another dose of the same medicine every time they were spotted. Now the strong-arm squads were back. Cops were warned not to use their nightsticks on inoffensive citizens and not to strike men on the head unless they were dealing with "real bad crooks. Then it doesn't make any difference whether they go to the insane asylum or to jail. They're enemies of society and our common foe."

The gangsters in the cities of the East found themselves increasingly constrained, hounded, and hunted by lawmen whose former impotence or acquiescence was now a fading echo of a past era. The fate of the notorious Gophers from Hell's Kitchen was a warning to all others. Police had once gone in fear of them. One leader of the gang, "One Lung" Curran, had blackjacked a policeman to steal his jacket as a coat for his girlfriend after she complained of the cold. That started a fashion among the Gophers' women, and a succession of bloodied policemen staggered back into their stations, beaten and stripped to their shirts. Now the Gophers were hounded by an alliance of policemen and a specially formed railroad corps who slugged harder, shot quicker, and clubbed and beat the once powerful gang out of the West Side railroad yards that had been its stronghold.

For his part, Monk was now a marked and vilified outcast on the streets that he had once ruled. Respectable citizens and crooks alike were informing on him, and people were running into Eldridge Street station every ten minutes, a policeman there said wearily, accusing Monk of all sorts of crimes. He was also constantly harassed and beaten by the police who had once been more or less willing partners in crime, but now saw the chance to settle scores for past indignities.

Despite his waning fortunes, Monk had married for the second time on September 8, 1911, in a ceremony at the New York City Hall. His wife, Worthy Cecilia Marven, was originally from Galveston, Texas; at just twenty years old, she was seventeen years Monk's junior. The address he gave on the marriage certificate was 116 West 116th Street, which does not correspond to any known address for him at that or any other time, and his listed occupation—clerk—was equally false.

Although the marriage certificate offered a choice of single, widowed, or divorced, Monk chose to describe himself as single. There is no record of any contact between Monk and his first wife, Margaret, since he had been sent to Sing Sing eight years before, but neither was there any record of a divorce or of Margaret's death, raising the strong possibility that Monk's second marriage was bigamous. His new wife's origins were as opaque as the fate of his first. Worthy listed no occupation, but most gangsters drew their wives and girlfriends from the pool of prostitutes they controlled or consorted with, and the assumption must be that the twenty-year-old Worthy Marven was a Texan girl "gone wrong" who had moved to New York and fallen in with Monk while working as a prostitute on the Lower East Side, probably under his control.

Although he exercised only a tiny fraction of the power he had held around the turn of the century, Monk was still bringing in money from small-scale crime and opium peddling. There was a rapidly expanding Chinese population in New York—most of them fleeing discrimination and xenophobia about the "Yellow Peril" in the West that had found legislative expression in the Chinese Exclusion Act of 1882. Demand for opium increased. The drug that the British had forced into China at the point of a gun and that had been widely sold to middle-class Americans in patent medicines and child soporifics was now perceived as a pernicious substance that the Chinese not only smoked themselves, but also used to subvert the morals of white men, and especially white women.

Chinese gangs were not yet a significant force in the New York underworld, and opium dens, although run by Chinese men, were usually white-owned. Battles were fought over control of the lucrative trade, and while Monk was now no more than a bit player in the gang wars on his former territory, on June 4, 1912, he was caught up in the aftermath of a bloody feud using pistols and bombs that began in a Chinatown saloon and spread to various parts of the city. The trigger for the violence may have been an attack on the current leader of Monk's former gang, "Big Jack" Zelig, who was shot in the neck and left in critical condition after he himself had shot up a saloon owned by a rival. With no fewer than six gang fights breaking out all over the city and running battles continuing for ten hours, it seemed to some a return to old-style gang violence.

Spurred to action by criticism of police impotence and incompetence, the strong-arm squads began a new roundup of gang members, and Monk was one of the victims. Acting on a tip, customs officials armed with axes and crowbars surrounded a tenement on East Thirteenth Street and smashed their way in. They claimed to have found a complete opium manufacturing outfit, and Monk himself smoking a pipe of the drug. It is conceivable that the evidence was fabricated; the order had come down from on high to rid New York of its gangsters, and, if relatively powerless now, Monk remained one of the city's most notorious figures. The arrest and conviction of Monk Eastman would satisfy the public that something was being done about gangsters, while leaving untouched more currently powerful gangland figures and their political and police accomplices.

The strong-arm squads, led by the ambitious and notoriously corrupt Lieutenant Charles A. Becker—who even had his own press agent to ensure his version of his exploits was always well-publicized—also raided a number of gambling dens. Those raids were the direct result of an appeal from the now aging and infirm Big Tim Sullivan to Police Commissioner Rhinelander Waldo and Mayor Gaynor. Big Tim complained that the owners of the gambling dens were not receiving their just returns on the hefty bribes and kickbacks they paid to the police, but it was a crass error to draw the mayor's attention to the corrupt relationship between police, city officials, and gambling-den owners. A short-tempered, unpredictable character with a bullet permanently lodged in his larynx after a failed assassination attempt, Mayor Gaynor prided himself on his morality and selflessness in the city's service and had pledged to stamp out corruption among public officials. As a result, Big Tim's intervention proved completely counterproductive; Gaynor responded by ordering that every gambling house be shut down.

Gaynor may also have been prodded into action by lobbying from Dr. Judah Magnes and the "Kehillah" (literally, "the communal body"), an organization formed by respectable Jews and dedicated to extirpating crime and the worst excesses of drugs, alcohol, prostitution, and gang activities from the Jewish districts of the Lower East Side. Their complaints had been ignored by police until Dr. Magnes paid a call on Mayor Gaynor and Commissioner Waldo; after that, police were regularly stationed in front of stuss houses, and by the time of Mayor Gaynor's death in September 1913, the Kehillah was able to claim that the criminal gangs had been broken up and the vice and crime that had infested the district for decades had been largely eradicated.

Big Tim Sullivan, already a spent force, died in the same month as Mayor Gaynor. Newspaper reports claimed he had lost

$700,000 in two years and shed sixty pounds from his once powerful two-hundred-pound frame. His mental condition had deteriorated so much, possibly as a result of tertiary syphilis, that he was "absolutely dominated by delusions of terrifying apprehension, fear, conspiracy, plot, attempts of poisoning, and efforts to do him bodily harm." He was taken to a sanatorium, but in September 1913 he escaped and disappeared. His mangled body, found on a railway line, was not identified for almost a fortnight, just as it was about to be shipped to Potter's Field for burial in a pauper's grave. The crowd of seventy-five thousand that lined the Bowery for his funeral procession included people from every walk of life, from statesmen and judges and actors to prizefighters and panhandlers.

The police raids led by Lieutenant Becker on Herman "Beansie" Rosenthal's gambling den after Sullivan's misjudged intervention had also triggered a chain of events that led to Rosenthal's killing, Becker's termination as head of the strong-arm squad, and his subsequent conviction and execution for Rosenthal's murder. Popular outrage at the affair ramped up pressure on police and politicians to demonstrate their integrity and incorruptibility, and a citizens' committee appointed to investigate corruption and graft reported that it was time for more radical efforts. Surprisingly, one of Tammany's most powerful figures, Charles F. "Silent Charlie" Murphy, had reached the same conclusion, recognizing that the old era was near its end. "New York City had emerged from its frontier stage."

The information passed on by the Kehillah made Jewish gangs and gangsters particularly vulnerable to any anticorruption drive, and many, of course, believed Monk to be Jewish. Whether or not he was truly guilty of the offense with which he was charged—manufacturing opium without a license—when he appeared before the United States District Court, he pleaded guilty and was sentenced to eight months' imprisonment. Monk served his time on Blackwell's Island, and on his release was given an ultimatum by the police: if he did not stay away from New York, he would be daily harassed, hounded, beaten with nightsticks, and arrested on any pretext. He duly left town, but moved only as far as Albany, where he lived on Lower Broadway. He led an apparently straight and honest life only until October 1914, when he was arrested and charged with burglary in Buffalo. He was discharged either for lack of evidence or after the intervention of some of his old Tammany friends from New York City. Driven out of town by the

Buffalo police, Monk returned to Albany.

There were reports that he had been seen back in Brooklyn soon afterward, "representing" the employers in a dispute with the stevedores' union, though his arrest for intoxication in Albany on February 28 of the following year suggests that any return to New York was only temporary. Meanwhile, Mayor John Purroy Mitchel, elected on a reform ticket after Tammany infighting had alienated voters, and his commissioners of police—first Douglas I. McKay, and then Arthur Woods, who took over in April 1914—were now completing the purge of the gangs that their predecessors had begun. During his first year in office, Commissioner Woods imprisoned more than two hundred of the most notorious crooks and thugs in the city, and gangsters against whom conclusive evidence could not be produced were hounded by detectives and routinely clubbed by uniformed patrolmen. More than ever, New York was no safe haven for Monk.

Like New York, the outside world was also changing. The war that had broken out in August 1914 had consumed all of Europe, burned through the Middle East and parts of Africa and Asia, and drawn in armies from across the globe. Before the war Britain and Germany had been each other's principal trading partners. With the war that came to an abrupt end and it became imperative for both countries to find alternative sources of supply of food, raw materials, and finished goods, and—insofar as war production allowed—alternative potential markets for their own exports. No markets for goods were greater and no industrial bases larger and more productive than those of the United States, and the European war had brought rising employment and growing affluence to New York's manufacturing and dockside districts. The railyards, roads, and docks were busy around the clock; manufacturing, shipping, construction, finance, and the wholesale and retail trades all benefited; and textile mills and engineering factories in particular were working flat-out, producing uniforms, arms, ammunition, and military equipment for export. There was work aplenty, and at least some of those traditionally vulnerable to the lure of the gangs must have opted for a perhaps less glamorous and lucrative, but undeniably quieter and safer, life in paid employment.

Although the United States still remained aloof from the fighting in Europe, Americans could not isolate themselves from the emotional impact of daily newspaper reports of battles, death, and destruction on an industrial scale, nor from the propaganda and psychological warfare waged by combatants seeking to influence American opinion and draw the United States into the conflict on their side.

Britain shared a common language and heritage with many Americans, but British power, imperialism, and arrogance were probably resented by even more of them. Germany, too, had links of culture and language to a substantial minority American population but was also widely perceived as militaristic and overly aggressive. The two sides adopted very different approaches to wooing the American public. German propaganda, largely disseminated through the bunds—German-American societies—across the United States, was targeted directly at the public but tended to be blatant, even crude, and its often strident and hectoring tone did not sit well with Americans.

If such an approach was often counterproductive, the British waged a much more subtle and delicate campaign, run by a propaganda bureau so secret that even most members of Parliament were unaware of its existence. Although there had been little prewar planning, Britain's first offensive action, within a few hours of the declaration of war, was the severing of the direct undersea transatlantic cables linking Germany with the United States. As a result, London had a monopoly of direct cable and telephone traffic with the United States and used it to take the initiative in the struggle for American public opinion.

American war reporters relied on the cables that Britain controlled, and that control was extended to the content passing through them both by direct censorship—a regular source of friction with the United States—and by skilled selection and manipulation of news content. Rather than making direct appeals to the American public—who in any case were unlikely to take kindly to being lectured by Englishmen—Britain devoted its efforts to influencing American opinion makers and providing the carefully chosen raw material from which columnists and editors selected the stories they would feature. As a result, the vast majority of stories about the war—including leaflets, cartoons, and features as well as hard news—that were put before the American people had originally been selected, modified, or created by British propagandists.

Their task was made easier by German actions. The unprovoked aggression against Belgium and France, and particularly the invasion and occupation of "poor little Belgium," had already cast Germany in an unsympathetic light even before atrocity stories of nuns being raped and babies bayoneted began to circulate. In the carnage and chaos of war, it was impossible to immediately disprove or verify such stories—

many of which later proved to be false—but they had an undeniable impact on American public opinion.

On May 7, 1915, the sinking of the *Lusitania,* with the loss of 128 American lives, signaled a sea change in attitudes toward the war and dealt a devastating blow to German hopes of keeping America neutral. In October of that year, the Red Cross nurse Edith Cavell was executed in German-occupied Belgium, and the reaction around the world was even more critical than it had been after the sinking of the *Lusitania.*

Although President Wilson still held back, and would even campaign in the 1916 election on the slogan "He kept us out of war," the die was now cast. American industry and finance were providing huge and still-expanding material support for the Allied war effort; the public—though horrified by the slaughter that had already seen millions killed—was increasingly on the Allied side; and among a growing number of American politicians, the question was no longer whether the United States would go to war, but when.

How much impact the march to war had on Monk at the time is not clear, but as the war clouds gathered over the United States, Monk's downward spiral continued. On May 17, 1915, the Albany chief of police flashed a warning over the wire, alerting police throughout the state to be on the lookout for an automobile in which a burglar was escaping with the proceeds of at least one robbery in the city. The thief was reportedly making hot tracks for New York, and the automobile was a very distinctive one: a Peerless seven-seater with a New York license plate and a coat of arms above the radiator cap.

Three Bronx detectives and two motorcycle policemen were stationed at the 242nd Street entrance to Van Cortlandt Park to intercept the thieves. By five o'clock in the afternoon they had watched at least fifteen thousand automobiles go past—then they caught sight of a seven-seater automobile with a coat of arms on the radiator cap, keeping close behind a trolley car. One of the motorcycle policemen flagged down the chauffeur, telling him he was breaking the speed limit, and the detectives, revolvers drawn, then jumped on the running boards on opposite sides of the car and pulled open the doors. Taken by surprise, the two men inside surrendered without a fight.

"Well, if it isn't Monk Eastman," one of the detectives said.

The two men were taken to the Bronx detective bureau, where Monk identified himself as William Delaney, a plumber, forty years old, but refused to give his address. His companion said he was Charles Murphy, thirty-eight years old, an "agent," of Albany, "known to the police in this city as a tin-horn gambler and tout." In the tonneau of the car the police found a suitcase containing at least a thousand dollars' worth of silverware, and some small pieces of jewelry. When detectives confronted him, Monk's only comment was, "Well, you have the silver, so go as far as you can, but you can't expect any help from me."

After word was sent to Albany of his arrest, Detectives Ryan and Mullen visited Monk's house at 71 Hamilton Street. There they found a woman—almost certainly Worthy—who gave her name as Mary Williams, but was recognized by Ryan as Monk's wife. Questioned at police headquarters, she admitted to a passing acquaintance with a man she knew as William Delaney, but denied that she lived with him, or that he stayed at the apartment, even though detectives found several pawn tickets for watches and jewelry bearing the name of Delaney. They also discovered a Colt .380 revolver and a box of cartridges.

Other incriminating articles found in the apartment included electric wires, drills, fuses, braces, flashlights, and other equipment used to blow safes or force entry into houses. When asked about them, "Mary Williams" denied all knowledge of them and insisted that they had been left there by workmen who had been making improvements to the house. Despite the "complete yegg [burglary or safe-cracking] outfit" found in the apartment, Albany police said that they did not believe that Monk had been actively engaged in the spate of burglaries that had hit the city and its neighborhood, but had acted more as a fence and a mastermind.

More than a thousand people crowded into Grand Central Terminal on May 19, 1915, to see the former "king" of the East Side gangsters and his codefendant taken under police escort to Albany. Another huge crowd was waiting at the Albany Union station, but detectives dodged it by taking their prisoners out through the subway and the American Express office. Only a month before, when brought before Chief Hyatt at police headquarters, Monk had pledged not only to "do right himself but to stop any 'suckers' from 'pulling jobs' in this city if he heard about them." Now he remained tight-lipped, though he did deny having ever lived at 71 Hamilton Street, where the revolver, burglary equipment, and pawn tickets had been found.

No one came forward to meet the three-thousand-dollar bail, and Monk and Murphy were held in custody. At their trial, Murphy was

sentenced to one and not more than two years for his part in the burglary. Monk, who pleaded guilty to charges of grand larceny, second
degree, and burglary, third degree, made an impassioned plea for a suspended sentence, swearing that he would reform and never again be
found in the criminal courts, and that he had well-to-do relatives in the
West—a reference to Monk's sister Ida in California, Worthy's family
in Texas, or, just possibly, to one of his wealthy uncle's children—who
had promised to care for him if he reformed. The judge was unmoved
and, after a brief deliberation, handed down a sentence of two years and
eleven months in "Little Siberia"—Clinton Prison, Dannemora. On
July 7, 1915, Monk passed through the steel gates to begin his sentence
as prisoner number 12,151. He still refused to give an address and listed
his occupation as plumber's helper.

Monk avoided further trouble while in jail and was released on September 11, 1917, after serving two-thirds of his sentence. In the time he
had been away, the East Side had continued its evolution. Spurred on
by Reform politicians, police had made huge inroads into the gangs and
had jailed many gang leaders, but two other, more subtle factors were
also at work. Trade unions, Jewish groups, and other social, political,
and welfare organizations were increasingly influential on the Lower
East Side, countering "the ethic of raw competition and predacity
which had hitherto held sway and from which the underworld culture
had drawn its strength and justification." The Jews of the Lower East
Side no longer depended on Tammany and the gangs for work or protection; that era was over.

Even before the direct involvement of the United States, the First
World War had also played a huge part in transforming the Lower East
Side, bringing unprecedented prosperity to the garment industry and
other Jewish trades, and to the docks, through which torrents of military and other goods were being shipped to Europe. The exodus of
Jews uptown, to the Bronx, or across the East River to Brooklyn and
Queens was also accelerating. At its peak the Lower East Side had been
home to at least 500,000 Jews. By 1916, that had already been reduced
to 313,000, and even that figure hid the aging of the remaining Jewish
population, whose members were less and less susceptible to the overtures of the remaining gangs.

Returning to the rapidly changing streets of his old domain, Monk
was at once subject to relentless police harassment, and within ten
days was again before the magistrates' court, this time on a probably

trumped-up charge of brawling. He was held overnight and discharged the following morning. He left no record of the thought processes he went through during that night in jail, but he had spent two-thirds of the previous thirteen years in prison, time enough in which to reflect on the path he had chosen and the course his life might take in the future. If he remained in New York, he would continue to drift from jail sentence to jail sentence, for even if he turned his back on crime, he must have known that he would never be treated with anything other than suspicion, hostility, and brutality by the police.

Whatever battles he fought with his conscience during that September night, by daylight Monk had made his decision. Until that moment, his whole adult life had been shaped by greed, crime, and gang violence. He had committed an endless string of robberies and assaults; lived off the earnings from theft, protection rackets, gambling, and prostitution; sold his brawn and his army of thugs to the highest bidder; and never once appeared to consider the consequences or the victims of his actions. Now, for almost the first time in his entire adult life, he made a decision that was not motivated—or not solely motivated—by self-interest.

Since April of that year advertisements pasted on bulletin boards and appearing in the Brooklyn newspapers had announced that the "Twenty-third Regiment of Brooklyn, now in Federal Service, desires recruits eighteen to forty-five years of age. Report at Armory, Bedford and Atlantic Avenues, Brooklyn, for physical examination and enlistment. Men of good moral character required. Men with dependent relatives not wanted." Monk fit at least some of those requirements, and at nine o'clock on the morning of September 21, 1917, he presented himself at the recruiting office and volunteered for active service, perhaps seeking in the army the sense of common purpose that he had once known with his gang.

Now forty-three, Monk deducted four years from his age to improve his chances of acceptance. He had no skills that were usable in civil society, but in one area he was an unequaled expert: he had seen more action than even the most grizzled U.S. Army veteran. The question that the New York National Guard—into which the 23rd Regiment of Brooklyn was to be merged—now had to answer was whether the violence and killing that had seen Monk stripped of his citizenship and sent to the United States' most notorious penitentiary could become acceptable when placed at the service of the state.

Tammany politicians had never troubled their consciences over that, and if there were any doubts in the minds of the recruiting sergeant and his superiors, they were quickly resolved. Monk had "showed that the quality of patriotism was not lacking even in the heart of a gangster." His criminal convictions for violence and gunplay were seen as no bar to service in war, and perhaps even a qualification for it; Monk Eastman was duly accepted as a doughboy in the New York National Guard.

Part II

II

O'RYAN'S ROUGHNECKS

W hen President Woodrow Wilson committed his country to war, the U.S. regular army was the same size as those of Chile, Denmark, and the Netherlands—countries with only a tiny fraction of the United States' population and wealth. The United States was even more deficient in artillery, aircraft, tanks, mortars, machine guns, rifles, grenades, shells, ammunition, steel helmets, and gas masks than it was in manpower; most Europeans—including the German High Command—assumed that America's major contribution to the Allied war effort would be to increase still further its supplies of credit, equipment, food, and munitions.

However, Americans took a different view, and new recruits like Monk were certainly not joining the army merely to load supplies for others to use. A collection of reasons for enlisting, assembled by an army newspaper, revealed diverse motivations, showing that simplistic notions of patriotism and duty were far from the whole story. One young man had enlisted because he wanted to have a chance to ride on a train, never having done so before; another wanted to learn self-control; another to get some excitement; and yet another, perhaps far from unique, had joined up "because the girls like soldiers." However, one reason might have been given by Monk himself: "I never did anything worthwhile on the outside, so I dedicated my life to my country, that I might be of use to someone."

Christened "Pop" by his army buddies, most of whom were at least twenty years younger, Monk became Private Edward Eastman, serial number 1207906, Company G, 2nd Battalion, 106th Infantry. He was one of the oldest men on active service with the American Expeditionary Force. The form that, like every recruit, he had to complete delved deep into his personal health, covering not only height, weight, eyesight, heart, nose, throat, and teeth, but also whether he "ever since childhood wet the bed when asleep . . . spat up blood," or had "convulsions, gonorrhea, sore on penis, hemorrhoids, flat foot." Surprisingly, syphilis as indicated by a positive Wassermann test—the first effective test for syphilis, devised by a German bacteriologist in 1906—was not in itself sufficient reason to reject a recruit, if other requirements were met, though syphilitics with open lesions or mental symptoms were refused. Perhaps fortunately for Monk, there was no question on the form relating to criminal records.

The 106th Infantry was a regiment composed entirely of men with Brooklyn connections; Monk had given his home address as 13 Union Avenue, Brooklyn—and for the first time in his adult life, it might even have been his genuine address. Whereas the sister regiment, the 107th Infantry—the "Silk Stocking Regiment"—included many sons of New York's wealthy, educated elite, almost all of the recruits to the 106th Infantry were workingmen; a breakdown of their occupations showed 390 clerks, 110 bookkeepers, 110 salesmen, 67 chauffeurs, 45 machinists, 25 electricians, 23 cooks, and 20 plumbers.

With the 105th and 108th Infantry and their supporting units, the

106th and 107th formed the 27th Division, soon christened "O'Ryan's Roughnecks" or "O'Ryan's Traveling Circus" after their commanding officer, Major General John F. O'Ryan. A "slight, soldierly erect figure, blue eyes steeled to keen observing, a firmly set mouth half-hidden by his closely cropped mustache," O'Ryan was a fervent advocate of improving the National Guard regiments to match the standards of the regular army. He demanded "trained dependability, disciplined initiative, and the Spartan spirit to 'will' success, no matter what the opposition," and imposed rigid training that closely simulated actual combat, including the use of live ammunition.

While the recruits began their basic training in the Bronx's Van Cortlandt Park, the more experienced National Guardsmen from the regiment had already been put to work in upstate New York, guarding bridges, aqueducts, and water treatment plants thought vulnerable to sabotage. The dangerous combination of darkness, tension, paranoia, and "spy fever" led to a series of incidents with suspicious persons near the Croton aqueduct and on the dark hillsides of the Catskills. More than a thousand German and Austrian seamen had already been interned on Ellis Island, and paranoia about enemy spies was so strong that even an innocuous organization like the Austro-American Naturfreunde Tourist Club, whose aims were "to bring to its members a healthier and happier life by leading them from the city's tumult into the quiet, clear invigorating country air," found their country walks interrupted by troops who suspected them of being saboteurs.

The lives of local residents in the Catskills were also heavily disrupted. A farmer—plainly not a regular letter-writer—wrote to the commanding officer of the 106th Infantry complaining that "the gates on the water works is all the times open by the solders and i cant get my cows whare be long thay rune all over and i want my rites and is gonto have it. i aint got no rite on the waterworks for thay halt me with the gun at me when i go for the cows tend to this rite away." In reply, one of the regiment's officers noted that leaving all the gates shut would require a trooper making a round-trip patrol to dismount and mount 344 times.

The water company protested that soldiers were smashing locks to shelter in its buildings, opening manhole covers and throwing things into the water supply, and burning wooden fences as fuel, but the most serious incidents saw them firing on suspicious figures, glimpsed in the darkness. One farmer claimed he had been repeatedly fired at while driving to and from his farm in his automobile, and a guardsman was shot dead by a comrade when his rifle discharged accidentally while the two chased after two suspicious figures.

Meanwhile, Monk and the other raw recruits had been issued uniforms, blankets, and an empty cot mattress or ticking to fill with straw. They were temporarily housed in a tented camp in Van Cortlandt Park, where conditions left much to be desired. The regimental surgeon complained of shortages of basic medical supplies and typhoid and smallpox vaccines, and criticized the glaring defects of the facilities. In spite of the fact that the expenditure of just fifty dollars would have solved the problem, two companies were without bathing facilities, while drinking water could be cut off at almost any time. There were also disciplinary problems with the new recruits. The commanding general complained that, contrary to his orders, enlisted men were carrying pistols when out on the streets. They were probably doing so only in the hope of impressing girls, but their regimental commander was strongly reminded that soldiers were only to carry arms when on authorized military duty.

Commanders and junior officers alike were also upbraided for the dilatory and tardy way they responded to orders from higher on the chain of command. "Our country is in an actual state of war, and defects and neglects that might have been condoned during annual encampments and maneuvers are now serious. The Division Commander trusts it will not be necessary to make examples of any offenders, regardless of rank, to impress upon all the seriousness of the present situation."

On September 29, 1917, escorted by veterans of the regiment, the men of the 106th Infantry marched through New York to the Twenty-third Street ferry. No one among the cheering crowds lining the streets to see them pass was aware that among the ranks of marching men, unrecognized by any of his former friends or his foes in the police department, marched Private Edward Eastman. After crossing the Hudson, the infantrymen boarded a train of the Central Railroad of New Jersey, bound for Camp Wadsworth, near Spartanburg in South Carolina, where they were to begin an intensive course of training in modern warfare.

The train was formed from old wooden Pullman sleepers that had been banned for passenger use and pensioned off many years before, but which had now been rescued from storage yards all over the country and brought back into use. The sleeping berths were not used, so the men slept on the seats. An order from the adjutant general required all railroad shipments of equipment to be loaded to the equivalent of 110 percent of the designated capacity of the car, and the troops, jammed closely together, would have been forgiven for thinking that the same ruling had been applied to them. They were fed from a kitchen car on stew or canned beans, corned beef, bread and butter, coffee, and bread pudding made from stale bread. The troops assigned to kitchen duty dragged "forty quart cans of this miserable stuff" along the aisles and spooned it into mess kits.

While they traveled slowly south, the new recruits had ample time to study a pamphlet issued to each of them, setting out their commanding general's military philosophy and his views on discipline, efficiency, and sexual activity, including a doom-laden warning about the dangers of resorting to prostitutes, headed "all prostitutes are diseased . . . There is a stinking, dirty disease which men acquire from prostitutes. It is called Chancroid. It causes the flesh to ulcerate, rot and fall away. Sometimes it causes a man's penis to rot off. When a crab loses a claw another one grows in place of it. But when a man loses his penis he never gets another. He may lose a leg and get a wooden leg. But a wooden penis . . ." Nonetheless, despite such dire warnings, young men who might be killed within a few weeks did not want to die virgins, and many resorted to prostitutes while in South Carolina, and later, in France.

Three miles outside Spartanburg, in the foothills of the Blue Ridge Mountains, Camp Wadsworth was reached by Snake Road, an unpaved and often washed-out rough track. Four-wheel-drive trucks carried the recruits from the railroad siding to a cotton field in full bloom "where the soft red clay was up to our ears. We sloshed around in it, we slept in it, and when it was dry and the wind blew, we even ate it." The camp was still a work in progress as they took up residence, with chain gangs of South Carolina convicts working on the roads.

The soldiers themselves had to clear the trees to make camp, the first manual labor that some of the former clerks in the regiment had ever carried out. There were few permanent buildings on the site, and no wooden barracks or permanent latrines, because the division was expected to be posted overseas before many weeks elapsed. Instead, to their mingled disappointment and disbelief, the men of the 106th Infantry were housed in neat rows of square army tents that seemed to stretch away as far as the eye could see. Each squad of ten or eleven men occupied a tent set over a wood floor with wooden walls about four feet high. A wood-burning, cone-shaped stove stood in the center, with a chimney poking out of a hole in the apex of the tent like the poles at the top of a wigwam.

The camp was crowded; a shortage of trained and trainable officers meant that a U.S. division of twenty-eight thousand men was twice as big as a British, French, or German division, and even the officers they did have were virtually untrained for the kind of warfare they would be entering. For officers trained at West Point prior to the U.S. declaration of war in the spring of 1917, the war in Europe might not have been taking place at all, and no attempt was made to draw lessons from it; "while the French bled to death before Verdun, the cadets at West Point inspected Gettysburg."

The overcrowding at Camp Wadsworth contributed to regular outbreaks of trouble. The 107th Infantry in particular was a volatile mix of blue bloods, Wall Street bankers, and upstate farmers. Despite orders emphasizing that at no time in their history had discipline been so important, it was far from good at first. A liquor still was found a few feet from where Major General O'Ryan's headquarters was to be sited, and fifty military police were on permanent patrol on the streets of Spartanburg to deter and control drunken soldiers. During inspections, O'Ryan found men wearing sweaters and overalls rather than military uniform, and half a company drilling while the rest slept or played games. O'Ryan addressed the officers about discipline and strict obedience to orders as soon as he arrived, but he described reveille the next morning as "the worst I have ever observed . . . Officers appeared to be unable to get men out." One sergeant of the 106th Infantry was still asleep in bed, and to O'Ryan's fury, it was revealed that "it was not customary in this regiment for the men to turn out on rainy mornings." Things were so bad at first that when other regiments of the 27th Division passed the 106th Infantry on the march, they taunted them about it.

The men of the 106th were also christened "Champs of the French Leave Brigade," with the worst record for the number of men absent from camp without leave. Those caught were shipped back to camp under guard, had the entire cost of their transport, food, and lodging for themselves and their guards deducted from their pay, and were then disciplined, usually by a spell in the newly erected barbed-wire prison stockade, so brightly lit that it was christened "Luna Park" by the sarcastic soldiers. As a result of the high incidence of French Leave among the 106th Infantry, the entire regiment was confined to camp and an example was made of Private William Kauffman, who was charged with desertion and sentenced to five years' hard labor in the disciplinary barracks at Fort Jay, New York. He could perhaps count himself fortunate that his sentence was not more severe, for desertion in time of war was a capital offense.

Camp Wadsworth also saw an occasional outbreak of the sort of criminal activity with which Monk had long been associated, including three privates convicted for passing counterfeit checks and sentenced to between five and seven years' hard labor. However, Monk submitted surprisingly quickly to the discipline of the regular army, and throughout the regiment's long stay in South Carolina, he was never involved in disciplinary proceedings, nor was he ever absent without leave.

The presence of so many soldiers sometimes provoked friction with the local inhabitants, and there was consistent hostility between the townspeople and the black 369th Infantry, who at first shared Camp Wadsworth, though they were rigidly segregated from the men of the 27th Division; the army even insisted that the division's black cooks be replaced by white ones. The mayor of Spartanburg was no less prejudiced, complaining to the War Department that "with their northern ideas about race equality" the black troops would expect to be treated "like white men. I can say right here that . . . they will be treated exactly as we treat our resident negroes. This thing is like waving a red flag in the face of a bull." The potential for severe disorder was demonstrated when African-American soldiers of the 24th Infantry rioted in Houston after rough treatment by the local population. Seventeen people were killed in the riots, and thirteen black soldiers were subsequently hanged for mutiny. In Spartanburg there were racial taunts and regular brawls until December 1917, when the War Department, alarmed by the events in Houston, hastily sent the 369th Infantry to France. There they trained with the French and, christened the "Harlem Hellfighters," distinguished themselves in several battles.

Fistfights between Spartanburg residents and white soldiers remained common, and there could have been no more reassuring figure to have at your side in a brawl than Monk. His scarred and battered face was probably sufficient warning to Spartanburg tough guys that this was one soldier it would be wise to avoid provoking. Any trouble there may have been for Monk and his buddies around the town was settled without the intervention of the police; neither Edward Eastman, William Delaney, nor any of Monk's numerous other aliases was ever written on the blotter at Spartanburg police headquarters.

The training program for Monk and his comrades had been expected to last only sixteen weeks. British instructors were brought in to supervise the training and, though some American officers found them intolerably overbearing, they did at least have experience of trench warfare and the conditions on the Western Front that their American allies would soon be facing. They laid great emphasis on physical fitness to "tighten the relation between the mind and muscle, so that the latter would become automatically and instantaneously responsive to the former, and the former instantaneously resourceful in applying methods to aid the latter when hard-pressed."

There were three hours of physical drill every morning and afternoon, and the men received additional instruction in unarmed combat from the redoubtable Frank Moran, a heavyweight boxer who had fought Jess Willard and Jack Johnson for the heavyweight championship of the world, and whose knockout punch, nicknamed "Mary Ann," was "first cousin to the kick of an artillery mule and sister-in-law of a bolt of lightning." One man from each company was detailed to take instruction from Moran, and they in turn trained the rest of their companies. It is doubtful if Monk needed much instruction in fistfighting, and boxing skills did not appear ideally suited to trench warfare, but Moran claimed that "it helps a man with his bayonet drill if he is a good boxer. It gives him quickness, confidence and strength. The English and Canadians who have gone over the top and have done some hot bayonet fighting tell me that it is just like a fistfight behind the shower baths when you run up against some Looie or Heinie in a trench: You watch 'is bloomin' heyes and you let im' 'ave it." The Pittsburgh-born Moran's attempt at a Cockney accent while recounting this was, the regimental newspaper reported, "the kitten's overalls."

Monk and his comrades also labored long and hard digging practice trenches on the hills behind the camp to simulate the battlefield conditions they would soon face. The practice trench system eventually covered a front of seven hundred yards, backed by eight miles of twisting, intersecting trenches, incorporating shelters, bombproof dugouts, reserve lines, and communication trenches. Colonel Vanderbilt, supervising construction of the trenches, had his engineers lay them out on a grid pattern like the streets of Manhattan, with which every member of the division was familiar. The main communication trenches were named Broadway and Fifth Avenue, and the cross-trenches were christened Thirty-fourth Street, Forty-second Street, and so on. The result was that every man could instantly orient himself and navigate his way through the system. Whether it would help them when they entered the less-helpfully named and laid-out trenches of the Western Front remained to be seen.

Having completed the trenches, they then discovered to their dismay that, just as on the Western Front, they would have to dig them all over again because the divisional artillerymen would be getting their practice by shelling the trenches. The artillery was sited a mile away, and the men detailed to repair the ruins were stationed far enough away to protect them from the shells and shell shock, but close enough to witness the destruction of their handiwork. The bombardment continued for an hour, and as soon as it stopped, the infantry and the engineers had to reoccupy and rebuild the shattered trenches in the shortest possible time.

The men also had to practice moving up and entering the trenches in complete silence and pitch darkness. At 8:30 on the evening of November 19, 1917, Monk and his comrades in the 106th Infantry were ordered to prepare at once to enter the trenches for a twelve-hour tour of duty. Sergeants rushed down the company street rousting out the men, who had been excused from their duties that afternoon and had mostly turned in for a nap. Carrying blanket rolls, haversacks, canteens, picks, shovels, rifles, and heavy equipment but no ammunition, the soldiers formed up, waited silently while every ninth man fell out to pick up a dark lantern that gave only a glimmer of light, and then moved off.

Just as would happen on the Western Front, a guide met the men at the entrance to the trenches. They followed the guide as best they could, "despite the fact you couldn't see the hat of the man in front of you, the red clay wall to your left, nor the firing step to your right." The trench was barely wider than the men, was slippery underfoot, and twisted and turned. The firing steps had also been revetted in places, and the stakes driven into the mud often caught on their overcoats or tore the laces of their leggings. "Occasionally a man stumbled or jammed his foot against a rock. Hoarsely but with vast emotion he cursed—cursed the war, the trenches, the Kaiser and like obnoxious things."

The platoons deployed into the support, cover, and firing trenches, lay on their stomachs on the parapet or stood on the firing step, about fifty feet apart, and settled down to watch and wait, peering into the ground mist. In front of them was "No Man's Land"—two hundred yards wide and punctuated by "a jaded barbed-wire fence, a narrow creek and a scant strip of woods." The men had been told that the penalty for falling asleep on sentry duty on the Western Front was death; they wouldn't be shot for sleeping in the Wadsworth trenches, but by the time their punishment had ended, they would wish that they had been.

As the hours crawled by, some men could not resist the temptation to raise their heads a little to peer out toward the enemy lines. Every time one did so, the field telephone would buzz and the "umpires" declared the man "dead." Two patrols were sent out, creeping silently over the parapet, but both were spotted at once and also declared casualties. The rest of their comrades remained on trench guard throughout the night, "through a fog that froze the marrow and a hard, dull bitterness of cold that contracted the innards." Their eyes tired and sore from peering into the mist, sentries shouted challenges at enemy soldiers who turned out to be scraps of paper or clumps of cotton bolls moving in the breeze, and when the enemy finally did come creeping along the creek bed and through the trees toward them, the sentries failed to spot them. The men were relieved at six in the morning, given a cup of scalding coffee, and led back to their shelters bleary-eyed, filthy, and utterly weary.

Although heavily censored, the reports filed by British observers were very critical of the American men's performance. The observers had entered the trenches undetected and calmly watched the Americans peering into the darkness, trying to spot the men who were already standing, unseen, behind them. The failure of some of the soldiers to keep absolute silence and avoid showing lights was also criticized, though in an effort to lessen the sting of the comments, it was claimed that the observers had also commented upon the excellence shown by men who had never before been on trench guard.

Each battalion in turn also went into the practice trenches for a forty-eight- or seventy-two-hour spell—Monk's Second Battalion began their first one at 9:00 p.m. on November 23, 1917—and was then subjected to a simulated gas attack using lachrymator (tear gas) and smoke bombs. Practice continued until every man could put on and adjust his mask within six seconds.

British and French officers also continued training the American soldiers on every other aspect of the war they would soon be fighting, from trench routine and trench raids to the dangers of booby traps and German subterfuges on the battlefield. British instructors also taught the men grenade-throwing; like almost all their weaponry and equipment, the grenades used were British. The steel, egg-shaped casing of the "Mills bomb" was scored with vertical and horizontal lines, like the lines of latitude and longitude on a globe, and when the grenade exploded, it fragmented along those lines, hurling lethal shrapnel in all directions. The thrower often pulled the steel firing pin with his teeth, and the grenade detonated about seven seconds later—in theory, enough time to throw it, but not long enough for the target to retrieve it and throw it back. The straight-armed throwing action taught by British instructors was more like bowling in English cricket than a baseball throw, and Americans often struggled to adapt to it. While tests showed that it was better than the baseball catcher's snap throw, the baseball outfielder's throw gave the greatest range and accuracy and was the one used by American troops. Monk had a natural aptitude for it and repeatedly proved himself to be among the most powerful, fearless, and accurate of grenade throwers.

Despite the best efforts of the instructors, training was often hampered by a lack of rifles, ammunition, and almost every other kind of weapon and military equipment. Even in February 1918, more than four months after they arrived at Spartanburg, the men were still being forced to use wooden guns and pipes as pretend rifles, trench mortars, and field guns. Live firing exercises with real rifles, trench mortars, and artillery required the construction of firing ranges at a site in wild country at Dark Corner, thirty-one miles northeast of Camp Wadsworth. The ranges spread across the lowlands at the foot of Glassy Rock, and the rock face, rising sheer for a thousand feet, was the backdrop to the targets.

While on the ranges, the recruits practiced loading with a clip of ammunition; sight-setting; and firing while standing, kneeling, sitting, and prone, and using a parapet, wall top, or the vertical edge of a wall, door, or tree. They were also given a "flinch test" in which the man being tested did not know whether his rifle was loaded until he pulled the trigger. Those who flinched at the discharge of the rifle could expect further hours on the ranges to stiffen their sinews. Monk, the veteran of more armed combat than even the most experienced member of the regiment, did not flinch or turn a hair, whether firing or under fire himself. He adapted so well to military life that he was soon promoted to private first class.

Monk and his comrades also practiced following a creeping barrage, forming a line one hundred yards behind the predicted point of shell bursts and then waiting as "shells whistled twenty feet over our heads and burst not a hundred yards in front of us. We were told to duck our heads. We did." The barrage sent rocks, earth, and trees skyward, and as it lifted and began to creep forward, the infantry advanced behind it, maintaining the hundred-yard gap between themselves and the curtain of exploding shells. This exposure to the kind of concentrated shell fire these raw soldiers would encounter on the Western Front made a profound impression upon them.

As fall turned to winter, the conditions at Camp Wadsworth became similar to those they could expect in the trenches on the Western Front: muddy and waterlogged. Monk and his comrades were even made to practice moving through the trenches with water up to their waists. Hot water was a luxury that few enjoyed, and cold-water shaving ensured that "no man was unshaved for Saturday inspection, but an awful lot of blood was spilled without bringing peace any nearer."

There were worse hardships to be endured during South Carolina's wettest, coldest, and snowiest winter in eighty years. Beginning on December 8, there was a ten-day cold snap, with thick snow and temperatures falling to sixteen degrees on the first night and getting progressively colder as the frost bit deeper. One company sergeant complained that there were now only two kinds of water: frozen and dirty. The conditions provoked a rising chorus of complaints about lack of blankets, hot food, hot baths, and wood for the stoves in each squad tent. Hard-bitten soldiers already serving on the Western Front would have had scathing comments to make about men complaining about such minor issues, but for the recruits of the 27th Division, shivering in their tents, still wearing their light khaki uniforms and with thin and often threadbare blankets, the cold was a terrible ordeal.

Snow filled the practice trenches; sentry duty and patrols continued for a while, as they would have to in Flanders and France, but were soon suspended. By then the camp rumor mill was already claiming that headquarters was covering up the news that as many as eleven soldiers had frozen to death. The rumors were so widespread that the 27th Division was forced to issue a statement that the percentage of deaths at

Camp Wadsworth had been no higher than in any population of thirty thousand people and that no one had frozen to death.

The conditions only increased the men's desire to be done with training and off to France, and rumors circulated almost daily about the date of their departure. As each date passed without any sign that they were to leave, frustration increased. The gloom deepened when Major General O'Ryan told a Senate committee that it would be another two months before his troops could be sent abroad, and even then they would need to undergo more intensive training before they were ready to face the enemy. "Officers and men should not be impatient to get abroad," he said. "There is enough war there for everybody."

Winter at last gave way to spring and, as the weeks drifted by, *The New York Times* was moved to wonder when the thirty-one thousand men of the New York Division would be going overseas.

They have had six months and more of training, much of it intensive. They have marched and counter-marched many hundreds of miles; they have dug trenches enough for a city's foundations; they have shot away cartridges and shells by the thousand; they have punctured dummies to rags with their bayonets; they have fought the enemy across No Man's Land and repulsed him with heavy losses; they have listened in trenches all night long for the raiders; they have gassed and been gassed; and how tired they are of waiting to go 'over there' . . . The Empire Division is needed in France, sorely needed, and the call should be sounded soon.

At the start of May 1918, the rumors of the division's departure for France at last hardened into solid fact: they would be leaving within the week. Private Edward Eastman and his buddies in the 106th Infantry put their affairs in order, including filling out the forms that detailed the next of kin to be contacted in the event of their death and to whom any unpaid wages and personal effects would be delivered. Unlike during his time in Sing Sing, when Monk had named his sister Lizzie as his next of kin, this time he listed his wife, Mrs. Worthy Eastman, but the only address he gave was "Persido" (Presidio), in the Big Bend area of Texas.

For the ex-prostitute wife of an ex-gangster who must still have been holding at least some of the proceeds from his past criminality, Presidio and Big Bend would have been a good bolt-hole. The border dividing the sun-baked dirt streets of Presidio from its Mexican neighbor, Ojinaga, was a porous one, little scrutinized by the authorities, and Presidio was "a gun on both hips kind of town . . . a place to go if you didn't want to be found." The population was largely transient, and few questions were asked of those who passed through or stayed to live there.

Although Worthy had family in Texas, they were in Galveston, seven hundred miles away, and if she was basing herself in Presidio, it was most probably because of its reputation as a no-questions-asked safe haven for those in trouble with the law. However, the clean air and bone-dry climate of the desert and mountain ranges north of Presidio, around the Big Bend town of Alpine, also drew a large number of sufferers from consumption and other chest complaints. The beneficial effects of the climate were regularly advertised in the New York newspapers, and it is also possible that Worthy was a consumptive seeking a healthier place to live than the damp, cold Lower East Side.

As her husband and his comrades made their final preparations for departure from Spartanburg, 231 of their fellows were told that their months of training had been wasted and they would not be making the voyage to France. Even though some of the worst physical specimens and those with physical or mental disabilities had been removed from the regiment before the move to Camp Wadsworth the previous fall, another 198 privates, 9 sergeants, 12 corporals, 4 wagoners, 3 cooks, 3 mechanics, and 2 buglers were now pronounced physically disqualified for service abroad but suitable for duty in the United States. The reasons ranged from flat feet and mental insufficiency to enlarged testicles, but even being underweight or having defective teeth was seen as reason enough to disqualify a man from arduous overseas service. A number of men, including several Austrians and two Turks, were also removed from the 106th Infantry's overseas roster as enemy aliens.

The remaining men, including Monk, made their final preparations for war. Senior officers of the division remained concerned about their men's level of training, discipline, and war-readiness, but events had now overtaken them. A last-ditch German offensive on the Western Front, launched on March 21, threatened to overwhelm the depleted British and French forces. On April 11, the British commander Field Marshal Sir Douglas Haig issued a last, desperate rallying call, as his troops stared defeat in the face: "With our backs to the wall and believing in the justice of our cause each one of us must fight on to the end.

The safety of our homes and the Freedom of mankind alike depend upon the conduct of each one of us at this critical moment." American troops were needed urgently in France to shore up the creaking Allied defenses and take the battle to the Germans; the 27th Division would now be thrown into the fight.

12

WE ONLY SEE OLD MEN AND BOYS

On May 6, 1918, the 106th Infantry left Camp Wadsworth for the last time and marched to Fairforest, about six miles west of Spartanburg, where they boarded a train to Jersey City. A quarter of a million men a month were now shipping out to Europe—the peak was reached in August 1918 when three hundred thousand embarked, the majority leaving from Newport News, Virginia, or Hoboken, New Jersey. Almost all men embarking for overseas from Hoboken were processed through Camp Merritt in New Jersey or Camps Mills and Upton on Long Island, where the camp personnel would receive, house, feed, inspect, and equip them. When the 106th Infantry boarded a ferry on the morning of May 8, many of the longer-serving men thought they were returning to the regiment's former base—Camp Mills at Mineola, Long Island. One of them shouted "Mineola!" and the response was "both instantaneous and electrifying; in one voice, raised to high heaven, the whole regiment shouted the magic word 'MINEOLA! MINEOLA!' " From that moment it became the battle cry of the 106th Infantry.

However, the ferry was not bound for Long Island. It steamed slowly along the Jersey shore, past the North German Lloyd and Hamburg-American piers, as the men crowding the rails cast wistful glances across the Hudson toward the New York skyline. Only the most naïve of those soldiers would have been expecting a home leave at this stage, on the eve of their departure for France and war, when the chances of a spate of desertions were much too high, but any lingering hopes they might have harbored were erased as the ferry docked at a row of Hoboken piers, alongside great troopships covered in camouflage paint.

Monk and his fellows boarded U.S. Navy Transport No. 36—the USS *President Lincoln*—an eighteen-thousand-ton German passenger liner that had been impounded and converted and was making its first run as a troopship. In the opposite berth, the mammoth USS *George Washington,* painted with "dazzle" camouflage to break up the ship's outline and already laden with men, was about to sail for France. In the early evening the great ship slid out of her berth and disappeared into the dusk.

The *President Lincoln* remained at the pier for two more days while other troops from the 42nd Engineers and 129th Infantry embarked. Even at this late stage, after an examination by the attending surgeon, a number of 106th infantrymen were found unfit for overseas service and were disembarked at 8:00 a.m. on Thursday, May 9. The following day, Friday, May 10, 1918, the ship was readied for departure. Card schools, circled by spectators, were already running in various parts of the ship. Other groups of men were pacing the decks, but most were "lounging along the rail with faces toward New York; no doubt we are all thinking the same thoughts. It grows hot and sultry; the afternoon drags."

As a precaution against sabotage or last-minute desertions, all the portholes were closed and the decks cleared an hour before the ship's departure time, leaving the men to wonder why they could not wave a last farewell to those watching from the pier and the ferry passengers. On the dot of five, without noise or fanfare, the great ship, dwarfing the tugs hauling it clear of the piers, slid away through the murky waters of the Hudson and disappeared almost at once into the mist hanging over the river. The laughter of the afternoon gave way to absolute silence. Those on board knew that many of them would never see New York again.

As the Manhattan skyline disappeared from sight, Monk must have felt as if the door had closed forever on his criminal past. He had turned his back on his old ways, trained hard, and learned military discipline. "Certain qualities which had been misdirected came under proper direction and when the 27th sailed for France, Private Eastman was as good a soldier as there was in the company." However, it is difficult to imagine that he did not take an active part in—and might well have taken control of—the incessant gambling aboard the ship. "There were continuously running crap games, Red Dog, poker and others I had never heard of. Some of those fellows never saw daylight during the whole trip."

After dark that evening, the last contact with home was lost as the pilot who had steered them downstream from the docks left the ship. Already the *President Lincoln* was rolling in the swell and the first men were succumbing to seasickness. The ship was tracking northeast, to rendezvous with the rest of its convoy for the perilous journey eastward through U-boat-infested waters. Lookouts were posted in the crow's nest and at intervals along the decks, alert for any sign of a periscope among the gray Atlantic rollers, a vigil that would be maintained until they made port.

At nine that night all lights except those in interior compartments were extinguished. Barely visible by day against the sullen gray Atlantic swell, the ship was a ghost by night, dark as the sky, every visible light extinguished. Seven troopships, with their dazzle camouflage "in most fantastic designs and colors," and escorted by a cruiser, USS *Huntington,* had formed the initial convoy, but during the night of May 11, another seven ships joined them, the largest troop convoy at that time: fourteen troopships in three line-astern columns of five, four, and five ships, carrying fifty thousand men between them. No gleam of light showed on any ship; even smoking on deck was forbidden, and nothing was to be thrown overboard, for a marauding U-boat could have used a tell-tale trail of debris to track them. Steaming without lights entailed the chance of an accidental collision with one of the other ships in the convoy, but it was a lesser risk than offering a well-lit target to prowling U-boats.

Conditions for the enlisted men were atrocious. They were packed in the holds in hammocks or long aisles of bunks, with wood frames and chicken wire supporting the straw-filled mattresses. These bunks were three or four tiers high, so that "the bottom man was almost on the floor while the top man was practically against the ceiling." The chicken wire also stretched, and the men on the bottom tiers were lying on the steel deck after a few days. In their dank, stinking quarters below-decks, without even room to sit upright, the men of the 106th Infantry endured a miserable crossing. At night all portholes were closed as a precaution against detection from submarines, and the ventilation was so poor that the smell from the holds was overpowering. When rough seas struck them, the sour stench of vomit was added to that of foul air and stale sweat, but they were at least fortunate that the influenza pandemic had not yet struck; later transports returned home with the bodies of many of the troops they had carried to France still aboard.

Just before dawn on the frigid, fog-bound morning of May 13, Monk was awakened by the moaning of the siren and the clanging of alarm bells. Like his fellows, he scrambled from his bunk and fought his way up the crowded companionways from the holds, but it proved to be nothing more than the first call to quarters for a practice drill in abandoning ship. It took only six minutes to clear the belowdecks areas of men, who then stood shivering on the deck until broad daylight, encased in bulky life belts. They were left to wonder "what chance the black gang [the coal stokers working in the bowels of the ship] will have in the event of disaster?"

The next morning the fog lifted and the troopships took turns at target practice. The *President Lincoln*'s four six-inch guns were fired at a huge cask, simulating a submarine's conning tower, towed on a cable behind another troopship. Soldiers packed the rails to watch, betting on the results of each shot.

As a commandeered former German liner and one of the largest troop carriers in the U.S. fleet, the *President Lincoln* was a doubly prominent target for German U-boats. The news that the kaiser had put a price on their heads had already spread through the ship, and though the convoy's escort was further strengthened by destroyers on May 15, that only signaled that the convoy was about to begin the most dangerous phase of the voyage. From then on, the captain took his meals and snatched what sleep he could without ever leaving the bridge, and every man aboard was ordered to wear or carry his life preserver at all times.

On May 21, 1918, the fleet entered the "Danger Zone": the U-boat–infested eastern Atlantic approaches to the Channel and the French ports. The cruiser USS *Huntington* left the convoy soon afterward, leaving the job of safeguarding the troopships to the faster and nimbler destroyers. Almost at once one of the troopships fell astern, signaling for assistance. A frisson of fear ran through everyone watching, but the ship's trouble was mechanical and, after swift repairs, she picked up speed again and rejoined the others.

As the escorts circled, the convoy steamed ahead in close formation, at full speed, with black smoke belching from the funnels. All hands were at full alert, but a stand-to at 2:30 in the morning on May 22 proved to be a false alarm, caused by a lookout spooked by hours of staring into the darkness. The men wore their life belts constantly now, and that night, at the suggestion of the ship's captain, everyone slept fully dressed, their boots on as well. They remained in their hammocks only a short while before the wailing of the ship's sirens and blasts on its whistle, accompanied by the sound of sailors running through the ship ringing handbells, signaled another stand-to in the small hours, triggered by reports of U-boat sightings off Brest.

May 24, 1918, dawned without further alarms. It was a beautiful morning and the men's spirits were lifted even more by the sight of land ahead: the coast of France. French patrol boats came out to meet the convoy while aircraft circled overhead and the destroyer escorts formed a protective screen as the troop transports, in single file, threaded the narrow inlet to the harbor, the only break in a rocky coast studded with reefs. As the *President Lincoln* nosed its way in, Monk and the other men at the rails saw "emerald-green hills, dotted here and there with tiny thatched-roof peasant houses, the bluest of blue waters, and the fleet of sailboats of all colors, some almost toy-like in size." Overhead, tethered barrage balloons strained against their moorings in the stiff onshore breeze.

The ship docked at Brest late that day, and the 106th Infantry spent that night aboard, before disembarking the following morning. They were luckier than they knew to have made the crossing unscathed; at 11:40 on the morning of May 30, 1918, their ship, carrying convalescent soldiers home to the United States, was torpedoed and sunk two hundred miles out on the return voyage. The U-boat wolf pack also accounted for the USS *Covington,* the ship that had flanked the *President Lincoln* on the voyage to France.

On May 25, the men of the 106th Infantry were ferried ashore. As they took their first steps on French soil, the strength of the regiment stood at 92 officers and 3,196 men. All the companies were short of officers—a reflection of the scarcity of suitably qualified men—but Monk's Company G was particularly badly served, consisting of 231 men but only 4 officers. Since line officers tended to suffer disproportionately high casualty rates because of their leading position in attacks, the shortage continued to prompt concern.

Struggling under the weight of their packs, the men formed up on the dockside before marching through the town and up the steep hill, lined with ancient houses. Curious French people watched them pass, and the war-weary civilians in their somber clothes were curiosities themselves to the new arrivals, almost all of them setting foot on European soil for the first time in their lives. The vast scale of French losses in the war was immediately apparent. There seemed to be few people who were not in mourning; almost everyone on the street was dressed in black. There were no young men to be seen, only women, old men, and boys. After a two-hour march, they halted at Fort Bougren, one of the ancient defenses of the port, and pitched their pup tents for a three-day rest. It puzzled them all greatly, since they had been doing virtually nothing but rest since sailing from Hoboken fourteen days earlier.

On May 28, 1918, the 106th Infantry marched back down the hill to the station. They traveled in three separate detachments, with Monk's Company G among four companies to leave at 11:30 that morning. The waiting trains hauled French boxcars, so small they seemed like toys and immortalized by the slogan stenciled in white paint on their sides: 40 hommes—8 chevaux (forty men and eight horses), though forty men could be accommodated in those cars only if they were all standing up. In each car were boxes of rations, supposedly enough to last three days. In groups of forty, the men were loaded into cattle cars still stinking of manure, and the train moved off. The journey passed with painful slowness, and the train was sometimes shunted into sidings and left for hours before jerking back into motion.

The commanding officer of the 106th had been ordered to prevent his troops from obtaining liquor, but there was little opportunity for them to do so. They were penned in their cattle cars and forbidden to leave for any reason, even though sanitary facilities were nonexistent. Trying to sleep at night was next to impossible. "We lay like sardines in a can. If one of us turned over, a dozen or so others had to do the same. If one tried to make the side door in an emergency, he crawled over all those between him and his goal. The cursing on such occasions was something to hear and would awaken everyone. Then we all cussed each other, France, the French railroads and the Army."

They traveled north and east for two days and nights, through Normandy in apple-blossom time, passing "checkerboard fields, broom-swept woods, past toy-like railroad stations, and road-crossings where papa or mama emerged from their little house near the tracks to lower and raise the crossing gates." The beauty of those surroundings made the contrast all the more pointed when they eventually arrived in the war zone at Noyelles-sur-Mer, near the major British base at Abbeville. Sleepy, stiff, and sore, they picked up their packs and began to march, hearing for the first time the ceaseless bass rumble of the heavy guns in the front lines.

The troops of the 27th Division bivouaced for miles around the Somme estuary, but on General Pershing's orders they were kept as far away from towns as possible, to minimize the VD rate. He was so obsessed by the potential impact of venereal disease on his troops that he ordered guards posted outside brothels to stop his men from patronizing them, and when he was told that prostitutes deliberately sought out foreign troops because they had more money, Pershing cabled the War Department to withhold part of each soldier's pay. Men who did contract VD were subject to trial by summary court-martial. General O'Ryan matched his commander's zeal by demanding that regimental and unit commanders of the 27th Division exercise the greatest care to ensure that no man escaped trial and punishment. Sufferers were also subjected to "extremely painful medical treatment which, it was suspected, was partly intended as a punishment and deterrent."

The bureaucratic and logistical chaos of war was never more evident than in the travails of the First Battalion of the 106th Infantry, which finally arrived by train at Noyelles at 2:15 on the morning of

May 30. There was no one there to greet them and direct them to their billets and, as the station was deserted, Major Ransom H. Gillet told his men to remain aboard until dawn. Just after daybreak, at about 4:00 a.m., a British officer appeared and told him to disembark and unload the equipment at once. The men stumbled from the cattle cars of the train, and unloading had been completed by 5:45 a.m. Fifteen minutes later another English officer arrived and told Gillet that breakfast was waiting at a rest camp a few minutes' walk from the station and that the battalion would be billeted at Crécy. However, first all the equipment that had just been unloaded from the train had to be moved again, into an open field, so that an incoming train could use the same space to unload. They then marched to the rest camp, and after a cold breakfast, they returned to the railroad yard.

Later that morning, two senior officers of the 27th Division appeared and issued orders about what each man should have in his pack and what should be done with his surplus equipment. While the men were unpacking, sorting, and repacking their equipment, their commander was informed that they would need to clear the area quickly, as another battalion was right behind them and would have to use the same ground. By the time all the clothing and equipment had been sorted and stowed to the officers' satisfaction it was 12:30 p.m., and Gillet was then ordered to take his men back to the rest area for lunch. When they arrived, they found Monk's Second Battalion already there. Since there was barely enough room for one battalion, let alone two, the resulting overcrowding meant that the First Battalion did not receive their full rations, nor have the chance to fill all their canteens before a British NCO told them to move out as yet another battalion was expected.

The promised guide to lead them to their billets did not appear until 3:10 that afternoon, and at that point, the First Battalion began the march to Crécy. By 7:30 that evening they had been marching for approximately eleven miles and were just a mile short of Crécy when yet another British officer rode up, told Gillet to halt the column, and informed him that they were on the wrong road and that there were no billets, no room, and no rations for them at Crécy. The battalion waited at the roadside while the British officer took Gillet to his office in the town and produced a map that showed the Americans were supposed to be billeted not at Crécy but at Canchy, a few miles away. Gillet then pointed out that it was now almost eight at night and his men had been on the move since four that morning, and were without food or water.

He therefore asked for trucks to take them to Canchy.

Another hour elapsed while thirty-five trucks were located and dispatched to where the battalion was waiting, and they were then driven to Canchy, arriving at 11:30. Inevitably there was no billet warden there to greet and direct them, and when one of the drivers took Gillet to the headquarters of the 27th Division, several miles away, he got lost, so it was two in the morning on May 31 when they arrived. The billet warden directed them to the house where the 27th Division had its headquarters, but it was in darkness, and no one came in answer to Gillet's fusillade of knocks. He went back to the billet warden, who sent him back to the house again. This time, in answer to a renewed barrage of knocking, a sergeant finally appeared, rubbing the sleep from his eyes. The sergeant took Gillet to another house to see a colonel, who sent him to see a captain in yet another house, who sent him and the sergeant back to the division's headquarters to make further inquiries by phone.

At 3:15 a.m. a weary Gillet gave up the attempt and decided to return to his troops, who had now been without food or water for almost twenty-four hours, his journey given added urgency by the truck driver's announcement that all the trucks would have to be back at their base by six that morning. A few miles down the road they met the troops in the other trucks, now under the care of yet another British officer, who was taking them to La Festel. There, as dawn was breaking, they at last found billets, but while his men settled themselves, Gillet made one final trip, to Coulonvillers, where he persuaded his commanding officer to give him some rations and water for his hungry and thirsty men. Such were the ways of great armies in wartime.

13

THIS REALM OF SILENCE

Although the commander of the American Expeditionary Force, General Pershing, had hoped to retain all American troops under his direct control, as a result of the "Abbeville Agreement," ten U.S. divisions, including the 27th, were sent to British sectors of the Western Front, where they would operate under overall British command. As a result, the 106th Infantry found itself at a British staging camp at Abbeville, where they spent their first night under fire. The town, incorporating a vital rail junction, was bombed every night, but while the raids sent British veterans sprinting to their dugouts, the men of the 106th, not yet realizing the horrors such raids could bring, "appeared to enjoy the performance as a child enjoys a circus." As searchlights sliced through the night sky, sometimes fixing an enemy aircraft like a moth on a pin, the roar of the antiaircraft guns pumping up a barrage of shells was counterpointed by the drum rattle of falling shrapnel and the sudden bass rumble of bomb explosions. Yet throughout this cacophony, the American troops remained in the open, "all standing and gaping heavenward, like Kansas gentlemen on a visit to New York."

After a brief sleep, Monk and his comrades were awakened at daybreak. They splashed their faces with cold water and then ate their first British Army breakfast. "The hot Irish cracked oatmeal with a big gob of jam on it, the bacon and the bread were wonderful. Why the 'Limey' had to spoil it with tea was more than we could understand or endure. Our howls of protest were heard all the way to General O'Ryan's headquarters, aided and abetted by those from every other unit in the Division. From then on we had coffee with all our meals."

Although there were complaints about British food, with the anonymous stew known as "McConachie" coming in for particular criticism, soldiers on British rations were much better fed than their counterparts, who were reliant on the American supply train. Most of those supplies arrived by the congested and lengthy rail route from Bordeaux, and General Pershing often had to choose whether a trainload of food or of ammunition would have priority. When at war, there could only be one solution to that problem, and as a result, his men were often forced to subsist on iron rations. By contrast, the 27th Division, fed via the much shorter British supply lines from the Channel ports, never went short of food.

On May 31, the 106th broke camp and the three battalions transferred to different areas of the Albert region, with Monk and the rest of the Second Battalion billeted in barns and cowsheds at Oneux-Neuville. There they were issued the rest of their battlefield equipment, including box respirators, gas masks, rifles, and bayonets, while all their excess clothing, shoes, and personal items were taken from them and put into storage. From now on they would have to carry all they owned on their backs. Each man had his razor and toilet articles, a pair of woolen socks, a suit of long johns, two blankets, a shelter half—one half of a pup tent—a tent pole and pins, a pair of shoes, an overcoat, a slicker or raincoat, a trench shovel, a Bowie knife, a revolver with ammunition, a first-aid kit, a mess kit, and a canteen for water. The full kit weighed around seventy pounds, and most men discarded some of it along the road; if challenged about it later on, they could claim that it had been lost in action. Steel helmets and gas masks were added burdens to carry, but only the insane or suicidal would have discarded them. American-made military equipment of any sort remained in such short supply that, like their rations, every piece of their uniforms, equipment, and weaponry—even their underclothes—was British. Even where U.S. military equipment was demonstrably better than its British equivalent, problems of logistics and lack of compatibility with existing Allied weapons or ammunition rendered much of it unusable.

The 106th Infantry's final training, on ground that had been fought over for years, was all with British troops and instructors, and they were lectured on every aspect of frontline operations, from gas drills to censorship rules. To instill confidence in their gas masks, American troops spent half an hour in dark cellars that were sealed and filled with greenish-yellow chlorine gas. They were also taught how to detect the various poison gases by their odors, and what precautions to take. One of the more astonishing statistics of the war was that a thousand high-explosive shells were required to cause one casualty, whereas every gas cylinder produced a casualty. All of the gases, particularly mustard and phosgene, were lethal if inhaled, but mustard gas also produced severe burns and blindness if it came in contact with the skin or eyes. Chlorine caused victims' lungs to fill with fluid and could "drown" them. Many of the gases clung to the ground, filling shell holes and seeping into unprotected dugouts, and remained virulent and deadly long after they had been spread.

At the end of their training, after a month without anything more than the most perfunctory wash, the entire 106th Infantry was given the luxury of a two-minute shower, albeit in cold water. The engineers had erected a crude framework on the banks of a creek, with five-gallon gas cans punched with holes acting as showerheads. A bucket line of men fed the showers with cold creek water, and ten or twelve men at a time took their turn underneath. One bucket of water descended on them at once, and after a minute for soaping up, another bucketful rinsed them clean. "If you didn't get thoroughly soaped or rinsed, it was your fault. You wiped yourself dry anyway."

On June 16, slightly cleaner and fresher, they began a punishing two-day march from Oneux to a new training base at

Gamaches-Moutiers, during which they crossed the infamous River Somme for the first time. A few soldiers dropped out of the march along the way, too ill or exhausted or with feet too badly blistered to continue, but Monk was not one of them. He was twenty years older than most of his fellows, and his health had been wrecked by his years in Sing Sing and the two major stomach operations he had required, yet his marching stride never slackened and his voice was never raised in complaint, no matter how many miles they trudged through mud and rain or heat and dust. At Gamaches-Moutiers, Monk and the rest of the Second Battalion were quartered in tents set among fields vivid with poppies and cornflowers. They remained there for four days, under the instruction of British veterans of the British 66th Division, a unit so depleted in numbers and morale by their horrific losses during the great German offensive that spring that it was a mere skeleton.

The 106th's British instructors, once naïve young soldiers themselves, were now hard-bitten veterans of the Somme and Passchendaele, and an instructor's first sight of the American troops was not encouraging for him or them. "My God," he said. "These are nothing but boys." A British corporal was even more offensive. Tired of American big talk about what they were going to do to the Germans, he expressed the fervent hope that "Jerry [the Germans] will smash them to atoms, for they are nothing more than human garbage, and this is the best I can say about them." The Australians expressed their views with a little more discretion, but were equally unimpressed by American officers, who "carried leather suitcases and umbrellas and looked more like commercial travelers than soldiers."

Although the American troops were raw, they were eager for the fray, and they were equally unimpressed with the war weariness and negativity that restricted the war aims of many British soldiers to obtaining a "Blighty" wound that would see them invalided out of the army and sent back to Blighty (Britain). The passivity and fatalism their instructors displayed in the face of a potential German attack also horrified the American troops. The British seemed resigned to being driven back by the next German attack, and appeared to have no aggressive spirit or desire to prepare for an offensive.

As they worked together, attitudes began to change. The Americans grew to have more respect for their British mentors' abilities and knowledge, and, whatever their tactical deficiencies, the American infantrymen had no shortage of spirit, which in turn communicated itself to the British. However, there remained a danger, as the U.S. Marines proved at Belleau Wood in that same month, June 1918, that reckless American bravery and the "profound ignorance" of the A.E.F.'s commanders at that time would lead to a profligate expenditure of American lives. After Belleau Wood it was remarked that "their dead, especially the dead of the Marine Corps, lay in beautifully ordered lines where the traversing machine guns had caught them." They had died in the same way as the British and French had during the first years of the war: shoulder to shoulder, in neat rows. Even British officers, serving in the most conservative army of all, found the American tactics astonishing. The U.S. Army went into battle in 1918 as if the Great War had just begun, and they had to discover the terrible realities of trench warfare for themselves.

There may even have been a subliminal feeling among American commanders that with Britain and France already having irrigated the battlefields with the blood of millions of their dead, an American blood sacrifice was also required. Perhaps only when General Pershing had laid down piles of American corpses like stacks of chips in a high-stakes poker game would he have earned the right to sit at the same table as his British and French counterparts Field Marshal Haig and Marshal Foch.

U.S. casualty rates could have been even worse. The German army that the A.E.F. faced in 1918 was not the same irresistible force that had swept the Belgian, French, and British armies aside in the early stages of the war. Most German divisions were now at least 50 percent under strength, and the elite Stoss divisions—the shock troops that had led the last great German offensive, in March 1918—had suffered even more severe losses of men. It is arguable that American casualties would have been far worse had their attacks not been launched against enemy troops who were already war-weary and badly demoralized, as the estimated forty thousand Germans who voluntarily surrendered to advancing U.S. forces seemed to confirm.

On June 21, the 106th Infantry marched out of Gamaches-Moutiers and, over the next few days, pausing at Guessoy-le-Montant, Neuilly l'Hôpital, Gorges, and Montrelet, they moved on, always eastward, toward the distant rumble of the guns at the front lines. Monk and his comrades were billeted in "every kind of haymow and cowshed . . . in orchards, fields and woodlands . . . in half-wrecked hovels." In the evenings they visited the local estaminets—British soldiers, unable to deal with French pronunciation, called them "just-a-minutes"—bars set up in the kitchen of a house, where beer, thin local wine, and a portion of the watery stew kept bubbling in a pot over the fire could be bought and letters home written while sitting on the rough wooden benches arranged against the walls. However, military police enforced a 9:30 p.m. curfew, clearing the estaminets and the streets.

At Montrelet, the men began the last phase of their combat training, before being sent into the lines for the first time. Much of the work done at Spartanburg was revisited, but new methods of warfare, developed since they left Camp Wadsworth, had to be learned as well. As a sign that they were nearing the front, enemy air raids took place almost every night. Beginning on June 29, still under the guidance and watchful gaze of seasoned British troops, the battalions were rotated into the reserve lines for brief periods, but returned to their billets to sleep. Military discipline still remained a problem, as was illustrated when, on their very first day in the trenches, despite having left their billets at 7:30 that morning, Monk's Second Battalion did not reach their allotted places in the line until after they had stopped for lunch, prompting a furious officer to demand that it should never happen again.

The following day, General O'Ryan circulated a letter to all the regimental commanders, expressing his disappointment with the performance of the division since its arrival in France, and in particular the shortcomings of its platoon and company commanders, which he blamed on a lack of the necessary sense of responsibility rather than any lack of knowledge. O'Ryan might have been genuinely aggrieved, but he might equally have been attempting to shake his men out of any complacency as they made ready to take their place in the firing lines.

On July 2, the 106th Infantry decamped and marched to a railhead, from where they traveled north to Arques, near Arras, arriving at ten that evening, after a twelve-hour journey. Any hopes of rest were punctured as they were formed up and marched out of town at twenty minutes to midnight. As required by military standing orders, they marched at a pace that covered two and a half miles in fifty minutes. After every fifty minutes, the soldiers rested for ten minutes, then marched on again. The timing was rigidly enforced; "between ten minutes of the hour and the even hour, no American soldiers in France will march but always will be found resting off the road and to the right. The reason for this order is obvious. This is a war of vast numbers. If companies, battalions and regiments were permitted to rest when they pleased, succeeding detachments would be constantly overtaking

Edward "Monk" Eastman in his prime (BROWN BROTHERS)

Police mug shot of Edward "Monk" Eastman, filed under what the NYPD believed was his real name: William Delaney (BROWN BROTHERS)

Louis Wolheim's career as a Hollywood tough guy was greatly helped by his physical resemblance to the notorious Monk Eastman. (COURTESY OF BRUCE CALVERT)

The pushcart market at Orchard and Rivington streets on a Sunday morning. Protection rackets targeting the pushcart vendors were a lucrative source of income for Monk Eastman's gang. (GEORGE GRANTHAM BAIN COLLECTION, LIBRARY OF CONGRESS)

One of the inhabitants of a cellar at Happy Jack's Canvas Palace— a dismal Pell Street lodging house (JACOB A. RIIS, LIBRARY OF CONGRESS)

A dingy, refuse-strewn court in a rear tenement at Baxter Street (JACOB A. RIIS, LIBRARY OF CONGRESS)

Chrystie Street, the rubble-strewn slum district that was
the site of Monk's headquarters, a dive called The Palm
(GEORGE P. HALL COLLECTION, NEGATIVE NO. 73849,
COLLECTION OF THE NEW-YORK HISTORICAL SOCIETY)

A dubious Lower East Side dive. The figure in a derby and a dark suit with
shiny buttons was probably the "sheriff" or "bouncer" of the dive; the
job was Monk Eastman's first step on the road to gang leadership. (ASBURY
PAPERS, COURTESY OF EDITH ASBURY)

SPANISH LOUIS   MONK EASTMAN   KID GRIFFO   YAKEY YAKE BRADY   EAT-EM-UP JACK McMANUS   JACK ZELIG

"Gun Men" of Two Rival Bands of the Underworld Using Bullet, Knife, and Dynamite on Each Other "For Business Reasons."

"HUMPTY JACKSON"

A SLIMY chapter of New York life has been brought to public attention by the gang feud that broke out during the early hours of last Monday morning in the back room of a Chinatown saloon, and that has since been blazonly continued with revolvers and dynamite bombs in various parts of the city.

The quiet, law-abiding, stay-at-home citizen may think that the existence of these gangs does not concern him, that their feuds, gun-fights, and murders are simply the most or less interesting outcroppings of the underworld...

New York's most notorious gangsters, including Monk Eastman and his bitter rivals Paul Kelly and "Yakey Yake" Brady (*NEW YORK TIMES*, JUNE 9, 1912)

Monk Eastman's political protector, "Big Tim" Sullivan (*center*) (LIBRARY OF CONGRESS)

Straw-hatted Tammany bosses "Silent Charlie" Murphy (*second from right*) and "Big Tom" Foley (*far right*) (BROWN BROTHERS)

Private Edward Eastman of Company G, 106th Infantry, photographed shortly before embarking for France (*A SHORT HISTORY AND ILLUSTRATED ROSTER OF THE 106TH INFANTRY*)

Men of the 27th Division struggling to scale a wall and leaping a practice trench during bayonet training at Camp Wadsworth (NATIONAL ARCHIVES AND RECORDS ADMINISTRATION, STILL PICTURES UNIT, COLLEGE PARK, MARYLAND)

A newspaper depiction of the 27th Division in action on the Hindenburg Line
(LIBRARY OF CONGRESS, PRINTS AND PHOTOGRAPHS DIVISION:
NEW YORK WORLD-TELEGRAM & SUN NEWSPAPER PHOTOGRAPH COLLECTION)

Scorched earth: the devastation left by the German armies as they retreated to the Hindenburg Line (IMPERIAL WAR MUSEUM, LONDON)

SCENES THE PHOTOGRAPHER SAW ALONG LINE OF GREAT PARADE

CIVIL WAR VETERANS WATCHING the PARADE

WOUNDED SOLDIERS SCRAMBLING for CIGARETTES

Gov. SMITH GREETS a DOUGHBOY FRIEND from the EAST SIDE.

The COLORS

ROOFTOP SPECTATORS

PASSING the REVIEWING STAND, 84th ST and FIFTH AVENUE

OLD LADY WHO CAME with her SERVICE FLAG, LUNCH and a SOAP BOX

Sergt. WAALER CUTTING SILKEN ROPE at VICTORY ARCH.

How one New York newspaper covered the homecoming parade of the 27th Division: The "doughboy friend from the East Side" being greeted by Governor Al Smith bears a more than passing resemblance to Monk Eastman. Six weeks after this photograph was taken, Governor Smith granted Monk a pardon, restoring the rights of citizenship he had lost after being convicted of a felony. The artwork next to the photograph shows the insignia of the New York Division, formed from the letters N Y D and the constellation Orion, a punning reference to the division's commanding officer, General O'Ryan. (*NEW YORK WORLD*, MARCH 26, 1919)

The body of Monk Eastman being carried out of Yannaco's funeral parlor in Williamsburg, Brooklyn, as Monk's former comrades formed an honor guard (LIBRARY OF CONGRESS, PRINTS AND PHOTOGRAPHS DIVISION: NEW YORK WORLD-TELEGRAM & SUN NEWSPAPER PHOTOGRAPH COLLECTION)

The funeral procession of Monk Eastman passing through the huge crowds lining the streets of Williamsburg (LIBRARY OF CONGRESS, PRINTS AND PHOTOGRAPHS DIVISION: NEW YORK WORLD-TELEGRAM & SUN NEWSPAPER PHOTOGRAPH COLLECTION)

preceding detachments and endless confusion would result." General O'Ryan had remarked that for every week of fighting a soldier would normally average ten weeks of marching and army routine, but sometimes the marching must have seemed to occupy even more time than that. Stragglers with blistered feet or who became ill were left by the roadside to catch up whenever they could.

On that night march, as they entered the city of Saint-Omer, a "mysterious, uncanny atmosphere seemed to grip the marching column; this was a dead city—repelling, silent as the grave. The unbroken rhythm of hobbed boots on rough cobbles, the absolute silence in the ranks and a full moon creating a shadowy regiment keeping step with the 106th, transformed the living into a ghost army on some unearthly mission." They passed through a labyrinth of twisting narrow streets with no light to guide them, not even a reassuring glow from the heavily boarded house windows. At intervals British patrols emerged from the shadows to challenge them, their bayonets flashing in the moonlight.

Beyond Saint-Omer, the regiment left the road and crossed the fields to a canal, which they then followed for miles. Hospital barges "moored to improvised docks bore mute testimony of their mission in those parts." The sight of rank upon rank of wounded soldiers was a sobering one for novice troops who knew that they would soon be in combat themselves. One group passed a hospital train and saw through the windows of each car wounded French soldiers swathed in bandages, many of which were bloodstained. "These soldiers were silent, motionless, staring out the windows and right through us. It was like we were not there or were wax figures." All that one of the Americans could say was, "Oh my. Oh my." For the first time he and his comrades were "face to face with the bloody facts of war."

The march continued until first light—3:35 a.m. on July 3—when the men of the 106th reached their billets at Lederzeele. Later that morning they marched eastward again, toward the front lines, hearing the menacing rumble of artillery growing louder with every step. It was a burning-hot day and their boots threw up suffocating clouds of dust from the road. As the sun rose higher and the heat grew more intense, their packs seemed to be getting heavier, the straps biting into their shoulders and their boots striking sparks as the soldiers dragged their feet over the cobblestone road.

At the end of that grueling two-day march, the 106th were quar-

tered in tents at Oudezeele, and began deploying in the East Poperinghe reserve area, alongside British and Australian forces, under
overall British command. They were now within range of the German
heavy artillery and were repeatedly shelled. As they dived for shelter,
they marveled at the Flemish farmers who continued to cultivate their
fields despite the constant bombardment—old men and women, young
boys and girls, all working in the fields seemingly as unconcerned by
the shelling as if they were miles behind the lines, seeking shelter only
when a shell fell very close to them.

The 27th Division had been allocated a three-thousand-yard sector
of the reserve lines at East Poperinghe, where the trenches scarred the
ripening wheatfields. Monk's Company G were billeted in an area that
included a schoolmaster's garden, and he promptly complained that his
fence had been broken, fruit stolen from his fig and cherry trees, and his
currant bushes stripped. The sight of so much fresh fruit after weeks of
army rations must have been an overwhelming temptation, though the
captain of Company G denied any involvement by his men and blamed
local children for the thefts. The men of the 106th were also instructed
not to damage the farmers' crops, but it was an almost impossible command to obey when they were simultaneously ordered to lay a thick
belt of defensive wire entanglements in front of their trenches. In any
case, orders for establishing firing pits required crops to be immediately
leveled to provide a field of fire of at least 250 yards in every direction.

Each of three regiments—the 105th, 106th, and 107th—had a
one-thousand-yard section of the lines to defend, with the 108th in
reserve. These American troops were holding the third and last line of
defense which, if breached, would mean the almost certain loss of the
Channel ports of Calais, Dunkirk, and Boulogne. The front line ran
down the valley east of Scherpenberg; the second line, barely deserving
the name, was a series of concrete pillboxes and machine-gun emplacements, but the system of defenses was unfinished and until now had
never been occupied by troops. Dug by the labor of Chinese "coolies,"
the trenches were so shallow that they gave minimal protection, the
machine-gun positions existed only on the map, and the barbed-wire
defenses were also nonexistent.

Along with their divisional comrades, the entire 106th Infantry
would now be occupied in constructing or completing these defenses,
and the battalions alternated between digging, sentry duty in the
trenches, and training and rifle practice on a range in the reserve area.

Continuous detachments were also sent from each unit to the front lines for observation and tactical study. They marched beneath the British observation balloons floating overhead on their wire cables, tethered to winches on trucks parked alongside the Scherpenberg road, and passed through Steenvoorde along a cobbled narrow street, lined with smoke-blackened brick houses. The brick-built church in the town square, its spire still undamaged by shell fire, had the same grimy, weathered look.

Between Steenvoorde and Abeele the men of the 106th crossed the Franco-Belgian border and were astonished to see customs officers of the two countries still presiding over the border from little huts and raising and lowering their barriers to allow the troops to pass through. The principal route for troops and supplies moving up to the front lines, the blood-soaked Steenvorde-Abeele road, was under artillery fire day and night. The surface was pocked and cratered, constantly repaired and as constantly cratered again. To minimize losses, intervals of five hundred yards were set between battalions, two hundred yards between companies, and one hundred yards between platoons. In the pitch darkness the infantrymen picked their way around the shell holes, marching in single file with ten to fifteen feet between individual men. Certain danger points were crossed at a run but, whatever the precautions, there were inevitable casualties, with several men killed or wounded by German shrapnel.

Beyond the village of Abeele, Mount Kemmel, "that metal-beaten, scarred old eminence which commanded a view of the North Sea," reared its "flat, sawed-off torso, once a proud peak, but four years of pounding by German and British artillery had given it a flat top. Up there along the skyline where Mount Kemmel stood, the smoke was rising from the battle front . . . The more we looked at that hunk of earth, the more menacing it became."

The weather was hot and very humid, and Monk and his comrades spent their detachments on the exhausting work of deepening trenches, digging machine-gun emplacements, setting up and clearing fields of fire, and stringing barbed wire. There were other, even less pleasant tasks. One group had to bury the stinking, bloated bodies of mules, which, killed by shell fire, had been lying in the hot sun for about three days. They borrowed a steel cable from one of the British observation balloon crews, dropped a loop over a mule's leg, and then hauled it over the ground to a shell crater deep enough to hold the bodies. Then one of the unfortunate soldiers had to retrieve the cable and make it ready for the next mule. When all the bodies had been moved in this way, while his comrades began shoveling dirt on top of them, he "sank to the ground, about as ill as any man could be . . . I could taste and smell that odor for several days."

The stench of putrefaction and the clouds of flies swarming everywhere should have been warning enough, but strict orders were issued to avoid drinking the groundwater from the streams, wells, ponds, and shell holes, which was so contaminated that it was unfit for any use. The men were warned of the consequences of an epidemic of diarrhea and dysentery and cautioned that a small percentage of men who had suffered dysentery remained infected, even though they were seemingly cured.

All Allied military activity in the area was under direct observation from the Germans on Mount Kemmel and the ridges that flanked it, and vulnerable to harassing artillery fire. At night American soldiers without dugouts slept in shallow scrapes they had made in the heavy clay soil, giving a little extra protection against shrapnel, though none at all against a direct hit. They soon learned to distinguish the different sounds of outbound shells from Allied guns and incoming projectiles from the German side and to tell roughly where shells would land and whether they needed to take cover. The long-range shells had "a peculiar plopping sound like they were slowly turning over and over in the air and traveling at a speed slow enough for one to see them." By contrast, the "whizzbangs" fired from a 77mm field piece had "landed and exploded before you could hear the sound of its approach. A barrage of these shells could throw the fear of God into any group of men and wreck their morale faster than any weapon in the German arsenal."

On the afternoon of July 14, the 106th Infantry was relieved and the Second Battalion marched back to Winnezeele before entraining once more on a narrow gauge railway, where a shortage of boxcars compelled them to travel on open flats in driving rain. They detrained and marched to Saint-Martin-au-Laërt. Although they were close to Saint-Omer, there was no possibility of any recreation in the town, the only nearby one of any size. No officer or enlisted man could visit Saint-Omer without the permission of his commander, approved and endorsed by headquarters, and even those few who did receive permission were warned that all brothels, whether licensed or unofficial, were out of bounds to officers and enlisted men alike.

Final training under the direction of the British continued, including practice maneuvers with battalions and companies, but whether the men of the 27th Division were yet ready for frontline combat was questionable. A report from divisional headquarters drew attention to a series of defects. Although officers had a considerable theoretical and technical grounding, their knowledge of their duties was less complete, and they often didn't even know what their responsibilities were. There were also innumerable complaints about their men having bayonets fixed and magazines loaded when away from the front lines; wearing caps instead of steel helmets; undermining trenches by digging into the face to create small dugouts; failing to care for their rifles; leaving their posts without authority; and showing a disregard for sanitation. Almost the only positive comment was the note of the troops' marked keenness when going out on patrol. The American chief gas officer also expressed alarm at their poor knowledge of and lack of preparedness for gas attacks. Some claimed they had not been told about mustard gas, and many officers and men were not carrying gas masks, even though they were in the danger zone and a gas attack could occur at any time.

No such reservations were expressed about Monk. It had been "a long trail from the saloons of Chrystie Street to the front line in France and in traveling it, a man's soul may undergo strange transformation." "An honest-to-God man . . . a real soldier," selfless, fearless, resourceful, cool under fire, and deadly with bomb, bayonet, or even bare hands, Monk was the finest soldier in his battalion. His commanders must sometimes have wished for a whole unit of his cohorts from the streets of the Lower East Side. Men like Monk, Gyp the Blood, Kid Twist, and Crazy Butch might even have frightened their own officers on occasions, but they would certainly have terrified the enemy.

14

THE NIAGARA OF SHELLS

O n July 23, the 106th Infantry began a two-day march back to the front lines. In the early hours of July 25, carrying only light battle packs and no blankets or pup tents, but laden with ammunition and equipment, they entered the trenches. In pitch darkness, led by a trench guide, they sloshed through the mud "over dismal wastes and trails made slippery by constant rains." There was no smoking or talking, and they followed one another at five-pace intervals, keeping their eyes fixed on the man ahead to avoid getting lost in the darkness.

It was just as they had trained to do at Camp Wadsworth, but now they did so to the accompaniment of the ceaseless roar of shell fire, the crash of trench mortars, and the crack and whine of rifle bullets, while their nostrils were filled with the stench that told of the unseen, half-buried dead all around them. There was a constant stream of casualties, one of the first, Private Isadore Cohen of Monk's Company G, suffering a severe shrapnel wound in his right arm. At Hallebast Corner and again at La Clytte, the shelling was continuous, and they had to take their chances and run in ones and twos through the showers of shells.

Monk and the rest of the 106th Infantry entered the reserve line at 4:20 that morning, with Mount Kemmel "looming up like the rock of Gibraltar on our right, while the shell-torn aspect of Ypres and the famous Passchendaele Ridge could be seen to the left." During their spring offensive, the Germans had dislodged the British from Mount Kemmel and Wytschaete Ridge, positions of great strategic value, and the Allied lines were now under close observation from there and subjected to artillery fire by day and night, inflicting a daily toll of casualties. In case any American troops had failed to realize it, orders reminded them that whenever they could see Mount Kemmel, the Germans could see them, and it was essential to use every scrap of cover when moving to or from the front lines. Although Monk and his fellows had experienced plenty of sporadic shelling before, this was their first taste of concentrated artillery and trench-mortar fire. It was an unnerving experience for all. Because the front line here was a salient—a tongue of Allied-held territory, surrounded on three sides by German positions—shells rained in from almost every direction, and men in the firing line often believed that they were being shelled by their own artillery when the firing was actually from enemy guns on the flanks or even in the rear.

The Second Battalion had remained in the reserve lines while their comrades took their first ten-day turn in the firing line, but at 9:15 on the night of August 2, along with the rest of the Second Battalion, Monk and his fellows in Company G received the orders "Action East Pop Line." They at once moved forward, accompanied by one limber carrying each company's ammunition and water. They brushed shoulders with the soldiers they were relieving—men gray with fatigue who did not even raise their eyes to acknowledge them as they passed—and as the Americans slipped and slithered through the mud, they had their first encounters with the omnipresent dead, stumbling over a body or a skeletal limb protruding from the floor of the trench like a tree root in a dark forest. As they approached the firing line, their progress was even slower. Every few minutes the Germans fired off a Very light and the Americans either "stood stock-still with our heads bent down so as not to expose our faces, or fell to the ground and froze, if there was time, until the light burned out."

The Second Battalion reached the front lines just before midnight, deploying behind the Wippenhoek Line, with two companies in the line and two in reserve. During their first days and nights in the firing line they were attached to the 18th Brigade of the 6th British Division. Working parties were formed every night from those in reserve to build shelters and dugouts, install rifle pits, and lay lines of cables. Like all fresh arrivals, the men in the firing line were also put on immediate sentry duty, to familiarize them with their surroundings and accustom them to being under fire. One sentry was permanently on watch, facing forward. "They do not turn about when spoken to by an officer or anyone, but answer the questions asked and still keep looking constantly to the front."

Spies were said to be a constant and real danger, and sentries were warned to arrest and turn over to their officers any strange officers or soldiers, regardless of their uniforms, if they did not show a proper written pass or identification card or give the password of the day. Sentries were relieved every two hours by day and every hour at night, when the strain of staring into the darkness could quickly play tricks on the eye and mind. Those awaiting their turn on sentry duty were permitted to sleep but kept their rifles close by, and for an hour around dawn and dusk there was a stand-to when "all men should be at their posts." Not all of them had to man the fire step, but all had to stand by.

The morning stand-down came when full daylight was reached. Monk and his comrades then had to clean their small arms, ammunition, and grenades to remove any trace of dirt, mud, or rust before the morning inspection by platoon leaders, who checked the dugouts, trenches, gun emplacements, latrines, and their men's arms, ammunition, and gas masks, and also the disposal of trash and human refuse. This was not simply a matter of hygiene. If even small quantities of empty cans, wastepaper, and other trash were allowed to accumulate, they could provide a reference point for enemy shell fire. Empty bags for trash were placed near every dugout, and the waste was then dumped in a shell hole and covered with earth if necessary, though there were plenty of shell holes with enough water to cover the refuse. Latrines were another serious problem. Sometimes it was possible to dig a latrine trench, and buckets were also used, but more often, especially in the front line during the daylight hours, men were "compelled to urinate or defecate almost in the exact spot where they must stay until darkness. The best that can be done in this regard is to clean up and disinfect thoroughly at night."

While on the front lines, Monk and his comrades huddled in trenches, dugouts, foxholes, or saps—short trenches used as forward observation posts, roofed with "elephant iron" (corrugated iron) and camouflaged with bags or burlap painted to match the surrounding ground. Pieces of turf, stones, dirt, small plants, and bushes were also added to make the cover look as natural as possible. The saps were barely wide enough for a man to enter, and only long enough for two men if they sat with their legs drawn up. Many of the American troops were almost paralyzed by fear. One sat with his back against the end of the foxhole, his legs pulled up under his chin and his arms and hands "clamped like a vise" around his shins. His whole body went into a muscle spasm. "I shook, I trembled, my teeth chattered. I was enveloped in a tremendous fear. I was beyond any ability to exert muscular control. The noise was deafening as the Niagara of shells, bullets and stones descended upon us . . . I tried to speak but I could not form any words, nor would a sound emerge from my mouth." As the fear abated, it was replaced by fury. "This kind of warfare in the filth and muck of the trenches (like a lot of woodchucks or rats) . . . This was no way to fight a war. It was un-American. Why don't we get out in the open and slug it out the way two men do?"

General O'Ryan made an inspection of the First Battalion of the 106th on August 2, 1918, immediately after they had been relieved by the Second Battalion, and fired off a complaint that what he saw was very unsatisfactory. Rifles were not cleaned, a Lewis gun was very rusty, and others were in little better condition. Many men, including some officers, were unshaven, a very serious issue; a daily shave was a military order because gas masks did not fit tightly to the faces of bearded or unshaven men, with the consequent danger of gas seeping around the edges of the mask. There were also complaints about the state of the men's clothing and boots, though in trenches that were often inches or feet deep in mud and water, that was scarcely surprising.

These new arrivals on the front lines, lacking the acquired knowledge and survival instincts of more experienced soldiers, often suffered a disproportionate number of losses, and casualty reports were now a part of the 106th's daily ritual. On August 4, two men from Monk's Company G, Private Errol K. Price and Private George Beliuk, were reported as missing, and the company's second lieutenant Frank P. Ulrich was wounded in the jaw by shrapnel. Three other men were also wounded. A battalion commander of the 106th Infantry stated that the casualties were unavoidable except for two, which were due to carelessness—one of them, Private John Foster, shot off the middle finger of his left hand while cleaning his rifle. Such accidents were always closely scrutinized, for some men deliberately wounded themselves in the hope of escaping the front lines and returning home. Enough cases of self-inflicted wounds occurred to suggest at the least "a surprising lack of care in the handling of rifles and pistols." Orders were given that every involuntary discharge of a weapon was to be assumed to be caused by carelessness and would inevitably lead to trial by court-martial. Any soldier convicted of willful self-wounding was to be sentenced to hard labor, to be served in "the most dangerous places where soldiers are required to perform labor": the front lines and No Man's Land. If the soldier had wounded himself too badly to serve his sentence at the front, he would instead receive a long jail term. Soldiers convicted of deliberate self-wounding were also forced to wear a brassard bearing the initials S.I.W. (Self-Inflicted Wound).

There was never any danger of Monk wearing such a brassard. Despite his age, he was always the first to volunteer or put himself in the line of fire. Herbert Asbury, also serving with the A.E.F., dismissively remarked that "the gangster invariably became a first-rate soldier, for his imagination was seldom equal to the task of envisioning either himself or his victim experiencing any considerable suffering from the shock of a bullet or the slash of a knife," but there was much more to Monk's bravery than that. The same determination that had raised him from a lowly dance-hall bouncer to the leadership of "the toughest gang of 'gorillas' that ever swaggered along the Bowery, kept him in the forefront of the battle" and he was praised by his commander for his bravery under fire. Bullets didn't bother the man who had acted as a forward fire controller in the Battle of Rivington Street beneath the Allen Street arches a dozen years earlier. As bullets flew around him at Kemmel Hill, Monk coolly directed fire. "When his comrades asked him what he thought of the war, he curled his lip and said he had fought the battle of New York," and afterward he was heard to say that "there were lots of dance halls in the Bowery tougher than that so-called 'Great War' of theirs."

However, the slow attrition of daily life in the trenches—the steady trickle of deaths from shrapnel, trench mortars, and sniper fire—was now whittling away at the men who had been Monk's constant companions for almost a year. One minute they were there, vital young men honed by months of training and outdoor living, and the next they were gone, just another khaki bundle of rags awaiting burial. The 27th Division's own ambulance companies and field hospitals were not sufficient to deal with the casualties, and they were often treated by British medical personnel; units of the East Lancashire field ambulances aided them throughout their time at East Poperinghe and Dickebusch Lake.

After a week of operating under the wing of the British, the Second Battalion of the 106th Infantry was left alone in the firing line for the first time on the night of August 10, 1918. While he was on the front lines, Monk's horizons were limited to the trench and the narrow slit of sky directly overhead. "How far above us it seemed . . . like a narrow, blue-black band of velvet ribbon, it was, studded by ten million stars." To raise his head even for a second would invite a bullet from one of the ever-alert German snipers, and, like all frontline soldiers, he had to come to terms with the paradox that, unless an attack was ordered, although he was no more than a hundred yards from the enemy, he might go weeks without seeing a German soldier at all.

On some nights he was ordered forward after dark to take his turn in a sap out in No Man's Land, observing the German lines. Keeping low to avoid being outlined against the night sky, he and his fellows rolled over the top of the trench wall and then crawled from shell hole to shell hole until they reached the cramped sap. There they would remain for twenty-four hours, through the cold of night and the burning heat of the day, before being relieved the following night. There was no room even to straighten their legs, and any stretching or movement might be their last; in No Man's Land movement meant death. Yet even here, in a dirt hole between the lines, each man shaved using his razor and a mug of his precious drinking water, to ensure that his gas mask would fit tightly to his face; if it did not, he would be dead in a gas attack.

Their overcoats were welcome during the night, but the sun beating down on their cramped quarters made the daytime conditions almost unbearable. They sweated "until we could feel the clammy dampness of our heavy underwear. We stunk because we were dirty." When they had emptied their water cans, they made use of them as latrines, and the stench compounded their misery. When finally relieved after dark, they could barely crawl out of their sap.

The men of the Second Battalion spent a torrid ten-day tour of duty, with Monk's Company G holding the hottest section of the line, and they suffered heavy losses before being relieved by British troops, the King's Shropshire Light Infantry, on the night of August 12. The men of the 106th then withdrew to Abeele Station to rest, Company G arriving there at 12:45 a.m. Reliefs were always carried out in secrecy, and infantry were not informed of the timing until shortly beforehand, but, as one British officer wryly observed, while the infantrymen might not know anything about their relief, every girl in the estaminets in the district would already have complete information about it.

While the Second Battalion had been on the front lines, King George V of England had inspected the rest of the 27th Division in the reserve areas. Reflecting the deep-seated hostility that still soured relations between the long-standing rivals who were now allies, the American troops paraded without their weapons because of British fears of an assassination attempt. A few days later, a further inspection was made by the United States General Read, who left disappointed, feeling the American troops were still defective in map-reading, scouting, patrolling, and rifle and hand-grenade practice.

There were also perennial complaints about lack of discipline in the 106th Infantry. The commanding officer of Monk's battalion noted that discipline might have been better had his men been paid since their arrival in France, and when challenged about their lack of "smartness in dress and manners," he testily pointed out that they had just emerged from a torrid spell on the front lines.

Indifference to basic hygiene was a concern, though it could not always be blamed on the men of the 106th. The commander of the Third Battalion listed some of the problems they had encountered on arrival at a farm site where they were billeted. The previous occupants had left fly-infested burlap bags full of rotten meat lying around, and an open pit in the backyard was two-thirds full of stinking ration tins, decomposing rabbit carcasses, bread, bacon rinds, potato peelings, and other food waste, all swarming with flies. The corrugated-iron latrine was left full to overflowing, and the American officers who had previously occupied the building had urinated on the floor of their quarters—"evidence plainly remained."

While Monk and his fellows alternated between further training and spells of duty on the lines, their wives, friends, and relatives at home, including Worthy, waiting in Presidio, Texas, had no idea whether their men were in action or in reserve, nor even whether they had yet deployed to the battle zone at all. Letters home were censored, and any more specific information than "somewhere in France" was crossed out in thick black ink. Relatives had to decipher what clues were offered in the censored news and propaganda that was published in the papers, or in the telegrams advising of deaths or wounds in action that were now arriving with increasing frequency at New York and Brooklyn addresses.

Between August 9 and 20, the three battalions of the 106th Infantry in turn had occupied the lines at East Poperinghe, and in that time they suffered steady losses that had already begun to seem routine. Twenty-six men were killed in action or dead of wounds, a further seventy-four men were wounded, and six more were gassed. Like the British, whose resignation, cynicism, and lack of ambition had so shocked them only weeks before, perhaps some of these American soldiers were now also coming to regard whether they lived or died as a whim of fate beyond their control. Had General O'Ryan himself not acknowledged in a bulletin issued as they prepared to enter the lines for the first time that "losses will result at times and in particular places from rashness, from timidity; from over confidence, from lack of confidence; from the exercise of good judgment as well as poor judgment"? What was that if not a reflection of the old soldier's fatalistic belief that "if a bullet's got your name on it . . . "?

O'Ryan had also noted that the most effective and valuable officers in peacetime sometimes disintegrated under the stress of battle, while others who had seemed mediocre in garrison or camp became real leaders in war. His comments must have resonated as the 106th Infantry's first frontline experience led to a series of changes among the NCOs. On August 19, even while they were still serving at the front, one corporal from Monk's Company G had been demoted, and two days later, immediately after they came out of the lines, another three corporals of Company G were reduced to the ranks and a private and three privates first class promoted in their place. Other companies of the regiment saw similar changes; no explanation was recorded for the demotions.

Whatever the merits or demerits of his NCOs and fellow soldiers, Private First Class Edward "Monk" Eastman's appetite for combat was undiminished by his early experiences on the front line. Determined not to "miss any of the big doings at the front," he had even insisted on remaining on the front line when his company was relieved. As his comrades made way for another company, Monk refused to leave. He first applied for transfer from the 106th Infantry to the Machine Gun Battalion, in order to stay in action, and when that was refused he approached the regimental surgeon, Major Larsen, and asked permission to remain with the relieving troops as a stretcher-bearer. Larsen agreed, and when his company withdrew to rest in the reserve areas, Monk stayed on duty in the frontline trenches and made constant forays into No Man's Land to rescue wounded men and carry them back to the dressing stations in the rear.

One wounded soldier offered Monk a fat cigar for helping him get to a field hospital. When Monk asked him: "Youse get this from a Boche?" The soldier said, "No, I was in Lieutenant Herbert Asbury's platoon on the Vesle front. He is like you, cares about us doughboys! A guy from the Y.M.C.A. came to La Pres Farm laden with boxes of cigars and wanted ten cents for each cigar. We had no money because the platoon had not been paid in months and Asbury asked the guy to give the cigars to the soldiers and look to Heaven for payment. When the guy refused, Asbury took his cigars away and kicked him in the pants. We all got two cigars, I saved one." It was a strange quirk of fate that Asbury should have made that unwitting, indirect gift to a man who ten years later would feature in the defining book of Asbury's literary career: *The Gangs of New York*.

On the night of August 22, the Second Battalion of the 106th marched back to the front lines. There were further casualties as they moved up. One man was wounded in a bizarre incident, accidentally shot when cartridges among a pile of blazing rubbish exploded, and the following night, August 23, Corporal John A. Kiernan of Company G was killed by shell fire as, rejoined by Monk, they reentered the lines at Dickebusch Lake. The British 6th Division withdrew that night, leaving the American 27th Division on its own on the front lines for the first time. If it was in part a reflection of the exhaustion of British troops involved in near-continuous fighting since March, it was also an acknowledgment of the growing confidence and competence of the "doughboys" who were shouldering the burden. The relief was completed by 10:40 that night, with the First and Third Battalions of the 106th in support in concealed trenches and the Second Battalion in reserve at Micmac and Hecla farms.

The German forces under the command of Prince Rupprecht of

Bavaria were expected to launch an assault at any moment, aiming to smash through the Allied lines and seize the Channel ports through which virtually all British men and war matériel were shipped. It was felt that the battered and depleted British troops holding the front line would be unable to withstand the shock of such an assault, and the 27th Division had been drafted in to hold the line at all costs, fighting in "this God-forsaken ground of shell holes and churned up earth, with its putrescent odors of death." The men rested by day, but between 9:00 p.m. and 3:00 a.m. each night they worked to repair and improve the defenses along the Dickebusch Lake–Scherpenberg Line.

With their comrades from the 27th Division, the 106th Infantry held the position for the next nine days despite heavy shelling with high explosive and mustard gas, which caused sixty-five casualties from burns. On August 24, Private Thomas F. Flood had his right arm blown off by an enemy incendiary bomb, losing a large quantity of blood, but his life was saved when one of his comrades in Company G—unnamed in accounts of the incident—volunteered to give two pints of his blood for a transfusion.

A succession of particularly virulent gas attacks was launched on successive mornings on August 26 and 27, and as the 106th Infantry's shelters were under enemy observation, they were unable to evacuate them. In one attack gas shells fell directly into the trench, catching the men by surprise, and some severe burns were suffered when mustard oil splashed on their thin clothing. Another group of a dozen men were also burned after walking through long grass and falling in a shell hole contaminated with mustard gas. To neutralize the gas residue, the shell holes were filled with earth and the contaminated ground and the clothing and skin of men affected by the gas were sprinkled with chloride of lime.

After the German forces suffered a defeat farther south, at Château-Thierry, information from prisoners and captured documents revealed that plans for the drive to the sea to seize the Channel ports had now been abandoned and the threat of a major German attack had evaporated. Plans for the 27th Division were accordingly changed and it was now tasked with capturing Mount Kemmel, the scene of some of the bloodiest battles of the war, which had seen it change hands numerous times. British veterans were astonished that the task of attacking it should have been assigned to such a "green" and untried unit.

During their training for the assault, the men of the 106th Infantry were issued a document titled "Principles and Methods to Govern Offensive Action." It included the surprising claim that "when immediate contact is obtained, the enemy will surrender. The best investigation the Division Commander [O'Ryan] has been able to make is that this statement is correct." It went on to cite the experience of the U.S. Marine Corps at Château-Thierry, where it was claimed that the losses they suffered were the result of poor precautions against gas attacks and poor tactics when crossing open ground to engage German troops; "when they got within fifty yards of enemy troops, the latter surrendered without fighting." It is impossible to say how Monk and his fellows weighed that optimistic view against the contradictory information that was also circulated among them stating that, in an earlier battle, the German machine gunners "appear to have been chained to their positions." The implication of that was clear: the Germans would be unable to withdraw or run away and would therefore fight to the death to save their own lives.

MORE THAN BROTHERS

After a week in the reserve trenches, the 106th Infantry began to move forward into the firing line on the evening of August 30, ready for the attack to be launched the next morning. They passed over shell-torn roads, jammed with vehicles and columns of men heading for the front lines, while streams of bedraggled, hollow-eyed men shuffled in the opposite direction. German aircraft bombed the advancing troops and long-range guns continued to rain down shells around them, but the 106th moved on, past Indus Farm and around the bend of the lake, where the "murky sheet of water seemed as silent as death itself. Not even a bullfrog croaked from its depths." They passed an advanced dressing station at Trappest Farm and a casualty clearing station at Esquellec, both reminders of the fate that awaited some of the men moving forward on that late summer night.

On this, the last night before their first taste of an actual attack, despite all his previous "battlefield" experience on the streets of New York, even Monk must have felt the same mixture of curiosity, excitement, fear, and regret as his comrades, together with the closeness, sometimes beyond even that shared with their families, that men felt toward their buddies in the face of war and death. As one of his fellows in that polyglot division wrote that night,

> Tonight we are more than brothers, for tomorrow may see things, and we know that shrapnel and bullets are absolutely unconscious of ancestry or creed, occupation or nationality. Among others we have Greek, Slav, Spanish, English, Swiss, the ever-present and irrepressible Irish, Italian and a descendant of an American Indian. We have Episcopalian, Methodist, Jew, Catholic, &c, but I feel sure we have tonight no atheist—nor will have until this is over.

A contact patrol of six riflemen and one Lewis-gun team of six men was sent out at once to locate the enemy. Before going out, they were stripped of all personal papers, letters, identity discs, regimental buttons, and numbers. They were also checked to ensure that there was nothing loose on them that might make a noise, because the least sound in No Man's Land—even as faint as the scrape of a belt buckle against a gun barrel or the tinny rattle of a strand of barbed wire against a bayonet—could be fatal. The patrols, usually consisting of an NCO and five men, had been taught not to lift their heads, but just to keep one eye looking ahead as they crawled forward a few yards apart, keeping their heads as close to the ground as possible and using their toes, knees, and elbows to push themselves along. Moving virtually inch by inch, they took advantage of any gunfire or other noises from the trenches to cover the sounds of their movement, and at times, fearing detection, they remained motionless for minutes on end.

If the Germans put up a single Very light, the patrol would remain motionless until it had burned out and then move on again. More than one light put up close to the patrol was usually a sign that the Germans had heard a noise or seen some suspicious movement. The advice then was to keep quiet for half an hour before moving ahead again. Even if standing upright when a Very light was fired, patrol members ran virtually no risk of discovery if they turned their faces away from the light and stood perfectly still. They were told that they could lie down if they wished, but it wasn't necessary, and might prove fatal if the movement caught the eye of a German sniper or machine gunner.

Company I had been ordered to move up behind the patrol and occupy Macaw Trench, but were forced to withdraw again almost at once when a breakdown in communications led their own artillery to target the trench for more than two hours. This also provoked heavy return fire from the enemy, which fell on the same trench. The shelling caused carnage among Company I—a lieutenant and thirty men became casualties—but what was left of the company still managed to form a defensive line and advanced by degrees during the night to reoccupy Macaw Trench, with Company G ranged alongside them on their right.

The Germans had been expected to fight to the death to defend Mount Kemmel, but the returning patrols reported that they had detected no signs of the enemy, and frontline companies also reported unusual quiet from the German lines during the night. This backed up intelligence from prisoners and intercepted communications suggesting that the Germans had suspected American forces were being massed and had begun withdrawing their forces to a more defensible line at Wytschaete Ridge. The fires burning all the way from Armentières to within six miles of Lille and in the Bertincourt region, between Bapaume and the Hindenburg Line, were further confirmation, as the Germans destroyed stores they could not take with them, a certain indication of an imminent retreat.

The Germans left machine-gun crews and snipers behind to hold the ground as long as possible. A prisoner interrogated early on August 31 believed that Kemmel Hill was already evacuated except by these screens of machine guns, and the whole terrain also remained subject to relentless German artillery fire. The machine-gun nests and sniping posts had tunnels leading to them and were camouflaged with turf and tall grass. The snipers wore different camouflage suits to blend with their surroundings, and concealed themselves in different hides. One sniper was spotted using a small pit hidden by some weeds, where he would drop after firing; another was hidden in the branches of a stunted willow.

American company commanders were informed of the German withdrawal and told to be ready to move forward at a moment's notice. Strong combat patrols were sent out to make and maintain contact with the enemy, taking with them men specially trained to seek out mines and booby traps. The main advance began at 11:30 that morning—perhaps in the hope of confusing the enemy, used to attacks launched at first light—but the Allied barrage was answered at once by the German artillery, which poured a torrent of gas and high-explosive shells onto the entire length of the front line, following it with trench mortars and machine-gun fire. In the face of this barrage, the 105th Infantry suffered heavy casualties but silenced a number of enemy heavy machine guns and advanced up the lower slope in bitter hand-to-hand fighting.

The 106th then took up the assault. The Third Battalion led the way, with the First Battalion in support, and although the Second Battalion was held in reserve, Monk's Company G was sent forward with the First Battalion in place of Company A, which had been heavily gassed, suffering such extensive casualties that it was too depleted to fulfill its part in the advance. Tasked with occupying Vierstraat Switch, the men of the 106th battled their way toward enemy machine guns sited in heavy brush about two hundred yards in front of them. Aided by Company G, the First Battalion reached their objective on the left of the advance, but the right flank was held up for some time by fierce fire from concealed machine-gun nests near Siege Farm, west of Vierstraat Switch, in which a further 15 men were killed, 53 wounded, and 106 gassed. However, the enemy machine guns were eventually eliminated with bombs and grenades, and the American troops then moved forward, crossing Cheapside and York roads. Although the intermediate ground still held many machine-gun nests and snipers, by five o'clock that afternoon the Americans were consolidating their lines along Vierstraat Ridge. They had suffered many casualties, but inflicted far more on the enemy.

At seven the next morning, September 1, 1918, the American attack resumed, with the 106th in the van, pushing forward past Dead Dog Farm as they attempted to force the enemy rearguard back from its last positions on the eastern slopes of Vierstraat Ridge and Mount Kemmel. The main body of German troops was meanwhile completing the retreat to Wytschaete Ridge, dominating the valley and the lower slopes over which the American troops would have to advance. They moved from shell hole to shell hole and across abandoned trenches, but concealed nests of enemy snipers and machine guns still studded the valley floor and lower slopes, and there was great confusion on the left flank as two battalions of the 106th became badly mixed up.

When the regimental commander, Colonel Taylor, went forward to investigate, he reported that Major Hildreth, commanding the Third Battalion, had "entirely lost control and seemed at a loss as to what to do." He relieved Hildreth of his command at once. Astonishingly, Hildreth was merely reprimanded and was restored to his position as battalion commander a few days later, though this must have been a reflection more of the regiment's desperate and rapidly worsening shortage of officers than of any confidence in his abilities.

At nightfall, the commanding officer of Company G reported that his men had suffered heavy casualties during the day, including the loss of nearly all their NCOs. He added that his men were "worn out and unfit for further service." Nonetheless, they were required to resume the advance the next morning. Reports were also received that a number of patrols were still out in front. Their locations were unknown, and as a result, it was impossible to put down a further barrage for fear of hitting them. During the night, replacement supplies of water, food, and ammunition were brought forward to the troops, much of the food carried in burlap bags, but the firing line remained restless, and at 4:00 a.m., when the 105th Infantry began to move forward on the left flank of the 106th, a heavy German barrage came down on the whole line.

During that night of September 1 through 2, Major Sidney G. de Kay, newly assigned to the 106th, had taken over command of the Second Battalion from its temporary commander, Captain Hetzel. As he took stock of the four companies under his new command, he found a somewhat dispiriting picture. Company E was somewhere on the south flank of the advance, though its exact location was unknown. Company G was in a trench, Company F was in shell holes, and the men of Company H were bringing up rations and ammunition.

De Kay eventually located Company E in a section of trench. They were under constant machine-gun and sniper fire, had been so heavily shelled that they had lost many of their noncommissioned officers, and had wounded men with them whom they were unable to evacuate. De Kay's orders were still to advance but, owing to the exhaustion of these and the other men under his command, and the heavy shell, shell-gas, machine-gun, and sniper fire, he resolved to continue the advance in small combat groups with automatic rifles and hand grenades, along each side of the sunken Vierstraat road toward the railroad track, where he could attempt to reorganize his men.

At 6:00 a.m. on September 2, Major de Kay met the commander of H Company, First Lieutenant Lennox C. Brennan, on the firing line and ordered him to go over the top and push forward with his company for a thousand yards to the railroad track, then pause and reorganize before advancing a further eight hundred yards to their objective, a line from Purgatory to Northern Brickstack on the shoulder of Wytschaete Ridge. When Brennan asked upon whose authority de Kay was issuing these orders, he was told that the battalion had been "sorted out" and de Kay had been placed in command.

There had been no artillery preparation, nor was any covering barrage planned, and when Brennan told de Kay that a creeping barrage was essential if their men were to achieve their objectives, he was waved away: de Kay told him that there would be no barrage and no request for covering fire; they were late and had to push forward at once. The exhausted 106th resumed their advance alongside the 105th, but suffered losses as soon as they went over. Although they had advanced some way up Chinese Trench by 11:30 that morning, they were halted by heavy machine-gun fire. The enemy positions were too strongly held for them to advance farther. While his men dug in, Brennan moved forward to survey the ground between them and their objective. He concluded that there was no good line of defense at the designated objective and tried to impress upon Major de Kay the folly of moving the line from a defensible position into a valley where there was no field of fire and where they would be a sitting target for the German machine guns. This argument took place not in some debating chamber, but in a frontline trench with shell, shot, and shrapnel filling the air around them.

Brennan was sent back to brief officers at regimental headquarters, where he discovered that the Third Battalion had also been "sorted out," with Captain Sullivan taking over command at 8:50 that morning. The regimental commander phoned the brigade commander at noon requesting permission to dig in on the line of the first objective and await relief there, but permission was refused. Ordered to advance, his men finally occupied part of Chinese Trench and even advanced a little beyond it.

De Kay and Captain Sullivan were now both claiming that it would be impossible to reach the objective; their units were seriously depleted by casualties, and the remaining men were exhausted and desperate for water and rations. However, Brennan, who had previously been urging caution, now told the regimental commander that with thorough artillery preparation and support he could reach and consolidate the objective line and clean up the intervening terrain. He was promptly given direct command of all that remained of the Second and Third Battalions and told to justify his claims.

At zero hour—five o'clock that afternoon—a barrage was to be laid along the entire regimental front, with particularly intense fire on the Purgatory–Northern Brickstack section. Five minutes later the barrage would lift and creep forward, allowing the troops to advance. The barrage would continue on the enemy positions for a further hour, by which time the objective should have been taken and consolidated. Monk and his comrades in G Company were to engage and destroy the machine guns in the Purgatory–Northern Brickstack pocket while the remaining companies advanced on the objective.

The men were all in their start positions at 4:45 p.m. Zero hour passed without any sign of the promised barrage; instead, at 5:15 p.m., a German barrage of high explosive and gas fell on them, so heavy it was almost impossible to move forward. Led by Lieutenant Archer, the men of Company G made progress during lulls in the shelling. Although "the rattle of the gang fighter's automatic is only the faintest echo of the roar of battle," Monk reveled in the fighting and close combat, setting the lead for his company as he had once done for his gang. "Crouched in a dugout while the barrage thundered above or creeping forward under machine gun fire," Monk was "always cool and courageous."

One of the most effective grenade throwers in the regiment, he spearheaded his company's attacks and personally destroyed several machine-gun nests. Belly-crawling through the mud under constant shell and machine-gun fire, he wormed his way forward using any cover—battlefield debris, craters, shell holes, even the bodies of the dead—until he was within range, and then threw his grenades with an outfielder's power and accuracy. If any of the German gun crew survived the blast, they were likely to be dispatched by Monk's bayonet.

Even though he was wounded in his left leg and right hand, Monk refused to seek treatment, remaining with his company at the heart of the fighting. One soldier recalled the shot of being hit as "a sharp pain when you are hit, and a shock that leaves you faint. This lasts about fifteen minutes, then the pain is gone, but a raging thirst sets in. I guess I smoked at least a dozen cigarettes in about twenty minutes." To Monk, a man who had been gutshot, scarred, and nicked innumerable times during his gangland career, the wounds would have been less of a shock.

While Company G was still battling to wipe out the machine-gun nests that were wreaking such havoc among the attackers, Brennan's cobbled-together command advanced in small groups. Each move drew further shell fire, on one occasion so heavy that they were unable to move for more than an hour. They eventually completed the occupation of Chinese Trench in the face of a heavy bombardment from Wytschaete Ridge, but stragglers turning back from G Company reported that they had suffered very heavy casualties and were being driven back. The blizzard of shells and machine-gun fire eventually forced Lieutenant Archer to order a withdrawal. The mopping-up companies then withdrew to the old Vierstraat line, where they could get some shelter, while the remainder of the troops held position and awaited nightfall. As Company G began to withdraw, despite his wounds and in full view of the enemy guns, Monk crawled to a dugout under enemy fire to help one of his fallen comrades—Sergeant Francis X. "Hank" Miller—back to the lines. " 'The Monk' was wounded," Miller later said. "He saw me fall with a bullet through my right shoulder. He crawled to me, picked me up and carried me to the rear. He saved my life."

After dark the men of E, F, and G companies fell back to the positions they had held that morning. Company H soon also withdrew, but the four companies of the First Battalion remained dug in, occupying a line along the railway at the foot of Wytschaete Ridge despite heavy barrages by artillery and machine guns. All the companies of the 106th were relieved by British troops during the course of that night. Major de Kay noted regretfully, though not without some satisfaction, that "the command I took charge of was worn out in forty-eight hours of the heaviest kind of work, during which time they had suffered heavy casualties and had been compelled to get little or no food, but the men responded to the call to go forward and continued to endeavor to clean up the machine gun nests and attack vigorously until absolutely stopped by machine gun fire."

Although the bravery of Monk and his fellow soldiers was not in doubt, de Kay admitted there had been confusion, even chaos, between the line officers, battalions, and companies of the regiment during the fighting around Vierstraat and Wytschaete ridges. While conceding that liaison between companies and battalions had been very poor, however, he blamed the difficulties in mopping up the German machine-gun nests on the fact that their organized plan of cross fire had been very little disrupted by American artillery.

The impact of that cross fire was shown in the casualty figures. During the action around Vierstraat and Wytschaete ridges, of the four companies of the Second Battalion, Company E had lost seven sergeants, nine corporals, and thirty-three privates; Company F lost one sergeant, four corporals, and twenty privates; Company G—the worst affected—lost one officer, one first sergeant, five sergeants, and thirty-eight privates; and Company H lost one sergeant, five corporals, and twenty-nine privates. A first sergeant of Company K and several other noncommissioned officers and runners were also killed when one of two concrete and brick pillboxes being used as a forward battalion headquarters was blown up by a delayed-action mine. The roof of the pillbox was a one-foot slab of concrete, covered by railroad iron, which in turn was covered by another one-foot slab of concrete, and about a foot of earth and grass on top of that. In the terrific explosion of the mine, the roof collapsed and all the occupants were instantly crushed.

Losses in the other battalions were not quite as severe as in the Second Battalion, nonetheless, in the regiment as a whole, 47 men had been killed, 267 wounded, and 41 gassed, and 7 more were missing in action and another 5 captured by the enemy. That casualty rate was equal to one-tenth of the original strength of the entire regiment when it disembarked in France, even before the steady attrition from gas, shell fire, shrapnel, sniper rifle, and machine gun had begun to whittle away its numbers. The dead—or those who could be found among the carnage of the battlefield—were buried in rows in a graveyard at Abeele, Belgium, the first of their countrymen to fight and die "in Flanders Fields." Strangely, it was among the duties of the regiment's mechanics to prepare the dead for burial, though after such losses, many others were compelled to lend a hand.

The surviving men of the 106th Infantry had come through their ferocious baptism of artillery, rifle, and machine-gun fire. They had taken Vierstraat Ridge, pushed their lines forward more than a mile in the face of ferocious opposition, and only their mounting level of casualties had prevented them from taking and holding their final objective. However, while they and the men of the other American regiments had undoubtedly been brave fighters, their losses had been heavier than necessary. A German officer reported that these still inexperienced American troops did not yet comprehend "how to utilize the terrain in movement, work their way forward during an attack, or choose the correct formation in the event the enemy opens artillery fire." Much of the blame for that had to be laid at the door of their officers, and Major Hildreth was only one of those whose abilities had been under question even before the 106th Infantry had embarked for France. First Lieutenant Fred E. Mayor and Second Lieutenants Lucius H. Doty and Harold deLoiselle had been reported to the inspector general as "professionally unfitted to hold their positions in the military service," yet they nonetheless embarked with their men. The commanding officer, Colonel William A. Taylor, reversed his opinion about deLoiselle after the regiment had been in France for a few weeks, and he was later cited for gallantry in action. However, Lieutenant Mayor failed to win the endorsement of his commander, and Colonel Taylor noted that, though Lieutenant Doty was "studious and takes a very good book examination," his battalion commander rated him as "having no qualities of leadership and states that his work as Company Commander . . . is unsatisfactory. Physically he would not rate above 6 [out of ten]." It was another vivid reflection of the paucity of good officers that, despite the withering assessment of his capabilities, First Lieutenant Doty had remained as second-in-command of Company G.

After the battle, the wounded Monk had been taken to a casualty clearing station and then to a British field hospital. The 27th Division's medical facilities were still insufficient to cope with the level of casualties they were experiencing, and once more, British, Australian, and Canadian units filled the gap. Monk would have empathized with the soldier who noted that when they cut off his clothes in the hospital, it was the first time he had removed his shoes in a month.

While his wounds were being treated, it was discovered that Monk had also been gassed, but had said nothing about it until then. Chlorine-gas casualties were particularly alarming. Fluid and blood filling the lungs would pour out of the casualty's mouth, and his efforts to breathe were distressing to watch, let alone experience. The treatment required the victim to lie facedown with his feet at least twelve inches above his head, to allow the lungs to drain. Afterward, if the victim was still alive, the advice was to keep him warm and avoid giving him alcohol or morphine, both of which slowed respiration. If he could be kept alive for two days he would recover, but the recovery was only partial. The effects of chlorine gas were permanent, damaging the lining of the lungs, and victims were never 100 percent healthy again.

Gas patients were all stretcher cases because any exertion increased the damaging effects of the gas and could prove fatal. Military regulations required a gas victim to be stretchered from the battlefield and kept in the hospital for a week for observation, but Monk had other plans. His crude speech, rough manners, and bruiser's appearance would not have endeared him to British officers and, in turn, he must have chafed at their rigid adherence to formalities, regulations and military etiquette, and a class consciousness that sometimes bordered on contempt. He had been in the field hospital only three days when he heard that the 106th Infantry was about to go back to the front lines. "Wanting to be in on the big show," without notifying the surgeon or even an orderly, he slipped away from the field hospital, still wearing his pajamas.

Confused, traumatized soldiers, often suffering from shell shock, were not an unknown sight near field hospitals in the rear areas, and no one tried to detain Monk as he made his escape. Pausing only at a salvage dump, where he exchanged his hospital clothing for a uniform and a pair of boots that roughly approximated to his size, Monk headed east, toward the angry rumble of the guns. Bandaged, unarmed, and still only partly equipped, he eventually made his way back to his unit. By leaving the field hospital without permission, he had made himself technically absent without leave, but none of his officers were ever likely to have punished him for a breach of discipline motivated solely by his desire to rejoin his unit in the firing lines, and when the 106th Infantry went over, Monk was with them.

16

THE MEN MUST GO FORWARD

During the night of September 2 through 3, the exhausted troops of the 106th had been relieved by the British 122nd Infantry. They trudged back across the Franco-Belgian border, leaving their billets at Micmac Farm at 1:30 a.m. and marching to Napier, where they boarded a narrow gauge railway to Rattekot, Saint-Eloi. After spending what was left of the night in tents there, they made a three-hour march the following night to Wayenburg and boarded another train, though they first had to shovel out the manure left by the animals that had previously been transported in it. They finally entrained at 1:30 a.m. on the morning of September 5, but did not reach Mondicourt until 6:30 that evening, and then faced another two-and-a-half-hour march before finally reaching their billets at Doullens. When they at last arrived, the surviving 12 officers and 654 enlisted men of the Second Battalion of the 106th ate for the first time in thirty-six hours.

They were quartered in the ancient stone citadel on a hill just outside Doullens, or in barns in the surrounding countryside. "There were prior tenants in these barns . . . some of them were quite large and every night they came out of their hiding places to chase each other over the blankets of the soldier occupants . . . We were involved in a serious training mission and were too tired to be bothered with rats. We just went to sleep, pulling our lone blanket over our heads." There were other prior tenants, too: "cooties"—lice—infested the men, their clothing, and their hay and straw bedding. Despite the army's attempts to delouse their troops, steaming or fumigating their uniforms to kill the lice while the men stood naked and shivering, they were louse-free only until they again lay down to sleep, when they at once became reinfested.

General Read, Commander of the Second Corps that included the 27th Division, had already made a request for replacements for his depleted ranks—now 62 officers and 2,547 men short. The request was not answered; the 27th Division received no replacements at all until late October 1918, by which time its fighting service was at an end.

The 106th Infantry remained in Doullens for a fortnight, reorganizing the depleted ranks, which were slowly being augmented by a trickle of returning wounded and gassed men, and reequipping and retraining, despite torrents of rain that left them once more knee-deep in mud and water. These tired and bloodied soldiers showed an understandable lack of enthusiasm for drill sessions during their rest period, drawing complaints from a regimental adjutant who noted that almost seven hundred men of the 106th and the other regiments of the division were "in billets at time of inspection . . . this number is out of all proportion and appears beyond reason."

There was also a problem with men going absent without leave, some of whom must have been classified as deserters. A report produced on September 6, 1918, showed that about fifty men had been AWOL at some time during the previous fortnight, with two companies particularly badly affected. Fifteen men from Company F were AWOL for at least part of that time, including eleven who had disappeared before the regiment's tour of frontline duty at Dickebusch Lake and Vierstraat Ridge and never returned. Seven men of Company I had been AWOL during the entire tour of duty, since early July. Whether they were ever found and what punishment was imposed does not appear to have been recorded, but the brigade commander made it clear that in every case, in addition to charges for being AWOL, he also wanted the men charged with misbehavior before the enemy. The implications of that were made clear in the relevant Article of War: Any officer or soldier who abandoned his post, incited others to do so, or threw away his weapon was liable to suffer "death or such other punishment as a court-martial may direct."

The men who had been involved in the brutal fighting around Vierstraat Ridge felt an understandable need to let off steam afterward, with predictable consequences. On September 14, 1918, a military policeman entered an estaminet in Doullens just in time to stop a brawl involving a dozen men of the 106th. There were about fifteen champagne bottles on the table in front of them and the men were "in a very nasty mood. I realized that if I endeavored to stop them from taking the champagne with them," the MP said, "it would mean trouble and probably necessitate the use of my gun." He got them outside, and after more fighting among themselves in the yard and on the road in front of the estaminet, he managed to get them started on the journey back to their billets.

However, they then assaulted two British YMCA workers who were out for an evening stroll. Although the culprits were arrested, the YMCA workers' superior, voicing the strong feelings of his staff and his YMCA executive, showed a remarkable degree of understanding in expressing the hope that the men would be dealt with as leniently as possible. His demand for action against "the sellers of strong drink, rather than the victims of it," echoed the debate on temperance and Prohibition that was dominating the domestic political agenda back in the United States.

Although they had been allowed a brief rest, the men of the 106th Infantry, like those in the other regiments of the 27th Division, were now in intensive training, practicing alongside British tanks for the first time. Their depleted state after the fighting on Vierstraat Ridge and Mount Kemmel was shown by the record of attendance for a tank demonstration on September 17, 1918, when almost half of the surviving members of the Second Battalion were missing, the majority of them wounded men who were still in the hospital. Depleted or not, a communiqué from General O'Ryan now informed them that in the near future they would be carrying out a mission of great importance, requiring them to serve as "shock troops." That mission, now being rehearsed by these still inexperienced soldiers, was to be an attack on the enemy's most formidable defensive system: the Siegfried Stellung—the Hindenburg Line.

Despite huge initial advances, the great German offensive that spring had not achieved its ultimate objective of dividing the British and French armies and breaking through to the Channel. It had also represented something of a last throw of the dice. Germany's economy, starved of raw materials by the British blockade of the North Sea ports, was struggling to supply enough war matériel and munitions for the troops, or even enough food and clothing for the population at home. German forces had suffered massive casualties, for which even the transfer of troops from the Eastern Front following the collapse of Russia into revolution could not compensate, and now the floods of fresh American troops arriving daily in Europe were tilting the balance of manpower ever more heavily in the Allies' favor.

The last German hopes of outright victory had evaporated when the great spring offensive faltered and stalled. Now, massed behind the fortifications of the Hindenburg Line, the German war aim was simply to weather whatever Allied storm might break against them, and then, negotiating from a position of rough parity, secure a peace that would allow them to retain as many as possible of the territorial gains in Belgium and France that they had made in the autumn of 1914.

When not carrying out their training and practice maneuvers, the men of the 106th Infantry and the other regiments of the 27th Division were told to get all the sleep they could. In between the endless hours of rehearsal for the attack and the sleep they were encouraged to get, Monk and his comrades also found time for some recreation, including a regimental athletics meet. There were also hundreds of stray dogs wandering the areas behind the lines, and many were adopted as pets by the American soldiers. Given his fondness for animals, it was no surprise that Monk found himself one, "a poor waif of a cur he picked up somewhere behind the lines in France" and took with him from billet to billet.

The 106th rested at Doullens until September 23, when they once more marched to a railhead and boarded the familiar boxcars, heading "in the general direction of the big show." The 15 officers and 635 men of the Second Battalion boarded their trains at 2:30 that morning, their numbers increased by the return of gassed and wounded men. In all, 39 officers and 2,058 surviving men of the 106th Infantry, accompanied by a baggage train of 60 limbers, journeyed by train to the dismal Tincourt area. Every soldier was burdened with a greatcoat, a British Lee Enfield .303 rifle, a hundred rounds of ammunition, and their rations for the day. A convoy of thirty trucks carried each battalion's additional ammunition: 140,000 rifle rounds, and 50,000 rounds for the Lewis machine guns.

Trains taking troops to the front traveled at five miles an hour, each locomotive pulling forty-eight boxcars with a total capacity of nineteen hundred men, capacity that was routinely exceeded by 10 percent. Soldiers went to great lengths to avoid being jam-packed into the stinking boxcars, and orders had to be issued to train commanders to stop men from riding on the roofs. As the trains rattled nearer to the front lines, the landscape they passed through was cratered by shell fire "like microscopic pictures of the moon." Once beautiful cities were "just heaps of brick and debris, not a living thing to be seen, even the trees all shot off, leaving nothing but stumps, which look like ghosts in the moonlight. The graveyards are turned upside down by terrific shell fire. The ground is covered with all the signs of a great battle—smashed guns of every caliber, wrecked tanks, dead horses and here and there a dead Boche overlooked by the burying parties."

The men of the 106th first realized that they were going directly into the line when the train rattled through war-ravaged Péronne, close to Saint-Quentin and Cambrai, where heavy fighting was still continuing. They passed through the war-scarred region around Albert and across the Somme, its banks pocked with shell holes and littered with barbed wire. The Germans had given up an area some fifty miles deep as they retreated to the Hindenburg Line, but they left behind a wilderness.

The Germans cut down trees, not even sparing the orchards; they set villages on fire and gutted towns, using explosives to demolish the buildings that fire alone could not destroy. They poisoned the wells, destroyed every road and railway bridge, tore up the rails, blew in the

embankments and tunnels, and detonated mines under every crossroads, leaving craters that made the roads impassable. The Germans also
left booby traps: steel helmets, pianos, door handles, the steps of dugouts or houses. They exploded when touched, costing the advancing
troops many lives. Only the hedgerows were left standing in this vast
wasteland, to serve as cover for concealed machine-gun nests.

Monk and his comrades eventually detrained at Tincourt after
a fifteen-hour train journey. They then marched to Villers-Faucon,
where they bivouacked under fire from enemy guns while a battery of
their own howitzers roared back throughout the night. The next night
they returned to the front lines, passing salvage corps hunting through
the wreckage for any war matériel that might be retrieved. Scores of
enemy dead lay strewn across this ground; the American troops had
been warned not to touch them in case they had also been mined by the
retreating Germans.

The 106th Infantry's route to the front ran due east, through the
village of Ronssoy. Just beyond it, they took over a position covering
four thousand yards of the front lines. Facing them were the formidably strengthened and ferociously defended outposts of the Hindenburg
Line, commanding a series of trenches running along a narrow plateau
two hundred yards or so from the eastern bank of the Saint-Quentin
Canal. A deep railroad cutting in front of the canal and a small river,
both strongly fortified, commanded the line of advance and exposed
attacking troops to fire from a warren of concrete machine-gun nests.
The rising ground beyond the formidable outworks was the main Hindenburg system, "stuck full, like pins in a pin-cushion, of all types of
automatic weapons of every caliber and breed."

Linking these fortified trenches were three strong points—
Quennemont Farm, Guillemont Farm, and the Knoll—a thousand yards
in front of the main Hindenburg Line defenses and connected to them
by switch lines (sunken communication trenches) and deep,
concrete-lined tunnels. These concrete bastions, with concealed dugouts and machine-gun nests every twenty to twenty-five feet, stood
on a high ridge, bare of trees. Artillery was ranged onto the sloping,
open ground in front of the strongpoints, where the densely tangled
barbed-wire defenses were designed to shepherd attackers into preor-
dained fields of fire so that they could be blown apart by shell fire and
raked by light and heavy machine guns, *Minenwerfer* (mine-throwers),
antitank guns, field guns, and powerful *Flammenwerfer* (flamethrowers).
"To a depth of six miles extended this foreground, gullied and hollowed

into spots where machine guns waited."

An offensive could not be successfully launched against the Hindenburg Line itself until the outposts had been neutralized, but successive attacks by British and Australian troops had failed, with British troops suffering a casualty rate of 80 percent. The American troops of the 27th Division were now to attempt what their far more numerous and experienced British allies had failed to do. Already depleted by combat casualties over the previous three months, the division was also now losing men to the influenza pandemic, which had begun to affect American forces around the middle of September. Moreover, since most of the division's fighting strength was being held back for the main assault against the Hindenburg Line, the 106th Infantry was to attempt this first herculean task alone; "in short, one regiment of the division was now to accomplish what five British divisions had repeatedly failed to accomplish."

General O'Ryan had nominated the 106th Infantry to make the attack, a curious decision since, after its earlier losses, it was already the weakest of the four regiments that made up the 27th Division, with only 41 surviving officers and 2,037 men. By comparison, the 105th Infantry had 73 officers and 2,659 other ranks, and the 107th and 108th both had more than 80 officers and almost 3,000 other ranks. The objective of the attack, supported by tanks and a rolling barrage, was defined as the occupation of the rearmost trenches of the outer line of the Hindenburg system, a distance of about eleven hundred yards from the American lines.

The keynote order was summed up in five words: "The men must go forward." All three battalions of the regiment were to attack together across the four-thousand-yard front. They were assured that the enemy troops defending the strongpoints would surrender, but "whether they do or not, the leading elements must go on, leaving to the mopping-up parties in the rear the task of dealing with them." All ranks were also warned that neither heavy shelling nor enemy counterattacks would be regarded as justification for withdrawal. The line was to be held irrespective of casualties.

The men of the 106th Machine Gun Company were given equally daunting orders. Their role would be crucial in slowing and halting enemy counterattacks, giving the American infantry time to prepare defensive positions or launch their own counterattacks. But every machine gunner knew that his life expectancy in a defensive action was estimated at just thirty minutes. He was expected never to "surrender his position or abandon his gun. He will disable it and defend himself to the last second of his life with every means at his disposal. These means are grenades, revolvers, clubs, stones, fists."

On the night of September 24 through 25, the 106th Infantry moved forward into the front lines, replacing the exhausted and woefully depleted British 18th and 74th Divisions. Monk and his comrades passed through the devastated town of Albert, reduced by constant shelling and bombing to a sprawling heap of rubble and dust. Beyond, rain had made the chalk roads slippery, and the shell holes were filled with stinking water, overlain with a film of mustard gas. The detritus of ferocious combat lay on every side: live shells and ammunition, bombs, rifles, shell craters so numerous that they pitted the ground like smallpox scars, collapsed trenches, twisted wire entanglements, endless rough graves, and many more bodies decomposing in the open for want of men to bury them. The Americans had to steel themselves against such sights and march on toward the baleful glow of shell fire and Very lights that marked the front lines.

For forty-eight hours before the attack, a continuous barrage had fallen on the German positions. The guns of nine artillery brigades, firing every twenty to thirty seconds, launched an avalanche of mustard-gas shells—the first time the British artillery had used the gas, long a German weapon—followed by a barrage of high explosive, shrapnel, and more mustard gas. In total, three quarters of a million shells were fired, creating "noise such as no mortal ear ever heard before." The results were revealed later, when the advancing troops "could not pass five feet without having to cross over the dead body of a German."

17

A SORT OF SACRIFICE

The attack by the 106th Infantry was to be launched at dawn on September 27, 1918. During the previous night, the mud and gray chalk, exposed in places by shell bursts, was overlain with a network of pegged white tapes, marking the jumping-off places for each unit, while strong patrols were pushed out well in front to protect those doing the pegging and taping. Through the remaining hours of darkness, men "murmured in low tones of Broadway and Bedford Avenue [in Brooklyn] and places about Times Square where they knew many of their friends were enjoying light and warmth and pleasure, and speculated on their chances of getting back to join them." At 3:30 in the morning, each company of the regiment, in one long single file, moved forward into the firing line. They could not use the main road, which was under enemy observation and regularly shelled, and instead followed a circuitous route along a less exposed road and across fields to the jumping-off point. Even then they were hindered by shelling and the difficulty of finding their designated places in the pitch darkness of a wet and moonless night.

To avoid alerting the Germans to the imminent attack, the rumble of tanks moving forward to their start positions was masked by the noise of a squadron of aircraft flying overhead. Four tanks had been assigned to each frontline battalion, three to advance with the first line, and one to follow in support, loaded with barbed wire and tools for consolidation. One four-gun platoon from the regiment's machine-gun company was also attached to each battalion. The infantry were approaching the assembly trenches when, alerted by noise or movement, the Germans fired a salvo of Very lights. Their blinding white light illuminated the American trenches, and seconds later German signal rockets went up, etching luminous pale green crescents across the sky. Almost simultaneously, an intense enemy machine-gun barrage began. "The momentary confusion is well nigh indescribable. Imagine men on the march, anticipating no opposition, suddenly thrown into bold relief, in a manner itself startling, and then, before recovering their equilibrium, exposed to withering fire." In the confusion, a number of stragglers from K Company of the 106th mistakenly attached themselves to Company M of the 105th Infantry.

By 4:30 that morning the broken battalions of the 106th Infantry were on their mark. Because they would have to advance rapidly under heavy German machine-gun fire, they had been ordered to leave their overcoats, blankets, and field kits at company headquarters and carried "only" a raincoat, assault rations, an extra water bottle, fighting equipment, four sandbags and a trench shovel, two hundred rounds of small arms ammunition, and five grenades per man. As dawn approached, all fell silent, checking and rechecking their equipment, fingering safety catches and testing the edges of bayonets, while drenching rain and mist soaked everyone.

The First Battalion, commanded by Major Gillet, took the right of the sector, with Captain Blaisdell leading the Third Battalion on the left, directly opposite the Knoll, and the Second Battalion, under Major Kincaid, holding the center ground, with Companies F and H in the van and Companies E and G in support. Major Kincaid, the division's judge advocate, had left his law books and gone out to command a battalion whose previous leader, Major de Kay, had been wounded within days of assuming command. Such was the shortage of officers after the losses in their previous battles that in many companies there were only sergeants in command, and the situation was made even worse by the bizarre practice of sending officers on detachment to training schools in aspects of military command, even as their units were about to enter the front lines to launch a crucial attack.

The 105th Infantry was to support the 106th and cover its flanks, and the machine-gun battalions of both regiments were to provide a machine-gun barrage, while Stokes mortars would add their firepower. On reaching their objectives, the troops were to fire success flares—rifle grenades bursting into three white lights. Allied reconnaissance aircraft flying overhead would also sound the Morse letter *A*—a short and long blast of a klaxon—as a signal for men in the frontline positions to fire red ground flares, lay groups of rifles parallel across the trench about a foot apart, and flash their polished tin discs, sewn on the insides of their respirator flaps, so that the observers could establish the position of the front line.

Sensing an attack, the enemy was still sending up rockets, while over the battleground, already pitted with shell craters, star shells were casting a lurid light. Stretched out, six feet apart, along a white tape line for a distance of four thousand yards, some eighteen hundred men, all with bayonets fixed, stood waiting for the moment to advance. They were laden with ammunition and grenades, gas masks hanging at their necks and steel helmets pulled low over their faces.

Though it was still only September, the morning was cold, with low clouds and a heavy mist. It was unusually quiet, the silence broken only by intermittent firing in the distance. Then, just as dawn was breaking, a single gun fired as a signal and then, with a thunderous roar, all the other guns opened up, right along the line. At once, colored lights and rockets could be seen going up from the enemy lines, SOS signals calling for a counterbarrage to protect them from the advancing American troops.

The artillery exchange created "the heaviest hail of fire any of us had ever seen or heard." "All along the front coalescent sheets of exploding flame bounce, seethe and creep forward, at the rate of one hundred yards every three minutes." Some 50 percent of the barrage was shrapnel, 35 percent high explosive, and 15 percent smoke to screen troop movements. Through it all "twangs and whines the wasp-like buzz of a barrage of copper-nosed bullets from ninety-six machine guns, each of which fires two hundred rounds a minute." The machine guns became so hot from constant firing that the gunners wore asbestos gloves and the cooling water in the jackets surrounding the guns continually boiled off and had to be replenished.

As the barrage lifted and crept forward, the 106th Infantry began to advance, shouting their battle cry, "Mineola! Mineola!" Almost at once they were enveloped in the smoke screen and lost to view. Some thought the concealing smoke, "so dense that a compass could not be read," was more damaging to the attackers than the enemy, and some of the American officers and men became almost totally lost for a time as they tried to advance.

Even though day was breaking, it was still dark enough for the flashes of shell bursts to be clearly visible and, as the men of the 106th advanced, "the sickening, whirring whine of machine gun bullets" was added to the din of explosions. "There is no sound in the world like it; with it comes death and wounds on every side." The reaction from the enemy had been instantaneous, and the near-simultaneous artillery barrage fueled later rumors that the Germans had been tipped off about the attack by a spy. Many American men and officers were killed before they had advanced even one stride; the First Battalion "jumped off on time and fairly melted away."

Half blinded by the smoke, the line officers of the 106th tried to lead their men forward with the aid of luminous compasses. The infantrymen fought their way from shell hole to shell hole under withering machine-gun fire. "All the strength and power and morale of the German army lay behind these [strong]points and their orders were to hold the line at all costs. They fought with every deadly weapon and contrivance known to modern warfare." Man after man of the 106th fell to the ferocious cross fire of German machine guns, but the advancing line kept moving forward through a blizzard of bullets and shells. "Rushing forward in an impetuous line . . . with their own barrage before them like a curtain of fire, it seemed as if nothing could stop them—as if they must win their objective."

The advancing American troops stormed and destroyed machine-gun nests, bombed and cleared enemy trenches, and moved with such speed that within an hour the Third Battalion had reached its first objective, and by 6:46 a.m. it was firing its success rockets to show that the Knoll had been taken. As one jubilant soldier of the 106th claimed, "When the time to charge came, we drove the Dutchman [*Dutch* and *Dutchman*—probably a corruption of the German *Deutsch*— were often used instead of *German*] out of the trench. When he saw us coming he ran for his life, but he ran right into his own barbed wire and we just mowed them down like flies on a wall." The First and Second Battalions also succeeded in reaching their first objectives, but although the 106th had gained a foothold in the three fortified outposts, they were not strong enough in numbers to completely drive out the defenders, and would now have to withstand the inevitable counterattacks.

Some troops were well into the German trenches in places, but in others they were held up by the barbed wire, and cut apart. Many companies had suffered terrible carnage among their men and were entirely without officers—almost all were killed or wounded. One observer was reminded of Pickett's Charge at Gettysburg. Once more, nothing had apparently been learned from four years of warfare against Germany; massed ranks of men with bayonets fixed again advanced in orderly ranks to be blown apart by shell fire and shrapnel or cut down by machine guns.

As the fighting continued, that fire came not only from the front and from the flanks, but increasingly from the rear, as German gunners emerged from concealed dugouts, communication trenches, and tunnels behind them. A disgruntled officer of the 105th Infantry complained that machine guns were being operated from areas that the troops assigned to mopping up were supposed to have cleared. Isolated on the battlefield and often confused about their position and their objectives, the remnants of the 106th dug in where they could and tried to hold the ground they had gained.

Guillemont Farm was deluged by shell fire as Company G and the rest of the Second Battalion bombed their way across the German trenches in hand-to-hand fighting, and once more Monk set an inspiring lead to his comrades. The Second Battalion briefly reached their overall objective, but there were many hidden dugouts and underground passages, and German troops and machine guns kept appearing in new or already cleared areas. One soldier of Company G reported that when German troops suddenly opened fire from a hidden tunnel, the concussion was so great that it tore the rifle from his hand.

Claims that the German machine gunners had to be tied to their weapons to force them to remain at their posts proved to be false propaganda. "Don't let anyone tell you they had to chain the German machine gunners to their guns," said one American officer. "Those Germans fought to the last. Not one quit before he was killed or wounded so badly that he could not fight." Yet the men of the 106th withstood repeated counterattacks and continued to try to advance in the teeth of the counterbarrage and the relentless machine-gun fire.

"Guillemont Farm and Quennemont Farm were hells. Our men died by squads trying to silence machine guns. Tanks went in to flatten out the nests, but were of no avail. A whole platoon of our men lay dead in a circle around the batch of nests. In the center their captain lay stark and cold." More and more of the tanks spearheading the attack ran over mines or were hit by antitank artillery, until all twelve of them were out of action. They had also inadvertently severed communications to Monk's Second Battalion; the telephone lines were torn out by the advancing tanks.

Even when the main advance had been stopped, individual soldiers and small groups continued to make their way forward, killing snipers and machine gunners and bombing dugouts. First Lieutenant William Bradford Turner displayed almost unimaginable—and ultimately suicidal—bravery. "Stumbling, groping in the dark through barbed wire entanglements in a veritable hurricane of machine gun bullets," he sprinted across open ground to a machine-gun nest, where he wiped out the entire crew with his pistol. He then ran twenty-five yards to the next machine-gun nest and shot another German, while his men killed the rest.

Turner and his men continued to advance, using tactics calculated to deceive and frighten the enemy. They stormed dugouts with grenades and rapid fire, creating the impression that the number of attackers was far larger than the reality. Despite mounting losses, they fought their way through four lines of trenches, killing several machine-gun crews. Even when wounded and out of ammunition, Turner still picked up a dead soldier's rifle and launched himself at another nest, bayoneting the gun crew before being overpowered and killed. His heroism later earned him the posthumous award of the 27th Division's first Congressional Medal of Honor. Around his body, men died in scores, and the roads leading back from the battlefield were choked with stretcher cases and walking wounded.

The fighting was most bloody around the Knoll, which changed hands four times that day. Both sides knew that they were fighting for control of terrain that would confer a vital advantage in the greater battle to come. At 11:40 a.m. reports stated that the enemy was in Guillemont Farm and cemetery and in some force in South Guillemont Trench, and forty minutes later the men of the 106th were counterattacked and driven off the Knoll. They reorganized and in turn counterattacked, forcing the Germans back with the help of artillery and machine-gun fire, but a report timed at 2:35 p.m. again stated that the Americans had withdrawn from the Knoll. The surviving members of the Second Battalion were eventually forced to drop back and occupy Claymore Trench, short of their final objective. The losses they had suffered made them too weak to advance farther, but they held their ground and repulsed several counterattacks.

"Everybody thought we were in contact with the outpost positions of the Hindenburg Line," Major Gillet later said, "but . . . we were up against the line itself. And a lousy, dirty, dangerous place it was." In fact, the 106th Infantry did not reach the actual Hindenburg Line, but what he perhaps meant was that the outpost positions were continually reinforced, and counterattacks launched by men emerging from the safety of their shelters within the main Hindenburg Line defenses. Mopping-up parties sent forward to break down the machine-gun nests and clear the dugouts and trenches behind the advancing American troops were bombed and strafed by German aircraft and counterattacked by endless numbers of fresh German troops. They poured out through concealed tunnels from the main Hindenburg Line defenses and filtered through the ravines and communication trenches into dugouts that the artillery barrage had scarcely touched. Enfilading fire and attacks from the rear stopped the American mopping-up parties from pressing forward, and left many of the companies and platoons of the 106th isolated behind German lines.

Confusion was as marked at the headquarters of the 106th as on the front lines. Battalion commanders complained that they were receiving no information at all from their advanced units; at no time during the day was any communication established with them. Returning wounded men were often the only source of information on the progress of the attack. When messages were received from the front, they merely reiterated that the position was obscure or not clear, and those reports claiming that the objectives were in American hands, with only pockets of the enemy to be mopped up, proved premature.

When General O'Ryan visited the headquarters of the First Battalion that afternoon to get direct information, he found that the battalion commander had lost touch with all his companies and had collected forty men to form a defensive line in the original frontline trench. Simultaneous reports from the Second Battalion indicated that the enemy was operating between the battalion headquarters and the advancing American troops. Consolidation of the earlier American gains was proving to be impossible. German counterattacks had regained at least partial control of the Knoll and Quennemont and Guillemont farms, and their machine gunners in the rear of the Americans were gradually forcing them to withdraw. As they did so, they left isolated groups of men holding out in shell holes.

At 6:30 that evening, one officer, brimming with misguided confidence, categorically stated that when he left the front line at 5:00 p.m., the Knoll, Guillemont Farm, and Quennemont Farm were in American hands, with only pockets of the enemy remaining to be mopped up. Another claimed that the Germans were occupying a small portion of the Knoll, but Guillemont Farm and Quennemont Farm were in American hands. In reality, most of the surviving remnants of the 106th Infantry's three battalions had reassembled in the original frontline trench, and at nightfall, while many of their comrades were still in trenches and shell holes ahead of them, the strongpoints of the Hindenburg Line were more or less back in enemy hands, although around them later were found German dead "thick as flies."

Some of the units of the 106th who had fought their way through the forests of barbed wire and the mazes of trench systems to break through to the German outposts were now holding a tenuous defensive line in isolated positions and were in urgent need of support. Among them was a platoon of Company F, by now numbering just twenty-five or thirty survivors, who had penetrated the German defenses east of Guillemont Farm. There, completely surrounded and with enemy troops bombing their way down the trenches toward them while others came through the communications trenches behind them, they held out until dark. At 7:30 p.m., the relieving troops of the 107th and 108th Infantry sent out four combat patrols to make contact, where possible, with these isolated units and establish a hop-off line for the next day's attacks, but they failed to find any men of the 106th Infantry and were met by such intense fire that minimal ground was gained.

Before going into action that morning, the men of the 106th had been given one final chilling instruction: "No man must be taken as a prisoner, but must fight to a finish"; "the supreme rule was kill or be killed." Such orders flagrantly contradicted instructions issued by the adjutant general just one month before, on August 26, 1918, following German press reports that some American soldiers had refused to give quarter to Germans who had offered to surrender. The adjutant general pointed out that such reports would only increase enemy resistance by instilling in their minds that they would be killed even if they tried to surrender. He then restated the policy of the United States Army: "An offer to surrender on the part of enemy soldiers not guilty of treacherous conduct will be accepted and these soldiers given food, shelter and protection strictly as laid down in the 'Convention Respecting the Laws and Customs of War on Land.' " But in the battleground before the Hindenburg Line, very few prisoners were taken on either side, and the fighting had cost the 106th dearly.

Dead and wounded men of both sides lay everywhere, strewn across the battlefield. Some wounded were brought in by the patrols of the 107th and 108th, but others remained out in No Man's Land all night, their cries weakening as the night went on and falling silent, one by one, as death claimed more victims. Many of the living wounded were again treated by British and Australian field ambulances and field hospitals; once more, there were simply not enough of the 27th Division's own medical personnel to cope with the casualties.

After they were relieved at three in the morning on September 28, Monk's Second Battalion faced a long, weary trudge back out of the lines before they could even think about rest. They marched to Villers-Faucon, where they were quartered in "elephant huts" [huts roofed with corrugated-iron sheets] and shelled billets. It was understandable that, though dog-tired, they were "proud to think that they had licked the stuffings out of the enemy and paved the way for the major operation of the 29th of September." The Second Battalion's war diary for that day also claimed that the objective had been reached and held successfully, and a counterattack repulsed with heavy enemy casualties. Certainly it was true that the 106th had shaken the morale of the German forces, claimed large numbers of enemy lives, and significantly weakened the German position, but the three strongpoints had not been taken and held. The front line was practically the same as it had been that morning.

There was no disgrace in the 106th's failure to achieve its objectives; far stronger British forces had repeatedly failed to capture the Knoll, Quennemont Farm, and Guillemont Farm. The 106th's lack of success might also have been partly due to its inexperience, but it was primarily the result of an unnecessarily complex and overambitious battle plan produced by the Allied commander of that sector, the Australian General Monash, and approved by the British General Rawlinson. It demanded a farther advance from the Americans than Monash had ever expected his Australian troops to achieve, and yet he had committed far too few troops to it. The three battalions of the 106th were allocated a front of about four thousand yards. They were well below strength even before beginning the attack and could hardly have been expected to make much of an advance even if they had all been at full battalion strength and fighting in open battle, rather than when the enemy troops were shielded by trenches and concrete fortifications. When the attack was resumed on September 29, the same front was occupied by two numerically stronger regiments—the 107th and the 108th—on the front line, with the 105th Infantry and what was left of the 106th in support, almost three times as many troops as had been committed on September 27.

There had also been a significant failure to learn the lessons drawn from observations of German tactics that were circulated to officers of the A.E.F. in May and June of that year, months before the battle of the Hindenburg Line. They drew attention to the use of infiltration and small columns in which the enemy advance guard would slip through any chinks in the defenses, with the infantry following force to exploit any breakthrough. Against poorly organized defenses, these tactics could succeed with only modest artillery support, or even without any artillery. The enemy would also use natural features like ravines and streambeds to penetrate the defenses and then turn right or left to roll up the defensive line. The comments on methods of attack make equally sobering—and prophetic—reading in the light of the 106th Infantry's experiences: "Advance by waves, even preceded by the creeping barrage is no longer enough, when the objectives to be taken are well defended, and could not be sufficiently destroyed previously by the artillery."

A further document drawing similar conclusions had been circulated in July, but if the officers of the 106th Infantry had read those reports—issued to all officers down to company commanders—there was little sign of appropriate measures being put into effect on the battlefield that day, though that is not to denigrate the courage of the enlisted men sent over the top. The fact that lacking any worthwhile support from the tanks, the 106th Infantry had still broken through the defenses and gained a foothold in the three enemy strongpoints, thus disorganizing the enemy's defense, was, General O'Ryan later said, "an extraordinary feat. The valor of the officers and men of the regiment is well indicated by the location of the bodies of their gallant comrades who fell in the battle and by the large number of enemy dead about them." His men had "fought like wildcats. I'd like to talk it over with some of the enemy who may still be alive who faced us on that day and see just what they thought of our advance."

The surviving soldiers of the 106th Infantry were "tired, spattered with mud, stiff and lame and scratched by barbed wire, oftimes half-dazed with shell shock," and they were stunned by the losses they had suffered. On the night before the attack, Monk's Second Battalion had reported 10 officers and 515 men present for all duty. Twenty-four hours later, just 5 officers and 241 men remained. The Third Battalion saw its numbers shrink from 12 officers and 484 men to 4 officers and 210 men, and the losses of the First Battalion were even more catastrophic. The night before the attack it had 6 officers and 491 men. When relieved twenty-four hours later, there were 4 officers and 98 men—a casualty rate of almost 80 percent. Only one of the line officers—those involved in the actual fighting—of the Third Battalion had survived; all those of Monk's Second Battalion were either dead or wounded; and all but one of the line officers of the First Battalion were killed or wounded. In total, 956 men of the 106th had been killed or were missing in action, wounded, or gassed, and a further 8 officers and 259 men had been captured.

Soldiers had to be quite seriously injured to be officially classified as wounded, and almost all the surviving men were carrying wounds of varying severity, so that at eleven o'clock the next morning, the 106th Infantry had just 9 officers—only 2 of them line officers—and 252 men present and ready for duty. Some of those survivors must have shared the mixed feelings of a soldier who declared, "The end of the world came today and yet here I am . . . I never was so happy and so proud in all my life and I never was so sad as I am now over all who died and showed wounds I shall see in dreams if I ever sleep again." So formidable had been the opposition and so insufficient in numbers the attacking troops that one officer pondered whether the 106th had been sent out as "a sort of sacrifice company to feel and prepare the way for future attacks on a grander scale."

18

THE HINDENBURG LINE

On the morning of September 28, 1918, without sleep since September 26, hungry and filthy, the men of the 106th lay in their billets in a stupefied state, completely exhausted from the ordeal they had endured. "They were quiet, perhaps with a feeling that they had done everything that could have been expected of them; yet they were aware that they would undoubtedly be called back into the lines."

Although now forty-four years old, Monk had never sought nor expected any concessions because of his age. He had fought as long and as hard as any of his comrades, and if they had to fight again, no one doubted for a moment that Monk would again be where the fire was hottest. However, there was no well-deserved rest for Monk, or for any of the exhausted men around him. The bloodied and battered remnants of the 106th Infantry—all of its available troops—were now to be organized into a provisional battalion of moppers-up, to follow the attack by the 107th and 108th over the top at dawn the next morning. Led by Major Gillet, in addition to the remnants of the fighting troops, "every officer and man of the 106th capable of shouldering a rifle . . . non-commissioned staff officers, cooks, clerks, teamsters and survivors lately relieved," were formed into three companies, X, Y, and Z, with a total strength of just 350 men—"the LAST offering of the 106th Infantry."

Immediately after issuing the order that might spell "the complete annihilation of the 106th Infantry," General O'Ryan appeared before the survivors to urge them to "finish the job. The response to this harangue was nothing more than the blank stare of men stunned by what appeared to them as brutal audacity." Noting their reaction, the general, "with great tact and apparent feeling"—not to mention a certain callous calculation—asked if they were happy to abandon their wounded comrades, who at that very minute were lying where they had fallen on the battlefield. The men of the 106th at once rose to his challenge. A good general is often said to require three characteristics above all others: intelligence, ruthlessness, and luck. No one had ever doubted O'Ryan's intelligence; now they would not doubt his ruthlessness, either. Whether he would prove to be lucky, too, would be decided by the events of the next forty-eight hours.

The regiments relieving what was left of the 106th—the 107th and 108th—had attempted to complete their job on the morning of September 28, pushing combat patrols forward to dislodge the enemy, but these attempts had resulted only in savage fighting and severe casualties without worthwhile territorial gain. The first objectives for the troops preparing to assault the main fortifications of the Hindenburg Line on the morning of September 29—part of an Allied assault along a front of approximately a hundred miles—would now be to complete the capture of the outpost strongpoints, which had cost the 106th so dearly.

The instructions issued to the machine-gun companies show the absolute determination that in this ultimate test, the New York division should not be found wanting:

1. This position will be held and the section will remain here until relieved.
2. The enemy cannot be allowed to interfere with this program.
3. If the gun team cannot remain here alive, it will remain here dead, but in any case, it will remain here.
4. Should any man, through shell shock or other cause, attempt to surrender, he will remain here—dead.
5. Should the gun be put out of actions, the team will use rifles, revolvers, Mills grenades and other novelties.
6. Finally, the position, as stated, will be held.

If the outposts could be neutralized, the main fortifications of the Hindenburg Line, built by the forced labor of thousands of prisoners and conscripted Frenchmen, would lie open to attack. But those fortifications were truly formidable. There were three deep trenches with concrete firing steps, each protected by a belt of barbed-wire entanglements twenty to thirty feet wide. If the first belt of wire was cut, there was another behind it, and still another beyond that. The trenches were as strong as human ingenuity and muscle could make them. Behind them was the Saint-Quentin Tunnel, built by Napoleon in 1811, now pressed into use as an underground barracks, a safe haven for fresh troops and a refuge for battle-weary ones. The tunnel formed an integral part of a multilayered defensive system, sited with such skill that it effectively denied the Allied artillery positions from which to attack it.

More than six thousand yards long, and ten to sixty yards belowground, the tunnel passed straight through a hill. The entrances at either end had been sealed with ferro-concrete walls four feet thick, containing upper and lower chambers, with machine gunners shielded from attack, firing through slits in the walls to cover the tunnel entrance. A series of barges moored on the canal inside the tunnel acted as barracks for the garrison, and passages and galleries had been cut through the rock to the firing trenches and the outpost positions, allowing reinforcements to reach them and wounded or exhausted troops to return to safety without being exposed to enemy gunfire or airplane observation. Nine separate galleries led to the fortified village of Bony alone, a stronghold immediately in front of the tunnel system. All the passages and their exits were heavily fortified and well camouflaged, concealing them from American observers and artillery spotters.

On either side of the tunnel, the canal ran through cuttings sixty feet deep in places, in the sides of which the Germans had built innumerable tunneled dugouts and concrete shelters. Concrete and armored steel machine-gun emplacements were concealed along the top edge of the cuttings. About four thousand yards behind the main trench lines was another double trench system, protected by huge barbed-wire entanglements and holding many more concrete shelters and machine-gun emplacements. The whole series of defenses, including several fortified villages, varied in depth from seven to ten thousand yards and formed a system thoroughly deserving of the formidable reputation ascribed to it. The Allied staffs had obtained a book describing the Hindenburg Line defenses and boasting that the section the New York troops were to attack was impossible for an attacking force to take. Even armed with the book, the Allied commanders did not know the half of it, for the book made no mention of the traps, mines, and secret tunnels that would prove so destructive to the American troops when the attack was launched.

During the night of September 28 through 29, despite heavy enemy fire, horse-drawn wagons brought forward rations, water, and ammunition. Supply dumps were set up just behind the lines, and pack animals were readied to carry fresh supplies forward as the troops advanced the next day. Assault rations were issued, and extra water canteens, pickaxes, shovels, grenades, flares, rockets, and great quantities of ammunition, carried in bandoliers and belts, were distributed, adding to the soldiers' burden.

The sky was overcast and the blackness of the night was broken only by the tracks of rockets seared across the sky, and the flashes of heavy guns. The German guns roared in answer, and the artillery duel took an increasingly heavy toll as the night wore on. The provisional battalion of the 106th formed up in the rear areas at 10:45 that evening. They were given a hot meal at eleven and then moved out at midnight, up the Ronssoy road. At once they found themselves part of a jostling mass of men, horses, trucks, and tanks, all competing for road space and trying to make progress toward the front. At last, the battalion left the congested road and struck off due east over the shell-torn fields. Ahead of them, the outlines of groups of men faintly silhouetted against the first graying of the eastern sky marked the position of the front lines. Knowing that a fresh attack must be imminent, the Germans were firing salvos of flares and rockets that created "a pyrotechnic display of blue, green and red, terrible in its import."

Already tired by the forced march that night and by the aftereffects of their battle, Monk and the rest of the provisional battalion arrived at their start position as support for the first wave just before zero hour on a bleak and rain-swept autumn day. However, one company became detached from the rest as they moved into the line, and had still not arrived at the jumping-off point as the attack began. The troops awaiting the signal to advance knew that many of them would soon be counted among the dead. The British gave all the American troops half a tumbler of rum before the charge: "a little of it will make a rabbit stand up and fight a bear." Then, at 5:50 on the morning of September 29, 1918, the big guns burst into life, said to be the most terrifying shellfire of the war.

Accompanied by tanks, the infantry was to advance behind a creeping barrage that would move forward twenty-five hundred yards and then remain static for fifteen minutes four hundred yards east of the tunnel, to allow time for mopping up and to interdict German reinforcements moving up from the rear. It would then creep forward again for another twenty-five hundred yards, and then continue falling on that point, a curtain of fire that—if the supply dumps of shells had not already been exhausted—would continue until the attacking troops had consolidated their gains and the inevitable German counterattacks had been repulsed.

Aerial reconnaissance had shown that pockets of soldiers of the 106th were still holding out in shell holes and isolated positions, and concerns had been voiced that, having survived the battle on September 27, the men occupying those positions ahead of the jump-off line would be shelled by their own men. However, the barrage tables had been predicated on the 106th achieving its objectives on September 27; the starting line for the shelling was the objective line that they had failed to reach, rather than the actual front line, one thousand yards farther back. It was claimed that it was impracticable to change the barrage tables to allow for this, and a request for a twenty-four-hour postponement of the attack to allow the revisions to be made was refused by the British. As a result, the barrage was laid down eleven hundred yards in front of the advancing troops' jump-off point, and actually fell on the far side of the hotly defended German strongpoints of the Knoll, Guillemont Farm, and Quennemont Farm. The only modest concession that could be wrung from the artillery commanders was that the barrage "lifts" would now be a hundred yards in four minutes, instead of a hundred yards in three minutes.

Between two barrages, their own well in front of them and the enemy's fifty yards behind them, and with machine-gun bullets spattering all around them, the American troops began to advance in a haze that was half mist and half smoke. The scene that confronted them was one of utter desolation: a wilderness of shell holes and collapsed trenches; ravaged earth; twisted and mangled thickets of barbed wire; abandoned rifles, helmets, and other equipment; and mangled corpses, all testifying to the terrible power of the Allied barrage. Yet the majority of the Germans had once more escaped the shelling in their deep shelters. They emerged so rapidly to take up the fight that some of the advancing Americans encountered the first enemy troops in force only about twenty-five yards from their starting tape. Despite this, prisoners captured in the early stages told their interrogators that the attack had been a surprise. Even if that was really true and not simply telling their interrogators what they wanted to hear, the Germans were soon directing withering fire at the advancing Americans, a hail of bursting shells, shot, and shrapnel, and continuous enfilading fire from machine guns on the flanks.

Just as on September 27, the early progress of the attack was deceptively rapid, although smoke from shell bursts and guns lay so thick over the battlefield that it was all but impossible for commanders to see what was happening. The fighting was some of the most bloody and ferocious of the entire war. Millions of machine-gun bullets raked the advancing troops, and by 9:10 a.m. there were reports that the Third Battalion of the 107th Infantry was suffering heavy casualties at Guillemont Farm.

Mark 5 Star tanks, the heaviest used by the British Army, each mounted with small cannon and six machine guns, were again spearheading the assault but, just as in the preliminary action, they were found to be virtually useless. Within ten minutes of the opening of the barrage, nine tanks had been destroyed. More were quickly put out of action, threatening the infantry's ability to get through the German barbed wire, but the 27th Division's engineers rushed forward and laid closely woven wire netting over the top of the wire entanglements. The infantry then pushed on over the barbed wire and toward the Hindenburg Line. As they advanced, the men of the 108th Infantry reported passing over small groups of the 106th Infantry, who were indeed still holding what ground they had gained in the fighting two days before.

In the original battle plan, the 106th Infantry had been scheduled to follow the 3rd Australian Division across the canal tunnel, but their losses in the preliminary attack had been so severe that this part of the plan was abandoned. Instead, the provisional battalion of the 106th was ordered forward behind the Third Battalion of the 107th Infantry, to assist in mopping up the Hindenburg Line, tunnels, and exits. After he had advanced with his men about seven hundred yards, Major Gillet was wounded by machine-gun bullets for the second time and, badly hurt, was stretchered to the rear. By eleven that morning the rest of the provisional battalion had reached the edge of Guillemont Farm, fighting their way through with ferocious determination, bombing enemy machine-gun nests and trenches.

Their losses were again substantial; out of the provisional battalion's fourteen remaining line officers, nine, including Major Gillet, were killed or wounded, and another was missing in action. One officer, engaged in hand-to-hand combat with a much bigger German, gouged out his opponent's eye and pinioned him with a finger hooked into the eye socket and a thumb clamped in his mouth until he could reach his knife and dispatch him. The 106th's Colonel Franklin Ward described the fighting as "murder, hell-to-breakfast carnage." In one sector the Germans formed a human chain, passing grenades forward to the lead men, who threw them in a constant stream. Yet no matter how many American soldiers fell, there were always others to take their places. The composite battalion of the 106th caught up with the 107th Infantry near Willow Trench and joined its fight, occupying trenches between Guillemont Farm and the Knoll, including the Knoll Switch Trenches, where the body of Lieutenant Turner still lay.

Information from the front lines was again obscure, confusing, or practically nil, and some reports were still claiming advances while others were citing withdrawals under heavy fire. The machine-gun fire was "thicker than flies in summer," so heavy that "a field mouse could not have crossed alive." One American corporal called it "a slaughter."

At 11:25, Lieutenant Brandt of the 106th Infantry, already wounded in the fighting, reported that the advance had halted, held up by machine-gun fire. Half an hour later an intelligence officer was still reporting that the Knoll had been captured, though, just as with the 106th's initial attack, the advance had actually stalled, with the 107th also pinned down by machine-gun fire from Guillemont Farm. Thick smoke and fog made it almost impossible to locate the machine guns that were wreaking such havoc. Throughout the rest of the morning they could make little progress against sustained enemy fire; they also faced German counterattacks, enfilading fire, and attacks from the rear by troops armed with machine guns and bombs, emerging from the concealed entrances of the underground passages of the tunnel. Orders before the battle had stressed the need to prevent this, and the Americans made repeated attempts to mop up the ground over which they had advanced, but the constant infiltration of fresh German troops behind them made it a thankless task.

By 2:15 the enemy was advancing from Bony, and the 106th and 107th were pulling back from the Knoll and Willow Trench. Yet within an hour the American troops were pushing forward again and, though the enemy counterattacked several times by bombing along the trenches, each time the Germans were driven off with very heavy casualties. As Australian and American troops tried to press forward again, machine-gun fire from Bony and Guillemont Farm to the west, the Macquincourt Valley, and the steep slopes east of the canal and north of Gouy brought such a heavy enfilading and cross fire to bear that it was impossible to advance against it. At four that afternoon a liaison officer was reporting that there were very few line officers still alive on the battlefield. Another twelve hundred American walking wounded were counted on the roads leading away from the front. As usual, troops had been ordered to advance without stopping to care for their wounded, who were to be evacuated by stretcher parties. They never appeared, and it was not until the following day that the regiment's medical officers and the regimental chaplain at last evacuated the large numbers of wounded men who had been lying, untreated, on the battlefield all night.

As attempts to advance continued, the number of casualties was still rising, and even the positions already taken or retaken were again under fire from machine gunners who had once more emerged from tunnels behind the attackers. When the Germans also launched a counterattack from the left flank, General O'Ryan sent in the 105th Infantry to support the 107th. Together with the remnants of the provisional battalion of the 106th, and with the 108th attacking the southern end of the tunnel, they held off the enemy and advanced a little farther. The lead battalion, now composed of survivors from all four regiments of the division, advanced as far as Gouy, far beyond its original objective, but brigade headquarters reported that the fighting in the Saint-Quentin Tunnel had been a massacre.

At sunset, the American front line, running almost north to south, passed through Knoll Trench with outposts in Knoll Switch and Willow Trench, on the western edge of Guillemont Farm, South Guillemont Trench, Claymore Trench, and south along the Hindenburg Line. By seven that evening, reports were coming in that things had begun to quiet down, but fighting continued long after nightfall and fresh casualties were still being reported well into the night. Attempts to resupply the fighting troops with ammunition, food, and water met with mixed success. When ration parties did not arrive, small details of men from regimental headquarters did their best to distribute food and water, but extra canteens sent up during the night arrived so late that it was impossible to fill them. Ammunition was also in short supply, though in some instances where Lewis-gun ammunition was exhausted, troops were able to use captured German machine guns and ammunition.

Before dawn the next morning more "iron rations" were served to the German defenses from artillery that had been advanced a mile and a half from the firing positions of the day before. The Australian artillery had so many guns in position that there was only thirty-five feet between each one. They were fired every thirty seconds for three quarters of an hour, with the result that seven guns burst from the intense heat, killing their crews. Fighting went on all morning, and at ten minutes to twelve another barrage was fired. Under its cover, the infantry advanced another four hundred yards. After holding a section of trench seven hundred yards in advance of the Hindenburg Line all night, under heavy shell and machine-gun fire, the remnants of the provisional battalion advanced still farther, mopping up another five hundred yards of trenches in desperate fighting.

Yet again Monk led by example, bombing machine-gun nests and wielding his bayonet in close-quarters combat with deadly effect. In an incident that left his fellow soldiers and officers openmouthed with astonishment, Monk also went over the top alone, on his hands and knees, carrying grenades with which to destroy an especially annoying German machine-gun nest. The German machine gunners spotted him, and their fire was so intense that Monk's pack was sheared from his back by the streams of bullets, but he kept on crawling forward until he was within reach of the machine-gun nest—and then silenced it and wiped out the occupants with a fusillade of grenades. "These incidents are told by Eastman's officers. He himself refuses to talk of his war experiences."

The unrelenting pressure was finally telling on the enemy, and at 1:50 that afternoon the aerial observers reported that the Germans seemed to be preparing to retreat. That prompted a third barrage at 2:30, when they "got all the hell on earth that any man could look for." An advancing American officer then found the tunnels leading from the trenches to the Saint-Quentin Tunnel "still as wine caves, dark and uninviting. Not a soul was in them. A few of our men went through them but the masses went over the hill above them." The retreating Germans were spewing out of the ground in hordes, and aircraft over-flying the battleground reported that the areas behind the tunnel were thick with running men. The remaining defenders trapped in the tunnel were bayoneted or bombed or taken prisoner, and by five past three, an observer dropped a note into the American front line: "The Hindenburg Tunnel is ours."

Australian troops were now relieving the 27th Division, but even though they had been cut to ribbons by the enemy machine-gun fire, many of the surviving American troops—whether driven by bloodlust, vengeance, or the desire to finish the task they had been set—refused to abandon the fight and continued to advance alongside the Australians. Among them was Monk, who was "in action throughout the entire Hindenburg Line show." The cooks, orderlies, and other miscellaneous men of the division thrown into the fighting had also advanced alongside the trained infantry, after the infantrymen spent five minutes showing them how to pull the ring of a grenade and how to throw it. Even the divisional chaplain, Father Kelley, went over the top three times, carrying a prayer book instead of a gun. His hair was said to have turned gray during the fighting.

When the battle was finally over and the weary American troops were relieved, the casualty toll was fearsome. One company of the 107th Infantry, which had begun the battle with 212 men, emerged from the fighting with only 12 unwounded, and a similar casualty rate was reported by almost all the units involved in the battle. However, enemy casualties had been even heavier, and the loss of the supposedly "impregnable" symbol of German resistance and intransigence dealt a devastating psychological blow to the German troops. Captured enemy soldiers were all "broken in body, spirit and morale . . . the will to war had simply run out of them." Their captors heard over and over again the same refrain: "The war is over, the Hindenburg Line is broken."

19

THE PHANTOM DIVISION

The next day dawned dry and hot, and in the aftermath of the battle a stomach-churning smell hung over the battlefield, "an odor unexplainable that issues not from dead animals, birds or fishes, but issues only from dead men upon whom the sun shines." Everywhere were dreadful sights that the soldiers would never forget. There were also other, hateful reminders of man's venality and corruption. "Human vultures" had been active during the night, and the bodies of American soldiers had been looted as they lay strewn over the battlefield. Wallets and personal possessions were removed, and in at least one case a dead man's finger was cut off to obtain the ring he had worn. Australian troops were strongly suspected to have been the culprits, but nothing could be proved and in the interests of inter-Allied harmony, the matter was dropped.

While the 3rd and 5th Australian divisions continued the advance beyond the Hindenburg Line, the 106th Infantry retired to Villers-Faucon during the night of September 30, though the last units did not arrive until the following day. Once more, these exhausted, shell-shocked, and battle-scarred men were quartered in elephant huts and broken-down billets. General O'Ryan remarked that "it is first depressing, then inspiring to see your units coming out after perhaps three or four days of continuous fighting, plastered with mud, more or less dazed from shell shock, many sick from gas fumes, all stiff from nights spent in shell holes, number slightly wounded who refused to be evacuated, and to note the dead, tired eyes flash with Division esprit the message—'Give us forty-eight hours in the hay, some "vin blink" and plenty of eats and then let us at them again.' "

While such tub-thumping comments no doubt boosted morale, a more sober evaluation suggested that the losses his men had suffered would have been lessened by better tactical appreciation. It was evident that the enemy tactics were to let the first wave of attackers pass through the defenses to a certain extent, and German soldiers would then emerge from emplacements, pillboxes, and dugouts, cutting off the first wave, who faced attack from in front and behind, as well as enfilading fire from the flanks. A critical Australian report claimed that the excitement of their first battle, together with the difficulty of locating all the dugout and tunnel entrances in the dense mist and smoke, made the American moppers-up move on without dealing with all the enemy who had taken shelter from the barrage during the initial advance and then emerged behind the Americans. When the smoke and mist at last began to clear, some troops, realizing how precarious their position had become, were able to pull back, but a considerable number were cut off and captured or killed.

Another observer also felt that the American moppers-up had been too anxious to join their comrades at the cutting edge of the attack, rather than completing the slow, tedious process of methodically clearing the ground and locating all the concealed dugouts and tunnel entrances. As a result, fierce resistance was still being encountered on ground over which the first wave had long since advanced. Even when battlefield experience had shown this to be a crucial flaw, attempts to remedy it were limited to vague, generalized orders to mop up thoroughly.

On October 2, the 106th Infantry began a brief rest period at Halle Wood, where its broken ranks were reorganized. It took some time for the regiment's casualty figures to be collated and forwarded to divisional headquarters, but when complaints were made to Colonel Franklin W. Ward, he replied—with more tolerance and forbearance than many might have mustered in such circumstances—that in the majority of cases, the first sergeant and company clerk, responsible for compiling the figures, had been killed or wounded, or was missing in action. He did not add that, in any event, filling in forms to satisfy bureaucrats at headquarters was hardly a priority for a regiment that had been so ravaged by one of the most bloody engagements of even that sanguinary war. When the statistics were finally produced, it was revealed that the 106th Infantry had suffered 1,185 battle losses in the seven days between moving up to the front lines on September 24 and being relieved after the battle of the Hindenburg Line. The regiment was now a "mere skeleton" and, in addition to the killed, seriously wounded, missing, or captured, almost all its effectives were also carrying lesser wounds of some sort, or suffering the aftereffects of gas or shell shock.

On October 3, the morning after their arrival at Halle Wood, burial detachments numbering two hundred men and accompanied by chaplains returned to the battleground surrounding the Hindenburg Line to begin the grisly task of identifying and burying their dead comrades. They were informed that they were to perform this duty as a tribute to their dead. The dead men's shoes were removed to be salvaged if in good condition, and the bodies were then wrapped in twelve-foot lengths of burlap for burial. The brother of Corporal Porter of Company G had seen Porter killed during the 106th Infantry's advance on September 27 and was almost deranged by it. He recovered his brother's body and buried it himself.

Fired on from time to time by the enemy, the men went about their melancholy work. Where the dog tags of the dead had survived, one was buried with the body, placed outside the undershirt but under the jacket to protect it from damage, and the other nailed to a peg, inscribed on both faces, and then placed at an angle of forty-five degrees, so that the inscription on the underside was shielded from the weather. If there were no pegs, burial parties were told to write the dead man's details on any piece of paper or cardboard, put it in a bottle or a tin can, and bury it almost its full length in the ground. In theory, the tag would later be retrieved by a graves register service officer, but in practice, shelling and fighting often obliterated all trace of the tag and the gravesite it marked, adding yet more to the millions of unidentified dead who had no known grave.

Units were to bury all soldiers, American, Allied, or German, but in fact, there was inevitably less appetite for burying the bodies of the enemy, and many were either left lying where they fell or were dumped in abandoned trenches or shell holes. Alongside the burial parties, salvage details including two officers and sixty-five men from the 105th Infantry were also at work, gleaning rifles, ammunition, grenades, and any other reusable equipment from the battlefield and the bodies of the dead.

On the afternoon of the fifth day, the burial and salvage details completed their work and set off to rejoin the rest of their comrades. Sorely depleted and with no prospect of any replacements, the 106th Infantry and the rest of the 27th American Division had begun the move back to the front lines on October 6, 1918. All this time the enemy had been in slow retreat, and a week's marching was required before contact was again made. The 106th Infantry first moved up to Tincourt Wood. Arriving at nightfall, during a heavy downpour, the men blundered through the dark forest and took whatever shelter they could find in caves and hastily improvised foxholes. The following afternoon they marched on to the shell-battered Hargicourt area, where the First Battalion bivouacked in the ruins of the town, while the Second and Third halted in and around Templeux, where their comrades from the burial details at last caught up with them.

On October 9 they began another night march, setting out for Bellicourt at dusk. The city lay directly behind the Hindenburg Line and the regiment had to pick its way through a morass of craters, tangled barbed wire, and shell-torn terrain. Persistent drizzle added to the misery of the troops and made conditions underfoot treacherous. Horse-drawn transport struggled even more than the infantry in the slippery, cloying mud. Wagons slid off the road and had to be hauled back by the sweating, cursing infantry, and when a medical cart overturned it had to be abandoned. When they finally reached the end of that march, the weary, mud-encrusted men again had to bivouac in the open fields.

Ahead of the 106th, the American 30th Division was still making advances against fierce German opposition. Enemy aircraft were very active, and to protect themselves from bombing, on this as on many other occasions, each man dug a shallow trench like an open grave and lay in it, safe from shrapnel, though not from a direct hit. At daybreak the shivering men emerged, cold and wet but otherwise unharmed.

While awaiting orders to again take their place in the firing line, some of the men of the 106th explored the now empty and abandoned Hindenburg Line. They found a scene of total devastation and desolation. The graves of some American soldiers lay practically on the jump-off line, the men having been killed before taking more than a few steps. Quennemont Farm had been completely demolished, and the trees in the orchard had been reduced to stumps that were so studded with shrapnel and bullets that they rang like iron when struck. The camouflaged machine-gun nests and strips of machine-gun ammunition were still in place around Guillemont Farm. Mountains of empty shells showed the extent of firing by the German defenders before they were overwhelmed, and the still-unburied bodies of German soldiers on the Knoll proved that it had also not been given up without a fearsome struggle.

Around the strongpoints, discarded first-aid packets, gas masks, and other American equipment revealed where the U.S. troops had occupied trenches as they fought their way forward. There were numerous concrete-lined passages leading down into the Saint-Quentin Tunnel, most of them blocked by the bodies of dead German machine gunners, and on the ravaged grass slopes lay the unburied bodies of hundreds of German infantrymen, intermingled with the as yet unburied remains of British and Australian soldiers. There was also evidence of how ineffective the artillery barrage that preceded the assault had been; engineers discovered only one destroyed machine-gun post along the entire length of the defenses from Bony as far as Bellicourt. Every other post was still intact.

After almost four years of static warfare, fought from trench systems that stretched, uninterrupted, from the Channel coast to the Swiss border—it was said that you could walk the entire distance without ever once coming aboveground—the "war of movement" that had characterized the opening months of the conflict had now been resumed. The aim of the Americans and their allies was now simply to maintain relentless pressure on the German armies, driving them back with continual attacks, giving them no rest or chance to regroup. The Allied commanders, seeing the daily returns of ground gained and German casualties, prisoners, and deserters, knew that the enemy forces were close to the point of collapse; there were no more troops on which they could call. One final push, one last rolling Allied offensive, might be enough to decide the war and force a German surrender.

Just after noon on October 10, the 53rd Brigade, including the 106th Infantry, received orders to move at once to the Montbrehain-Brancort area, and then be prepared to move farther into action on one hour's notice. Leaving behind the ravaged area around the Hindenburg Line, they began a long march eastward across open country and through the battered towns of Neuroy, Joncourt, and Ramicourt, to Montbrehain, where they bivouacked for the night. It was a brief rest; their orders, again underlined, required them to move on at daybreak.

As they formed up again at first light, enemy artillery launched a sudden barrage. Several men were hit by shrapnel before the regiment escaped the town, making for Premont. Australian troops had recently fought their way through Montbrehain, and in an attempt to slow their advance the Germans had saturated the town with heavy concentrations of "Green Cross"—tear gas—which affected the 106th as well. On the night of October 11 through 12, they marched on, following a British guide, and at daybreak they rested in Butry Wood west of Busigny, but hardly had they thrown off their packs than the enemy began to shell the area with gas and shrapnel.

The Second Battalion continued their advance from the wood and completed the march to their position in the reserve trenches that morning, relieving the 30th Division. It had been a difficult, frustrating march, taking nine hours to cover nine kilometers, for the Germans had blocked all approaches to Busigny by felling trees and telegraph poles, and, in the absence of pioneer troops to clear the way, Monk and his fellows had to pick their way through tangles of wire, poles, tree trunks, and improvised barricades.

Alongside the 105th Infantry, the 106th deployed along a fifteen-hundred-yard front, in close support of the 107th and 108th in the firing line. They remained there for four days, during which their working parties and formations were so regularly and so accurately shelled that it seemed as if "some sinister agency informed the enemy of every movement within the American lines." The duration and intensity of the shell fire increased each day, and it was almost a relief to the troops when, on the night of October 16, they were ordered to move up to the Selle River, where the retreating German troops had now dug in on the far bank. Normally a modest waterway, the Selle was swollen by heavy fall rains, and the enemy had blown up the bridges and dammed the river downstream, flooding some of the low-lying lands on the western bank.

Once more, the German artillerymen seemed to have sensed the impending battle, for the afternoon of October 16 saw such ferocious shelling that the men of the 106th were forced to huddle in slimy trenches in the marshy ground. Despite constant enemy shelling with high explosive and gas, the regiment advanced that night to take its place on the jump-off line, supporting the 105th and 108th. As an anti-gas precaution, all American soldiers were required to add two teaspoonsful of bicarbonate of soda to the water in their canteens, which could be used to clean off and neutralize any gas or liquid residue adhering to their gas masks, skin, or clothes.

The 106th Infantry now had a rifle strength of just four hundred men, and the 27th Division as a whole was so depleted by the loss of men killed or wounded—reduced to about twenty men per company, one fifth of its strength little more than a month before—that it was now nicknamed the "Phantom Division." As the infantrymen groped their way forward in the dark, slipping in the mud and stumbling over ruts and potholes, shell bursts claimed a steady toll of yet more dead and wounded. A high-explosive shell burst immediately behind one company, wiping out most of a platoon. Casualties had to be left where they fell, for others to treat, and once more Monk and his comrades had to harden their hearts and close their ears to the screams and cries of wounded comrades writhing under the terrible effects of gas poisoning.

German shelling continued all night, interspersed with gas attacks, but by 4:20 on the morning of October 17 the 106th had formed up on the white tape stretched across the ground. They deployed in artillery formation with greatly extended intervals between platoons and companies, waiting in a downpour that had turned the chalky ground into gray mud, while a thick mist made having any sense of location or direction virtually impossible.

The task of the infantry spearheading the attack was to cross the river and assault the heavily defended German positions at the top of the slope leading up from the far bank. The river had been reconnoitered during the previous night and was found to be fordable, except for a few deep holes in the riverbed. But General O'Ryan was in no doubt about the serious obstacle presented by the river, with its steep approaches, absence of bridges, and high embankments on the far side, bristling with machine guns, antitank guns, and *Minenwerfer,* supported by artillery. The terrain in that area was also unusual in that all the fields were bordered by hedgerows, which provided perfect cover for machine gunners.

After a sixty-minute silent period before zero hour, an hour-long barrage, launched at 5:20 a.m. on October 17, breached the enemy barbed-wire defenses in several places. At 6:20, as the barrage lifted and began to creep forward, the infantry started over the top, the first wave wading the river while the engineers began trying to place light bridges for the use of the second wave.

The heavy fog and rain that had rolled in at two that morning showed no sign of clearing, and the infantry advanced into an almost impenetrable murk of mist and yellow smoke; once more the smoke-screen proved as much of a hindrance as a help to the attacking troops. It was impossible to see more than a few feet, and compass bearings proved unreliable. Almost at once the first wave began to fall behind the barrage. The 106th Infantry moved up in reserve, so that when the 105th Infantry started to advance from the first objective, the 106th was just west of the Selle River and ready to cross. The mist was so dense that a machine-gun nest on the ridge to the east of the railway was completely missed by the first wave and not discovered until it began firing on the supporting troops, delaying their advance until the 106th Machine Gun Company eliminated the problem.

Ten heavy tanks were to cross the Selle after the infantry and advance in support of them, but the much-vaunted tanks again proved of very limited value. Having moved south to cross the river, they then lost their way in the fog, and only two tanks joined the battle at all—both of which were soon destroyed by shell fire. One of them had reached the village of Arbre Guernon before it was disabled, where it lay blocking the crossroads and drawing fire.

Monk's Second Battalion reached the river by sliding down the embankment onto the heads of a company of the 102nd Engineers still engaged in the futile attempt to lay footbridges across the river. After fording the river and climbing the slippery banks, the battalion attacked and mopped up, crossing a trench system cratered by shell fire, which proved a formidable obstacle. They then entered Saint-Martin-Rivière and cleared the town, silencing the enemy guns from which heavy firing had been coming, and taking numerous prisoners.

The Second Battalion moved on to a railroad a thousand yards east of the town and took cover under the embankment—about forty feet high—unaware that enemy troops were occupying dugouts on the other side, within a few yards of them. When this startling discovery was made, Monk led his comrades in scaling the embankment and bombing the enemy dugouts. More prisoners were taken, and the Second Battalion marched their captives forward with them, making them identify enemy positions. Using captives as human shields breached the rules of warfare, but the weary and now battle-hardened New Yorkers were less concerned with legal niceties than with ensuring the survival of as many of their remaining comrades as possible.

Fierce resistance at Jonc de Mer Ridge was overcome by rifle fire and a frontal attack, with the Second Battalion clearing the trenches at the point of the bayonet. They were then held up by machine-gun nests hidden in hedges and thickets just outside Arbre Guernon, fulfilling the prophecy contained in their battle orders that the main resistance might not come from the village itself but from the hedges flanking the road to the northwest. Strong patrols eliminated the machine guns, and the Second Battalion then linked up with the 105th Infantry and established a line of resistance just east of the main road. The other battalions of the 106th were digging in along a sunken road west of Arbre Guernon, ready to hold this line for the night.

As Monk and a comrade worked their way forward, mopping up enemy positions with bombs, bullets, and bayonets, they came across a young German soldier huddled in a dugout and paralyzed with fright. He was only fifteen years old but looked even younger. In these dying days of the war, in a last desperate attempt to hold the line, the Germans were throwing their last reserves of manpower—the young, the old, the wounded—into the fight. The boy made no effort to defend himself, staring helplessly up at them as Monk's buddy raised his rifle. He was about to shoot the boy when Monk pushed the gun's barrel down. "Don't shoot," Monk said. "He's only a kid." They took him prisoner instead and sent him under guard to the rear as they continued to advance. The boy owed his life to Monk.

By now, the 106th Infantry had crossed the crest to the east of the river and advanced two miles, but they had suffered more heavy casualties. The First Battalion was down to ten officers and thirty-eight men, and the others were little stronger. Along with the other exhausted men of the 27th Division, they were due to be relieved that night, but the

British commander, General Sir Henry Rawlinson, informed General O'Ryan that unforeseen circumstances would prevent this and asked whether the American troops would be willing to hold their lines until the following morning. With a confidence shading into hubris, O'Ryan replied that they would not only be willing to hold their ground but would make a further advance if the Australian artillery supplied a barrage.

O'Ryan's plan called for the 106th to leapfrog the 105th during the advance, but the 106th was now so numerically weak that it could not assume that responsibility. Instead, Monk's Second Battalion was merged with what was left of the 105th Infantry, and they went over the top together toward La Jonquière Farm on the morning of October 18. Their battle orders predicted that the farm, occupied by a full German unit, strongly entrenched, would be a major obstacle, occupying a commanding position, with extensive cover surrounding it and concealed approaches on the enemy's side.

It was another gray, mist-laden morning, and barely light enough for observers to distinguish the trees outlined against the skyline from the groups of men moving like ghosts through the smoke and mist. A barrage was put down at 5:30 but was answered almost immediately by a furious enemy counterbarrage, and in "one of those unfortunate military miscalculations which result in the infliction of greater losses upon your own men than upon the enemy," the targeting for the Allies' barrage was so inaccurate that the 105th and 106th Infantry's sector was deluged with shells from their own guns.

In a system of warfare dependent on cooperation between different units and synchronization of their movements, sometimes even to the minute, potentially disastrous mistakes were inevitable. This was one such occasion. As a result of a delayed or misunderstood order, the barrage that should have fallen two hundred yards in front of the infantry began fifty yards behind them, and when it lifted and began to creep forward, it swept right through them. Desperately seeking whatever cover they could find, many men huddled against the eastern bank of the road, but some companies didn't know whether to go forward or back or remain where they were. When the barrage had passed, their handful of officers and NCOs managed to reorganize them and get them moving forward, but they had been nearly annihilated by their own fire and left behind many wounded or dead comrades.

As they advanced under heavy machine-gun fire, the Phantom

Division, with a paper strength of almost 15,000 men, had been able to field no more than 850 rifles, and that included the cooks, order-lies, and other noncombatant troops who had been pressed into action. Most of those 850 were suffering the effects of previous wounds or gas attacks before they even began advancing. Held up once more by hidden machine-gun nests and repeated counterattacks supported by artillery, the attackers lost touch with the 30th Division on their flank and had to dig in until contact could be reestablished. The First and Third Battalions of the 106th meanwhile offered what feeble support they could to the attack, but no further advance was made or attempted, and the day's fighting ended with the front line pulled back a little to a road on the eastern slope of the ridge above the Saint-Maurice River. The 106th Infantry had lost another eighty-one men to wounds during the course of the day, and among them was Monk, who had again been hit as they pressed home their attack. Once more, he was treated at a British field hospital, and once more he returned immediately to the firing line.

That evening, determined to squeeze the last ounce from his exhausted men, O'Ryan issued orders for another advance, and in the latter part of the night and the early morning, the attack was resumed. It met no opposition, except from La Jonquière Farm, where the 106th had to make a bitter advance attack to capture or destroy enemy machine-gun nests. There had been such a heavy dew during the night that it looked like frost, and the men of the 106th, lying in the long grass as they waited for the signal to attack, were soaked to the skin, but at a whistle blast, they rose from the grass and the shouts of "Let's go! Let's go!" were answered by their battle cry: "MINEOLA! MINEOLA!" Although they were weary to the core of their being, they summoned the energy to attack with renewed ferocity, storming the machine-gun nests and wiping out gun crew after gun crew. One badly wounded German "begged to be put out of his misery; he was accommodated on the spot."

When the Second Battalion reached the Mazingheim road, they found their way blocked by a high stone wall. The road was exposed to enemy fire but they crossed by rushes, breached the wall with pickaxes, and then pushed on again, covered by the First and Third Battalions. They crossed an orchard, marked on the map as a danger spot; the splintered trees and trampled hedges gave evidence of the fierceness of the fighting as they eliminated yet more nests of machine guns and snipers, and occupied La Jonquière Farm. As they cleared the farmhouse, they found two badly wounded American soldiers, lying on stretchers. They had been treated by enemy field-ambulance men, and when the Germans were forced to retreat, they left the wounded Americans in the farmhouse with water and rations within reach. Monk could have been forgiven for thinking that the care the enemy had given to the two men was a return for the mercy he had shown to the boy soldier from the same German unit a couple of days before.

The 106th Infantry's own casualties from shelling, machine-gun, and sniper fire continued to mount. Under covering fire from their own Vickers machine guns, patrols went out, crawled to within throwing range, and then bombed the nests of snipers and machine gunners with grenades; several more of their own men were killed or wounded as they did so. Intense bursts of shelling continued throughout the night, and once more the men of the 106th Infantry were forced to endure the cries for help from their wounded comrades in No Man's Land, without being able to help them. At five o'clock the next morning, the enemy again shelled their positions.

The Second Battalion of the 106th now held a line along the west bank of the Saint-Maurice River, though enemy snipers and machine guns remained active. Patrols destroyed four German machine-gun nests and killed several snipers, but the 106th were driven back by heavy machine-gun fire. They regrouped and advanced again, and by nightfall they had achieved all their objectives. Fourteen hundred German soldiers had been taken prisoner, and by degrees the enemy had been driven back, incurring heavy casualties every time they tried to make a stand, and forced to abandon ammunition, machine guns, trench mortars, and rifles as they fled for their lives.

Once more the enemy had been driven out of strong defensive positions by the sheer aggression of the American attackers. Many more German troops had been killed, wounded, or taken prisoner, and the remainder were now so debilitated and demoralized that when the 106th Infantry pressed forward in two waves in one final attack, they met practically no opposition at all. Many of the officers described it as "the prettiest fight of our war"; it also proved to be the last.

20

ALWAYS SHALL WE HONOR THEM

On the night of October 20, 1918, the remnants of the 106th Infantry, with an effective strength of only 180 rifles—little more than a twentieth of the numbers with which they had first entered the lines just three months earlier—were relieved by British troops. The Second Battalion made way for the First West Yorkshire Regiment at 9:30 that evening and, as they withdrew, utterly exhausted, "the column moved on its nerve alone," the stronger among them carrying double loads and supporting their weaker comrades. During the march back to Escaufourt, they were given hot chocolate and crackers from a rolling kitchen, though some of the men, marching from memory and instinct, were barely aware of it. From time to time an exhausted man fell in his tracks and was cursed awake by those who tripped over him.

Over the next four days they marched slowly westward, bivouacking each night under the stars. On the morning of October 24, in a chill atmosphere of rain and fog, the regiment reached a railhead at Roisel where a train was waiting to carry them to their designated rest area. They stacked their arms and began to relax in the false hope of soon entraining. They were still there in early evening, when an ominous roar and a terrifying crash brought them stumbling to their feet. "Roadbed and rails, wagons and teams shot skyward" as a delayed-action land mine, planted by the retreating enemy at the intersection of the railroad tracks and the road, exploded. A group of prisoners of war working near the railhead burst out laughing; for some, it was the last thing they ever did. Several British and American men had been killed in the blast, and in revenge for the explosion and the laughter, a number of POWs were shot on the spot by British guards. Grabbing their rifles, several men from the 106th Infantry also ran toward the POWs, but a hastily formed line of guards prevented any further bloodshed.

With their train destroyed and the railhead devastated, the bone-weary troops of the 106th were then forced to make another night march in driving rain to Tincourt. They then had to wait alongside the railroad tracks for five hours before crawling wearily into boxcars from which artillery horses had just been unloaded. The train eventually pulled out at 3:40 on the morning of October 25, and pounded and bumped its way back to Corbie, arriving there at 1:15 that afternoon. From there they marched one final time to the stuffy little hamlet of Bussy-lès-Daours, where they could at last lay down their packs and arms and rest.

While Monk and his fellows were still enduring their marathon journey, his wife, Worthy, must have read devastating news. On October 24, 1918, the local newspaper carried the story that "Friday's casualty list contained the name of Edward Eastman of Presidio, Texas, killed in action. He is the first man from the Big Bend District to be mentioned on these lists." It was the second time in his life that Monk had erroneously been listed as dead by a newspaper—*The New York Times* had also reported his death after he was gut-shot and taken to Gouverneur Hospital in 1901—but such tragic mistakes were not infrequent during the war. Monk's wounds and his treatment at a British or Australian dressing station rather than an American one may have contributed to the confusion and led to him being listed as missing in action or dead. However, no correction to that report appears to have been published, and when, if ever, Worthy realized that it was false is not known. Like many of her Big Bend neighbors, Monk's wife seems to have disappeared from the official records without a trace, and it is conceivable that she never discovered that terrible error and went to her grave believing that Monk had been killed in action.

Other than the conscription of some of its young men, life in Big Bend was little altered by the war, but great changes were sweeping the United States, and nowhere more so than in New York. From the turn of the century to the outbreak of war in Europe, there had been almost continuous growth and rising prosperity right across America. The number of people employed in manufacturing had increased by 65 percent, and the value of industrial output, salaries, and wages had all doubled. In a ten-year period, it was estimated that one-third of New York's Italians and Jews had left manual labor for semi-skilled or skilled work, or for self-employment. A recession beginning in 1914 had been threatening that prosperity, but the war in Europe ended that, causing rocketing demand from the Allies for foodstuffs, manufactured goods, and war matériel, and boosting the U.S. economy to such an extent that by the time of the U.S. declaration of war in April 1917, more than $2 billion in goods had already been supplied to the Allies, principally Britain.

Many American corporations laid the basis of their postwar global dominance during the war years, and American farmers had also scrambled to cash in on the soaring demand for wheat and other agricultural produce. Marginal lands went under the plow, and intensive cultivation and mechanization increased, with the number of gasoline-powered tractors quintupling during the war years. With Europe's farms depopulated of young men to work the land and much of the land itself devastated by the war, the United States became the prime supplier of food to Britain, France, and some of the other Allies. However, poor harvests in 1916 and 1917 led to shortages for domestic consumption and export. Herbert Hoover, appointed by President Wilson as the head of a new Food Administration, introduced the idea of voluntary "Wheatless Mondays" and "Meatless Tuesdays," with Americans at home going without a little of their food to supply the Allies and feed the U.S. troops in training at home and serving abroad.

Cards were issued, instructing American housewives in economy and conservation and suggesting "Victory Menus" with alternatives to meat, though such dishes as "stewed lima beans with milk" would not have struck everyone as an adequate substitute for a steak or a pot roast. It was claimed that the meatless days at the Waldorf-Astoria in New York alone saved two thousand pounds of beef a week. Many parts of the country went even further, observing "Gasless Sundays," "Sugarless Mondays," "Meatless Tuesdays," "Wheatless Wednesdays," "Porkless Fridays," and "Two Meal Saturdays." Such measures were not enough to prevent food shortages, however, and sugar was so scarce that stores ran out completely.

Tobacco was also in short supply, as the U.S. Army bought huge quantities for its troops. The majority of smokers before the war had used pipes or cigars, but the greater convenience of cigarettes led to their wholesale adoption by soldiers. Issued along with their rations, cigarettes were the only luxury that men in the trenches could enjoy, and virtually all of them smoked. Those who opposed supplying doughboys with cigarettes were accused of being traitors, and General Pershing even made the extraordinary claim that "what we need to win this war [is] tobacco as much as bullets. Tobacco is as indispensable as the daily ration; we must have thousands of tons without delay."

Huge loans to the Allies tied American finance and prosperity ever more closely to an Allied victory, though U.S. government propaganda still justified the war in terms of lofty aims and ideals, stressing that the Americans were fighting for peace, freedom, and justice for all individuals of all nations, including Germans.

Despite such rhetoric, many Americans felt a less than overwhelming enthusiasm for the conflict. Socialists dismissed it as a businessman's war, but opposition was not confined to the Left. An Akron, Ohio, newspaper said that the nation had "never embarked on a more unpopular war" and only seventy-three thousand of the one million men needed had voluntarily enlisted in the six weeks following the declaration of war, forcing the introduction of conscription. In some Americans' eyes, the "war to make the world safe for democracy" was also signally failing to safeguard democracy at home. Although he had led his nation into the war, Wilson had warned of the danger it would pose to American society: the American people, he said, would "forget there ever was such a thing as tolerance. To fight you must be brutal and ruthless and the spirit of ruthless brutality will enter into the very fiber of our national life, infecting Congress, the courts, the policeman on the beat, the man in the street." That was not markedly different from the socialist Max Eastman's prophecy that it would not be a war for democracy at all; "we will Prussianize [militarize] ourselves and will probably not democratize Prussia."

Xenophobia was rampant. German-language books were publicly burned in several places, including Spartanburg; sauerkraut was renamed "Liberty Cabbage," and the hamburger became the "Liberty Sandwich." Hollywood weighed in with luridly titled films like The Beast of Berlin and The Claws of the Hun that fueled anti-German feeling. Citizens with foreign accents or names were instantly suspect, irrespective of their actual nationality or whether they were fresh off the boat or American-born, and in the U.S. heartland in particular, due process often gave way to lynch law and the rule of the mob.

Police, courts, officials, and government were often passive—and sometimes active—conspirators in an assault on American civil liberties, as the rights to free speech and thought, habeas corpus, and a fair trial came under attack. Free speech was now apparently tolerated only when the sentiments it expressed accorded with the views and policies of the U.S. government and did not include the right to criticize the decision to go to war, conscription, or the conduct of the war.

Federal prosecutors also showed extraordinary zeal in targeting individuals. In one of the more extraordinary cases, the maker of The Spirit of '76, a film depicting British atrocities against American colonists during the War of Independence, was sentenced to ten years' imprisonment by a judge who told him that the film "tended to question the good faith of our ally, Great Britain." The irony of the official listing of the case as U.S. v Spirit of '76 seemed to elude everyone.

Conscientious objectors were treated with uniform harshness. Even those whose religion forbade them to take up arms were persecuted; forty-five Mennonites were sentenced to twenty-five years in jail for refusing to wear army uniforms. The postmaster general took powers to ban from the U.S. mail any publication criticizing America's war effort; seventy-five periodicals, the majority of them socialist publications, were put out of business as a result, and there was growing industrial and social unrest, as socialism, Marxism, and anarchism claimed increasing numbers of adherents among the industrial poor and the unemployed.

Conflicts between companies and their increasingly organized and vocal employees created conditions that, with one eye on events in Russia, some feared might even be prerevolutionary. Gangsters like Monk had long been used as strike-breakers for hire, but the gangs could no longer provide sufficient men to intimidate workforces that often numbered in the hundreds if not thousands, and companies hired in other "goons," private detectives, vigilantes, and even the National Guard to break strikes and labor disputes.

The Alien Enemies Act of 1798 had been widely used to intern some of the 3.5 million immigrants from Germany and the territories of the Austro-Hungarian empire, but the 1917 Espionage Act and the 1918 Sedition Act gave the government even more draconian powers, not only against espionage and sedition but against any form of dissent. Fines of up to ten thousand dollars and twenty-year jail sentences were imposed on offenders.

The state and the police now had the freedom to interfere in almost every area of American life; as the attorney general remarked, "It is safe to say that never in its history had the country been so thoroughly policed." If that had already proved to be dangerous for aliens, pacifists, socialists, and union organizers, it also threatened to be bad news for criminals like Monk, should he attempt to resume his old career once the war was over.

Soon after Monk and his comrades arrived in Bussy-lès-Daours, the 106th Infantry received their first replacements since leaving Spartan-burg the previous spring. The new boys, National Army men, had not faced combat at all, and there must have been an almost unbridgeable gulf between them and the surviving veterans.

Despite growing rumors about peace proposals, the 106th resumed intensive training, preparing the new arrivals for the regiment's impending return to the front lines. On the morning of Sunday, November 10, as the 27th Division was about to begin the trek back to the Western Front, a bugle sounded, calling the surviving members to attention. Against the backdrop of the French hills, snowcapped and blue-tinted in the chill of the morning, the 27th Division Memorial Review was held in honor of the memory of their comrades. Although the dead had been buried in or near the battlefields where they fell, and burial services held over their graves, General O'Ryan felt that the survivors would still want to participate in a ceremony to commemorate their lost comrades and claimed that no soldiers had ever been more motivated by "the higher military ideals," nor more disciplined. If that remark would once have provoked incredulous looks from those familiar with the disciplinary record of the 106th Infantry at Spartanburg, their subsequent conduct on the battlefield had more than wiped the slate clean.

The snow-covered ground on which Monk and the other veterans of the 106th stood shoulder to shoulder to honor their dead seemed to heighten the stillness of that somber scene. Fourteen months earlier, they had left for Camp Wadsworth, South Carolina, marching in the shadow of the skyscrapers of New York with the cheers of their fellow citizens ringing in their ears. Six months ago they had disembarked at Brest and marched up the hill from the harbor through the narrow streets, past throngs of French civilians curious to see these young American "saviors" of their land. Now there were no spectators, and the only visible building was the war-ravaged cathedral of Corbie in the distance. Their equipment was battered, their uniforms threadbare, and the once numerous companies were now hardly bigger than platoons. They were gaunt and tired, many bore wound stripes on their arms, and their drawn faces were almost unrecognizable as those of once brash, cocky young men.

Accompanied by their retinues of staff officers, Generals Pershing, Read, and O'Ryan walked past each file of troops. General Pershing inspected every single man and paused to talk to many of those who wore wound stripes or decorations. His progress was "so slow it seemed we would be there in our rigid position forever . . . this thing would never end." Even when the inspection was at last over, the troops were still kept rigidly at attention. They watched from the corners of their eyes as the staff officers formed a circle around General Pershing, all facing outward, and the watching soldiers were left to wonder if theirs was the only unit ever to have to stand at attention while its commander emptied his bladder. The New York Division remained at attention while their massed bands played not a martial air, but a hymn in memory of all those men whose places in the ranks now stood empty. After a two-minute silence, the generals took the salute as, regiment by regiment, the troops marched past the dais. A pack of about twenty of their adopted stray dogs trailed after the soldiers, as if taking part in the ceremony.

The 106th Infantry and their sister regiments had fully earned the battle honors and the praise heaped upon them by the generals who watched them pass in review that cold November morning, but the men and their families had paid the heaviest possible price. The 106th Infantry had been over the top more times than any other regiment in the division, and had "the honor of being first over in every engagement, which to us is the greatest honor of all." They had not been the first to break through the Hindenburg Line—that honor had fallen to their fellow regiments—but, as General O'Ryan acknowledged, "It was undoubtedly the fierce attack of the 106th Infantry which broke the morale of the enemy and made possible the subsequent attacks by the remainder of the division."

Monk had fought at East Poperinghe; the Dickebusch Line; Vierstraat Ridge; the Knoll, Guillemont Farm, and Quennemont Farm on the Hindenburg Line; and at the Selle and Saint-Maurice rivers. His commanding officer, Colonel Franklin W. Ward, described Monk's record as exceptional, and there was probably no soldier in the entire 27th Division who was more inspirational to his comrades, more cool under fire, more brave in leading attacks, more willing to remain in the front line even when his regiment was being relieved, or more selfless in risking his own life to save others. His heroics at Vierstraat Ridge, the Hindenburg Line, and the Selle River alone make it difficult to comprehend why he was not cited for bravery.

The citations among other men of the regiment and the rest of the division include a number whose feats appear far less selfless and impressive than those of Monk, yet he was awarded no decorations for his valor. The death of Monk's Company G commander and the loss of all the other company officers during the fighting may have meant that he was denied simply by the ferocious toll of dead and wounded among them. Officers wrote up the battle reports and citations for bravery— one reason, cynics might have said, for the disproportionate number of officers who received medals for bravery—and many of the heroics performed by Monk may have been witnessed only by other enlisted men. The replacement officers may have been unaware of Monk's actions when compiling reports for their superiors, or the commendations may have come from the less unimpeachable sources—at least in staff officers' eyes—of NCOs and other ranks.

Monk was not alone in being overlooked. Of the eight men of Company G cited for valor after the war was over, only three were privates, the rest being sergeants, and none of the three privates had played any part in the actual fighting. One was a runner cited for delivering messages "between battalion headquarters, company and platoon headquarters under heavy fire and displayed unvarying coolness," and the other two were stretcher-bearers at Mount Kemmel, cited for "devotion to duty and tireless energy under fire."

The other possible explanation for Monk's failure to win the medals his bravery should have earned him is that his troubled past had counted against him; perhaps someone among the senior regimental or divisional officers knew that he was a convicted felon and had vetoed a citation. However, although Monk had no Congressional Medal of Honor or other military award, he had earned the unconditional respect and admiration of the most important judges: the men who served alongside him. If ever anyone had redeemed a terrible past by his present actions, Monk Eastman was that man.

His regiment had borne the brunt of the 27th Division's losses. It had lost 663 men at the Hindenburg Line alone, and in all sustained 1,955 casualties, including 1,496 wounded, 376 killed outright, and another 83 who died later of their wounds. On October 27, a report on the current strength of the regiment, company by company, had shown that, while the headquarters company still retained 5 officers and 199 men, the fighting companies had been cut to pieces. Monk's Company G alone had 52 men killed. They had no line officers at all, and just 56 men. None of the other eleven infantry companies in the regiment had more than 60 enlisted men still standing, and many of those were suffering from the aftereffects of wounds, gas, and shell shock. In less than four months' service on the front lines, the total fighting strength of the regiment had been reduced by two-thirds. Losses in the 27th Division as a whole were massive; out of a paper strength of around 14,000 men, 236 officers and 7,901 men were casualties, and 1,659 had died, including 1,329 killed in action, 253 who died later of wounds, and the remainder from disease, primarily influenza, or accident. In the two infantry brigades that composed the 27th Division, only 850 rifles remained when the Armistice "terminated the World's Greatest Show on the morning of the 11th of November."

Although Allied commanders knew that the war was about to end, many attacks scheduled for that morning still went ahead, with hundreds more men condemned to fall in one final, futile assault on territory that would have been handed over to the Allies anyway under the terms of the Armistice. Even in that monstrous meat-grinder of a war,

never had there been such pointless deaths. The artillery also continued to fire right up until the eleven o'clock deadline, expending shells
not merely in a final act of vengeance against the Germans, but also in
the gun crews' pragmatic knowledge that any not fired would have to
be carried back by them from the front lines. That night there was a
last orgy of firing, though this time it was a fireworks show, as all the
remaining front and reserve line stocks of rockets, flares, star shells, and
bombs were blasted off. As their comrades in other divisions celebrated,
the men of the 27th Division were now so remote from the front lines
that they were not even aware that the Armistice had been signed until
General O'Ryan encountered two Australian soldiers on the road outside his headquarters who demanded to know why he wasn't celebrating.

After the suspicion, condescension, and sometimes hostility with
which the American soldiers had first been greeted by their allies, there
was now unstinting praise for their contribution to the Allied victory.
Having lauded the 27th Division, Britain's commander in chief, Field
Marshal Douglas Haig, heralded the Anglo-American alliance as the
start of a new era. "I rejoice to think that in the greater knowledge and
understanding born of perils and hardships shared together, we have
learnt at last to look beyond old jealousies and past quarrels to the essential qualities which unite the great English-speaking nations."

General O'Ryan's reply gently punctured some of Haig's hyperbole about the kinship of "English-speaking nations" with a reminder
that his troops, "being Americans, are the descendants of many races
and peoples, some of them having no sentimental or other ties with
Great Britain. It is natural to assume that they entered upon the service
of their Division with widely varying notions respecting British soldiers and the soldiers of her colonies." However, he then sugared the
pill by acknowledging that "upon the completion of our service, we
carried with us respect and admiration for your soldiers, both officers
and men."

The five thousand new troops added to the 106th and the other
regiments of the 27th Division would now never see action, though in
that they were far from unique, for most doughboys never even saw a
shot fired in anger. Even those who saw action were in the firing line
for an average of just seven days; Monk and his fellows had seen almost
continuous action for four months.

The 106th Infantry remained in the Corbie area for a further two weeks. Their billets were less than satisfactory, and when winter began to bite, the lack of heating was so keenly felt that the number of compensation claims for damages from French property owners increased dramatically, as furniture, doors, and windows were broken up and used for fuel. Commanding officers were ordered to take the necessary steps to prevent vandalism, but to the relief of men and officers alike, they were transferred on the night of November 27, marching to the railroad station just before midnight. After a twenty-four-hour journey, cooped up in the familiar horse cars, they then endured a further infuriating two-hour wait on the train after its arrival at Le Mans, where they were held by railway officials, before the men finally disembarked at 2:15 on the morning of November 29. They then marched to Le Breil, three miles away, arriving, worn out, at 5:45 in the morning.

Monk and his comrades stayed in Le Breil for three months, continuing to undergo training, inspections, and army "bull," five days a week, beginning at 7:45 a.m. In addition to one hour's close-order drill every day and three hours daily of field exercises, formation for attack, patrols, and advance guards, each battalion was required to hold one maneuver exercise each week, and target practice also continued.

The veterans of the 27th Division failed to share their commander's enthusiasm for continued training; absenteeism from maneuvers held just before Christmas 1918 ran at about 25 percent, and in addition to 1,328 enlisted men, 28 officers were also missing. Longer-term absentees, men sentenced to imprisonment for being absent without leave, had been granted amnesty soon after the Armistice, but this did not signal a general relaxation of discipline. Reports that enlisted men had been discarding some items of their equipment and selling others led to General Order No. 106, issued at the end of December, requiring the mens' shoes, gas masks, helmets, and slickers to be carefully checked; any soldier found to have disposed of them was threatened with a summary court-martial. Pistols and revolvers stolen or salvaged during operations and kept by many men as souvenirs from the battlefield were also confiscated.

The disciplinary tone had been set by a memorandum issued just after the Armistice, announcing that "owing to changed conditions of service it is now practicable to devote much attention to the details of personal appearance of men and precision in all details of their life." Orders forbidding the wearing of sweaters over their shirts when outside their quarters, or requiring enlisted men to salute automobiles, on the assumption that automobiles would always contain officers—"not enough attention is being paid to this order"—might almost have been calculated to provoke the exhausted survivors of a conflict that had claimed so many lives.

There were also a few more serious breaches of discipline like brawls and thefts, and allegations of many more that were rejected as not proven. To minimize friction with the local inhabitants, the rules governing soldiers' off-duty behavior were circulated both to the men and to the townspeople. Soldiers had to be in their billets by 9:30 every evening, and French citizens were asked not to allow any soldiers to be in their homes or places of business after 9:15 p.m. Soldiers were only allowed in estaminets between noon and 1:00 p.m. and 5:00 p.m. and 8:00 p.m., and it was illegal to sell soldiers any alcoholic drinks except light wine and beer. Even so, drink may have fueled an incident in which, after a brawl with a soldier from Company G or H of the 106th, a soldier from the 102nd Field Signals allegedly had his ear cut off.

As they had done for most of their time in France, the men of the 106th Infantry were once more living in a sea of mud. Shortages of cooking stoves meant their food was often late and cold, and when they were issued with replacement underwear, it was already infested with lice. Faced with such living conditions and irritated by petty rules and complaints, the enthusiasm of the men of Monk's Company G for further military service could be gauged by the reply to a memorandum seeking volunteers to remain in France and serve with the 16th Salvage Company, clearing the battlefields of ordnance and reusable equipment and materials. Only ten men from the entire regiment expressed interest, and of those, two were men held for being AWOL, who were trying to avoid being sent to a labor battalion, and another was volunteering for anything that would keep him in France because of his "infatuation with a Parisienne."

The rest of the men wanted only to be gone from France and on their way home, and in the absence of any definite news about when they would be embarking, the rumors flew thick and fast. Christmas provided a brief distraction, though it must also have provoked a renewed longing among the American troops to be home with family and friends. They tried to make the best of it, putting up a Christmas tree on the village green and taking up a collection to buy toys for the kids in town. Monk and his comrades had been given Christmas Day off, with no duty other than guard duty, but it was a very brief reprieve. The hated drill and practice maneuvers resumed on December 26, and on New Year's Eve the regiment assembled at Saint-Michel for an inspection and review, finishing with a march of twelve miles through sticky mud and drenching rain.

Cigarettes, cigars, and candy were freely distributed in an attempt to keep up the men's spirits—in a single month, the American Expeditionary Force issued a billion cigarettes, twenty-two million cigars, and "three million rounds of candy"—and a schedule of leaves in the United Kingdom was also arranged. One officer and sixteen other ranks from each regiment went at first, and the numbers were slowly increased, though they were never to exceed 10 percent of a regiment's strength. It is doubtful whether Monk ever took advantage of the opportunity. He preferred to spend his spare time working toward a qualification; his grade of Army Mechanic was finally confirmed on March 1, 1919.

To the continuing anguish of their families at home, even at this late stage, sixty members of the regiment, including seven from Company G, were still posted as missing in action, though there was little realistic hope now of them ever being found alive. Officers had the heartrending duty of replying to letters from relatives seeking news of their missing loved ones, or details of their death.

Decisions also had to be made over the fate of those definitely dead and buried. General O'Ryan had asked company commanders for their men's views on whether the bodies of the dead should be repatriated or remain buried near where they fell in battle. The men of Company G were unanimous that the dead should lie undisturbed where they had fallen, and 86 percent of their fellows in the 106th Infantry agreed. Many of the grieving relatives at home shared that view, but others wanted their dead repatriated and were vigorously supported by a lobbying campaign of breathtaking cynicism mounted by the "Purple Cross," a newly created group funded by American funeral directors eager to profit from the thousands of burials that would result. Some funeral-industry organizations and publications were brazen enough to openly discuss the profits to be made, and they even offered to send sufficient embalmers to France—at government expense—to ensure the return of every "American Hero . . . in a sanitary and recognizable condition."

In the end, like Theodore Roosevelt, whose youngest son, Quentin, was killed in the war, thirty-one thousand American wives and parents believed that their dead husbands and sons would have wished to remain among their fallen comrades. As Roosevelt wrote to the army chief of staff, "Mrs. Roosevelt and I . . . have always believed that where the tree falls, let it lay." Twenty-five thousand parents and wives still disagreed and opted to have the bodies of their loved ones returned to the United States for burial, though not all got their wish. Well over one thousand of the American dead, lost without a trace in the shell-cratered battlefields, had no known graves.

Rumors that the 27th Division was about to head home continued to circulate, but finally, on February 20, 1919, the 106th Infantry regiment started to move back to Brest. They had already been inspected for vermin on January 31, but, before being pronounced fit to be embarked for home, every American soldier had to be inspected again, deloused, and pronounced free from any communicable diseases. The 106th Infantry had been designated for earliest movement, and they were first to pass through "Bathing, Delousing and Re-Equipment with Clothing, Inspection, Verification of Records, etc.," at the "Dirty Camp" at Belgian Camp, a process that took four or five days. They then boarded the 40 hommes—8 chevaux boxcars for the last time for the journey to Brest, during which many of them were probably reinfested with lice.

On arrival, Monk and his fellows were assigned to Pontanezen Barracks, to be remembered without fondness for its mud and slippery "duck boards," though "it was nothing compared to the trenches." There were many complaints about conditions at the camp, but they were probably less attributable to the now familiar mud, cold, and discomfort than to the frustration of being camped within sight of the port and the ships that could take them home, but still without a firm date of departure. Disease was also rife. The great Spanish influenza epidemic that had claimed more lives worldwide than even the Great War itself was still carrying off men, and the childhood diseases of measles and mumps remained prevalent. Fostered in the unsanitary and often stagnant air of the dugouts in the reserve areas, such diseases had hospitalized many victims and continued to infect men at the Pontanezen Barracks.

It is probable that Monk was one of those who caught influenza. The gassing he had suffered in combat had made his lungs more vulnerable to infection, and on December 2, 1918, he reported sick. Within two weeks Monk's condition had deteriorated so much that he was sent to the hospital. Unlike many of his comrades, however, Monk recovered, and by January 2, 1919, he was back on duty, though still excused from drill; he returned to full duty a week later.

On February 24, the men of the 106th Infantry at last received the orders they had long been awaiting and marched the five miles down the road to Pier 5 at Brest. They took their final step on French soil at ten past eleven that morning, before boarding the lighter Tudno for transfer to their troopship, the USS Leviathan, at anchor out in the harbor. They were the first of 10,343 officers and men of the 27th Division to board.

The Leviathan was one of six big transports—the others being Agamemnon, Mauretania, Harrisburg, Louisville, and Pannonia—assigned to carry American troops home. An impounded and converted German liner, the Leviathan was the fastest and, at fifty-four thousand tons, by far the largest of the fleet, more than twice the size of the next largest ship. Capable of carrying as many as twenty thousand troops in a single voyage, she always traveled alone because she could outrun any convoy or submarine. Loading continued all that day and the next, when the ship was also coaled and the baggage craned aboard. They sailed on the high tide at 12:30 p.m. the following day, February 26, 1918, a gray and rainy day. Included in the souvenirs that Monk was taking home were "ten homing pigeons and his trench hat, bearing bullet holes."

Part III

21

THE FIGHTERS THAT
THEY WERE

The Leviathan and one of her sister ships, the Mauretania, returned home together on March 6, 1919, bearing a total of about 13,700 New York troops. The pilot boat that met the Leviathan off Ambrose Channel Lightship delivered mail, newspapers, and an official letter of greeting from Mayor Hylan, but the first official welcome came from a flying boat sent by the Aeronautical Exposition and manned by C. J. Zimmerman, who flew out to sea early in the morning, met the Levi-

athan ten miles off Sandy Hook, and, circling low, dropped two canvas bags containing messages of welcome onto the deck of the ship. A
fleet of boats carrying members of the city and state official reception
committee and upstate representatives had also left the Battery at eight
that morning to rendezvous with the ship as it came up the channel,
and the Knights of Columbus sent out a boat laden with cigarettes and
candy for the returning heroes—the first of many such gifts they would
receive. A flotilla of other boats, chartered by friends and families of
returning servicemen, also sailed to greet the ship. In all, more than
fifteen thousand people were packed on the eighteen ships that sailed
down the bay to greet them.

The Leviathan slowed as she reached Quarantine, allowing the welcoming flotilla to form an escort around her, and then steamed slowly
on. "From the moment the huge Leviathan became visible to the welcoming fleet in the morning mists off Quarantine, until the last soldier
stepped aboard the last train in the embarkation station at Hoboken,
thousands strained their eyes to catch glimpses of those who returned."
The men on board let out shouts as they glimpsed old familiar landmarks along the Brooklyn and Jersey shorelines, and there was a huge
cheer when the white sands of Coney Island came into view.

Under a bright sun, the harbor was dotted with craft of all kinds,
and the sea wall at the Battery was black with people cheering and waving flags and handkerchiefs. General O'Ryan stood on the flying bridge
of the ship, acknowledging the greetings of the reception committee
and the cheers of the spectators. Every porthole of the ship seemed to
frame a smiling face, and the decks were jammed with soldiers. Ships
sounded their foghorns and the Bands of the Port of Embarkation
struck up as the great ship nosed in to dock at Pier 4 at Hoboken, but
the noise was almost drowned by the cacophony of shouts and cheers
from the waiting crowds, all desperate to identify their own returning
heroes, and the answering yells from the men lining the decks.

The ship docked at twelve minutes past eleven that morning, but
it was more than half an hour before the first of three gangplanks was
lowered and the first soldier—an officer of the 106th Infantry—rushed
down to plant his feet on American soil. All day the streets near the
army piers in Hoboken were so crowded with people hoping to catch
at least a glimpse of the returning heroes that traffic came to a complete stop, but if families had hoped for a dockside reunion with their
long-absent husbands, fathers, brothers, and sons, they were to be dis-

appointed. Only officials were admitted to the pier, and relatives had no opportunity to catch even a glimpse of the individual soldiers.

Alongside the thousands of men pouring down the gangplanks was a large number of dogs. Hardly any of all the scores of strays that individual soldiers had befriended and adopted had been given official permission to return home with the regiment on the USS Leviathan, but many had made the journey as stowaways, smuggled aboard, often rolled in blankets inside the men's packs. The enlisted men were not alone in wanting to bring back their pets and mascots; their commander, General O'Ryan, brought a Belgian police dog, "Fique," with him. After the dog attached himself to the division at Alençon in Belgium, his name was added to the official muster rolls and his blanket decorated with two service stripes and one wound stripe after he was slightly injured by shrapnel. The men of the headquarters company of the 106th were less successful with the thirteen-year-old Flemish orphan boy whom they had unofficially adopted. They tried to take him back to the United States with them after the war, but military police refused to allow him to board the troopship.

Eleven hundred men on board the Leviathan were still sick or wounded, including two hundred cases of the influenza that continued to claim lives. They were helped down the gangplanks long after the other men had disembarked, but thirty were so ill that they were kept aboard the ship for another night. Monk and his comrades did not disembark until four that afternoon, and they were then transferred by waiting ferries to Long Island City and by train to Mineola, Long Island. They arrived at 8:45 that night, and the first sight of Mineola triggered a barrage of shouts of the 106th's battle cry. They then marched to Camp Mills, but homecoming celebrations were put on hold as the men were placed in strict quarantine until they had gone through the sanitation process. Despite the delousing at Belgian Camp, the majority of men and their kit were still infested with the lice they had first acquired in the trenches and French billets, and as soon as they arrived they were covered with liquid soap and kerosene and then given hot showers while their clothing and bedding were fumigated.

It was after midnight by the time the last men from the Leviathan reached Camp Mills, by which time the earlier arrivals had already gone through the cleaning process and the baths were waiting for the last arrivals. Fifty-four medical officers presided over the examination of every man, and as soon as the cleaning process was complete, half the men at Camps Mills and Merritt were given forty-eight-hour leave passes, and upon their return the other half were sent on leave. All the men were either discharged or transferred to another camp within four days, making room for the next contingent of homecoming troops. Camps Upton, Devens, and Dix took most, with the overflow going to Camp Meade or Camp Merritt.

On March 24 the men of the 106th Infantry, with the rest of the five thousand men of the Brooklyn contingents of the 27th Division, arrived in the city on eight special trains. Their comrades in the 106th Machine Gun Battalion had not been billeted with the rest of their regiment and were transported from Camp Merritt to Jersey City on the Erie railroad and then ferried over to Manhattan. They took the subway from Wall Street and emerged at Atlantic Avenue in Brooklyn, where a huge crowd was waiting to greet them.

Led by Colonel Franklin W. Ward and preceded by two hundred mounted policemen and the men of the Brooklyn State Guard, the 106th Infantry marched through the streets of Brooklyn with all the equipment they had carried when they went over the top at the Hindenburg Line, excluding their hand grenades and the machine-gun battalion's weapons, which had been taken from them in France. They wore their tin hats and light field packs slung across their backs, carried gas masks, and had rifles with bayonets fixed. They marched in their platoons, sixteen abreast, from Bedford and Atlantic Avenues to Park Place and Flatbush Avenue, and then to Prospect Park West, where two reviewing stands had been erected, one built by carpenters of the Todd Shipyard, who did the work without pay. The stands could hold 20,000 people, only a fraction of the 125,000 applications for seats that had been received.

People had been claiming vantage points on the route since well before dawn. Many of the earlier arrivals had brought their breakfast with them, but others relied on the sandwich and hot dog men, who were already doing a roaring trade. The masses that jammed the streets along the line of march and overflowed well up the cross streets formed by far the largest crowd ever gathered in Brooklyn. The "wild men," as the Brooklyn soldiers who first swarmed over the outposts of the Hindenburg Line were described in diaries found on captured and dead Germans, marched beneath a canopy of American flags, banners, and welcoming ribbons, fluttering in the breeze in bright sunshine.

Many of these same men had paraded through the streets before going off to war, but they were different now. Their uniforms were battle-worn, and the naïveté and youthful enthusiasm that had shone from so many faces then had gone. "With set faces that betrayed no interest in mere display, with a step that carried them tirelessly over the distance but had no parade ground snap . . . they were impressive because they looked—with guns carried easily instead of smartly, bundled in their big coats, encumbered with packs and gas masks—rough and tough, the fighters that they were." They seemed to have aged far more than the year that they had been away, with a look in their eyes that spoke of things seen that made the gang wars of the Lower East Side seem like the playground bickering of infants. "The straight lines cut into their faces by facing death and dealing with it . . . were not relaxed by the pleasure which they must have felt at the reception . . . These stern countenances struck a kind of awe into the crowd. One glance was enough to show that these were men just returned from the bloody battlefield with their experiences stamped on their features."

The crowd's reaction had been subdued by these silent, grim-faced, marching men, but there were cheers and laughs as three regimental mascots appeared—two dogs and a young goat. One of the dogs, a collie, wore a blanket with the division insignia and two wound stripes. The dog had been adopted by the regiment while they were in training at Spartanburg and had been on the front lines with them, suffering wounds at Vierstraat Ridge (machine-gun bullet, left foreleg) and the Hindenburg Line (shrapnel, neck). He had also been marked AWOL from June 20 to 22, 1918, but that was the sole blemish on his service record, and he was the only dog officially cited by his commander, Colonel Franklin W. Ward, for distinguished service with the A.E.F. The dog was guest of honor at a dinner of the Brooklyn Democratic Club at the Commodore Hotel after the parade, his invitation bearing the promise of a silver collar and three extra bones.

Although the sight of the animals drew smiles and applause from spectators, "the spell of the grim fighters was not entirely broken until the veterans who were no longer under military discipline came along." They included Brooklyn men from other units like the Rainbow Division, the Camp Upton Division, and the marines. Some had already been mustered out of the service, others were wounded convalescents, and they marched along in the rear, smoking, chatting, shouting, and waving at friends. Brooklyn hospitality had been lavished upon them before they started and at intervals during the march, to such an extent that most of them were laden with doughnuts, buns, candy, and sausages. They had eaten all they wanted by the time they reached the official reviewing stand at Prospect Park and Ninth Street and began using the surplus as missiles in a lighthearted food fight. Sharp orders from their officers restored some order, but sausages and buns continued to fly from their ranks at intervals as they marched on.

The parade ended at Fifteenth Street, and after leaving their weapons and equipment in the armories, Monk and his fellows attended dinners for enlisted men and noncommissioned officers at 150 different hotels and several armories, followed by "general jollification and entertainment." More cigarettes, candy, and chewing gum were distributed to each man, courtesy of the Knights of Columbus, and eight thousand Ward Baking Company cakes were handed out. Across the East River, a monster boxing carnival was being held in Madison Square Garden to entertain the troops, and scores of theaters added special showings at which only uniformed men were admitted.

There was little time for sleep before leaving for the following morning's parade in Manhattan—the greatest parade in the city's history. Grandstands had been erected along fifty-one city blocks, thus surpassing, as the 27th Division's official historian proudly noted, the seating capacity of the Roman Colosseum. Fifth Avenue, "the Appian Way of the New World," had been thronged all day and far into the night. From the Washington Arch to Sixtieth Street, Fifth Avenue was "a modern fairy land of color and illumination, a blazing golden way," its decorations the "most pretentious and artistic ever seen, expressing three sentiments: the note of triumph, the note of memorial and the note of carnival and jubilation." Lights of more than a hundred thousand candlepower had been arranged along the route, and searchlights played on the decorations at the three places of honor—the Victory Arch at Madison Square, the Court of the Heroic Dead at Forty-second Street, and the Arch of Jewels at the Plaza.

Pristine white sand covered Fifth Avenue from Twenty-third to Twenty-sixth streets, flanked by a colonnade of pylons that held four huge balloons, tethered by colored ropes and decorated with Allied flags and glittering metal spirals. The Altar of Liberty was surrounded by massed Allied flags, and the Victory Arch stood, brilliant white and twelve stories high, above Madison Square. Golden shields emblazoned with the 27th Division's crest hung from the trees between Fortieth and Forty-second streets. At the Court of the Heroic Dead, outside the New York Public Library, two tall pylons bore gleaming golden eagles with spread wings, while golden spears and more shields bearing the divisional crest supported a purple curtain fringed with gold and inscribed with the 27th Division's battle honors.

Above the list of battles was a copy of a letter written by Abraham Lincoln to the mother of six boys who lost their lives in the Civil War: "I feel how weak and fruitless must be any words of mine which should attempt to beguile you from the grief so overwhelming, I pray that our Heavenly Father may assuage the anguish of your bereavement and leave you only the cherished memory of the loved and lost, and the solemn pride that must be yours to have laid so costly a sacrifice upon the altar of freedom." Below that text, half-shrouded by the purple curtain, was a huge roll of honor inscribed with the names of the dead and the heroic deeds of the 27th Division.

Sightseers and friends and relatives of soldiers had poured into the city from upstate, and every hotel was so packed that "even the best friend of the manager" would have struggled to find a place to sleep. Enterprising people with apartments or offices overlooking the parade route were hiring out space to stand and watch from their windows for a few dollars a time, and one person with a room near Forty-second Street was asking three hundred dollars for a day's hire.

The grandstands stretched for two and a half miles along Fifth Avenue, and the city's parks had also been stripped of their benches. Twenty-five hundred were placed between Eighteenth and Twentieth streets and seven hundred near the public library, as front-row seats for six thousand wounded and convalescent soldiers and the few remaining veterans of the Civil War. Convalescents from the Grand Central Palace Hospital viewed the parade from the backs of trucks parked in the side streets from Forty-fifth to Fifty-first streets, while the shell-shocked men from the Gun Hill Road Hospital were seated with 275 Red Cross nurses in a stand at Sixtieth Street.

Hundreds of improvised stands had been erected for employees of the shops and offices lining Fifth Avenue. Building after building was festooned with banners and welcome home signs, and the flag of the 27th Division also hung from hundreds of improvised poles. On each flag, the divisional insignia, the stars of the constellation Orion—a punning reference to the name of the division's commander—and the letters nyd (New York Division) were picked out in crimson on a black background. The colors also had symbolic significance: "the black for iron, the crimson for blood—The Iron and Blood Division." The façade of one store bore an American flag covering five stories, and smaller flags were grouped around a replica of the great seal of New York State, topped by "27" picked out in blue lights. Thick ropes of greenery were strung from flag to flag, and there was scarcely a window that did not contain a flag or a placard.

Clear skies and sunshine and a gentle northerly breeze greeted the 27th Division as they set out together for the last time, heralded by two airplanes, one said to be piloted by air ace Eddie Rickenbacker, that flew straight up Fifth Avenue, below the roof levels of the buildings on either side. Flying higher, they performed aerobatics above the rooftops.

The procession itself was led by a symbolic tribute to the dead: a flower-decked and flag-draped funeral caisson, drawn by eight horses and bearing a catafalque laden with a great laurel wreath and huge masses of flowers, filling the air with their fragrance. The caisson was followed by a group of soldiers carrying an enormous service flag bearing 1,973 gold stars—one for every member of the division killed in the war. As the great golden service flag came into view, its stars glittering in the light of the noonday sun, the crowds removed their hats and bowed their heads.

Wounded men in trucks and automobiles came next, followed by the police department band, playing Sousa's "Stars and Stripes Forever," and behind them came the officers and men of the 27th Division, marching in their individual platoons, twenty abreast and in such close order that the rear rank man's steel helmet was under the bayonet of the front rank man in the next platoon. The 106th Infantry had formed up on Ninth and Tenth streets, between Fifth Avenue and Broadway, before taking their place in the parade. They wore their dark green helmets displaying the division insignia and had light packs, filled canteens, and overcoats with belts and sidearms. All their equipment, except their contaminated gas masks, had been brought home from France with them.

The parade halted for five minutes on the hour and half hour, and, whether marching or at rest, the men had been warned to maintain the military discipline that had brought their division "the respect of the world." There was to be no gum-chewing; no conversation in the ranks; no smiling and waving to relatives, friends, or acquaintances;

and no flowers, ribbons, or unauthorized badges or decoration of any kind.

As the procession approached the Victory Arch, the bands stopped their triumphal music and buglers played a salute to the colors while a single soldier, Sergeant Reidar Waller, selected for his heroism in battle as a winner of the Congressional Medal of Honor and the British Distinguished Service Medal, stepped forward. He cut the silken rope stretched across the entrance to the arch with his bayonet, while the guns of the forts along the river fired a salute.

At the Court of the Heroic Dead by the public library, a wreath of purple orchids was carried from the caisson by an honor guard of seven veterans of the Civil War and two of the Spanish-American War, and was laid at the foot of the roll of honor, surrounded by wreaths and flowers from other states and cities. While the wreath was being laid, a band played a funeral march. The spectators bared their heads and the uniformed veterans remained at attention until the last note had died away. The caisson was then led slowly away, and as the service flag reached the Court of the Heroic Dead, a community chorus of young boys sang "The Battle Hymn of the Republic," after which "many persons wiped their eyes."

Ever since his abrupt disappearance from the streets in September 1917, almost no one in the whole of New York City knew what had become of Monk Eastman. Now he was back, toting a gun on Fifth Avenue, but for once with no fear of arrest. "The gang"—a group of his old friends and acquaintances lining the sidewalks around Twenty-third Street—was out in force to greet him, and when the 106th Infantry appeared, "yells of 'Hello Monk' came from the throats of East Side admirers." Most of his army comrades knew him only as "a good pal and a brave soldier who was always ready to put his comrades and country above himself." Not until the parade did they discover that Private Edward Eastman and Monk Eastman the New York gangster were one and the same. A newspaper photograph published the next day showed Governor Alfred E. Smith—notoriously corrupt and Tammany to his fingertips—resplendent in a shiny top hat, leaning out of the front row of the reviewing stand to shake the hand of a doughboy friend from the East Side. The man whose hand he was shaking bore more than a passing resemblance to Monk.

It took the parade five hours to cover the five-mile route up Fifth

Avenue. The head of the procession, bearing the tributes to those buried in graves in Belgium and France, moved in slow and solemn silence, but the rest of the procession, the wounded riding in motorcars and the "effectives" striding along, were greeted by roars that never ceased. An estimated three million people had lined the route, jamming the sidewalks from curb to building line, leaning from every window and the roof edges high above them. Every seat in every stand was filled.

Many of those who had paid for grandstand seats found that they had invested in worthless bits of pasteboard, for when they arrived, they found their seats already taken by people who showed no willingness to give them up, and who had often paid for them as well. A few who had bought tickets from reputable agencies managed to get their money back, but "those who bought from irresponsible speculators got nothing but a bit of experience for their money." At some stands, attendants sold the reserved seats to the first persons who came along and then refused to do anything for the rightful owners when they appeared.

Thousands of people stood on chairs and boxes, craning their necks for a better view, and every cross street was dense with people for at least half a block in both directions. As they tried to snatch a better view of the parade, those nearer to Fifth Avenue were pushed forward until the crush was so great that the police lines were swept aside and the avenue was flooded with a swirling mass of humanity. Each time it happened, the parade ground to a stop. At Madison Square the press of spectators forced the procession to halt for nearly half an hour. The best efforts of mounted policemen using their horses to push back the people, police chauffeurs using their automobiles and motorcycles as "tanks," patrolmen on foot, and soldiers and sailors among the crowds resulted in the clearance of only a narrow pathway. Before General O'Ryan could lead his men under the Victory Arch, they were forced to break their platoon formation and swing into the familiar column of fours, the campaign marching formation that was rarely used on parade. O'Ryan was nearly thrown by his horse as the crowd pushed against it.

The crowds also later blocked Fifth Avenue in the Fifties, and again at Seventy-ninth Street. Men, women, and children were trampled underfoot; scores fainted, and three people died in the crush: a police captain had a heart attack, an insurance clerk was knocked down and run over as police struggled to clear the way, and a salesman fell down an airshaft from his viewing place high on a rooftop and suffered fatal injuries. Another dozen people were injured falling from trees that they had climbed for a better view, or from rooftops that were almost as densely packed as the streets below.

Thirty thousand boxes of lunch had been prepared for the marchers, but their rations were also augmented by a constant fall of manna from above, causing officers to observe that never in the history of the 27th Division had its discipline been put to a greater test. General O'Ryan had ordered his men to "parade at attention," but the distractions of family and friends calling to them from the crowd and the gifts of cigars, cigarettes, and candy showering on them from the buildings, sidewalks, and grandstands were hard to resist.

Although some of the men kept their eyes straight ahead whatever the distractions, not everyone was able to resist temptation, especially in the periods when the column was at rest. People dropped packs of cigarettes, bananas, and apples from the upper stories and rooftops, and "the boys didn't let many of them hit the asphalt and only laughed at the tingling in their fingers." Wounded soldiers watching the parade from curbside seats joined the scramble for cigarettes and money that came fluttering down like snowflakes from on high. When a shower of money—including coins wrapped in dollar bills—sandwiches, and cigarettes descended on the heads of the wounded men in the grandstands in front of the Netherland and Savoy hotels, many of them "forgot they were wounded" in the scramble for the gifts.

At intervals, the procession halted while delegates of public organizations and private enterprises presented boxes of candy and sandwiches. At the American Tobacco Company's offices at Eighteenth Street, tobacco and cigarettes were tossed to the boys, and at Fifty-ninth Street the official lunch wagon of the police department, a truck thirty feet long and six feet wide, dispensed fifteen thousand sandwiches and six thousand apples. New York had never seen such a parade.

After the parade, fifty thousand places for dinner at forty hotels and restaurants had been offered—almost twice as many as the number of soldiers. What was described as the city's biggest banquet featured a specially designed menu card detailing notable incidents from the 27th Division's history, including, of course, the storming of the Hindenburg Line. The same menu was served at all the venues:

Olives   Mixed Sweet Pickles
Grape Fruit
Fresh Vegetable Soup
Half Roast Broiler (1½ pounds)

Boiled Sweet Potato   Green Peas
Apple Pie
Neapolitan Ice Cream
Large Coffee with Milk and Sugar
Cigarettes   White Rock

Unfortunately, the organizing committee had displayed rather more enthusiasm than efficiency, and tickets for dinner were not distributed until well into the afternoon, by which time many of the men had drifted away with friends and relatives or made their own arrangements to eat. The Hotel McAlpin, asked to prepare dinner for five hundred soldiers, served only seventy-two, and the Commodore Hotel served only one-third of the eighteen hundred men they had been told to expect. Meanwhile, Monk led "the East Side delegation"—comrades of the 27th Division from his old Lower East Side turf—on a parade of his old haunts, ending with "a dinner to Eastman," a feast served at Pistanis on Kenmare and Elizabeth streets.

22

VICTIMLESS CRIMES

The next morning, March 27, 1919, hundreds of people gathered in Brooklyn at the Atlantic Avenue Terminal of the Long Island Rail Road to give the 106th Infantry a rousing final send-off as Monk and his comrades boarded trains for Camp Upton. A wartime camp of hurriedly erected two-story frame barracks sixty miles east of New York City, among the pine bush and white sands of Eastern Long Island, Camp Upton was where Monk and all his comrades were to complete the last formalities before their discharge from the service. At intervals of a few minutes, twenty-five trains, each eleven to fifteen cars long and packed with men, arrived at the terminal at the south center of the camp. As the trains pulled in, officers jumped into the cars and ordered the men out double-quick; within three minutes, each train had been emptied and sent back on the spur to the main line, returning to Jamaica by the South Shore Division.

On arrival at Camp Upton, each man was given a package containing cigarettes, chocolate, chewing gum, matches, and stamped cards. To minimize the risk of unauthorized excursions and interregimental troubles, visits by relatives and friends were not encouraged; the sections were at a remove from the station and widely separated from one another. Before their discharge could become effective, the soldiers had to sit through eight lectures, including talks on compensation, insurance, morale, and labor; fill out endless paperwork (eleven forms had to be completed for each man); settle their accounts; and undergo a physical examination.

Along with the rest of his comrades, Monk's formal discharge was completed on April 2, 1919. Each discharged man received a bonus of sixty dollars, and when the last one had been paid, the regiment was formally disbanded and ceased to exist. All the officers and men then boarded trains for New York, though they first had a long march back to the station from their section of the camp. Monk was given an honorable discharge and his papers were marked "Excellent." He had fought with extraordinary bravery for his country, but he remained deprived of the rights of citizenship, including the right to vote, because he had been convicted of a felony. However, as Monk boarded the train, he carried in his shirt pocket an envelope containing a petition bearing the signatures of his regimental officers, including the commanding officer, Colonel Franklin W. Ward; Captain Robert S. Cleaver; Captain Robert G. Conrow; the regimental surgeon, Major Larsen; and Lieutenant Joseph A. Kerrigan, who was Monk's direct superior. The petition had also been signed by every man in Company G and 150 other members of the 106th Infantry. Monk delivered the petition to supreme court justice Morschauser, who would personally present it to Governor Al Smith. The officers of the regiment also wrote letters to the governor, testifying to Monk's excellent conduct while in the service, his loyalty to his unit and his comrades, and his bravery in action.

On May 2, 1919, Governor Smith duly received the petition, supported by a letter from Justice Morschauser, who had become interested in Monk's case after meeting him. "Eastman came to see me here in Poughkeepsie and I was impressed with his desire to make good, if he had an opportunity," Morschauser wrote. "He volunteered his services for his country and made good, offering his life to the end that law and order should prevail in the world."

The letter of support from Colonel Ward drew attention to the fact that Monk had volunteered rather than been conscripted, and noted that "his record throughout the war has been exceptional and his service has been honest and faithful." Major Larsen was willing to vouch for the fact that after the 106th was withdrawn from the front lines, Monk had stayed on duty as a stretcher-bearer, "exhibiting great bravery," and Captain Cleaver had seen firsthand Monk's service at Kemmel Hill and the Hindenburg Line, where he displayed the "utmost courage and devotion to duty . . . he has been an excellent soldier and has made a good record."

In an observation that would have astounded the officers of the New York City Police Department, Captain Conrow also noted that Monk was "a quiet, disciplined soldier, who never gave any trouble . . . He bears an excellent reputation in the company for soldierliness and bore himself admirably under fire. Toward all comrades he evinced the greatest kindness and devotion." After describing Monk's heroism in battle, Lieutenant Kerrigan noted that Monk's conduct had also been exemplary and he had never been reported for absence without leave or any other offense. He had given Monk an excellent character on his discharge and believed that he "should be rewarded for the wonderful work done by him in the line and his honest and faithful service since his enlistment."

monk eastman wins new soul, the Tribune proclaimed in its front-page report on the petition. After sober consideration, on May 8, 1919, Governor Smith duly restored citizenship to the "one time 'bad man' of the East Side, survivor of a hundred gun fights, political ward heeler, repeater at the polls and finally convict . . . because of his exceptional record in the army overseas." As Monk confided to a friend, "Army life has made me over. I'm going to stick. If a fellow makes good wearing the uniform, his work is appreciated." The New York Times noted that "his own testimony on that score might not be readily taken, were it not backed up enthusiastically by those above him, [but] every man with human instincts will be glad to extend his hand to 'Monk' Eastman, the bad boy who had something in him."

However, questions still remained about the true extent of citizen Eastman's reform and redemption, and he refused to reveal to reporters where he was going to live or the nature of the work he had been offered. In fact, using the qualification as a motor mechanic he had gained in the army, Monk found work with Charley Jones, an old friend and former member of his gang who had gone straight and built an auto repair business on East Twentieth Street. For several months Monk appeared genuine in his desire to go straight, but a new and formidable temptation had emerged: Prohibition—"the father of the modern gangster."

The Great War had provided firm evidence that the United States had replaced Britain as the world's dominant power. The U.S. economy was already by far the most dynamic since well before the turn of the century, and now U.S. industrial output exceeded the combined production of Europe's three richest countries—Britain, Germany, and France—and by 1913 accounted for 35 percent of the world's total industrial production. America's political influence and military power had not reflected that economic strength, but now the United States had flexed its muscles. The nation that at the time of the declaration of war with Germany in April 1917 ranked equal with Finland in the size of its armed forces had armed, equipped, trained, and shipped to France two million soldiers by the time of the Armistice, barely eighteen months later. Although isolationism would remain a potent force in domestic politics, the United States was now the major figure on the world stage, and a perverse demonstration of that fact came when the American refusal to join the League of Nations rendered that organization impotent from the very start.

If the balance of world power was shifting toward America, her greatest city, New York, was also undergoing another seismic shift. The criminal gangs that had been driven to the point of extinction were now rising again as a direct consequence of the imposition of Prohibition, and the profits to be made dwarfed by far those that Monk had been able to achieve. Even at the peak of his powers, his annual returns from his criminal enterprises were probably counted in tens or, at most, hundreds of thousands of dollars; the major gang leaders of the Prohibition era would soon be calculating theirs in tens of millions.

The strength of the temperance movement in rural America had produced enough votes for the Eighteenth Amendment, prohibiting intoxicating beverages, to be ratified in January 1919, but it was believed to be unenforceable without further legislation, and in October 1919 Congress accordingly passed the National Prohibition Act, more widely known as the "Volstead Act" after its Republican sponsor, Representative Andrew J. Volstead from Minnesota. President Woodrow Wilson at once vetoed the measure, but Congress overrode the veto the next day. Distracted by the great issues of war and peace, the Spanish flu epidemic, and the increasing incapacity through ill health of President Wilson, the American electorate had now allowed a rump of almost exclusively rural and Protestant voters to turn the entire nation "dry."

The Volstead Act came into effect on January 16, 1920; nationwide prohibition was now in force. The act established penalties, including a search-and-seizure clause, against establishments selling liquor, while perversely continuing the taxation of alcoholic beverages. Private stocks of liquor bought before the act went into effect could be retained, and beer manufacture was permitted to continue, but only if brewers reduced the alcoholic content to 0.5 percent or less.

However, the principal consequence of Prohibition was not to turn the population of the United States into teetotalers overnight, as its proponents had hoped, but to secure the dramatic rebirth and regrowth of the previously moribund gang culture, and the fight to control bootlegging was more ferocious in New York than in any other American city—even Chicago. In a truly bizarre reversal, the once vilified gangsters would also acquire—albeit temporarily—the mythic status of folk heroes and community servants, American Robin Hoods committing "victimless crimes" to bring succor to a thirsty nation.

Much of the legitimate alcohol for medical or industrial use, housed in bonded warehouses on the Manhattan and Brooklyn waterfronts, found its way into bootleggers' hands through theft or forged medicinal withdrawal permits. A Brooklyn man, Edward J. Donegan, was said to have made more than two million dollars in two years after acquiring a set of blank permits and a rubber-stamp facsimile of the liquor administrator's signature. Bootleggers also loaded cargo ships with alcohol legally purchased in Europe. The ships were met in international waters just outside the three-mile U.S. territorial limit by fleets of fast speedboats that ran the contraband into coves and jetties the length of Long Island Sound. One of the leading rumrunners was Monk's old adversary Paul Kelly. Garbage scows operated by the members of his Scow

Trimmers Union went out to sea to dump New York's garbage every day, and it was easy for the scows to rendezvous with rum ships while out in the harbor. Booze was also trucked from Canada while many excisemen, like their counterparts in the Coast Guard, took bribes and looked the other way. Illicit breweries and distilleries within the United States also churned out everything from fine bourbon to rotgut hooch and sold it at a huge profit to speakeasies, clubs, restaurants, bars, brothels, and backstreet dives.

Police departments from which at least some of the corruption and criminality had been driven now found themselves again riddled with policemen on the take. Prohibition also put millions of ordinary, normally law-abiding citizens on the wrong side of the law, either as consumers or producers of illicit booze. Within months of the Volstead Act being passed, thousands of homes throughout the United States were being transformed into small-scale distilleries and breweries. In North Tarrytown, New York, the sewer inspector was forced to ask the town's inhabitants not to flush prune pits, grain, potato peelings, and other detritus from the stills, because they were clogging the drains. Mrs. Viola M. Anglin, deputy chief probation officer for New York City, testified that in each of the districts of her sixteen probation officers there were between one and two hundred stills, and not just in cigar stores, delicatessens, and other commercial premises, but "in the homes of the people who live in the tenements . . . any child in New York who knows anything about the city at all, can point out a still in his own neighborhood—can point out a speakeasy."

The gangs were now back on the streets of the Lower East Side, albeit in far lesser numbers than in Monk's prime, and bootleg alcohol was sold to bar, brothel, and speakeasy owners from "curbside markets" on Kenmare, Broome, Grand, and Elizabeth streets, only a stone's throw from police headquarters. When Monk disappeared from his old haunts and failed to appear at the garage for several weeks, police at once suspected that he had tired of honest toil and slipped back into criminality, though friends hinted that he had grown tired of New York and left the city to make a fresh start in a place where there would be less temptation to return to his old criminal ways. Some felt that he had at last fulfilled his pledge to go West and had joined Worthy in the Big Bend area of Texas. However, police treated those claims with derision, insisting Monk "couldn't be any further from the Bowery and Chrystie Street than the police would take him." Their cynicism soon seemed justified. If he really had gone West, it proved a short-lived move, and within weeks he was on a rampage around his old haunts and was seen drunk in a Brooklyn saloon at Broadway and Driggs Avenue.

He did not return to work at the garage, but instead took another job obtained for him by a Democratic politician in Brooklyn. In company with another reformed East Side gangster, he worked as a loading foreman and was paid in cash per load by the truckmen. At the end of each week the two men shared the profits and started a "booze party" that might last all weekend. However, there were rumors that Monk was once more active in racketeering, and according to one criminal, he was certainly involved in car theft. It was claimed that in May 1920, Monk and three other men stole a Cadillac, a shiny blue landaulet "with nickel plate a-plenty, sparkling like a bridal gift," parked outside Big Tom Foley's speakeasy, in plain sight of the criminal courts building. Although the thieves were unaware of the fact, the car belonged to Fanny Brice, star of the Ziegfeld Follies on Broadway and wife of one of Arnold Rothstein's henchmen, Julius "Nicky" Arnstein. Rothstein, who in his early days as a loan shark had hired Monk and his gang as "muscle," was one of the most feared of the new wave of gangsters, the real-life model for Meyer Wolfsheim in The Great Gatsby and Hyman Roth in The Godfather. Although he denied it, Rothstein was widely believed to be the brains and the money behind the 1919 "Black Sox" baseball scandal—the fixing of the World Series of America's national pastime.

After the theft of the Cadillac, word was put out on the streets by a henchman of Big Tom Foley that if the car was not returned at once, there would be fatal consequences for those involved. It was said that within half an hour, Monk drove up in the Cadillac, offering profuse apologies for the error. "It's a good thing we got word in time," Monk was purported to have said. "Half an hour more and nobody would have recognized it."

Such stories were flatly contradicted by Charley Jones, who claimed that, having been given the chance to live clean after his war service, Monk had turned his back on his old ways. When Jones heard that Monk was going on the level, he had taken him into his automobile business, and although Monk had soon tired of the business, Jones claimed that it was because he was finding even that too lively for his tastes and perhaps too fraught with temptations to resume the old sort of life. Monk had then crossed the bridge, said Jones, and gone back to Brooklyn, taking a furnished room at 801 Driggs Avenue—an ordinary rooming house in an ordinary neighborhood, "within a biscuit toss of the Williamsburg Bridge and within the shadow of the Williamsburg police court." He had opened a pet store on Broadway specializing in birds and settled down to live "the quietest life a man could live." However, Monk's Polish landlady at Driggs Avenue, where he had indeed lived for seven months, said that though he kept pretty much to himself, he spent most of the daylight hours asleep and his evenings out, which hardly sounded like the typical daily routine of a pet-shop owner.

Brooklyn police said Monk was working as a bouncer in a crap joint near Flushing Avenue and Broadway. New York police went further, claiming that there was already reason to believe that Monk's reformation had been much less genuine than many people believed.

Whatever the truth, even if he really had reformed, Monk still could not escape his past, and the very qualities that had made him such an admired and inspiring comrade in the army—candor, openness, patriotism, courage in the face of danger, and a willingness to risk his own life for the greater good—might also have made him a perceived threat to some elements of the underworld. The governor's pardon and the press portrayals of Monk as a reformed good citizen might on their own have been enough to start questions forming and rumors circulating in gangland circles. Perhaps, too, someone remembered the curious incident ten years earlier when, while recovering from a stomach operation in an Albany hospital, Monk had been given a round-the-clock police guard.

On the evening of Christmas Day 1920, Monk went to an all-night restaurant, the Court Cafe, at the corner of Broadway and Driggs Avenue in Williamsburg, where he was seen talking to two girls and a tall thin man carrying a traveling bag. Soon after midnight, he left in the company of some friends and was driven to a Manhattan basement cabaret, the Blue Bird Cafe, on the corner of Fourth Avenue and Fourteenth Street, "the northern boundary of the asphalted domain which once he ruled by right of might." Long known as Pabst's Rathskeller, the Blue Bird had been taken over and renamed the Café Chateau-Thierry—though no one but the owner used the name—by Willie Lewis, a prizefighter turned soldier who had owned it long enough to have gotten himself badly shot there.

Monk, who was in the habit of going to the Blue Bird every Saturday night, was with friends, several of them members of his old gang whom it was said he had continued to see regularly. The party gathered at a big table and had plenty to drink. They chatted in low tones, turned now and then to greet friends, and appeared to be having a good time, though Monk was getting drunker and drunker. According to other accounts the party was boisterous and there was considerable singing, with Monk taking the lead. When a woman cabaret singer came in with a party of friends, the two groups joined forces and more singing and drinking followed. Monk was said to have talked a great deal about his record as a gang leader and a war hero and been very boastful. "Do you know who I am?" he was said to have asked. "I'm Monk Eastman, the gang leader who made good; the guy that went over there and came back a hero and was made a good citizen by Governor Smith." The cabaret singer and her companions eventually departed after "a hilarious time."

Later, "always likely to be quarrelsome, self-assertive and domineering," according to police, Monk was said to have gotten into an altercation, and other members of the party had to separate the disputants. Angry and outraged, Monk left the place almost at once. He staggered into the street at about 3:45 and apparently started for the downtown subway station, probably intending to go home to Brooklyn, but as he reached the subway entrance on the south side of Fourteenth Street he was shot five times with a .32-caliber pistol. "He crumpled up on the sidewalk. A trickle of blood ran along the cement."

Monk was found by two patrolmen. They bent over him and, despite the bullet wounds he had suffered, they were able to detect a faint heartbeat. However, he had suffered bullet wounds to the left chest, heart, stomach, pancreas, and second lumbar vertebrae and, although a taxicab took him to St. Vincent's Hospital, he was dead when taken to the operating room. One bullet had pierced his heart, passed through his stomach, and embedded itself in his backbone. That wound was cited as the direct cause of death. Another shot had hit his right arm, and two more shots hit his left arm—suggesting that Monk had tried to shield himself with his arms as the gunman fired at him. The fifth shot apparently struck something else and then ricocheted, lodging in Monk's overcoat with insufficient force to pierce the cloth. A bullet hole in the coat, near his heart, was two inches in diameter and covered with powder marks, showing that the fatal shot had been fired at point-blank range.

DRAPED IN BLACK CLOTH

Monk's body was taken to the morgue and docketed as that of an unidentified man. Bodies in the holding rooms lay on a zinc table, and in hot weather a spray of cold water fell constantly from a showerhead and was carried away by a drain beneath the table; in the depths of winter, the biting cold was enough to delay decomposition until the coroners and undertakers had done their work. A postmortem examination revealed a good deal of grain alcohol in Monk's stomach. The body of the man whose face was once familiar to every detective lay unrecognized for two hours before it was identified by two old-timers—policemen who had known Monk in his heyday.

A label on the inside coat pocket of the good suit of clothes he had been wearing when shot was marked e. eastman. oct. 22 1910. no 17434. w.b. That identified the suit's makers as Witty Brothers of 50 Eldridge Street, and Henry Witty confirmed that he had made the suit for Monk. "We have made clothes for him for nineteen years. The last suit we made for him was delivered October 21 this year." Still not completely satisfied with that identification, detectives took fingerprints from the body and compared them with those held at police headquarters, definitively establishing his identity.

Contrary to a lurid and entirely fictional newspaper report of Monk shooting back in his last moments, he had been unarmed when he was killed. "That fact, even more than the mystery of his murder, was the talk of the Lower East Side last night. The Monk was killed while unarmed." John A. Ayres, a printer, was the only witness to come forward, even though he said that Monk had been killed in the sight of ten or more people, several of them within fifteen or twenty feet. Ayres was in a restaurant on the other side of the street, and when he heard the first shot he rushed outside and saw a man lying on the sidewalk across the street with his arms over his face. "A man was standing over him," Ayres said, "and as we reached the window, we saw him fire four more shots into the man on the sidewalk." The murderer "bent over his victim a moment, presumably to make sure he was dead," then ran to a taxicab moving slowly up Fourth Avenue. "He ran out as if he expected it," Ayres said. The taxi slowed and the killer jumped onto the running board. Ayres saw the man throw something out of the window as he got into the taxi. Someone shouted, "Stop him!" but the taxi drove off. Ayres said that he was warned by one of the men who had been in the restaurant, "If you try to mix in this, you'll get killed," so he had stayed where he was for fifteen minutes and then caught a cab home.

A cheap, nickeled .32-caliber revolver with five empty chambers in the cylinder was later found on the steps of the B.R.T. subway entrance at Union Square, by the same policemen who had been first on the scene after the shooting. Suggestions that the gun might have been Monk's were laughed off by police. "The Monk wouldn't carry a cheap gat," one plainclothes officer said. "The man who planted that 'Young America' beside the body of the Monk didn't know him. If he was packing a gun, it would be one of the best . . . As far as we can learn, the Monk hadn't packed a gun in months."

Perhaps forgetting past shootouts like the Battle of Rivington Street, Police Commissioner Enright cited Monk's killing as proof that

> there is a new kind of crime abroad in the land . . . it is the "Wild West" sort of crime. We used to read about it in dime novels . . . but it is only since the close of the war, where many young men learned to use firearms for the first time, that we began to have this form of spectacular crime . . . We had assaults and robberies in the old days, but the implement was the slug iron, the sandbag or brass knuckles. The gun . . . was not so much in evidence.

As they turned their attention to the search for Monk's killer, New York police were forced to confess that the Penn Street address they had for him was false. They had no idea where he had been living and were ignorant of most other aspects of his life, as was demonstrated by their insistence that Monk and his father were both really called William Delaney, and that his parents were still alive—his father had died in 1888, his mother in 1903. They then released details of Monk's rap sheet—his criminal career as far as they knew it—listing some of the aliases he had adopted:

> John Eastman, December 1902: New York City, assault, discharged
> Joseph Morris, August 1903: Freehold, NJ, felonious assault, discharged
> William Delaney, December 1903: New York City, suspicion of homicide, discharged
> William Delaney, December 1903: twice arrested as a suspicious person and twice discharged
> William Delaney, April 1904: felonious assault, ten years in Sing Sing, by Recorder Goff
> John Marvin, Buffalo, burglary, discharged
> William Delaney, July 1915: Albany, burglary, two years and eleven months in Dannemora

Even that was a far from complete account of Monk's criminal career. The police claim that Monk had first been arrested in 1902 was ten years wide of the mark; in fact, he'd been arrested in 1892, and he was convicted and sent to Blackwell's Island for three months in 1898. Police were so much in the dark about the killing that it was first alleged that Monk might have been shot somewhere else and then thrown from a taxicab outside the subway. Although police now embarked on a belated roundup of gangsters and former associates, they admitted that no immediate arrests were expected, for the leads they were following were "as vague and shadowy as the life of Eastman since he forsook his old haunts and ways of crime."

Robbery was ruled out as a motive for Monk's killing when his pockets were found to contain $144, a heavy watch and chain, two pairs of gold spectacles, a bunch of keys, and a Christmas card addressed to "E. Eastman." It was signed with the name "Lottie" and postmarked Brooklyn, but that was all the police knew about the woman. Yet again they displayed their ignorance about him when claiming that Monk "was understood to have had a wife who died several years ago, but his closest friends did not believe he ever married again, nor did they know of any woman with whom he had been closely associated." The fact that he had been living alone in a single room was enough to persuade police to state that Monk had "tired of women . . . Once, years ago, he was 'turned in' by a 'moll' and since then he often had been heard to voice rather positive opinions about the opposite sex." How this belief chimed with their disclosure that they were seeking the woman, Lottie, who had signed Monk's Christmas card, in the hope of learning something of importance, was not explained.

Police kept watch on the morgue, seeking to detain someone who might aid them in their search for the murderer, but the only person who went to the morgue to view Monk's body was Charley Jones, who said he would take charge of his old friend's body and arrange his funeral if no one else came forward. "He was a good guy," Jones said. "I'm trying to find some of his folks. If I can't, I'll take care of the body. He was regular, he'd do as much for a pal. I'll come through for him as I know he'd come through for me."

Jones volunteered his interpretation of his old friend's death, suggesting that some "young squirt gunmen" eager to make a name for themselves in Monk's former kingdom might have shot him out of sheer bravado. Jones then somewhat diminished the impact of his previous statements about Monk's reformed life by adding that if he was "over in Manhattan after all this time on any business, you can bet it was big business and no piker affair."

With little or no hard evidence, other theories about Monk's death were soon being circulated, and almost the only thing on which all concurred was that Monk had not merely been shot in a drunken argument. One theory, probably originating with the police since it insisted that Monk's real name had been William Delaney, claimed that the killing was the result of a gunman's vendetta and that Monk had been "associating with professional gamblers. He had no known means of support but had plenty of money," an assertion at least partly borne out by the $144 found on his body. Another newspaper report, based on yet more anonymous police sources, suggested that the killing was premeditated and the real reason for Monk's death was a dispute about the profits from drug peddling and bootlegging.

The narcotics squad added their weight to that theory, stating that Monk was the head of an organized band of drug sellers, employing twenty agents. In an attempt to substantiate those claims, New York police then fed newspapers with reports supposedly emanating from the Brooklyn police that Monk had taken up with a criminal gang there that had been planning an old-style shootout in the streets with a rival gang. Brooklyn police immediately refuted those claims. Captain Daniel J. Carey, head of detectives in the section of Williamsburg where Monk had been living, said he had led a quiet and apparently respectable life since he moved across the river. Far from knowing that Monk had joined a new gang or rejoined his old one, and that the rival gangs were arming for battle, Carey said the Brooklyn police did not even have Monk under surveillance, and he had last been seen a few months before by a detective who had known him during his criminal career. "I am not Monk Eastman anymore," he had told the detective. "Tell the world that I am going straight."

Corroboration of that appeared to be offered by his furnished room on Driggs Avenue, a dismal, unheated little bedroom for which he paid $2.50 a week. Even when that address had been passed on to the New York police by their counterparts in Brooklyn, a search of the property and an examination of Monk's belongings failed to yield any useful clues. The police were later forced to admit that they had found no evidence that Monk had been involved in any sort of large-scale crime; if he was making big profits from drug running and bootlegging, there was little sign of it in his dingy furnished room in Williamsburg. Monk had claimed to be a bartender at the Court Cafe at Broadway and Driggs Avenue, not far from the house, though in reality, police said, he was employed as a bouncer—bringing his life full circle from his early days at the New Irving Dance Hall in the 1890s.

Yet another theory about the crime, believed by many in the underworld, was that Monk had been shot because he was suspected of being an informer. "Whipped by drink and drugs . . . a victim of cocaine and opium for years . . . 'Monk' had squealed and for that had made himself a marked man, doomed to die." Despite his claims that Monk had not been seen for months and his denials of having him under surveillance, Captain Carey was said to have paid a second visit in ten days to Monk's room on Driggs Avenue on December 23, just three days before the killing. That fact alone might have been enough to mark Monk out for a gangland execution, but in addition, two officers from the narcotics squad had also called on Monk in the same month. Still loyal to the code by which he had lived all his adult life, Monk had refused to give them information, but rumors about his involvement with the police persisted, and one officer conceded that it would be no surprise if Monk had been shot because someone thought he had "squealed." Others claimed that Monk's boasting had become tiresome to his associates, though that alone scarcely seemed enough to merit a death sentence.

Police sources then backtracked, further muddying the waters. In a curiously worded statement they "would not deny" that they had secured information leading to the exposure of an opium ring, but they then went out of their way to deny that Monk had been killed for informing. Instead, they stressed their belief that Monk, "drunk and quarrelsome, had brawled once too often," claiming that he had been particularly aggressive since retuning from the war. Whatever the truth of that, it was widely believed that the police, whether eager to avoid deterring other potential informers or for some other, more opaque reason, had invented the story of Monk's involvement in bootlegging.

Newspapers also interviewed Morris Pockett, who claimed to be Monk's best friend and insisted that Monk made an "honest" living selling pigeons he had coaxed to the roof of his building back to their rightful owners for twenty-five cents each. Pockett denied that Monk was involved in any crime and said that his only excursions to Manhattan were weekly trips to a Turkish bath. He and some of Monk's other friends cited his kindness to children and animals as proof that "he really wasn't a 'bad guy.' "

Like Pockett, Monk's comrades from the 106th Infantry dismissed all the calumnies against him, and two comrades, John J. Boland and

Monk's former platoon sergeant, "Hank" Miller, whom Monk had rescued from the battlefield at Vierstraat Ridge, put up funds for a burial with full military honors. "Mr. Edward Eastman did more for America than presidents and generals," Boland said with some hyperbole. "The public does not reward its heroes. Now they are calling Mr. Eastman a gangster instead of praising him as one of those who saved America. But we'll do the right thing by this soldier and give him the funeral he deserves."

After a death certificate, number 33332, Manhattan County, was issued, listing Monk's occupation as a machinist in the auto trade, his body was taken from the dead house—the morgue at First Avenue and Twenty-sixth Street—to be prepared for the funeral. Monk's wife did not put in an appearance. If Worthy—last heard of living in the Big Bend area of Texas—was aware of his death, or even alive herself, there was no trace of her at the morgue, or at the funeral parlor of A. C. Yannaco on Metropolitan Avenue in Brooklyn, where his body was taken. When his two married sisters, Lizzie Reynolds and Francine Wouters, perhaps shocked by the killing and fearing unwelcome publicity, also failed to claim the body, the medical examiner surrendered it to Monk's army comrades. Soon afterward a man wearing the uniform of a chief petty officer in the U.S. Navy arrived at the dead house and asked to see Monk's body. Told it had already been removed, the man, who refused to give his name, said, "I'm sorry I didn't have the chance to see him again. It was Monk Eastman who set me going straight. I met him twenty years ago on the Bowery. I was a sailor then and what he had to say to me made a big difference."

In the funeral parlor's cold, marbled back room, Monk's body was prepared and dressed for burial, surrounded by stacked coffins and the ritual satin shrouds in which women were buried: "white ones for dead virgins, lavender for the young married, purple for the middle-aged and black for the old." Monk then lay in state in the funeral parlor, dressed in his army uniform. The American Legion wounded men's button with a silver crest in the center was pinned on his left breast, with the insignia of the 27th Division on the left shoulder, three service stripes on the left sleeve, and two wound stripes on the right. Monk's name, the dates of his birth and death, and the simple legend our lost pal. gone but not forgotten were inscribed on a silver plate on the lid of the oak coffin. Mrs. Yannaco told reporters that, though several men and women had visited the funeral parlor to see the body, they showed no signs of grief and appeared to her to be "mere curiosity-seekers rather than old partners of the Cherry Hill battles in the days before 'the Monk' thought of regeneration and restored citizenship."

On the evening of December 30, a whiskey-sodden wake that lasted all night took place in one of the Lower East Side bars on Monk's old turf, and at two o'clock the following afternoon, New Year's Eve 1920, he began his final journey. Well before the scheduled time for the funeral, a corps of detectives had spread themselves throughout the neighborhood. Two men who had been among the party in the Blue Bird Cafe on the night of the shooting were arrested, though police later admitted that neither was the killer, who was still at large.

While police patrolled outside, the Reverend James H. Lockwood, pastor of the South Third Street Methodist Church, gave a brief address at the funeral parlor. "It is not my province to judge this man's life," he said.

> His Creator will pass judgment; He possesses all the particulars and is competent to judge any soul. It may startle you to hear me say I wish I had known this man in life. We may have been reciprocally helpful. It has been said there is so much bad in the best of us, so much good in the worst of us, that it does not become any of us to think harshly of the rest of us. That is one way of saying "let him that is without sin cast the first stone."

The pastor said he had been told of many incidents in Monk's life that showed he was made of "the right kind of stuff."

After the address, two dozen of Monk's former comrades from the 106th Infantry, under Lieutenants Michael J. Davidson and Edward McNeeley, formed an honor guard, and the coffin, draped with the American flag, was borne out of the funeral parlor on the shoulders of eight uniformed veterans. Despite the thin fall of gray, gritty snow cloaking the ground, a crowd of several thousand men, women, and children had gathered outside the funeral parlor long before the procession departed; one estimate put the crowd at ten thousand.

The pallbearers led the funeral procession along South Fifth Street to the Williamsburg Bridge Plaza, and then on to Keap Street, where they halted while the coffin was transferred to a hearse for the long climb to Cypress Hills Cemetery. The windows of the tenements along the route were filled with faces staring down, silent, as the cortege of six black limousines and twenty horse-drawn carriages moved slowly past. Thousands lined the sidewalks, and thousands more fell into line behind the column of mourners, their breath hanging like mist in the still, frosty air, as the cortege made the five-mile journey through the snow. Although it was rumored that Monk's sisters were among the crowds thronging the sidewalks, friends failed to spot them, and Mrs. Yannaco subsequently revealed that Lizzie and Francine had paid their last respects to their brother at the funeral parlor late the previous night.

Despite the bitter cold, the first groups of mourners, the majority of them women, had begun to arrive at Cypress Hills as early as two o'clock that afternoon. "Mothers with lines of hardship on their faces trudged along the soggy roads behind carriages bearing crying infants to the farthest end of the grounds," where Monk's body was to be laid to rest. Each train arriving at the cemetery gates brought further mourners until by 4:15, when the procession appeared, there were six hundred people from all walks of life waiting beside the freshly dug grave in the cannon grounds of the cemetery, the site of the long-demolished Cannon Street Baptist Church.

Mere curiosity alone was not enough to explain the presence of so many on such a harsh winter's day. Like his army comrades, the majority of Lower East Siders must have been there because in some way Monk had touched their lives. For them at least, memories of past kindnesses—a handout of money or food when they were destitute, a dose of rough justice enacted on their oppressors—must have outweighed the wrongs he had inflicted. The people of the Lower East Side, an often despised and ignored underclass, had turned out to pay their last tribute to one of their own.

Several thousand more mourners arrived behind the cortege as it turned in through the gates of Cypress Hills and the oak coffin was carried into the chapel of rest. There Monk lay in state as a line of serving officers and men filed past, paying their last respects. They included Monk's former divisional commander, General O'Ryan, several officers from his old regiment, and many former doughboys with campaign medals pinned to their jackets. There were others there, too: police; sharp-suited mobsters and their bodyguards; a few scarred and aging street toughs, uncomfortable in their unaccustomed, ill-fitting suits; and more throngs of poor Lower East Siders, all paying homage to New York's most celebrated gangster and most unlikely war hero.

When the coffin was carried to the gravesite, the mourners spilled over the pathways and climbed onto the other graves for a better view, trampling the fresh-fallen snow into gray and grimy slush. After Pastor Lockwood had read the committal, Sergeant Miller of Company G walked slowly forward and spoke.

> The character of Eastman—I knew him as "Pop" when he was a buddy of mine—has been blackened in the press. But we knew him as an honest-to-God man. He was a real soldier. He saved my life on September 2, 1918, when our company was attacked and caught near Vierstraat Ridge. "The Monk" was wounded. He saw me fall with a bullet through my right shoulder. He crawled to me, picked me up and carried me to the rear. He saved my life. He was a real man. That's why I cannot forget and why I am here.

After Miller's eulogy, the curiosity-seekers were allowed to file past the casket to take a last look at the face of the dead gangster. A number of detectives stood by the casket and carefully scrutinized everyone who passed.

Then the coffin lid was closed and Monk was lowered into his last resting place, a grave near that of his mother. There was a dry rattle as General O'Ryan scattered a handful of dirt on the coffin, then a lone bugler sounded taps. As the last notes of the bugle hung in the air, the mourners remained motionless, perhaps remembering not just Monk Eastman, but all those old comrades lost in East Side gang wars or buried in Flanders mud.

A rifle squad of men from his old regiment stood ready to fire three volleys over Monk's grave, but another figure, a man in clergyman's robes—probably the divisional chaplain, Father Kelley—then stepped out of the crowd. "No matter how bad a man is, there's always some good in him," he said. "Eastman was a gunman, but not at heart. There were many heroic things he did during the war that never reached the ears of those over here." Like Pastor Lockwood, Kelley told of Monk's encounter with the fifteen-year-old German youth. "Monk's companion was about to end the boy's life with a bullet," Kelley said. " 'Don't shoot' cried the 'killer.' 'He's only a kid.' The boy was made a prisoner. That boy's life was spared, and I am sure that, together with his mother, he prays for 'The Monk.' " As he stepped back into the ranks of mourners, there was a moment's silence and then, at a command from Lieutenant Davidson, rifle shots sounded a requiem. As the echoes faded, the crowds began to file away into the gathering dusk of that cold December afternoon.

Even as the funeral was taking place, police had produced yet another leak about the cause of Monk's death. It was now grudgingly admitted that Monk had been acting as a police spy. Described on the morning after his death as "a reformed gangster who could not go right," he was now being hailed by his former comrades in the 27th Division as "a hero who had paid the price of his recovered citizenship by losing his life to the swift, relentless vengeance of the underworld." However, those claims were ridiculed by Monk's former gang members. Throughout his life, no matter what threats were made or inducements offered, Monk had adhered to the underworld code, and those who knew him refused to believe, on no more solid evidence than yet another unattributable leak from police headquarters, that he had become an informer.

The search for his killer continued, but it appeared directionless, and police statements remained contradictory. Forty-eight hours after the shooting, they had still been insisting that the suspect, supposedly an old crony of Monk's and a member of his gang, had not left New York, though, as one observer noted, it was obvious that their information did not extend to his present whereabouts. When it was pointed out that more than thirty-six hours had elapsed between the killing and the questioning of the first witnesses, and that the criminal—if there was only one—had had ample time to flee New York, the feeble response from the police was that they "did not believe their case had been weakened by the lapse of time, as they had to 'work it out in our own way.' " Despite their claims that Monk had been killed for informing, the police were also forced to concede that they were still far from certain of the motive.

Two days later, the arrest and interrogation of two material witnesses—William J. Simermeyer, the chauffeur who drove Monk and five other men from Brooklyn to the Blue Bird Cafe on the fatal night, and Sylvester Hamilton, a member of the party—produced a breakthrough. Police announced that they were now confident that Monk had been shot and killed by a man who had entertained him and five friends at a dinner in the Blue Bird Cafe immediately before the killing. He was, they said, a Williamsburg man whose business was "both legitimate and illegitimate"—a prosperous businessman who was also on intimate terms with many criminals.

Contradicting earlier claims of a furious argument between Monk and his killer, Hamilton insisted that "not an angry word had passed up to the time the slayer began to shoot at Eastman," and police were now also forced to admit that, in complete contradiction of their earlier claims, the killer had left the city immediately after the murder. The killing was now said to be premeditated, and police claimed that Monk had been invited to the dinner to ensure that there would be no interference with the murderer's plans.

On December 31, 1920, the district attorney's office released the name of the suspect: Jeremiah "Jerry" Bohan, a "dry agent" (Prohibition Enforcement Agent). Although they stopped short of naming him as the killer, the statement that Bohan was not at his home, was known to carry a gun, and had been arrested in connection with a previous shooting in Williamsburg, and that of three customers of the Blue Bird Cafe on the night of the shooting who were still unaccounted for, "we want Jerry Bohan most of all," was probably enough of a hint for even the most dim-witted bystander.

On January 4, 1921, there was an astonishing development, as Jerry Bohan walked into the Lee Avenue police station in Brooklyn, voluntarily surrendered to police, and confessed to the killing, though he claimed he had shot in self-defense. Bohan said that Monk had "got mussy over nothing" in the Spatz Cafe in Brooklyn some months before and had threatened to shoot him, but the quarrel had then been patched up. On Christmas night they were in the Blue Bird Cafe with four other men when an argument broke out over tipping the staff and the piano player. Bohan claimed that when that had been settled, he was walking away from the Blue Bird alone when Monk grabbed him from behind, whirled him around, and told him that he had been "a rat" ever since he got the Prohibition job. At the same time, Bohan asserted, Monk, who was subsequently found not even to be armed with a penknife, "dropped his hand in his right coat pocket." At that instant, Bohan said, remembering how Monk had threatened him before, he drew his own pistol and emptied it into Monk's body. He also claimed that the arrival of the taxicab in which he escaped was merely a coincidence and not evidence of premeditation on his part.

Bohan's story was contradicted by the testimony of the other witnesses in the case, and his bizarre claim that he and Monk had fallen out over the tip at the Blue Bird Cafe was denied by the waiters there. They insisted that Bohan had not been one of the six companions with whom Monk shared his last marathon drinking session. It was also revealed that Bohan had a long criminal record. He had been tried and acquitted for the killing of Joe "The Bear" Faulkner in Brooklyn in 1911, and had been arrested four times for disorderly conduct. During the war he had again been arrested under the "Work-or-Fight" law, and then got a job on the Brooklyn waterfront "representing" the stevedore's union, which was having trouble with the employers. Monk was "representing" the employers at the same time, and it was "thus the two met and became friendly enemies."

Bohan had been fired from his job as a Prohibition agent as soon as it was known that the police were looking for him, but why he returned to New York, gave himself up, and voluntarily confessed to the killing was not revealed by him or the police. It is possible that he feared Jersey justice—a revenge shooting by one of Monk's former gang members—more than the justice administered by the City of New York, or he may have struck a deal to plead guilty in return for money, or for other crimes being ignored.

Three months after Monk's funeral, one of his old gang, Edward Herberger, traveled to New York from Philadelphia to avenge his old boss. It was said that one of the ties that bound them was that they had once been arrested together on the Williamsburg Bridge, charged with picking a pocket. Herberger arrived in Brooklyn and went to the Court Cafe, the favorite haunt of Monk and many of his old followers. When he walked in, Herberger announced that he was looking for an old enemy of his pal, Monk, and dropped many hints about what he would do if he found the men he was after, but Bohan was behind bars and none of the other men Herberger named were to be found. As he sat in the Court Cafe, "brooding, with his head in his hands, his disinterested motive for the visit to New York seemed to ebb away" and, according to the cafe owner, Joseph Germanhauser, Herberger suddenly jumped to his feet, drew a revolver, and said, "I guess I have got to work." He then held up the cafe owner, robbed him of two thousand dollars, and fled. He was identified by Germanhauser from the portraits of Monk's friends and criminal associates held in the Rogues' Gallery at police headquarters, and Philadelphia police arrested him a week later. When they searched his lodgings, along with most of the two thousand dollars, they found some opium, a set of safecracking tools, and a photo of Monk draped in black cloth.

The man Herberger had been seeking, Jerry Bohan, was initially imprisoned in the Tombs without bail, and his trial did not take place until a year after the killing. After pleading guilty to manslaughter in the first degree, Bohan was sentenced to from three to ten years, three months in prison. Received at Sing Sing on January 5, 1922, he was paroled on June 23, 1923, after serving just seventeen months of his sentence, giving rise to further suspicions that there was more to Monk's death and Bohan's confession to the killing than had ever been revealed.

THE WAY THINGS HAVE CHANGED

Like the lawlessness of the Old West, the era of Monk Eastman in the "Wild West" gangland of the Lower East Side had passed into history, his death signaling the last rites for the old-style gangs and the dawn of the new age of organized crime. Although gangsters still strode the streets of New York, they were of a very different breed. Monk had priced his jobs at a handful of dollars and always liked to keep his hand in by inflicting an odd beating himself, a habit that put him on the path to his downfall. His successors walled themselves off from the violence perpetrated by their minions and, fueled by the liquor gold rush of Prohibition, became extremely wealthy, if not wholly respectable, businessmen.

Rooted in the "romantic" East Side past, public perception of the modern gangsters lagged behind the reality. Writing fifteen years after Monk's death, the Pulitzer Prize–winning reporter Meyer Berger remarked that most people still thought of gangsters and racketeers as "loafers with turtle-neck sweaters, cauliflower ears and protruding maxilla, who beat their women and punt their offspring around the flat. That type passed out of existence during the liquor gold rush . . . Your modern racket boss, when he isn't in Miami to avoid embarrassing questioning by loutish policemen . . . if he kicks mamma around once in a while, for old time's sake, he does it in the privacy of his own home."

Old-style gangsters might mutter scornful remarks into their beers about gang bosses with secretaries, receptionists, and smart offices in fashionable districts, but these new gangsters wouldn't have dreamed of dirtying their manicured hands with a little Monk-style street-fighting; they enjoyed wealth, power, and influence beyond the dreams of Monk Eastman in his prime. They resented being described as gangsters and preferred to describe themselves as businessmen and their gang as their organization.

As Meyer Berger sardonically noted, "the muscle" used for intimidation or to carry out the murders that were incidental to the business were not allowed to "clutter up the premises, because it wouldn't look nice," and most of the racket bosses also aspired to a place in society commensurate with their wealth. Ciro Terranova, the boss of the Harlem rackets, loved

> a canter in the park or among the lovely hills of Westchester, because you meet such interesting people on the bridle path . . . The East Side crime-school graduates, once devoted to pinochle and stuss, have taken up bridge . . . and discuss end-plays and squeezes with as much zest as they used to discuss a particularly neat skull fracture or eye displacement . . . Born in cold flats on the East Side and accustomed to taking their night's ease on pool tables when the skull-fracturing and nose-busting wasn't paying dividends . . . the present big-shot bosses are making up for it in the most luxurious penthouses in the city.

The few survivors of the old gangs and the old ways, like Humpty Jackson—when last heard of, the owner of a Harlem pet shop—could only shake their heads at the way things had changed.

Like the Dead Rabbits and Whyos before him, Monk had been an old-school gangster, fighting and brawling his way to the top of the heap and leading from the front in the bloody, brutal gang battles to consolidate his power. Yet he also anticipated the modern gangland era, developing the sophisticated rackets that his successors would utilize and overseeing the organization of rival gangs into federations that might sometimes feud with one another, but could also collaborate for their mutual benefit. He created the template and laid the foundations that Murder Inc., the Syndicate, and the Cosa Nostra would build upon.

He was undoubtedly a gangster, a bruiser, a burglar, a liar, a thief, a thug for hire, a pimp, and an occasional opium peddler, but the litany of his crimes and misdemeanors does not begin to tell the full story of Monk Eastman. He covered his tracks so well that even the most basic facts of his existence were open to question. Barely anyone knew his real name, his genuine age, or his true address. Even the police showed themselves unable to keep track of all his numerous arrests and convictions under a string of aliases, and they continued to file his records under "William Delaney," believing to the end that it was his real name. They also believed that he was illiterate, but it stretches credulity to imagine that a man who could not read would have had newspapers delivered to his cell or required his subordinates to produce written reports of their crimes. Nor, if he was merely an ill-educated thug, would he have taken time to save a young sailor from his own youthful folly on the Bowery—an act of kindness the man still remembered and treasured twenty years later—nor risked his life to rescue his wounded comrades on the battlefield, nor intervened to prevent another member of his company from taking the life of a terrified German boy soldier. His army comrades had no doubts about Monk's character, and their feelings must have been shared by those thousands of poor citizens of the Lower East Side, the majority women, who traveled across the East River to Williamsburg and Cypress Hills and stood for hours in the bitter winter cold just to attend his funeral.

No matter how cynical his motives or how illicit his means of earning money, Monk—like his old political patron, Big Tim Sullivan— saw to it that much of it found its way into the pockets of the desperately poor inhabitants of his Lower East Side kingdom. He was no Robin Hood, and the Lower East Side was emphatically no Sherwood Forest, but his acts of kindness and generosity; his love of children and animals; the loyalty and affection he inspired, even in some of his rivals; the testimonials to his character from those—like the officers of the 106th Infantry, Charley Jones, and Morris Pockett—who had no vested interest to protect; and above all, Monk's courage and dedication to others in the furnace of the battlefields of the Western Front argued of a far more complex character than the brutal, mindless thug his detractors described. He had lived most of his life in the shadows of the underworld, but he emerged into the light and by his actions redeemed some, perhaps all, of the many crimes he had committed. In a life characterized by venality, he also proved himself capable of selflessness and altruism, even risking his life to save others, the most Christian act a man can perform.

An enigma throughout his life, Monk Eastman went to his grave leaving a score of unanswered questions behind him. When he spoke for the record in court, or in police or newspaper interviews, he almost invariably lied. He left not a single word written in his own hand, made no deathbed confession, and left no last will and testament. The true extent of the reformation of "Citizen Eastman"; the ultimate fate of his wives, his children, his property, and the fortune he made from his crimes; and the real reasons for his killing on that cold December night remain unknown to this day.

ACKNOWLEDGMENTS

I owe a huge debt of gratitude to the many, many people who have assisted me in my research into that elusive character, Monk Eastman. In Britain, my particular thanks to the Book Supply Team at the British Library's newspaper section at Colindale, North London—Audrey O'Sullivan, Pat Hanna, Norman, Joyce, Jeff, Spud, Pravin, Mark, Pat Fitzgerald, Geraint, Andy, Dick, and Robert—who went far beyond the call of duty to help me in my research. My thanks also to the staff of the National Archives in Kew; the British Library in St. Pancras and its "out-station" at Boston Spa in Yorkshire; the Ilkley Library; the Leeds Library; Kevin, Carole, Ross, and the rest of the staff of my excellent local bookshop, the Grove Bookshop in Ilkley, West Yorkshire, who tracked down and obtained some obscure publications for me; Paul Anning and Mark Bukumunhe of Annings Ilkley, for their painstaking digital imaging of what is almost certainly the last remaining paper copy of The World, March 26, 1919; and Simon Wilkinson of swpix. com for his expert help and advice on photography.

In Israel, my thanks go to Professor Shlomo Yotvat, and to Esther Lichtenstein and Hadassah Assouline at the Central Archives for the History of the Jewish People. In the United States, my grateful thanks to the staff of the General Research Division in Humanities 315, the Microform Reading Room, the Irma and Paul Milstein Division of United States History, Local History, and Genealogy, and the Dorot Jewish Division at the New York Public Library; the New York City Municipal Archives; the New York State Library Reference Section, Manuscripts and Special Collections, and the New York State Archives at Albany; the Library of Congress (Madison, Adams, and Jefferson Buildings) in Washington, D.C.; the McKeldin Library at the University of Maryland in College Park; the U.S. Army Center for Military History, Collins Hall, Fort McNair, Washington, D.C.; and the National Archives and Record Administration in Washington D.C. and at College Park, Maryland.

Thanks also to Jim Gandy at the New York State Military Museum and Veterans Research Center at Saratoga Springs; Leilani Dawson at the Brooklyn Historical Society; Meletta Bell at the archives of Big Bend, Texas; Jodye Stone and Verna Bonner, Big Bend, Texas; John Chapman in Chicago; Bonnie Nelson at the Lloyd Sealy Library, John Jay College of Criminal Justice; Paul Boag at Proquest; Valerie Swan Young at Cypress Hills National Cemetery in Brooklyn; Thomas C. McCarthy of the New York Correction History Society; Ron Arons; Michael Harling; Beth Spinelli of the New York City Police Museum; the staff of the Lower East Side Tenement Museum; the New York County Surrogate's Court; Jill Slaight at the Department of Rights and Reproductions, New-York Historical Society; and Bruce Calvert of the Silent Film Still Archive.

Among the many very helpful NARA staff I encountered, special thanks to William G. Seibert, R. Reed Whitaker, Kimberlee Ried, and Timothy Rives. My thanks also to Eli Paul, museum director, and James M. Barkley, education program coordinator, at the National World War I Museum in Kansas City, Missouri; and to Ed Tracy, executive director of the Taiwani Foundation, and Colonel James Pritzker and the staff of the excellent Pritzker Military Library in Chicago. Walter Bradford of the U.S. Army Center for Military History provided much useful information, and my thanks also to Martin Gedra, archivist at NARA; Mitchell Yockelson, investigative archivist, Office of the Inspector General at NARA and author of the excellent Borrowed Soldiers; and Lori Miller, for hunting down material held in the National Personnel Records Center in St. Louis, Missouri. My sincere thanks also to Coreen Hallenbeck for her meticulous additional research work for me in the New York State Archives in Albany, and to Sean McCrohon for his enthusiastic, indefatigable, and invaluable work for me at NARA in Washington, D.C., College Park, and elsewhere. My special thanks are due also to the late Edith Evans Asbury, to Barbara Ross of the New York Daily News, and to Roch Dunin-Wasowicz, for their collective help in enabling me to consult the papers of the late Herbert Asbury, which had lain undisturbed in a Manhattan basement since Mr. Asbury's death in 1963.

As ever, I'm indebted to my British agent, Mark Lucas, and to Alice

Saunders at Lucas Alexander Whitley in London, and to Kim Wither-spoon, David Forrer, and Rose Marie Morse at Inkwell Management in New York. I'm also very grateful to Barry Fast for his help and his insights into New York, the manuscript, and—most vital of all—where to go for dinner in Manhattan.

Particular thanks are due to my editor, Andrew Miller, and to Andrew Carlson at Alfred A. Knopf in New York, whose thoughtful and insightful critiques of the early drafts of the book were invaluable to me. I'm also grateful to Maria Massey, Sara Eagle, and the rest of the team at Knopf and Vintage, including the legendary and now honorably retired Ashbel Green.

Finally, my thanks to the Royal Literary Fund for the Fellowship awarded to me in 2007–2009, and to the fellowship officer, Steve Cook, for his help and support. I also acknowledge with great gratitude a grant toward the costs of my American research from the Authors' Foundation at the Society of Authors in London.

Every effort has been made to contact copyright holders and the author will be pleased to hear from the descendants or administrators of any copyright holders he has been unable to trace.

Glossary

all-sorts drink also known as "dog's-nose" or "swipes," made from wringing out the cloths used to wipe the counters in dives and low groggeries

amusers operators who threw snuff or pepper in victims' eyes; under the pretext of offering help, an accomplice then robbed them

anglers petty thieves who used hooked sticks or fishing lines through mailboxes or open windows to steal property or keys

badger man who, after his woman accomplice had lured a victim to her room for sex, would burst in posing as an irate husband and confront the victim, but then allow himself to be mollified with cash

bag of nails total confusion, like a shaken-up bag of nails

ballum-rancum ball at which all the dancers were criminals or prostitutes

barrel-boarder lowest kind of drunken sot (because they often slept draped over a barrel or on bare wooden boards)

bat streetwalker who worked at night (also known as an *owl*)

bedizened dressed in gaudy fashion

betting his eyes a punter who watches a game but doesn't bet

Billingsgate swearing (after the foul language of the porters at London's Billingsgate fish market)

billy club or bludgeon

blind pig; blind tiger illegal bar concealed behind an innocuous-looking storefront

blink shut your eyes to what is going on around you

boardinghouse the Tombs, or any prison

booster shoplifter

bounce evict with violence

bucket shop worst type of bar; a dive where beer was sold by the bucket

bufe dog

bufe-napper dog thief; rogue

bull cop

bull traps thieves who impersonated cops

bundle woman; girlfriend

bundle thief robber specializing in targeting women

cab brothel

cadet recruiter of prostitutes; pimp

cant thieves' argot (also known as *flash*)

cap name; join in or assist with a job

capper confederate, especially one who makes false winning bets at cards to
    encourage victims to play

cherry young girl

chopped up stolen goods divided into smaller lots and hidden in different
    places

City College the Tombs

cold pig victim robbed of his clothes; a dead body

cop policeman (from the copper badges worn by the first police under Mayor
    Fernando Wood)

courtisans shyster lawyers, especially at the Tombs

cramped killed; murdered; hanged

crimps seamen's boardinghouses, run by corrupt owners who would drug
    or blackjack their victims and sell them as crewmen to the captains of
    outward-bound ships

crow sentry

cut up turned out to be

cut up very fat turned out to be very rich

daylights eyes

dip, dipper pickpocket

dog's-nose see all-sorts

doorman lookout

doubler a punch hard enough to make someone double up

drab disreputable woman; hag

dropper operator; part of a wallet-dropping gang

dustman dead man

earth-bath grave

elbow turn corner; get out of sight

facer brim-full glass; person who blocked pursuers of a criminal

fence receiver of stolen goods

flash, the thieves' argot (also known as *cant*)

flat sucker; mark

floorer knockout punch

four-flusher a cheat, a bluffer (from a poker player who lays down four cards
    of the same suit, keeping his other card of a different suit half-hidden in
    the hope of persuading the other players that he has a flush)

Friday-face dismal (executions originally took place on Fridays)

gat gun

glim, glimmer eye

goads cappers

goo-goos reformers (derisive contraction of "good government")

gorilla, guerilla enforcer, gang member

grafter con man; thief

groaners church and funeral thieves

groggery bar; dive
gropers blind men
gun pickpocket; thief (probably derived from the Yiddish gonif)
gun-moll woman pickpocket
hard metal
heeler operator, part of pocketbook gang, who trod on the heels of the victim
    to draw his attention to the dropped wallet that was the bait in the scam
high tide plenty of money
hog in armor blustering officeholder
hog in togs well-dressed idler
hoist steal by climbing through window
hook pickpocket; thief
hush-stuff bribe paid to a witness to buy silence
Island, the Blackwell's (now Roosevelt) Island, especially the penitentiary
jammed killed; murdered; hanged
Jersey justice rough justice
jinglers coins
kettle pocket watch
kidsman a Fagin
kiting restless; on Wall Street, wild speculation
knockout drops chloral hydrate, or any drug that rendered the victim uncon-
    scious
knucks brass knuckles; pickpockets
lamp eye
layout faro or stuss term; the oilcloth or green baize on which one of each
    card, ace to king, is pasted; players placed their bets on the card of their
    choice before the pack was turned over
leather wallet
leg bail absconding while on bail
lighthouse lookout
long large price
low tide nearly broke
lush drink; a drunk
lush-roller, lush-worker thief preying on drunks
mab whore
mack pimp
moll woman
moll-buzzer pickpocket specializing in targeting women
moon month (usually describing imprisonment, e.g., "He's gone to the Island
    for a moon")
mosh eat and leave without paying
mount give false testimony
mounter one who gives false testimony
mugwump do-gooder
my uncle pawnbroker
nailed arrested

nippers tool used by hotel thieves for turning keys from outside

nook-and-corner men thieves lurking in the shadows or obscure hiding places

office nonverbal signal or information

officer one giving nonverbal signals or information

on a/the string sending someone on a fool's errand; flirting with or luring a sucker

on it easy and dishonest living, e.g., as a prostitute

owl night streetwalker (also known as a *bat*)

panel-crib place fitted with a sliding panel, false wardrobe, or other concealed opening or door for the robbery of a victim occupied with a prostitute

panel-thief one carrying out robberies in a panel-crib

peached turned police informer; squealed

penny-weighter sneak thief specializing in switching fake gems for real ones

picker-up roper-in, drawer of suckers to gambling dens, saloons, or brothels

piker one who bets very small amounts

pipe fiend opium smoker

poke pocketbook

prospecting looking for a victim or something to steal

rabbit rowdy person

rabbit-sucker young slummer

rag-water drink of all kinds, sometimes literally the wringings from the cloth used to wipe the bar

red gold; a cent

right bower right-hand man, derived from the name for the jack of trumps, the second-highest card in the game of euchre

rocked in a stone cradle born in prison

roped led on; led astray; tricked

roper-in drawer of suckers to gambling dens, saloons, or brothels

rounder one who hangs around stuss games but does not play

running through not allowing a sucker to win even a single bet

sachem Tammany boss (from a Native American term for a wise man or chief)

school gang of thieves

scratch cash; roll of bills not carried in a pocketbook; also, a line drawn in the middle of a boxing ring—anyone not "up to scratch" at the start of a round was ruled to have lost

second-story men men who broke into buildings through second-floor windows; the term could also carry an implication of cowardice: second-story men were too scared to climb higher, and too frightened of a confrontation with a house-owner to break in on the first floor

shady glim dark lantern

shanty black eye

sheeny Jewish thief; low thief

sheriff bouncer

side pocket saloon in out-of-the-way or unexpected place

sifting going through a purse or pocketbook

skin purse

skull head of the house; boss

slap down cash price of admission

slungshot type of blackjack; heavy weight contained in a leather or cloth sling

smoke lies told to conceal the truth

snake sly thief; one who hides in a building to let in his accomplices after dark

spit out free; remove

stalls accomplices who would get in the way of pursuers

stargazers prostitutes (because they spent most of their time on their backs)

start, old start the Tombs

stiff a corpse; but also anything printed

stun cheat

stuss also known as "Jewish faro," a card game in which cards were dealt from a metal box, faceup, and placed on the "layout," where the bets had been laid by gamblers betting on which card would be turned over next

swaddler "The End Is Nigh" type of street-corner speaker who drew a crowd so that his pickpocket accomplices could go to work

swipes see all-sorts

take the shine out lower someone's self-esteem

tooth music enjoying a meal; good food

touch theft; proceeds of theft

trinkets knife and revolver

turf racecourse

up the spout pawned (from the spout or chute through which bulkier items were sent to a different floor of the pawnshop)

vampire blackmailer preying on "respectable" men who patronized prostitutes

Venus curse venereal disease

waxy light-fingered

weeding taking part of money or goods, but leaving enough to avoid arousing suspicion

whipped cheated; beaten

white slave trade prostitution

wind money

wire pickpocket

working the rattler carrying out robberies on streetcars

yegg burglar; safecracker

NOTES

ABBREVIATIONS

A.E.F.—American Expeditionary Force

AMHI—American Military History Unit

NARA—National Archives and Records Administration; unless otherwise specified, NARA refers to records held at the National Archives at College Park, Maryland

Prologue A LOT OF LITTLE WARS

7 FIVE FOOT SEVEN B0100, Physician's Register, Sing Sing Prison.

8 "THE AFTERMATH OF SMALLPOX" and "AN ODD DANDIFIED TOUCH" Rich Cohen, Tough Jews, 44.

8 "A LOT OF LITTLE WARS" Herbert Asbury, The Gangs of New York, 256.

11 ONE NAVAL OFFICER New York Times, December 29, 1920.

I THE HALL OF TEARS

14 OSTERMAN Herbert Asbury, The Gangs of New York, 256.

14 BORN IN DECEMBER 1873 Census of the United States, New York (Manhattan), New York City, Greater New York, roll T9_896; page 389.1000, ED 610, image 0781; Census of the United States, New York (Manhattan), New York City, Greater New York, roll T623 1092; page 5B, ED 240; Sing Sing Admissions Register, April 23, 1904, NY State Archives, B0 143, page 157, vol. 36, box 14; State of New York, Certificate and Record of Marriage 4106, February 8, 1911.

14 SAMUEL HAD BEEN BORN, ANGLO-SAXON ORIGINS, and A METHODIST PASTOR Borough of Manhattan, death certificates 33332, 29833; New York Times, December 31, 1920.

14 THOMAS McSPEDON and VIOLENCE, CRUELTY Census of the United
15 States, New York Ward 19, District 2, New York, New York, roll

M653_815; page 0, image 600; Ninth Census of the United States, New York Ward 13, District 3, New York, New York, roll M593_1031; page 70, image 140; T; New York Times, November 24, 1877.

15   1880 CENSUS, DIED OF CONSUMPTION, and DESCRIBING HERSELF AS A WIDOW Census of the United States, New York (Manhattan), New York City, Greater New York, roll T9_896; family history film: 1254896; page 389.1000, ED 610, image 0781; New York Death Certificate 29833; Trow's New York City Directory, 1878, 1880; Trow's New York City Directory, 1887.

15   93 SOUTH THIRD STREET and ALLEGED THAT MONK'S PARENTS Lain's Brooklyn City Directory, 1883–1899; Asbury, The Gangs of New York, 256.

15   TIMOTHY EASTMAN Census of the United States, New York Ward 19, District 9, New York, New York, roll M593_1042; page 230, image 463; Ninth Census of the United States, New York Ward 19, District 21, New York, New York, roll M593 1005; page 408, image 251; New York Times, January 19, 1859, October 13, 1893.

16   "chose for his school" New York Daily Tribune, December 27, 1920.

18   "TRIUMPH OF MECHANICS" and "A SPARKLING GEM" Sydney Brooks, "London and New York," 297; Edward K. Spann, The New Metropolis, 137.

18   BANDIT'S ROOST and "SOME FORM OF CREEPER" Luc Sante, Introduction to Jacob A. Riis, How the Other Half Lives, xvii, 17; Geoffrey Moorhouse, Imperial City, 82.

18   "JEW BREAD," "AN ENGLISH WORD," and "THE PIG MARKET" Betty Smith, A Tree Grows in Brooklyn, 30; Jacob A. Riis, How the Other Half Lives, 91, 89.

19   "WITH RARE IMPARTIALITY" Henry Collins Brown, ed., Valentine's Manual of Old New York, 16–17.

19   "THE KIND OF DIRTY PEOPLE" and "THE SCUM OF IMMIGRATION" Methodist Bishop James Cannon, quoted in Stephen Fox, Blood and Power, 14; Eliot Lord et al., The Italian in America, 190–91.

20   ONE IN SEVEN EAST SIDE and "ONE FINDS THE BLACKEST" Walter Scott Andrews, "A Study of the East Side Courts," 23, 22; Charles Gardner, The Doctor and the Devil, 41.

21   "THE SUICIDE WARD," INFANT MORTALITY RATES, and "THE RICH FLED" Justin Kaplan, Lincoln Steffens, 61; Riis, How the Other Half Lives, 53, 85, 133, and note, 228; Howard Zinn, A People's History of the United States, 213.

21   "TREAD IT EVER SO" and "THE TRACK OF A TORNADO" Riis, How the Other Half Lives, 11.

21   "IN THE COMMON TRENCH" Ibid., 132–33.

22   "OLD HAGS" Helen Campbell, Thomas W. Knox, and Thomas F. Byrnes, Darkness and Daylight, 364, 374, 371.

23   FIFTY THOUSAND INDUSTRIAL ACCIDENTS and "A SIGN WOULD GO UP" Zinn, A People's History of the United States, 317–19.

23 "TAINTED MEAT" and "FRAGMENTS OF BREAD" Campbell, Knox, and Byrnes, Darkness and Daylight, 402–3; Ezra R. Pulling, "Report of the Fourth Sanitary District," 16.

24 "PAPER WASN'T WORTH MUCH" Smith, A Tree Grows in Brooklyn, 5.

24 "278 JUVENILE PRISONERS" and "FRIGHTFUL WHISKEY" Jacob A. Riis, A Ten Years' War, 155–56; Asbury, The Gangs of New York, 225.

24 "WILD AS HAWKS," TWO HUNDRED FOUNDLINGS, and "AN ODD COIN-
25 CIDENCE" Campbell, Knox, and Byrnes, Darkness and Daylight, 154, 517; Riis, How the Other Half Lives, 141, 143, 134.

2 BLACKER THAN A WOLF'S THROAT

27 "BRUTAL IN FACE" Helen Campbell, Thomas W. Knox, and Thomas F. Byrnes, Darkness and Daylight, 359–60.

27 "I GAVE MY NAME" Court of General Sessions, People of the State of New York versus William Delaney, alias Monk Eastman, 260.

27 AT CONEY ISLAND New York Times, September 25, 1893.

27 MONK'S FIRST ARREST, WILLIAM MURRAY, and ON THE ISLAND New York Times, December 28, 1920; The Sun, April 13, 1904; Court of General Sessions, People of the State of New York versus William Delaney, alias Monk Eastman, 271–72.

28 A THOUSAND SILVER DOLLARS Albert Fried, The Rise and Fall of the Jewish Gangster in America, 28.

28 THE NIGHT COURT George Kibbe Turner, "Tammany's Control of New York by Professional Criminals," 128.

28 "THE USE OF THE FIRST" Theodore A. Bingham, "The Organized Criminals of New York," 30.

28 "A DIVE NOTORIOUS" and A BLOODIED HEAP Jay Robert Nash, Blood-letters and Bad Men, 189; Jorge Luis Borges, A Universal History of Iniquity, 33.

29 "DANCING ACADEMIES" Benjamin Antin, quoted in Fried, The Rise and Fall of the Jewish Gangster, ix.

29 "BOISTEROUSLY DRUNK" and "IT WAS NOT UNUSUAL" John M. Oskison, "Public Halls of the East Side," 38–40; Herbert Asbury, Sin in New York, Asbury Papers, manuscripts box 1; 4, 9.

29 "THE FOULEST OF ALL" and "TOUGH RACKETS" Herman Melville, quoted in Timothy J. Gilfoyle, "Street-Rats and Gutter-Snipes," 4; Verne M. Bovie, "The Public Dance Halls of the Lower East Side," 32.

29 "HE BULLDOZES THE MERCHANTS" Abraham H. Shoenfeld papers, P3/1768, 109–10.

30 "WERE IN THE HABIT," "A BLOW BEHIND THE EAR," and "FORTY-NINE NICKS" The Sun, June 20, 1909; Henry Collins Brown, ed., Valentine's Manual of Old New York, 21; Herbert Asbury, The Gangs of New York, xvi.

30 "WITH AN APTITUDE" and "I ONLY GIVE HER" Asbury, The Gangs of New York, 257.

30   "A PIMP, A THIEF" and "HE LEARNS HOW" Turner, "Tammany's Control of New York," 122; Gilfoyle, "Street-Rats and Gutter-Snipes," 6; Abraham H. Shoenfeld papers, P3/1768, 107.

31   "THOSE LITTLE BOYS" Washington Post, May 27, 1906.

32   "A TRIUMPH OF EFFICIENCY" Tyler Anbinder, Five Points, 74.

32   "SLAUGHTER ALLEY" and "BLACKER THAN A WOLF'S THROAT" Campbell, Knox, and Byrnes, Darkness and Daylight, 89; Stephen Crane, "New York Sketches," in Last Words, 159.

33   "ALMOST IMPOSSIBLE TO PASS" quoted in Anbinder, Five Points, 89.

33   "NO WASTE" Jacob A. Riis, How the Other Half Lives, 108.

33   A SINGLE BLOCK and "THE MOST CROWDED BLOCK" Moses King's 1893 Handbook of New York City, quoted in Nathan Silver, Lost New York, 74; Tenement Commission report 1903, www.immigrantheritagetrail.org.

33   40 PERCENT TO BE A FAIR AVERAGE and A QUARTER TO A THIRD HIGHER Riis, How the Other Half Lives, 7, 11.

34   "PACKED IN LIKE HERRINGS," "ONE MAY SLEEP," and "REVOLVERS" Campbell, Knox, and Byrnes, Darkness and Daylight, 423; Riis, How the Other Half Lives, 70; Howard Zinn, A People's History of the United States, 238.

34   "TOUCHED UP WITH DRUGS," ON BAYARD STREET, and "THE WASHINGS OF THE BAR" Riis, How the Other Half Lives, 61; Campbell, Knox, and Byrnes, Darkness and Daylight, 358, 198–201, 496.

35   "THE THEATER OF," "EXPLORED THE BOWERY," and "SHOW YOU THE BOWERY" "Bowery Amusements," 14; M. B. Levick, "Tough Girl of New York Remains Only a Memory"; Alvin Harlow, Old Bowery Days, 501–5.

35   "IF YOU WILL STAND FOR" and STREETCAR CONDUCTORS Gilfoyle, "Street-Rats and Gutter-Snipes," 3; Harlow, Old Bowery Days, 501–5.

35   "THE MOST BRILLIANTLY" and "AN ANEMIC" Levick, "Tough Girl of New York"; Julian Ralph, "The Bowery," 234; Theodore Dreiser, quoted in Luc Sante, Low Life, 67.

36   "COMBINED ELEMENTS" and "FREE and EASYS" Sante, Low Life, 64, 113.

36   DIME MUSEUMS cf. Robert Bogdan's Freak Show: Presenting Human Oddities for Amusement and Profit (University of Chicago Press, 1988) for a fuller exploration of the phenomenon.

36   "COCAINE ROW" and "DIVES and HOUSES" Abraham H. Shoenfeld papers, P311768, 153; Ezra R. Pulling, "Report of the Fourth Sanitary District," 15; Riis, How the Other Half Lives, 159.

37   CHLORAL HYDRATE Benjamin P. Eldridge and William B. Watts, Our Rival the Rascal, 288–89.

37   "THE NEARER THE RIVER" Campbell, Knox, and Byrnes, Darkness and Daylight, 360.

37   OOZED THROUGH THE WALLS Pulling, "Report of the Fourth Sanitary District," 2, 11.

38   "GENERATIONS" OF PROSTITUTES Sante, Low Life, 180.

3 AS A POOL REFLECTS THE SKY

39   THIS "MODERN GOMORRAH" Herbert Asbury, "Gangland USA," 14; Lewis J. Valentine, Night Stick, 124.

40   "AN ABYSS OF MANY GENERATIONS" and "FORMALLY CAST THEM OFF" Lincoln Steffens, Autobiography, vol. I, 246; George Kibbe Turner, "The Daughters of the Poor," 47.

40   "EVERY AFTERNOON, JUST LIKE MECHANICS" and "AS A POOL REFLECTS THE SKY" Alvin Harlow, Old Bowery Days, 501–5; Gustavus Myers, History of the Great American Fortunes, quoted in Howard Zinn, A People's History of the United States, 233–34.

41   "SALESMAN, BIRDS" and LARGE PROFITS United States of America, Bureau of the Census: Twelfth Census of the United States, 1900, New York (Manhattan), New York City, Greater New York, roll T623 1092; page 5B, ED 240; Harlow, Old Bowery Days, 501–5.

41   A TOUGH SCHOOL and "OBJECTS FOR TARGET PRACTICE" "Young Mayors Govern a Once Unmanageable School," New York Times, May 29, 1910.

41   "HARD-FISTED, TOUGH-FACED" and "TOITY-TOID" Brooklyn Eagle, December 27, 1920; F. Raymond Daniell, "The Big Business of the Racketeer."

41   "MONKEY-LIKE FACE" and CLAMBERING UP and DOWN George Kibbe Turner, "Tammany's Control of New York by Professional Criminals," 122; New York Times, December 27, 1920.

42   "LONG JOHN" GARVEY Thomas Byrnes, Professional Criminals of America, 23.

42   "BEAT UP A GUY" and "THE EASTMAN PAVILION" Herbert Asbury,
43   The Gangs of New York, 258, 257.

43   HUNG OUT IN TWO STORES New York Daily Tribune, April 26, 1903.

43   $75,000 ANNUALLY and "A SORT OF LICENSED BANDIT" Asbury, "Gang-
44   land USA," 18, 17; Turner, "Tammany's Control of New York," 122.

44   "I WANT FIFTY" New York Times, June 9, 1912.

44   "A REAL GANGMAN" Abraham H. Shoenfeld papers, P311768, 151, 110.

44   TWENTY THOUSAND FULL-TIME PROSTITUTES and FIFTY CENTS Herbert Asbury, Sin in New York, Asbury papers, manuscripts box 1; 1–2; Albert Fried, The Rise and Fall of the Jewish Gangster in America, 7.

44   "HALF-EXPOSED WOMEN" and "STAKHANOVITE OF SEX" Edwin G.
45   Burrows and Mike Wallace, Gotham, 805, 996, 1163.

45   "SOUBRETTE ROW," "JENNIE THE FACTORY," and "ON CERTAIN DAYS" Timothy Gilfoyle, City of Eros, 165; Abraham H. Shoenfeld papers, P311768, 210; Asbury, Sin in New York, Asbury papers, manuscripts box 1; 6, 12.

45   "THE TREASURE-LADEN," "THE MORGUE," and McGURK'S SUICIDE HALL Asbury, The Gangs of New York, 234, 207; Mike Dash, Satan's Circus, 31n.

46 THIS WAS THE HEYDAY and THE LATTER'S ACOLYTES New York Daily Tribune, April 26, 1903; The Bookman, December 1905, 303.

46 "BY WAY OF TESTING" and "IF LITTLE KISHKY" New York Daily Tribune, April 26, 1903; Alfred Henry Lewis, "The Cooking of Crazy Butch."

47 "THE HEART OF THAT," "ALL TRAINED," and "THE RASCAL NOTICE" Lewis, "The Cooking of Crazy Butch"; Asbury, The Gangs of New York, 226.

47 MOST EFFICIENT BLACKJACKERS and "THE FIRST OF THE GANGSTERS" Asbury, The Gangs of New York, 234, 247; New York Times, May 13, 1915; Leo Katcher, The Big Bankroll, 276, 238.

48 "NOT TENDER" Helen Campbell, Thomas W. Knox, and Thomas F. Byrnes, Darkness and Daylight, 513, 95.

48 ARNOLD ROTHSTEIN Katcher, The Big Bankroll, 23.

48 A COMPREHENSIVE LIST Jenna Joselit, Our Gang, 25, 44; Asbury, The Gangs of New York, 211.

49 "A BLONDE OF STRIKING APPEARANCE" and "THE CONSPIRACY" New York Times, November 11, October 22, 1903.

49 TRACED A SCORE and "IN THE THREE YEARS I WAS" Chicago Daily Tribune, December 27, 1920; Turner, "Tammany's Control," 122; New York Daily Tribune, April 26, 1903.

4 A MODERN ROBIN HOOD

51 REVOLVERS INSTEAD OF CUES New York Daily Tribune, April 26, 1903.

51 "A HOSTAGE TO FORTUNE" and "SECURE THEIR HARD-" George Kibbe Turner, "The Daughters of the Poor," 53–54; Albert Fried, The Rise and Fall of the Jewish Gangster in America, 19; Frank Moss, The American Metropolis, quoted in S. S. McClure, "The Tammanyizing of a Civilization," 118–19.

51 THOROUGHLY PROFESSIONAL CRIMINALS New York Daily Tribune, April 26, 1903.

51 "THE GANG NEEDED THE POLITICIAN" George Kibbe Turner, "Tammany's Control of New York by Professional Criminals," 123.

52 "THE SWELLEST GINMILL" Alvin Harlow, Old Bowery Days, 501–5.

52 "NEVER TASTES TOBACCO," "THE POLITICAL BOSS OF DOWNTOWN," "THE KING OF THE UNDERWORLD," and "POLITICALLY HE IS CORRUPT" Alfred Henry Lewis, "The Modern Robin Hood," 186; Tammany Times, November 4, 1895; Daniel Czitrom, "Underworlds and Underdogs," 539; Hutchins Hapgood, Types from City Streets, 58.

52 "REPULSIVE ENOUGH" and "THE SCENE OF MORE MURDERS" The World, April 18, 1889; Herbert Asbury, Chinatown, Asbury papers, manuscripts box 1, 3.

52 "THE SOCIETY OF POLITICIANS, PIMPS" Turner, "Tammany's Control of New York," 121.

53 "WORD IS LAW" and "HARRISON GOT ONE MORE" Turner, "Tammany's Control of New York," 126; Czitrom, "Underworlds and Underdogs," 541, 538; Albert Fried, The Rise and Fall of the Jewish Gangster in America, 53.

53 TEN THOUSAND DOLLARS, "THE GREAT DANCING HALL," and "LEADS THROUGH THE HAPPY" Lewis, "The Modern Robin Hood," 186; Turner, "Tammany's Control of New York," 132.

54 "NOT A SPLINTER" Lewis, "The Modern Robin Hood," 186; John Carter, "Master of Manhattan," 203.

54 "THINK OF THE HUNDREDS" Quoted in Werner, Tammany Hall, 449–50.

54 CONTROLLER METZ and $80 MILLION Gustavus Myers, History of Tammany Hall, 338; Lewis, "The Modern Robin Hood," 186.

55 SHOESHINE STAND and "I SEEN MY OPPORTUNITIES" The Old Time Saloon, Asbury papers, manuscripts box 1, 7; William L. Riordan, Plunkitt of Tammany Hall, 310.

55 "GUERILLAS" the words guerillas and gorillas seem to have been used interchangeably by writers of the era.

55 "ANY POLITICAL WAVERING" and "THE NERVOUS HEBREWS" Lewis J. Valentine, Night Stick, 125; New York Daily Tribune, April 26, 1903.

55 IMMUNITY and "YOUTHS WHO, ALONE" The Sun, June 20, 1920, October 11, 1903; New York Times, June 9, 1912.

55 PARTICULARLY TRUE IN cf. Turner, "The Daughters of the Poor," 53–54.

55 "WORD WAS SENT OUT" Brooklyn Eagle, November 1, 1901.

56 "STRONG ON THE SIDE," "MORE THAN ONCE," and THE GRAVE-YARDS Jacob A. Riis, How the Other Half Lives, 61, 71; New York Times, November 2, 1903.

56 "DISORDERLY RESORTS" Brooklyn Eagle, November 1, 1901.

56 "BRING DOWN A LOT OF FOOTBALL-PLAYING" and "A REGULAR COM-
57 MISSARY" Big Tim Sullivan, quoted in Czitrom, "Underworld and Underdogs," 549; Turner, "Tammany's Control of New York," 122–25.

57 "MET WITH INDIFFERENCE" New York Times, November 4, 1903.

57 "OLD-TIME IRISH RESIDENTS" and "PROBABLY EXCEEDED ALL PREVIOUS" Turner, "Tammany's Control of New York," 133.

57 FIVE TO TEN VOTES and "GUYS WITH WHISKERS" Ibid., 123; Brooklyn Eagle, November 1, 1901; Big Tim Sullivan, quoted in Harlow, Old Bowery Days, 501–5.

58 "LIKE A CROWD OF" Turner, "Tammany's Control of New York," 132–33.

58 QUIET DAY AT THE POLLS and "A RIDDLE" New York Times, November 4, 1903.

58 BIG TIM SULLIVAN PERSONALLY PROVIDED, "WORKING THE RATTLER," and "THE POLITICIANS ALWAYS SPRUNG HIM" Czitrom, "Underworlds and Underdogs," 546, 129; New York Daily Tribune, April 26, 1903;

Herbert Asbury, The Gangs of New York, 256.

59   "INSTANTLY THE WORD WAS PASSED" New York Daily Tribune, April 26, 1903.

59   "OVER THEM HIS POWER" and "THE CONDUCT OF THE POLICE" Lewis, "The Modern Robin Hood," 186; Turner, "Tammany's Control of New York," 124.

59   "OUR PEOPLE COULD NOT STAND" Lincoln Steffens, Autobiography, 256.

59   "TO HELL WITH REFORM!," "TAMMANY IS NOT A WAVE," and "A NEW, PERFECTED SYSTEM" Virgil W. Peterson, The Mob, 92; a "reform chief of police" quoted in Steffens, Autobiography, vol. 1, 281; Lincoln Steffens, "The Real Roosevelt," in Ainslee's Magazine, December 1898.

60   "THE GOVERNMENT OF THE," "CORRUPTION WITH CONSENT," and "THE PEOPLE ARE NOT INNOCENT" Turner, "Tammany's Control of New York," 125; Alexander B. Callow Jr., Introduction to Gustavus Myers, The History of Tammany Hall, ix; Lincoln Steffens, The Shame of the Cities, 14, 290, 292.

5 THE ROGUES' GALLERY

61   EIGHTY OF THE ONE HUNDRED Raymond A. Mohl, The Making of Urban America, 98.

62   THE U.S. MURDER RATE and "PERFECT DEVILS" Henry Collins Brown, ed., Valentine's Manual of Old New York, 3; Helen Campbell, Thomas W. Knox, and Thomas F. Byrnes, Darkness and Daylight, 511.

62   LOCUST WOOD, "SLAUGHTERHOUSES" and AN UNNERVING DRUMMING SOUND Campbell, Knox, and Byrnes, Darkness and Daylight, 512; Edwin G. Burrows and Mike Wallace, Gotham, 1,192; Brown, ed., Valentine's Manual, 24.

62   NUMBER 5,844 and ARRESTED MEN The Argus (Albany), May 18, 1915; Campbell, Knox, and Byrnes, Darkness and Daylight, 693.

62   PICTURES OF THE MOST NOTORIOUS, "NO END OF DIRKS," and "A SEN-
63   SATIONAL MINUTENESS" Abraham H. Shoenfeld papers, P3/1768, 131–42, 141; Campbell, Knox, and Byrnes, Darkness and Daylight, 525; Jacob A. Riis, How the Other Half Lives, 164.

63   IN THE 1890S THE GOING RATE, "OF COURSE THERE ARE COPS," and
64   ANY DISTRICT REMOTE Virgil W. Peterson, The Mob, 89; Cornelius Willemse, quoted in Mike Dash, Satan's Circus, 55; Brown, ed., Valentine's Manual, 11.

64   THERE WAS A GAP Campbell, Knox, and Byrnes, Darkness and Daylight, 167.

64   WALL STREET HAD ONCE and A HABITUAL CRIMINAL Ibid., 520.

65   WITH THE COMPLIMENTS OF and A HANDSOME $500 GOLD WATCH Ibid., 520–21; Steffens, Autobiography, 221–22.

65   "FENCE OFF THE GOOD" Riis, How the Other Half Lives, 120–21.

65   "WE SEE THE POWERS" and ENTERTAINING SEVERAL CITY OFFICIALS

66　Peterson, The Mob, 94; Herbert Asbury, Sin in New York, Asbury papers, manuscripts box 1, 7.

66　"RUSTIC INNOCENCE" and "TO PROTECT and FOSTER" Charles Parkhurst, Our Fight with Tammany, 5; Charles Parkhurst, My Forty Years in New York, 126–30.

66　"WHILE WE FIGHT INIQUITY," "POLLUTED HARPIES," and SLUM and WHOREHOUSE Peterson, The Mob, 87; New York World, February 15, 1892; Justin Kaplan, Lincoln Steffens, 118.

66　"THE COAT WAS CUT" Charles Gardner, The Doctor and the Devil, 17.

67　"HEY WHISKERS," "SOLICITING MEN," and "WOULD NOT PERMIT" Gardner, The Doctor and the Devil, 24–26, 56; Asbury, Sin in New York, Asbury papers, manuscripts box 1, 5.

67　"ONE OF THE MOST INFAMOUS," "SHOW ME SOMETHING WORSE!," and IN EACH ROOM WAS Charles Gardner, The Doctor and the Devil, 56, 52.

67　TEA and COOKIES Luc Sante, Low Life, 286.

67　"TRUE IN NO OTHER," "URGENT BUSINESS," and "WITH APPROPRIATE

68　SUBTRACTIONS" S. S. McClure, "The Tammanyizing of a Civilization," 126–27; Gustavus Myers, History of Tammany Hall, 278; V. O. Key, "Police Graft," 624; Peterson, The Mob, 86.

68　"WE WILL PARADE" Theodore Roosevelt, quoted in Peterson, The Mob, 90.

68　"WIDE OPEN" and $680,000 OF ICE COMPANY STOCK Gustavus Myers, History of Tammany Hall, 283; Dash, Satan's Circus, 24n.

69　"OPERATORS ENCROACHING," PAID THIRTY THOUSAND DOLLARS A YEAR, "THERE'S MORE LAW," and PROPERTY SPECULATION IN JAPAN Key, "Police Graft," 629; Peterson, The Mob, 89; Asbury, Sin in New York, Asbury papers, manuscripts box 1, 3; Steffens, Autobiography, 252.

69　SOMETHING OVER THREE MILLION DOLLARS and "GAMBLING HOUSE COMMISSION" William Devery, quoted in Lincoln Steffens, The Shame of the Cities, 294; New York Times, March 9, 1900; Landesco, Prohibition and Crime, quoted in Key, "Police Graft," 631.

70　"A GRAFT-RIDDEN TOWN" and "PAID DEAR TRIBUTE" Abraham H. Shoenfeld papers, P3/1768, 199; Myers, History of Tammany Hall, xvi.

6 THE GANGLAND CODE

71　UPMARKET SUBURB United States of America, Bureau of the Census, Twelfth Census of the United States, 1900, Queens Ward 4, Queens, New York, roll T623_1149; Pages 19B, 20A, ED677; Census of the United States, Brooklyn Ward 28, Kings, New York, New York, roll T624_982; page IB, ED 917, image 495.77; Census of the United States, Brooklyn Ward 28, Kings, New York, New York, roll T624 973; page 12A, ED 695, image 747.

72   "THE BY-BLOW OF" Jorge Luis Borges, A Universal History of Iniquity, 32.

72   BAT JARVIS P. G. Wodehouse, Psmith Journalist, chapter 4.

72   "A FEUD CODE," "GREAT ITALIAN BAND," "A BLAND HEATHEN," and

73   "AN ODOR OF STALE BEER" New York Times, September 20, 1903; George Kibbe Turner, "Tammany's Control of New York by Professional Criminals," 122, 125; The Sun, October 11, 1903.

73   PAOLO CORRELLI The Sun, October 11, 1903.

73   "AFTER THE COMMON CUSTOM," AN ITALIAN BANK, and "ACQUIRED SOME REPUTATION" Turner, "Tammany's Control of New York," 124; The Sun, October 11, 1903.

73   SALVATORE LUCIANA, SELLING HEROIN and MORPHINE, and "ARTICHOKE KING" George Walsh, Public Enemies, 45; Craig Thompson and Allen Raymond, Gang Rule in New York, 23; Robert J. Kelly, Encyclopedia of Organized Crime in the United States, 293–94.

73   "DAPPER" PAUL KELLY, "EXQUISITELY SCENTED," and "WHICH THE

74   BOWERY ACCEPTS" Lewis J. Valentine, Night Stick, 126; Richard Harding Davis, "The Defeat of the Underworld," 11; The Sun, October 11, 1903.

74   HE SPOKE FOUR LANGUAGES and "ONE OF THE FLASHIEST" Herbert Asbury, The Gangs of New York, 254–55.

74   PERCHED ON TOP and "FLABBY and EPICENE" Valentine, Night Stick, 125; Borges, A Universal History, 32–33.

75   "MONK HADN'T A REAL" and "A SOFT EASY-GOING" New York Times, December 29, 1920; Alvin Harlow, Old Bowery Days, 501–5.

75   "PEGGY" . . . DONOVAN Also sometimes described as "Piggy" Donovan, cf. New York Times, September 9, 1923.

75   "PEGGY DONOVAN, WITHOUT WARNING" New York Times, April 15, 1901.

75   "TWO MEN GRABBED ME" New York Times, April 14, 1901.

76   "THE DONOVANS WERE HEARD" and "DIED IN THE GOUVERNEUR" New York Times, April 14, 15, 1901.

76   A FIVE POINTER WAS DECOYED and "MONK GOT HIS MAN" Asbury, The Gangs of New York, 259; New York Daily Tribune, December 27, 1920.

76   "A JAGGED CONFLUENCE" and MONK WAS SET UPON New York City Guide, 117; Asbury, The Gangs of New York, 259.

77   "A VERITABLE WILD WEST" New York Times, September 30, 1902; New York Daily Tribune, April 26, 1903.

77   NIGGER MIKE's Asbury, The Gangs of New York, 258; Stephen Jenkins, The Greatest Street in the World, Asbury papers, box 8.

77   CHINESE CRIMINAL GANGS cf. Moses King's Guidebook, quoted in Edwin G. Burrows and Mike Wallace, Gotham, 1,131; Herbert Asbury, Chinatown, Asbury papers, manuscripts box 1, 1.

77   THOMAS COMINSKY New York Times, April 22, 1902.

77   "SAID TO BE OF THE EASTMAN," "LOOKING FOR THE ENEMY," and

78   "POUNCING ON THE KNOTS" New York Times, September 30, 1902.

78   THIRTY-FIVE MEMBERS New York Times, October 5, 1902.

78   "A DISGRACE TO THE CITY" New York Times, October 6, 1902.

78   "BIG DAVE" BERNSTEIN, EXCHANGE OF SHOTS, and "ANYWAY, I'LL SETTLE" New York Daily Tribune, April 26, 1903; New York Times, March 9, 1903; The Sun, June 20, 1920.

79   "NO ONE KNOWS" and JOHN "MUGSY" BAYARD New York Times, August 18, 19, 1903; New York Daily Tribune, April 26, 1903; New York Herald, August 18, 1903.

79   "A FRIEND OF MONK," "THE WICKEDEST STREET," and "PRESSED A REVOLVER" New York Times, August 8, 1903; New York Herald, August 8, 1903.

79   FEMME FATALE and "LAID VIOLENT HANDS" New York Times, June 9, 1912; New York Daily Tribune, April 26, 1903.

80   THIRTY-THREE MEN and "A LABYRINTH" New York Times, March 28, 1903.

80   A CONFERENCE BETWEEN New York Times, October 12, 1902.

81   "THE REPRESENTATIVES OF THESE" and "THE GANG REACHED THE OLD" New York Times, October 6, 12, 1902.

7 THE WOLF OF WALL STREET

83   "I'M PAID FOR DRIVING" New York Times, May, 5, July 29, 11, 13, 1903.

83   A FEW DRINKS The World, October 14, 1903.

83   FOUR BURLY MEN The Monmouth Democrat, September 3, 1903.

83   ON JULY 9, 1903 The Sun, October 13, 1903; New York Herald, October 13, 1903; The Monmouth Democrat, September 3, 1903; New York Times, July 10, 1903; The Freehold Transcript, July 31, 1903.

84   "ARREST ME, WILL YER?" The Freehold Transcript, July 31, 1903; New York Herald, July 29, 1903; New York Times, August 2, 1903, June 21, 1909; George Kibbe Turner, "Tammany's Control of New York by Professional Criminals," 123; The Monmouth Democrat, October 15, 1903.

84   "WHOSE REAL NAME IS WILLIAM," 93 SOUTH THIRD STREET, and "TAKE THAT FELLOW" New York Times, July 29, 1903; Lain's Brooklyn City Directory; Uppington's General Directory of Brooklyn; New York Herald, August 1, 1903.

84   "WHO IS THIS MAN" and "SPOKE BITTERLY" New York Daily Tribune, August 1, 1903; New York Herald, August 1, 1903.

84   CONTRADICTED BY A BARMAN The Freehold Transcript, July 31, 1903.

85   "A FOUR-FLUSHER" and "LICKSPITTLE" New York Times, July 30, 1903; William S. Devery, quoted in New York Times, November 2, 1903; New York Herald, August 2, 1903.

85   "ARE YOU NOT AN EX-CONVICT?" New York Times, August 2, 1903.

85   "IT WAS THOUGHT BETTER" New York Daily Tribune, August 2, 1903.

86   "MUCH ELATED" and A FISHING EXCURSION New York Times, Au-

gust 1, 2, 1903; The World, August 6, 1903.

86   "STRENUOUS EFFORTS" and "AT PRIMARY ELECTIONS" New York Daily Tribune, August 1, 1903; New York Times, July 29, August 4, 1903.

86   "WHEN I GET OUT" New York Daily Tribune, August 1, 1903; New York Times, August 4, 1903; New York Herald, August 7, 1903.

86   THE PRISONERS WOULD "SQUEAL" and "THEY ARE THE FELLOWS" The
87   Sun, August 7, 1903; New York Herald, August 7, 1903; The Freehold Transcript, August 7, 1903; New York Daily Tribune, August 2, 1903; New York Times, August 1, 1903.

87   CELL NUMBER I and SHOOT ANYBODY SCALING The Freehold Transcript, August 7, 14, 1903; New York Herald, August 8, 1903.

88   A FRESH ALARM and "THE CASES ARE BAILABLE" New York Herald, August 8, 1903; The Sun, August 8, 1903; The Monmouth Democrat, August 13, 1903.

88   "THE GREAT MONK EASTMAN" New York Times, July 31, August 10, 1903.

88   "PACKED IN THE CELLS" and "EASTMAN IS THE ONLY" New York Times, August 9, 1903; New York Daily Tribune, August 8, 1903.

88   "I GUESS IT DIDN'T," "ORGANIZED SPECIFICALLY," and "THE ARREST OF
89   THESE" New York Times, August 9, 1903; New York Herald, August 9, 1903.

89   "I WOULD NOT HAVE WALKED" and "SCOURED FOR LUXURIES" The Freehold Transcript, August 14, 1903; New York Herald, August 8, 1903.

89   "MERELY A BUSINESS" New York Herald, August 15, 1903; The Monmouth Democrat, August 20, 1903.

89   THE DAY BEFORE THANKSGIVING New York Daily Tribune, December 27, 1920; New York Times, February 3, 1904; Court of General Sessions, People of the State of New York versus William Delaney, alias Monk Eastman, 255–56.

89   "LEG BAIL" and "IT IS DIFFICULT" New York Times, September 4,
90   1903; The Monmouth Democrat, September 3, 1903.

90   "A PRECAUTION UNUSUAL," "NEWLY CLIPPED," and "NERVOUS, THIS MAN WHO" New York Herald, October 13, 1903; New York Times, October 13, 1903; The World, October 14, 1903.

90   "HAD TO GET THE BOYS" The Sun, October 15, 1903.

90   "I AM ALWAYS INTERESTED" Ibid.

91   WANTED A RICH and "'LEAVE IT ALL TO ME'" The Freehold Transcript, October 16, 1903; The Sun, October 15, 1903.

91   JUSTICE WALTER BRINLEY The Freehold Transcript, October 16, 1903; The Monmouth Democrat, October 15, 1903.

91   "NEVER" and COULDN'T READ The Sun, October 14, 15, 1903.

91   "NO, I NEVER CARRY" and "ANYONE CAN TELL A DETECTIVE" The
92   Sun, October 15, 1903; The World, October 14, 1903.

92   "DOVETAILED WITH CONSIDERABLE" New York Times, October 17, 1903; The Sun, October 15, 1903.

92   "IF YOU HAVE NO" The Sun, October 17, 1903; New York Herald, October 17, 1903.

92   "THERE MAY BE ONE" and ACCEPT THE VERDICT The World, October 14, 1903; New York Times, October 17, 1903.

92   "HONEST MONMOUTH COUNTY" The Sun, October 17, 1903.

92   "MANIFESTED CHILDISH" New York Times, October 17, 1903.

92   "WELL, PERSONS WHO HAVE" and "NOT NECESSARILY A CONFESSION"

93   The Sun, October 17, 1903; The Freehold Transcript, October 23, 1903.

93   SINISTER RUMORS and "AS IF A GAME" *New York Herald,* October 17, 1903; *New York Times,* October 17, 1903.

93   "NO MORE GUNS" New York Herald, October 17, 1903.

93   "THE REIGN OF TERROR" and "WHEN I SAY" Ibid.

8 THE BATTLE OF RIVINGTON STREET

96   TYPICAL BOWERY TOUGHS and THE FURIOUS LAST FUSILLADE New York Times, September 17, 1903.

96   STUSS A card game, also known as "Jewish faro."

96   "FIFTY FOOT CREVASSE" New York Times, January 5, 1928.

96   PERPETUAL SHADOW cf. the photograph in the New York Daily Tribune, April 26, 1903.

96   A HUNDRED WOMEN ON EVERY The American Hebrew, March 8, 1929, quoted in Jenna Joselit, Our Gang, 46.

96   FIFTY MEN ALREADY INVOLVED, "THEIR PARAPETS OF IRON," and "A
97   LOT OF THE GUYS" New York Herald, September 17, 1903; Jorge Luis Borges, A Universal History of Iniquity, 35; Herbert Asbury, The Gangs of New York, 261.

97   MEN ON THE ROOFTOPS New York Daily Tribune, September 17, 1903.

97   A SQUARE MILE OF TERRITORY New York Herald, September 17, 1903.

97   MICHAEL DONOVAN and JOHN CARROLL New York Times, September 17, 1903; New York Daily Tribune, September 17, 1903.

98   JOSEPH MORRIS New York Times, September 17, 1903.

98   ITS CHAMBERS WERE STILL and DETECTIVE McCOY Ibid.; New York Daily Tribune, September 17, 1903.

99   "ALONG THE LINE OF THE FIGHTING" New York Times, September 17, 1903.

99   "LOLLY" "Lally" in some versions.

99   MEYERS New York Times, September 18, October 17, 1903.

99   "EACH GANG DANCED WITH" The Sun, June 11, 20, 1909.

99   POLICE COMMISSIONER FRANCIS V. GREENE New York Times, September 18, 24, 1903.

100 WE MOURN and "THERE WAS NO CEREMONY . . ." New York Times, September 20, 1903.

100 "THIS MEETING IS" and "I THINK WE HAVE SUCCEEDED" Ibid.

100   A SCORE OF POLICEMEN   New York Daily Tribune, September 22, 1903.

101   "TO GET A DOSE"   The World, September 22, 21, 1903; New York Times, September 23, 1903.

101   "AS RECKLESS and DESPERATE" and "THIS BRIGHT FACED"   New York Herald, October 2, 1903; Kansas City Star, October 3, 1903.

101   "TESTIFIED THAT SHE WAS INCORRIGIBLE," "ABUSED HER IN SUCH,"

102   and "BARELY FIVE FEET"   New York Times, September 27, 1903; Kansas City Star, October 3, 1903.

102   "GLORIED IN HER WICKEDNESS"   Kansas City Star, October 3, 1903.

102   "SHE CARRIES A GUN, JUDGE"   New York Times, September 27, 1903.

102   "A KIND OF SPARROW"   M. B. Levick, "Tough Girl of New York Remains Only a Memory."

103   GERRY SOCIETY   Now known as the New York Society for the Prevention of Cruelty to Children.

103   BEDFORD REFORMATORY   Now the Bedford Correctional Facility.

103   "BIG FELLOWS IN POLITICS"   New York Times, October 5, 1903.

103   "YOU'SE GO TO ENTIRELY" and "A SURPRISE TO THE GROUP"   New York Times, October 5, 1903; New York Herald, October 6, 1903.

104   "RIGHT BOWER"   The name for the jack of the trump suit, the second-highest card in the game of euchre.

104   "THE REDOUBTABLE KING EASTMAN" and BANNED IN EVERY STATE   The Sun, October 11, 1903; Dennis Brailsford, Bareknuckles, 8.

104   "HELLO YOU RUNT"   The Sun, October 3, 1903.

105   "SHIMSKY OPENED"   Ibid.

105   "WIPE UP DE EARTH"   Asbury, The Gangs of New York, 264.

105   "TOUGHS IN COCKED DERBY HATS"   Borges, Universal History, 35–36.

106   "COULD FACE THE SEARCHLIGHT"   The Sun, December 30, 1903.

106   "WHETTED THEIR APPETITES"   Ibid.

107   ARMED GANG MEMBERS   New York Times, September 9, 1923.

108   THEY REACHED 161ST   The Sun, December 30, 1903.

9 THE TOMBS

109   TO BLACKJACK A MAN and STAGGERING OUT OF JACK'S   Herbert Asbury, The Gangs of New York, 265; Court of General Sessions, People of the State of New York versus William Delaney, alias Monk Eastman, 6–7.

109   TWO ROUGHLY DRESSED MEN   Some versions, e.g., Asbury, Gangs of New York, 265–66, describe only one Pinkerton's man, but the trial transcript makes clear that there were two.

110   "THE WAYWARD SON"   Court of General Sessions, People of the State of New York versus William Delaney, alias Monk Eastman, 6–7; New York Times, April 15, February 3, 1904.

110   "SHOOT FIRST and THEN"   Asbury, The Gangs of New York, 266; New York Times, February 3, April 20, 1904.

110   BRYAN LATER TESTIFIED Court of General Sessions, People of the State of New York versus William Delaney, alias Monk Eastman, 12.

110   2060 SECOND AVENUE The Sun, June 20, 1920.

111   "INCORRUPTIBLE" PINKERTON New York Daily Tribune, February 3, 1904; Richard Wilmer Rowan, The Pinkertons, 142.

111   "ONE OF THE BEST" Wilmer Rowan, The Pinkertons, 142; *The Sun*, June 20, 1920.

111   "WILLFULLY, FELONIOUSLY" and "UP THE RIVER" Court of General
112   Sessions of the Peace, Case Number 45,672, February 4, 1904; New York Times, February 5, 1904.

112   "MEETING THEIR EYES" Helen Campbell, Thomas W. Knox, and Thomas F. Byrnes, Darkness and Daylight, 337.

113   SHYSTER LAWYERS Ibid., 347.

113   "COLD-HEARTED, HUMORLESS" and "NOT ENOUGH GLOOM" Mike Dash, Satan's Circus, 241, 252.

113   PACKED WITH EAST SIDE TOUGHS New York Times, March 2, 1904.

114   FIFTEEN OF HIS GANG MEMBERS New York Times, March, 30, April 2, 1904.

114   TEN DAYS LATER New York Times, April 12, 1904.

114   MONK'S SISTERS New York Times, March 5, 29, 1904; The Sun, April 13, 1904.

114   DRESSED BETTER, "LET GO OF HIM YOU," and "LIKE THE BARK" New York Times, April 13, 1904; The Sun, April 13, 1904.

115   ELEVEN PAGES OF THE TRIAL TRANSCRIPT Court of General Sessions, People of the State of New York versus William Delaney, alias Monk Eastman, 260–70.

116   "TWENTY GLASSES" Ibid., 250–55.

117   "HELD WALLACE" Ibid.

117   "WONDER AT THE NERVE" and POLICE CONSPIRACY New York Times, April 15, 1904; New York Herald, April 15, 1904.

117   "NEVER IN MY EXPERIENCE" New York Times, April 15, 1904; New York Herald, April 15, 1904.

118   MONK SEARCHED THEIR FACES, "IN THE LANGUAGE," and "THANKS GENTS" New York Herald, April 15, 1904; New York Times, April 15, 20, 1904.

118   "I HAVE ORDERED THE DEFENDANT" New York Times, April 20, 1904.

118   "THE CIRCUMSTANCES OF THE CASE" Ibid.

118   "NOBODY BEGRUDGED THE MONK" New York Times, November 30, 1911.

118   GEORGE COAN New York Daily Tribune, April 21, 1904.

119   "WELL, I'M GOING" and "HOLY SMOKES!" New York Times, April 23, 1904; New York Daily Tribune, April 23, 1904.

119   "THAT HOUR GOIN' UP" and "BURIED HIS FACE" Quoted in Campbell, Knox, and Byrnes, Darkness and Daylight, 73; New York Daily Tribune, April 23, 1904.

120   "WERE IT NOT FOR THE IRON BARS" and "NOTHING THAT IS

HUMAN" Lewis E. Lawes, *Twenty Thousand* Years in Sing Sing, 209.

120   "EXPERIENCED CONS ANSWERED" Ibid., 192, 201–2.

120   TAR and TIN ROOFER and "COMPLEXION DARK" New York State Archives, B0143, vol. 36, box 14, page 157.

121   THE USUAL BATH and TWO LEGAL RIGHTS Lawes, Twenty Thousand Years in Sing Sing, 192–193.

121   "UNFIT FOR THE HOUSING OF ANIMALS" Grand Jury Report, Westchester County, June 19, 1913, quoted in Denis Brian, Sing Sing, 75–77.

121   "REPUGNANT and DANGEROUS" Ibid.

121   "THE WHOLE SYSTEM UNDER WHICH" New York Times, November 18, 1913.

122   "THIS SITUATION IS AS DEPLORABLE" and KNOCK ON THE DOORS OF THE DARK CELLS Grand Jury Report, Westchester County, June 19, 1913, quoted in Brian, Sing Sing, 75–77; Dash, Satan's Circus, 286.

122   WHIPPINGS, "WATER CURES" http://www.correctionhistory.orglhtml/chronicl/state/html/nyprisons.html.

122   "IT'S THE LEATHER COLLAR" Gustavus Myers, History of Tammany Hall, 370–71.

122   THIRTY-THREE MALE and TWENTY FEMALE Lawes, Twenty Thousand Years in Sing Sing, 201–9.

123   BRUSHES, MATTRESSES, PILLOWS Ibid.

123   "AN ENDLESS LINE" Ibid.

124   "ODIFEROUS APPEARANCE" and RABBI S. BRAVERMAN Ibid., 206–7; Brian, Sing Sing, 65.

124   THE ELECTRIC CHAIR and "THE DANCE HALL" Mark Gado, Stone Upon Stone: Sing Sing Prison, chapter 4; Brian, Sing Sing, 63.

124   "BURN IT DOWN!" New York Times, May 31, 1914.

124   "SOME ALARMED" and "DID SOME FIST WORK" New York Times,
125   April 27, 1904.

125   HARRIS STAHL and HAD FIVE MORE OF FITZPATRICK'S MEN New York Times, November 2, 1904; Jay Robert Nash, Bloodletters and Bad Men, 625.

125   "OLD-TIMERS" and "THEN HOW DOES IT" New York Times, November 9, 1904.

125   CELERY TONIC and DICK FITZGERALD George Kibbe Turner, "Tammany's Control of New York," 123.

126   A SINGER IN THE IMPERIAL MUSIC HALL and FORCED HIM TO JUMP New York Times, June 9, 1912; Nash, Bloodletters and Bad Men, 625.

126   "HELD SIX BULLETS" and "I WOULDN'T HAVE" New York Times, May 15, June 9, 1912.

126   "THE SPECTACLE OF" and FIFTY TO A HUNDRED THOUSAND New
127   York Times, June 9, 1912; Turner, "Tammany's Control of New York," 123.

127   "EVIDENTLY THE GANG WANTED" and "EAT 'EM UP" New York Times, August 6, May 27, 1905.

127 "LAST REPORTED AS RUNNING" and "A LURKING CAT" New York Times, June 9, 1911, November 24, 1905; Turner, "Tammany's Control of New York," 125.

128 MEMBERS OF THE MORELLO FAMILY and INTERNATIONAL LONGSHOREMEN'S New York Times, September 20, 1912; Virgil W. Peterson, The Mob, 111; Craig Thompson and Allen Raymond, Gang Rule in New York, 361.

10 A NAPOLEON RETURNED FROM ELBA

129 TAMMANY PROTECTORS New York Times, June 20, 1909.

130 "CONDUCTED HIMSELF ADMIRABLY" and "ONE OF HIS INTELLIGENCE" The Sun, June 20, 1909.

131 "SOME INTERNAL TROUBLE" and "OH, I'VE BEEN" New York Times, September 16, 1909, June 21, October 8, 1910; New York Herald, October 8, 1910.

131 "THE WILD and WOOLY" and "A NAPOLEON RETURNED FROM ELBA" New York Times, September 16, 1909, October 8, 22, 1910; New York Daily Tribune, December 27, 1920.

131 "STONE BROKE" and "MOST OF HIS OLD MOB" F. Raymond
132 Daniell, "The Big Business of the Racketeer"; New York Times, June 21, 1909.

132 A "LOBBYGOW" and "HE WON'T WANT TO SHOW" A Review of the World 5 (May 2, 1911):20–21; John R. Chamberlain, "Gangsters Have Lost Their Last Big Name"; New York Times, October 30, 1927.

132 "CARVE GUYS UP" Jay Maeder, Big Town Biography, 27; Abraham H. Shoenfeld papers, P311768, 112.

132 MANY OF MONK'S and BREAK THE BACK Chamberlain, "Gangsters Have Lost"; New York Times, October 30, 1927; Herbert Asbury, The Gangs of New York, 306.

132 AN OLD MAN and USING OPIUM Albert Fried, The Rise and Fall of the Jewish Gangster in America, 36; New York Times, June 9, 1912; The Sun, December 27, 1920.

133 "A SEETHING REALM," AN ESTIMATED NINE THOUSAND, and GROWN TO TWENTY-FIVE THOUSAND Ronald Sanders, The Lower East Side Jews, 43; Jacob A. Riis, How the Other Half Lives, 71; Luc Sante, Low Life, 137.

133 THE KNOWLEDGE THAT The Sun, December 27, 1920.

134 A "WIDE-OPEN TOWN" and "A COMBINATION OF INTERESTS" Quoted in Virgil W. Peterson, The Mob, 103; William McAdoo, Guarding a Great City, 52.

135 "I WAS HEAD OF THE DEPARTMENT" Theodore A. Bingham, "The Organized Criminals of New York," 62.

135 "COMMON PATROLMEN" and "SENT TO DO CAPTAIN'S WORK" New York Times, April 20, 1907.

135 "PERMIT THE POLICE TO CLUB" Herbert Asbury, "Gangland USA," 16;

New York Times, September 20, 1912.

136   "REAL BAD CROOKS" Cornelius Willemse, Behind the Green Lights, 30.

136   THE NOTORIOUS GOPHERS Asbury, The Gangs of New York, 235; New York Times, September 30, 1934.

136   ELDRIDGE STREET STATION New York Times, June 21, 1909.

136   MARRIED FOR THE SECOND TIME State of New York, Certificate and Record of Marriage 4106.

137   THE CHINESE EXCLUSION ACT and A PERNICIOUS SUBSTANCE Peter Kwong, The New Chinatown, 13–14; Edwin G. Burrows and Mike Wallace, Gotham, 1,130.

137   THE TRIGGER FOR THE VIOLENCE New York Times, June 9, 6, July 24, 1912.

137   SPURRED TO ACTION New York Herald, July 24, 1912.

138   BIG TIM COMPLAINED THAT New York Times, July 24, 1912.

138   THE "KEHILLAH" Abraham H. Shoenfeld papers, P311758, 3.

138   LOST $700,000, "ABSOLUTELY DOMINATED BY," and THE CROWD OF

139   SEVENTY-FIVE THOUSAND New York Times, September 20, 1912; Daniel Czitrom, "Underworld and Underdogs," 557; New York Sun, September 16, 1913.

139   ROSENTHAL'S KILLING See Mike Dash, Satan's Circus, for a vivid and comprehensive account of the Becker affair.

139   "NEW YORK CITY HAD EMERGED" Leo Katcher, The Big Bankroll, 95; Report of the Citizens Committee appointed at the Cooper Union meeting, August 12, 1913, 6–7, quoted in Gustavus Myers, History of Tammany Hall, 358–359.

139   BLACKWELL'S ISLAND, STAY AWAY FROM NEW YORK and DRIVEN OUT OF TOWN Annotation, Sing Sing Admission Register, New York State Archives, B0143, page 157, vol. 36, box 14; Albany Times Union, May 8, 1919; New York Times, December 27, 1920; The Argus (Albany), May 18, 1915.

140   "REPRESENTING" THE EMPLOYERS New York Times, January 4, 1921.

142   MAKING HOT TRACKS The Argus (Albany), May 9, 1919.

142   AT LEAST FIFTEEN THOUSAND New York Times, May 18, 1915.

142   "WELL, IF IT ISN'T MONK," "KNOWN TO THE POLICE IN THIS CITY,"

143   and "WELL, YOU HAVE THE SILVER" Ibid.; The Argus (Albany), May 18, 1915.

143   MARY WILLIAMS The Argus (Albany), May 18, 1915.

143   "COMPLETE YEGG" The Argus (Albany), May 18, 21, 1915.

143   "DO RIGHT HIMSELF" The Argus (Albany), May 18, 20, 1915.

144   REFORM and NEVER AGAIN and NUMBER 12,151 New York Times, July 2, 1915; Physician's Register, Clinton Prison, B0100, New York State Archives.

144   "THE ETHIC OF RAW" Fried, The Rise and Fall of the Jewish Gangster, 87.

144   313,000 New York Bureau of Jewish Social Research, Jewish Communal Survey of Greater New York, 3–7, quoted in Fried, The Rise and

Fall of the Jewish Gangster, 87.

145 "TWENTY-THIRD REGIMENT OF BROOKLYN" and SEPTEMBER 21, 1917 Colonel Frank H. Norton to Postmaster, April 13, 1917, 391 United States Regular Army Mobile Units, 1821–1942, Records of the 106th Infantry Regiment, [NM-93] 2133 box 1642, NARA; Abstracts of WWI Military Service, New York State Archives, B0808.

145 DEDUCTED FOUR YEARS and "SHOWED THAT THE QUALITY OF PATRI-
146 OTISM" New York Sun, May 9, 1919; Abstracts of WWI Military Service, New York State Archives, B0808.

II O'RYAN'S ROUGHNECKS

149 CHILE, DENMARK Gary Mead, The Doughboys, 13.

150 A COLLECTION OF REASONS and "I NEVER DID ANYTHING WORTH-WHILE" Trench and Camp, November 1917.

150 "POP" and SERIAL NUMBER Gas Attack, March 1918; Abstracts of WWI Military Service, New York State Archives, B0808.

150 106TH INFANTRY The designation was changed from the old 23rd Regiment to the 106th Infantry on October 31, 1917; 120 Records of the A.E.F. (WWI), Records of the 27th Division [NM-91] 1241, box 1, NARA.

150 "EVER SINCE CHILDHOOD" Physical Examination for Enlistment, 120 Records of the A.E.F. (WWI), Records of the 53rd Brigade [NM-91] 254, box 369, NARA.

150 13 UNION AVENUE and ALMOST ALL OF THE RECRUITS B1357, NY Bonus Card 235, NY State Archives, Albany; List of Occupations, 391 United States Regular Army Mobile Units, 1821–1942, Records of the 106th Infantry Regiment [NM-93] 2133, box 1638, NARA.

151 "SLIGHT, SOLDIERLY" and "TRAINED DEPENDABILITY" Trench and Camp, March 1919; New York Times, September 11, 1917, December 15, 1918.

151 "SPY FEVER" and "TO BRING TO ITS MEMBERS" New York Times, February 15, 1917, April 8, 11, 1917; Washington Post, April 8, 1917; Correspondence of Colonel Frank H. Norton, 391 United States Regular Army Mobile Units, 1821–1942, Records of the 106th Infantry Regiment [NM-93] 2133, box 1643, NARA; GH Scull, Fifth Deputy Commissioner, City of New York Police Department, to Major General John O'Ryan, April 10, 1917; Tourist Club "Naturfreunde" leaflet; 391 United States Regular Army Mobile Units, 18211942, Records of the 106th Infantry Regiment [NM-93] 2133, box 1643, NARA.

151 "THE GATES ON THE WATER WORKS" and 344 TIMES Correspondence of Colonel Frank H. Norton, 391 United States Regular Army Mobile Units, 1821–1942, Records of the 106th Infantry Regiment [NM-93] 2133, box 1643, NARA.

151 REPEATEDLY FIRED AT and DISCHARGED ACCIDENTALLY Ibid.; New

152   York Times, February 15, 1917.

152   FIFTY DOLLARS and THE COMMANDING GENERAL COMPLAINED Surgeon, 23rd NY Infantry to Commanding Officer, June 1, 1917, 391 United States Regular Army Mobile Units, 1821–1942, Records of the 106th Infantry Regiment [NM-93] 2133, box 1640, NARA; Memorandum from Lieutenant Colonel Franklin W. Ward, Adjutant, July 23, 1917, 120 Records of the A.E.F. (WWI), Records of the 53rd Brigade [NM-91] 254, box 369, NARA.

152   "OUR COUNTRY IS IN AN ACTUAL STATE" Adjutant to Organization Commanders, August 9, 1917, 120 Records of the A.E.F. (WWI), Records of the 53rd Brigade [NM-91] 254, box 369, NARA.

153   EQUIVALENT OF 110 PERCENT and "FORTY QUART CANS" O.Q.M. Circular Letter No. 159, July 5, 1917, 120 Records of the A.E.F. (WWI), Records of the 53rd Brigade [NM-91] 254, box 369, NARA; William F. Clarke, Over There with O'Ryan's Roughnecks, 22.

153   ALL PROSTITUTES and "THERE IS A STINKING" http://www.oryans roughnecks.org

153   "WHERE THE SOFT" and CHAIN GANGS Clarke, Over There, 22; New York Times, December 15, 1917.

154   THE TOP OF A WIGWAM Clarke, Over There, 23.

154   "WHILE THE FRENCH" quoted in Gary Mead, The Doughboys, 144.

154   A LIQUOR STILL, WHILE THE REST SLEPT, and "THE WORST I HAVE" Spartanburg Herald, August 9, September 8, 1917; Mitchell Yockelson, Borrowed Soldiers, 46; Memorandum for Colonel Wood, December 9, 1917, 120 Records of the A.E.F. (WWI), Records of the 27th Division [NM-91] 1241, box 6, NARA; Gas Attack, March 1919, 27; The General Principles Governing the Training of Units of the American Expeditionary Force, 120 Records of the A.E.F. (WWI), Records of the 27th Division [NM-91] 1241, box 5, NARA.

154   "CHAMPS OF THE FRENCH LEAVE," THE ENTIRE COST, and "LUNA PARK" Gas Attack, December 8, 1917, March 8, 1919, 27; Headquarters, Coast Defenses of Southern New York, April 18, 1918, 391 United States Regular Army Mobile Units, 1821–1942, Records of the 106th Infantry Regiment [NM-93] 2133, box 1651, NARA.

155   WILLIAM KAUFFMAN and DESERTION IN TIME OF WAR New York Times, November 30, 1917; Adjutant to Commanding Officer, Company H, June 6, 1917, 391 United States Regular Army Mobile Units, 1821–1942, Records of the 106th Infantry Regiment [NM-93] 2133, box 1651, NARA.

155   COUNTERFEIT CHECKS and HOWEVER, MONK SUBMITTED New York Times, April 8, 1918; New York Daily Tribune, April 2, 1919.

155   RIGIDLY SEGREGATED, "WITH THEIR NORTHERN IDEAS," SEVENTEEN PEOPLE WERE KILLED, and THE "HARLEM HELLFIGHTERS" Memorandum to all Commanding Officers, 391 United States Regular Army Mobile Units, 1821–1942, Records of the 106th Infantry Regiment [NM-93] 2133, box 1638, NARA; quoted in Stephen L. Harris, Duty, Honor, Privilege, 85; Arthur Little, From Harlem to the Rhine, 52–70;

Mitchell Yockelson, Borrowed Soldiers, 22

156 INTOLERABLY OVERBEARING and "TIGHTEN THE RELATION" Kenneth Gow, Letters of a Soldier, 237; Robert Sutliffe, Seventy-First New York in the World War, 42–43.

156 "FIRST COUSIN TO THE KICK" and "THE KITTEN'S OVERALLS" Gas Attack, November 1917, 3.

156 COLONEL VANDERBILT Harris, Duty, Honor, Privilege, 66.

157 AT 8:30 New York Times, November 20, 1917.

157 "DESPITE THE FACT" and "OCCASIONALLY A MAN STUMBLED" Sergeant Joseph Robins, quoted in Walter G. Andrews, The Story of a Machine Gun Company, 37.

158 "A JADED BARBED-WIRE" Gas Attack, December 15, 1917, 19–20.

158 "THROUGH A FOG" Ibid.

158 HEAVILY CENSORED New York Times November 26, 1917.

158 MONK'S SECOND BATTALION and LACHRYMATOR General Orders No. 4, November 14, 1917, 120 Records of the A.E.F. (WWI), Records of the 53rd Brigade [NM-91] 254, box 370, NARA; 120 Records of the A.E.F. (WWI), Records of the 27th Division [NM-91] 1241, box 5, NARA.

159 BOWLING IN ENGLISH CRICKET and MONK HAD A NATURAL Gas Attack, December 15, 1917; From C.O., Co.C, 106th Infantry, to C.O., 1st Battalion, 106th Infantry, July 19, 1918, 391 United States Regular Army Mobile Units, 1821–1942, Records of the 106th Infantry Regiment [NM-93], 2133 box 1645, NARA; Trench and Camp, April 8, 1919.

159 WOODEN GUNS 120 Records of the A.E.F. (WWI), Records of the 27th Division [NM-91] 1241, box 5, NARA.

159 SIGHT-SETTING and "FLINCH TEST" Ibid., box 6, NARA.

160 PRIVATE FIRST CLASS The New York Evening Telegram, December 30, 1920; Abstracts of WWI Military Service, New York State Archives, B0808.

160 "SHELLS WHISTLED" Rutherford Ireland, History of the Twenty Third Regiment N.G.S.N.Y., 258–59; Harris, Duty, Honor, Privilege, 101; Gas Attack, December 15, 1917, 6.

160 "NO MAN WAS UNSHAVED" Gas Attack, December 15, 1917, 10.

160 SIXTEEN DEGREES and TWO KINDS OF WATER Memorandum for Colonel Wood, December 9, 1917, 120 Records of the A.E.F. (WWI), Records of the 27th Division [NM-91] 1241, box 6, NARA; Harris, Duty, Honor, Privilege, 92.

160 THE CAMP RUMOR MILL Gas Attack, December 23, 1917.

161 "OFFICERS and MEN" New York Times, December 16, 1920.

161 "THEY HAVE HAD SIX" New York Times, March 5, 1918.

162 "A GUN ON BOTH HIPS" Interview with Verna Bonner, September 2008; Ronnie C. Tyler, The Big Bend, 149.

162 PHYSICALLY DISQUALIFIED and FLAT FEET Acting Adjutant to Commanding Officer, 106th Infantry, April 11, 1918, 391 United States

Regular Army, Mobile Units, 1821–1942, Records of the 106th Infantry [NM-93] 2133, box 1646, NARA; Surgeon, 106th Infantry to Commanding General, 27th Division, May 4, 1918, 391 United States Regular Army, Mobile Units, 1821–1942, Records of the 106th Infantry [NM-93] 2133, box 1646, NARA.

162   "WITH OUR BACKS" Field Marshal Douglas Haig, quoted in http://www.firstworldwar.com/source/backstothewall.htm.

12 WE ONLY SEE OLD MEN AND BOYS

164   THREE HUNDRED THOUSAND EMBARKED and "BOTH INSTANTANEOUS"
165   Order of Battle of the United States Land Forces in the World War, 505, 516; Rutherford Ireland, History of the Twenty Third Regiment N.G.S.N.Y., 261–62.

165   U.S. NAVY TRANSPORT Manifest USNT President Lincoln, NARA.

165   UNFIT FOR OVERSEAS and "LOUNGING ALONG THE RAIL" HQ 106th Infantry, On Board US Navy Transport, May 8, 1918, 391 United States Regular Army, Mobile Units, 1821–1942, Records of the 106th Infantry, [NM-93] 2133, box 1646, NARA; Ireland, History of the Twenty Third Regiment, 263.

166   "CERTAIN QUALITIES" and "THERE WERE CONTINUOUSLY" Trench and Camp, April 8, 1919; William F. Clarke, Over There with O'Ryan's Roughnecks, 29.

166   "IN MOST FANTASTIC DESIGNS" Ireland, History of the Twenty Third Regiment, 264.

167   "THE BOTTOM MAN" and AT NIGHT ALL PORTHOLES Gary Mead, The Doughboys, 104, 144; Clarke, Over There, 28.

167   JUST BEFORE DAWN Ireland, History of the Twenty Third Regiment, 266.

168   PRICE ON THEIR HEADS Ibid., 265.

168   A STAND-TO Ibid., 269.

168   "EMERALD-GREEN" Quoted in Stephen L. Harris, Duty, Honor, Privilege, 105.

169   TORPEDOED and SUNK and USS COVINGTON: Order of Battle of the United States Land Forces in the World War, 511; Ireland, History of the Twenty Third Regiment, 271.

169   231 MEN Special Orders, No. 140, Headquarters Base Section No. 5, May 24, 1918, 391 United States Regular Army, Mobile Units, 1821–1942, Records of the 106th Infantry [NM-93] 2133, box 1645, NARA.

169   THERE WERE NO YOUNG MEN Gas Attack, March 1919, 42–43; diary of Major General Hugh Drum, quoted in Mead, The Doughboys, 100.

169   40 HOMMES and IN GROUPS OF FORTY Clarke, Over There, 32; Leslie W. Rowland, The 27th Division Crashes Through, 3; Ireland, History of the Twenty Third Regiment, 271–72.

170   THE COMMANDING OFFICER and "WE LAY LIKE SARDINES" Superintendent ATS to CO, 106th Infantry, May 27, 1918, 391 United States

Regular Army, Mobile Units, 1821–1942, Records of the 106th Infantry [NM-93] 2133, box 1645, NARA; Clarke, Over There, 32.

170   "CHECKERBOARD FIELDS" Clarke, Over There, 32.

170   HE WAS SO OBSESSED and "EXTREMELY PAINFUL" Donald Smythe, Pershing: General of the Armies, 14; Mead, The Doughboys, 114; cf. also Adjutant to all Commanding Officers, June 27, 1918, 391 United States Regular Army Mobile Units, 1821–1942, Records of the 106th Infantry Regiment [NM-93] 2133, box 1646, NARA; Yockelson, Borrowed Soldiers, 56.

170   MAJOR RANSOM H. GILLET and WITHOUT FOOD OR WATER Major
171   Ransom H. Gillet to Commanding Officer, 106th Infantry, June 3, 1918, 391 United States Regular Army, Mobile Units, 1821–1942, Records of the 106th Infantry [NM-93] 2133, box 1643, NARA.

13 THIS REALM OF SILENCE

174   "APPEARED TO ENJOY" and "ALL STANDING" Rutherford Ireland, History of the Twenty Third Regiment N.G.S.N.Y., 272; Stephen L. Harris, Duty, Honor, Privilege, 112.

174   "THE HOT IRISH" William F. Clarke, Over There with O'Ryan's Roughnecks, 33.

174   FORCED TO SUBSIST John S. D. Eisenhower, Foreword to Mitchell Yockelson, Borrowed Soldiers, xi.

175   MOST MEN DISCARDED SOME Clarke, Over There, 33.

175   A THOUSAND HIGH-EXPLOSIVE 120 Records of the A.E.F. (WWI), Records of the 27th Division [NM-91] 1241, box 5, NARA.

175   "IF YOU DIDN'T GET" Clarke, Over There, 36.

175   GAMACHES-MOUTIERES and A MERE SKELETON War Diary, 2nd Bat-
176   talion, 106th Infantry, June 16–17, 1918, 120 Records of the A.E.F. (WWI), A.E.F. General Headquarters, War Diaries [NM-91] 26, box 2694, NARA; Station List of Unit, 120 Records of the A.E.F. (WWI), Records of the 27th Division, Historical Files, [NM-91] 1241, box 9, NARA; Ireland, History of the Twenty Third Regiment, 272.

176   "MY GOD," BIG TALK, and "CARRIED LEATHER" John Bessette, Lecture at York St. John's University, January 19, 2008; diary of Robert Cude, quoted in Mitchell Yockelson, "Brothers-in-Arms," 87, 7.

176   NO AGGRESSIVE SPIRIT Lieutenant William S. Conrow, 102nd Engineers, 120 Records of the A.E.F. (WWI), Records of the 27th Division [NM-91] 1241, box 6, NARA.

177   "PROFOUND IGNORANCE" and "THEIR DEAD" Gary Mead, The Doughboys, 173, 180.

177   ESTIMATED FORTY THOUSAND John Ellis, Eye Deep in Hell, 181.

177   ALWAYS EASTWARD, "EVERY KIND OF HAYMOW," and 9:30 P.M.
178   CURFEW Commanding Officer to Commanding General, June 27, 1918, 391 United States Regular Army, Mobile Units, 1821–1942, Records of the 106th Infantry [NM-93] 2133, box 1632, NARA; War Diary, 2nd Battalion, 106th Infantry, June 21–24, 1918, 120 Records of the

A.E.F. (WWI), A.E.F. General Headquarters, War Diaries [NM-91]
26, box 2694, NARA; Leslie W. Rowland, The 27th Division Crashes
Through, 4.

178　ENEMY AIR RAIDS and STOPPED FOR LUNCH　War Diary, 2nd Battal-
ion, 106th Infantry, June 27, 1918, 120 Records of the A.E.F. (WWI),
A.E.F. General Headquarters, War Diaries [NM-91] 26, box 2694,
NARA; Rowland, The 27th Division Crashes Through, 4; U.S. Army
Field Message, CO 53 Infantry Brigade to CO 106th Infantry, June 29,
1918, 391 United States Regular Army, Mobile Units, 1821–1942,
Records of the 106th Infantry [NM-93] 2133, box 1646, NARA.

178　SHORTCOMINGS OF ITS PLATOON　General John O'Ryan, Circular Letter
to all Commanding Officers, June 30, 1918, 120 Records of the A.E.F.
(WWI), Records of the 27th Division [NM-91] 1241, box 6, NARA.

178　AS REQUIRED BY MILITARY and "BETWEEN TEN MINUTES"　The General
Principles Governing the Training of Units of the American Expedition-
ary Force, 120 Records of the A.E.F. (WWI), Records of the 27th Division
[NM-91] 1241, box 5, NARA; General John O'Ryan, Circular Letter
to all Commanding Officers, June 30, 1918, 120 Records of the A.E.F.
(WWI), Records of the 27th Division [NM-91] 1241, box 6, NARA.

179　"MYSTERIOUS, UNCANNY"　Ireland, History of the Twenty Third Regiment, 275–76.

179　"THESE SOLDIERS WERE SILENT"　Clarke, Over There, 38.

179　LEDERZEELE　War Diary, 2nd Battalion, 106th Infantry, July 3, 1918,
120 Records of the A.E.F. (WWI), A.E.F. General Headquarters, War
Diaries [NM-91] 26, box 2694, NARA; Abstracts of WWI Military
Service, New York State Archives, B0808.

180　AS THEY DIVED　Maurice J. Swetland and Lilli Swetland, These Men, 127.

180　FRESH FRUIT, LAY A THICK BELT, and FIRING PITS　CO, Company G to
CO 106th Infantry, July 20, 1918, 391 United States Regular Army,
Mobile Units, 1821–1942, Records of the 106th Infantry [NM-93]
2133, box 1633, NARA; Swetland and Swetland, These Men, 127;
Confidential Memorandum, Headquarters 27th Division, 120 Records
of the A.E.F. (WWI), Records of the 27th Division [NM-91] 1241, box
3, NARA.

180　SYSTEM OF DEFENSES　Clarke, Over There, 44; Rowland, The 27th
Division Crashes Through, 4.

181　RAISING and LOWERING　Clarke, Over There, 60, 41–42.

181　FIVE HUNDRED YARDS WERE SET BETWEEN　Field Order No. 33, August
20, 1918, 120 Records of the A.E.F. (WWI), Records of the 27th Division, Historical Files—53rd Brigade [NM-91] 1241, box 7, NARA;
Clarke, Over There, 45.

181　"THAT METAL-BEATEN" and "FLAT, SAWED-OFF"　John F. O'Ryan,
History of the 27th Division: New York's Own, 22–23; Clarke, Over
There, 41–42.

182　"SANK TO THE GROUND"　Clarke, Over There, 65.

182　THE MEN WERE WARNED　General Orders No. 73, August 26, 1918,

General Orders No. 75, August 28, 1918, 120 Records of the A.E.F. (WWI), Records of the 27th Division, Historical Files [NM-91] 1241, box 6, NARA.

182   "A PECULIAR PLOPPING" Clarke, Over There, 45.

182   SAINT-MARTIN-AU-LAËRT and NO OFFICER OR ENLISTED War Diary, 2nd Battalion, 106th Infantry, July 14, 1918, 120 Records of the A.E.F. (WWI), A.E.F. General Headquarters, War Diaries [NM-91] 26, box 2694, NARA; General Orders No. 88, 391 United States Regular Army, Mobile Units, 1821–1942, Records of the 106th Infantry [NM-93] 2133, box 1653, NARA.

183   SERIES OF DEFECTS and THE AMERICAN CHIEF GAS Secret Bulletin No.5, Headquarters, 27th Division, August 19, 1918, 120 Records of the A.E.F. (WWI), Records of the 27th Division, Historical Files [NM-91] 1241, box 6, NARA; Chief Gas Officer to Asst. C. of S., G-3, France, July 28, 1918, 120 Records of the A.E.F. (WWI), Records of the 27th Division [NM-91] 1241, box 6, NARA.

183   "A LONG TRAIL" and "AN HONEST-TO-GOD" New York Daily Tribune, April 2, 1919; The New York Evening Telegram, December 30, 1920.

14 THE NIAGARA OF SHELLS

184   "OVER DISMAL WASTES" Rutherford Ireland, History of the Twenty Third Regiment N.G.S.N.Y., 279; War Diary, 2nd Battalion, 106th Infantry, July 23, 1918, 120 Records of the A.E.F. (WWI), AEF General Headquarters, War Diaries [NM-91] 26, box 2694, NARA.

185   ISADORE COHEN and HALLEBAST CORNER William F. Clarke, Over There with O'Ryan's Roughnecks, 52; War Diary, 2nd Battalion, 106th Infantry, July 30, 1918, 120 Records of the A.E.F. (WWI), A.E.F. General Headquarters, War Diaries [NM-91] 26, box 2694, NARA.

185   "LOOMING UP" and IN CASE ANY AMERICAN Gas Attack, March 1919, 42–43; Field Orders, No. 4, July 21, 1918, 120 Records of the A.E.F. (WWI), Records of the 27th Division, Historical Files—53rd Brigade [NM-91] 1241, box 7, NARA; Ireland, History of the Twenty Third Regiment, 277.

185   "ACTION EAST POP" and "STOOD STOCK-STILL" War Diary, 2nd
186   Battalion, 106th Infantry, August 2, 1918, 120 Records of the A.E.F. (WWI), A.E.F. General Headquarters, War Diaries [NM-91] 26, box 2694, NARA; Clarke, Over There, 52.

186   "THEY DO NOT TURN" 120 Records of the A.E.F. (WWI), Records of the 27th Division [NM-91] 1241, box 9, NARA.

186   "ALL MEN SHOULD" Ibid.

187   "COMPELLED TO URINATE" Necessary Personnel, Functions and Duties, 391 United States Regular Army, Mobile Units, 1821–1942, Records of the 106th Infantry [NM-93], box 1634, NARA.

187   BAGS OR BURLAP, THE SAPS WERE BARELY, and "I SHOOK, I TREM-BLED" Confidential Memorandum, Headquarters 27th Division, 120

Records of the A.E.F. (WWI), Records of the 27th Division [NM-91] 1241, box 3, NARA; Clarke, Over There, 55, 56, 65.

187 RIFLES WERE NOT CLEANED Adjutant to Commanding Officer, 106th Infantry, September 12, 1918, 391 United States Regular Army, Mobile Units, 1821–1942, Records of the 106th Infantry [NM-93], box 1643, NARA.

188 A BATTALION COMMANDER, PRIVATE JOHN FOSTER, and "THE MOST DANGEROUS PLACES" Commanding Officer, 1st Battalion, 106th Infantry, to C.O. 106th Infantry, August 4, 1918, 391 United States Regular Army, Mobile Units, 1821–1942, Records of the 106th Infantry [NM-93], box 1646, NARA; War Diary, 2nd Battalion, 106th Infantry, August 10, 4, 1918, 120 Records of the A.E.F. (WWI), A.E.F. General Headquarters, War Diaries [NM-91] 26, box 2694, NARA; General Orders No. 75, August 28, 1918, 120 Records of the A.E.F. (WWI), Records of the 27th Division, Historical Files [NM-91] 1241, box 6, NARA.

188 "THE GANGSTER," "THE TOUGHEST GANG," PRAISED BY HIS COMMANDER, and "WHEN HIS COMRADES" Herbert Asbury, The Gangs of New York, xvi; New York Daily Tribune, April 2, 1919, December 27, 1920.

189 BRITISH MEDICAL PERSONNEL Order of Battle of the United States Land Forces in the World War, 131.

189 "HOW FAR ABOVE" Gas Attack, December 15, 1917, 19–20; War Diary, 2nd Battalion, 106th Infantry, August 10, 1918, 120 Records of the A.E.F. (WWI), A.E.F. General Headquarters, War Diaries [NM-91] 26, box 2694, NARA.

189 "UNTIL WE COULD FEEL" Clarke, Over There, 57.

190 THE HOTTEST SECTION and EVERY GIRL IN THE ESTAMINETS New York Daily Tribune, April 2, 1919; lecture by Captain Stead, 120 Records of the A.E.F. (WWI), Records of the 27th Division [NM-91] 1241, box 5, NARA; War Diary, 2nd Battalion, 106th Infantry, August 12, 1918, 120 Records of the A.E.F. (WWI), A.E.F. General Headquarters, War Diaries [NM-91] 26, box 2694, NARA.

190 ASSASSINATION ATTEMPT and DEFECTIVE IN MAP-READING John Walker, Official History of the 120th Infantry, 13; Mitchell Yockelson, Borrowed Soldiers, 88.

190 PERENNIAL COMPLAINTS and "SMARTNESS IN DRESS" Questionnaire, 106th Infantry, 2nd Battalion, July 26, 1918, 120 Records of the A.E.F. (WWI), Records of the 27th Division [NM-91] 1241, box 9, NARA.

190 "EVIDENCE PLAINLY" Commanding Officer, 3rd Battalion, 106th Infantry, to Lieutenant Colonel J. M. Wainwright, Inspector General, 27th Division, August 11, 1918, 391 United States Regular Army Mobile Units, 1821–1942, Records of the 106th Infantry Regiment [NM-93], 2133 box 1642, NARA.

191 "LOSSES WILL RESULT" Bulletin No. 41, June 14, 1918, 120 Records of

the A.E.F. (WWI), Records of the 27th Division [NM-91] 1241, box 6, NARA; Ireland, History of the Twenty Third Regiment, 280.

191   REAL LEADERS Bulletin No. 41, June 14, 1918, 120 Records of the A.E.F. (WWI), Records of the 27th Division [NM-91] 1241, box 6, NARA; Special Orders No. 232, Headquarters 106th Infantry, August 21, 1918, 391 United States Regular Army Mobile Units, 1821–1942, Records of the 106th Infantry Regiment [NM-93] 2133, box 1653, NARA.

192   MONK REFUSED TO LEAVE New York Daily Tribune, April 2, 1919; The World, March 27, April 9, 1919.

192   "YOUSE GET THIS" Herbert Asbury, letter to his brother, quoted by Frances Carle (Asbury), http://herbertasbury.comlbillthebutcher/eastman.asp.

192   CORPORAL JOHN A. KIERNAN and MICMAC and HECLA New York Times, December 15, 1918; War Diary, 2nd Battalion, 106th Infantry, August 22, 23, 1918, 120 Records of the A.E.F. (WWI), A.E.F. General Headquarters, War Diaries [NM-91] 26, box 2694, NARA; Commanding Officer, 106th Infantry to Commanding General, 27th Division, September 9, 1918, 391 United States Regular Army, Mobile Units, 1821–1942, Records of the 106th Infantry [NM-93] 2133, box 1643, NARA.

193   "THIS GOD-FORSAKEN" Clarke, Over There, 55; J. Leslie Kincaid, "The 27th New York's Guard Division," 1.

193   MUSTARD GAS and THOMAS F. FLOOD Commanding Officer, 106th Infantry to Commanding General, 27th Division, September 9, 1918, 391 United States Regular Army, Mobile Units, 1821–1942, Records of the 106th Infantry [NM-93] 2133, box 1643, NARA; Missing in Action/Wounded Notices 1918, Brooklyn Standard Union October–December 1918.

193   SPRINKLED WITH CHLORIDE Joseph L. Gillmann, handwritten report, August 27, 1918; Reg. Gas Officer to Commanding Officer, 106th Infantry, August 28, 1918; 391 United States Regular Army, Mobile Units, 1821–1942, Records of the 106th Infantry [NM-93] 2133, box 1645, NARA.

193   BRITISH VETERANS WERE Leslie W. Rowland, The 27th Division Crashes Through, 4.

194   "PRINCIPLES and METHODS" and "APPEAR TO HAVE BEEN CHAINED" Stanley H. Ford, Lieutenant Colonel, G.S., Chief of Staff, June 26, 1918, 120 Records of the A.E.F. (WWI), Records of the 27th Division [NM-91] 1241, box 6, NARA; Confidential Memorandum, Headquarters 27th Division, 120 Records of the A.E.F. (WWI), Records of the 27th Division [NM-91] 1241, box 3, NARA.

15 MORE THAN BROTHERS

196 "MURKY SHEET" and ESQUELLEC Stephen L. Harris, Duty, Honor, Privilege, 170; Maurice J. Swetland and Lilli Swetland, These Men, 134.

196 "TONIGHT WE ARE MORE" Private Angelo Ferraro, quoted in New York Times, March 23, 1919.

197 THEY WERE TOLD 120 Records of the A.E.F. (WWI), Records of the 27th Division [NM-91] 1241, box 5, NARA.

197 MACAW TRENCH C.O., Company I, 106th Infantry, to Commanding Officer, 106th Infantry, September 7, 1918, 120 Records of the A.E.F. (WWI), Records of the 27th Division [NM-91] 1241, Box 75, NARA.

197 DESTROYED STORES New York Times, September 5, 1918.

197 A PRISONER and MACHINE-GUN NESTS Orders No. 3, August 31, 1918, 120 Records of the A.E.F. (WWI), Records of the 27th Division, Historical Files [NM-91] 1241, box 7, NARA; Commanding Officer, 2nd Battalion, 106th Infantry, to Commanding Officer, 106th Infantry, September 7, 1918, 391 United States Regular Army, Mobile Units, 1821–1942, Records of the 106th Infantry [NM-93] 2133, box 1643, NARA.

198 VIERSTRAAT SWITCH and INFLICTED FAR MORE Commanding Officer, 106th Infantry, to Commanding General, 27th Division, September 9, 1918, 391 United States Regular Army, Mobile Units, 1821–1942, Records of the 106th Infantry [NM-93] 2133, box 1643, NARA; Leslie W. Rowland, The 27th Division Crashes Through, 4.

199 GREAT CONFUSION Swetland and Swetland, These Men, 136; Commanding General, 53rd Infantry Brigade, to Commanding General, 27th Division, September 10, 1918, 120 Records of the A.E.F. (WWI), Records of the 27th Division [NM-91] 1241, box 75, NARA.

199 "ENTIRELY LOST CONTROL" Commanding General, 53rd Infantry Brigade, to Commanding General, 27th Division, September 10, 1918, 120 Records of the A.E.F. (WWI), Records of the 27th Division [NM-91] 1241, box 75, NARA.

199 "WORN OUT" Commanding Officer, 2nd Battalion, 106th Infantry, to Commanding Officer, 106th Infantry, September 7, 1918, 391 United States Regular Army, Mobile Units, 1821–1942, Records of the 106th Infantry [NM-93] 2133, box 1643, NARA.

200 "SORTED OUT" C.O., Company H, 106th Infantry, to C.O., 106th Infantry, September 6, 1918, 391 United States Regular Army, Mobile Units, 1821–1942, Records of the 106th Infantry [NM-93] 2133, box 1643, NARA.

200 THE FOLLY Ibid.

200 THE REGIMENTAL COMMANDER and WITH THOROUGH ARTILLERY
201 Commanding Officer, 3rd Battalion, 106th Infantry, to Commanding Officer, 106th Infantry, September 7, 1918; Commanding General, 53rd Infantry Brigade, to Commanding General, 27th Division, September 10, 1918; 120 Records of the A.E.F. (WWI), Records of the 27th

Division [NM-91] 1241, box 75, NARA; C.O., Company H, 106th Infantry, to C.O., 106th Infantry, September 6, 1918, 391 United States Regular Army, Mobile Units, 1821–1942, Records of the 106th Infantry [NM-93] 2133, box 1643, NARA.

201　PURGATORY–NORTHERN BRICKSTACK C.O., Company H, 106th Infantry, to C.O., 106th Infantry, September 6, 1918, 391 United States Regular Army, Mobile Units, 1821–1942, Records of the 106th Infantry [NM-93] 2133, box 1643, NARA.

201　"THE RATTLE OF THE GANG" New York Daily Tribune, April 2, 1919.

201　ONE OF THE MOST EFFECTIVE Trench and Camp, April 8, 1919.

201　"A SHARP PAIN" Corporal James Toole, quoted in Mitchell Yockelson, Borrowed Soldiers, 173.

202　THE BLIZZARD OF SHELLS C.O., Company I, 106th Infantry, to Commanding Officer, 106th Infantry, September 7, 1918, 120 Records of the A.E.F. (WWI), Records of the 27th Division [NM-91] 1241, box 75, NARA.

202　MONK CRAWLED TO A DUGOUT and "'THE MONK' WAS WOUNDED" The New York Evening Telegram, December 30, 1920; Albany Times Union, May 8, 1919.

202　"THE COMMAND I TOOK" Commanding Officer, 2nd Battalion, 106th Infantry, to Commanding Officer, 106th Infantry, September 7, 1918, 391 United States Regular Army, Mobile Units, 1821–1942, Records of the 106th Infantry [NM-93] 2133, box 1643, NARA.

203　A ONE-FOOT SLAB Commanding Officer, 2nd Battalion, 106th Infantry, to Commanding Officer, 106th Infantry, September 4, 1918, 391 United States Regular Army, Mobile Units, 1821–1942, Records of the 106th Infantry [NM-93] 2133, box 1646, NARA.

203　PREPARE THE DEAD Necessary Personnel, Functions and Duties, 391 United States Regular Army, Mobile Units, 1821–1942, Records of the 106th Infantry [NM-93], box 1634, NARA.

204　"HOW TO UTILIZE" Major General Hamann, quoted in Yockelson, Borrowed Soldiers, 109.

204　"PROFESSIONALLY UNFITTED" and "STUDIOUS and TAKES" Adjutant to Commanding Officer, 106th Infantry, June 12, 1918, 391 United States Regular Army, Mobile Units, 1821–1942, Records of the 106th Infantry [NM-93], box 1634, NARA; Headquarters, 106th Infantry, October 6, 1918, 391 United States Regular Army, Mobile Units, 1821–1942, Records of the 106th Infantry [NM-93], box 1634, NARA; Commanding Officer to Commanding General, 27th Division, June 13, 1918, 391 United States Regular Army, Mobile Units, 1821–1942, Records of the 106th Infantry [NM-93], box 1634, NARA; Headquarters, 106th Infantry, June 7, 1918, 120 Records of the A.E.F. (WWI), Records of the 27th Division, Historical Files—106th Infantry [NM-91] 1241, box 9, NARA.

204　MONK WOULD HAVE EMPATHIZED New York Times, December 15, 1918; Trench and Camp, April 8, 1919.

204 HAD SAID NOTHING and THE TREATMENT REQUIRED Trench and Camp, April 8, 1919; 120 Records of the A.E.F. (WWI), Records of the 27th Division [NM-91] 1241, box 5, NARA.

205 MONK HAD OTHER PLANS and "WANTING TO BE IN ON" Trench and Camp, April 8, 1919; Albany Times Union, May 8, 1919.

205 A SALVAGE DUMP and WHEN THE 106TH INFANTRY WENT Chicago Daily Tribune, December 27, 1920; Trench and Camp, April 8, 1919.

16 THE MEN MUST GO FORWARD

206 DURING THE NIGHT OF and SHOVEL OUT THE MANURE William F.
207 Clarke, Over There with O'Ryan's Roughnecks, 73; Commanding Officer, 2nd Battalion, 106th Infantry, to Town Major, Doullens, September 6, 1918, 391 United States Regular Army, Mobile Units, 1821–1942, Records of the 106th Infantry, [NM-93], box 16343, NARA.

207 "THERE WERE PRIOR TENANTS" Clarke, Over There, 73.

207 GENERAL READ G-1, GHQ, American EF, C of S-1 14, September 7, 1918, 120 Records of the A.E.F. (WWI), Records of the 27th Division, Historical Files [NM-91] 1241, box 1, NARA.

207 "IN BILLETS AT TIME" Commanding General, 53rd Brigade, to Commanding Officer, 106th Infantry, September 12, 1918, 391 United States Regular Army, Mobile Units, 1821–1942, Records of the 106th Infantry [NM-93], box 1636, NARA.

208 MISBEHAVIOR BEFORE and "DEATH OR SUCH OTHER" Commanding General, 53rd Brigade, to Commanding Officer, 105th Infantry, 106th Infantry, September 10, 1918, 391 United States Regular Army, Mobile Units, 1821–1942, Records of the 106th Infantry [NM-93], box 1638, NARA; Articles of War, http://www.loc.gov/rr/frd/Military_Law/AW-1912-1920.html.

208 "IN A VERY NASTY" Statement of Evidence, Sergeant Clarke C. Macpherson, 102nd Military Police, 391 United States Regular Army Mobile Units, 1821–1942, Records of the 106th Infantry Regiment [NM-93] 2133, box 1638, NARA.

208 "THE SELLERS OF STRONG DRINK" Statement, John S. Warne, British YMCA HQ, Doullens, September 19, 1918, 391 United States Regular Army Mobile Units, 1821–1942, Records of the 106th Infantry Regiment [NM-93] 2133, box 1638, NARA.

209 DEPLETED OR NOT AND A MISSION OF GREAT Commanding Officer, 2nd Battalion, 106th Infantry, to Commanding General, 27th Division, September 17, 1918, 391 United States Regular Army, Mobile Units, 1821–1942, Records of the 106th Infantry [NM-93], box 1640, NARA; John F. O'Ryan, Story of the 27th Division, 243.

209 TOLD TO GET ALL and "A POOR WAIF" John H. Eggers, 27th Division, 9; New York Times, December 28, 1920.

210 THE 15 OFFICERS and 635 MEN Gas Attack, March 1919, 42–43; War

Diary, 2nd Battalion, 106th Infantry, September 23, 1918, 120 Records of the A.E.F. (WWI), A.E.F. General Headquarters, War Diaries [NM-91] 26, box 2694, NARA.

210   FORTY-EIGHT BOXCARS, "LIKE MICROSCOPIC PICTURES," and "JUST HEAPS" Orders No. 92, September 21, 1918, 120 Records of the A.E.F. (WWI), Records of the 27th Division, Historical Files [NM-91] 1241, box 2, NARA; Orders No. 22, September 22, 1918, 120 Records of the A.E.F. (WWI), Records of the 27th Division, Historical Files—106th Infantry [NM-91] 1241, box 9, NARA; Tristram Tupper, New York Evening Post, March 25, 1919; Kenneth Gow, Letters of a Soldier, 387.

210   PÉRONNE and THE GERMANS CUT DOWN Clarke, Over There, 75; Sir Frederick Maurice, The Last Four Months, 128.

211   WARNED NOT TO TOUCH Maurice J. Swetland and Lilli Swetland, These Men, 143; Gas Attack, March 1919, 42–43.

211   FACING THEM WERE and "STUCK FULL" John F. O'Ryan, History of the 27th Division: New York's Own, 24; Trench and Camp, March 1919.

211   "TO A DEPTH" Trench and Camp, March 1919.

212   "IN SHORT, ONE REGIMENT" Swetland and Swetland, These Men, 151.

212   THE OCCUPATION OF Eggers, 27th Division, 7.

212   "THE MEN MUST GO" and "WHETHER THEY DO" Ibid., 7–9.

212   "SURRENDER HIS POSITION" Clarke, Over There, 37.

213   "NOISE SUCH AS NO MORTAL" and "COULD NOT PASS" Private Angelo Ferraro, quoted in New York Times, March 23, 1919; A Short History of the 106th Infantry, 4.

17 A SORT OF SACRIFICE

214   "MURMURED IN LOW" Trench and Camp, March 1919; Commanding Officer to Commanding General, 27th Division, October 3, 1918, 391 United States Regular Army Mobile Units, 18211942, Records of the 106th Infantry Regiment [NM-93] 2133, box 1643, NARA; History of Company M, 105th Infantry, 120 Records of the A.E.F. (WWI), Records of the 27th Division [NM-91] 1241, box 9, NARA.

215   "THE MOMENTARY CONFUSION" History of Company M, 105th Infantry, 120 Records of the A.E.F. (WWI), Records of the 27th Division [NM-91] 1241, box 9, NARA; Operations Report of the 27th Division, A.E.F., covering the period September 23 to October 1 1918, 120 Records of the A.E.F. (WWI), Records of the 27th Division [NM-91] 1241, box 3, NARA.

216   SUCCESS FLARES Maurice J. Swetland and Lilli Swetland, These Men, 152; Field Order No. 47, 120 Records of the A.E.F. (WWI), Records of the 27th Division, Historical Files [NM-91] 1241, box 2, NARA; John F. O'Ryan, History of the 27th Division, New York's Own, 28.

216   "THE HEAVIEST HAIL," "ALL ALONG THE FRONT," and "TWANGS and
217   WHINES" O'Ryan, History of the 27th Division, 37; Franklin Ward,

Between the Big Parades, 123; Rutherford Ireland, History of the Twenty Third Regiment N.G.S.N.Y., 292.

217   "MINEOLA!" and "SO DENSE THAT A COMPASS" John H. Eggers, 27th Division, 5; Commanding Officer, 105th Infantry, to Commanding General, 27th Division, October 5, 1918, 120 Records of the A.E.F. (WWI), Records of the 27th Division [NM-91] 1241, box 3, NARA.

217   "THE SICKENING, WHIRRING" and "JUMPED OFF ON TIME" Eggers, The 27th Division, 5; Summary of the Operations of the 27th Division, 120 Records of the A.E.F. (WWI), Records of the 27th Division [NM-91] 1241, box 2, NARA.

217   "ALL THE STRENGTH" and "RUSHING FORWARD" J. Leslie Kincaid, "The 27th New York's Guard Division," 2–3; New York Times, March 2, 1919; Trench and Camp, March 1919.

218   "WHEN THE TIME TO CHARGE" New York Times, October 13, 1918; Operations Report of the 27th Division, A.E.F., covering the period September 23 to October 1, 1918, 120 Records of the A.E.F. (WWI), Records of the 27th Division [NM-91] 1241, box 3, NARA.

218   CARNAGE and GETTYSBURG Operations Report of the 27th Division, A.E.F., covering the period September 23 to October 1, 1918, 120 Records of the A.E.F. (WWI), Records of the 27th Division [NM-91] 1241, box 3, NARA; Eggers, 27th Division, 10; Frederick Palmer, quoted in Mitchell Yockelson, "Brothers-in-Arms," 9.

218   A DISGRUNTLED OFFICER Commanding Officer, 105th Infantry, to Commanding General, 27th Division, October 5, 1918, 120 Records of the A.E.F. (WWI), Records of the 27th Division [NM-91] 1241, box 3, NARA.

218   MONK SET AN INSPIRING LEAD and THE CONCUSSION WAS Albany
219   Times Union, May 8, 1919; The Evening Telegram, December 30, 1920; Missing in Action/Wounded Notices 1918, Brooklyn Standard Union, October–December 1918.

219   "DON'T LET ANYONE" Major Raphael A. Egan, quoted in O'Ryan, History of the 27th Division, 14.

219   "GUILLEMONT FARM" and TORN OUT O'Ryan, History of the 27th Division, 26; Commanding General to Commander-in-Chief, American EF, December 15, 1919, 120 Records of the A.E.F. (WWI), Records of the 27th Division, Historical Files [NM-91] 1241, box 1, NARA.

219   "STUMBLING, GROPING" History of Company M, 105th Infantry, 120 Records of the A.E.F. (WWI), Records of the 27th Division [NM-91] 1241, box 9, NARA.

220   THE FIGHTING WAS MOST Kincaid, "The 27th New York's Guard Division," 2–3.

220   GUILLEMONT FARM and CEMETERY and TOO WEAK TO ADVANCE Operations Report of the 27th Division, A.E.F., covering the period September 23 to October 1, 1918, 120 Records of the A.E.F. (WWI), Records of the 27th Division [NM-91] 1241, box 3, NARA; History of Company M, 105th Infantry, 120 Records of the A.E.F. (WWI), Records of

the 27th Division [NM-91] 1241, box 9, NARA; Swetland and Swetland, These Men, 162.

220   "EVERYBODY THOUGHT" Quoted in Stephen L. Harris, Duty, Honor, Privilege, 216.

220   AT NO TIME and OBSCURE OR NOT CLEAR   Commanding Officer to
221   Commanding General, 27th Division, October 3, 1918, 391 United States Regular Army Mobile Units, 1821–1942, Records of the 106th Infantry Regiment [NM-93] 2133, box 1643, NARA; Major General John F. O'Ryan, Operations Report, 27th Division, A.E.F., May 29–September 22, 1918, folder 5, entry 270, RG 120, NARA.

221   WHEN GENERAL O'RYAN   Commanding Officer to Commanding General, 27th Division, October 3, 1918, 391 United States Regular Army Mobile Units, 1821–1942, Records of the 106th Infantry Regiment [NM-93] 2133, box 1643, NARA; 27th Division, Summary of Operations in the World War, 18.

221   CATEGORICALLY STATED and "THICK AS FLIES"   Operations Report of the 27th Division, A.E.F., covering the period September 23 to October 1, 1918, 120 Records of the A.E.F. (WWI), Records of the 27th Division [NM-91] 1241, box 3, NARA; Kincaid, "The 27th New York's Guard Division," 2–3; General O'Ryan, quoted in New York Times, April 11, 1919.

221   TWENTY-FIVE OR THIRTY and MINIMAL GROUND   Swetland and
222   Swetland, These Men, 162; 54th Brigade, Unit History, 120 Records of the A.E.F. (WWI), Records of the 27th Division, Historical Files [NM-91] 1241, box 7, NARA.

222   "NO MAN MUST," "THE SUPREME RULE," and "AN OFFER TO SURRENDER"   Major General John F. O'Ryan, Operations Report, May 29–September 22, 1918, 120 Records of the A.E.F. (WWI), Records of the 27th Division [NM-91] 270, box 5, NARA; Eggers, 27th Division, 9; Secret Bulletin No.6, Headquarters 27th Division, August 26, 1918, 120 Records of the A.E.F. (WWI), Records of the 27th Division [NM-91] 1241, box 6, NARA.

222   QUARTERED IN "ELEPHANT HUTS," "PROUD TO THINK," and CERTAINLY IT WAS TRUE   War Diary, 2nd Battalion, 106th Infantry, September 28, 1918, 120 Records of the A.E.F. (WWI), A.E.F. General Headquarters, War Diaries [NM-91] 26, box 2694, NARA; Gas Attack, March 1919, 42–43; Summary of the Operations of the 27th Division, 120 Records of the A.E.F. (WWI), Records of the 27th Division [NM-91] 1241, box 2, NARA; History of Company M, 105th Infantry, 120 Records of the A.E.F. (WWI), Records of the 27th Division [NM-91] 1241, box 9, NARA.

223   GENERAL MONASH   Mitchell Yockelson, "Brothers-in-Arms," 10; Field Notes, Action of 27th Division Against that Portion of the Line near Bony, 120 Records of the A.E.F. (WWI), Records of the 27th Division [NM-91] 1241, box 2, NARA.

223   INFILTRATION and "ADVANCE BY WAVES"   GHQ, A.E.F., France,

May 23, 1918, 120 Records of the A.E.F. (WWI), Records of the 27th Division [NM-91] 1241, box 5, NARA; Stanley H. Ford, Lieutenant Colonel, G.S., Chief of Staff, June 26, 1918, 120 Records of the A.E.F. (WWI), Records of the 27th Division [NM-91] 1241, box 6, NARA.

224 "AN EXTRAORDINARY FEAT" and "FOUGHT LIKE WILDCATS" General John F. O'Ryan, letter to Commanding Officer, 106th Infantry, October 22, 1918, quoted in Ireland, History of the Twenty Third Regiment, 302; General O'Ryan, quoted in New York Times, April 11, 1919.

224 "TIRED, SPATTERED" and LOSSES Eggers, 27th Division, 12; Operations Report of the 27th Division, September 23 to October 1, 1918, 120 Records of the A.E.F. (WWI), Records of the 27th Division [NM-91] 270, box 3, NARA. (Some of the losses may have been double-counted after initially being listed as missing in action.)

224 "THE END OF THE WORLD" and "A SORT OF SACRIFICE" Private
225 Angelo Ferraro, quoted in New York Times, March 23, 1919; History of Company M, 105th Infantry, 120 Records of the A.E.F. (WWI), Records of the 27th Division [NM-91] 1241, box 9, NARA.

18 THE HINDENBURG LINE

226 "THEY WERE QUIET" John F. O'Ryan, History of the 27th Division: New York's Own, 14.

227 A PROVISIONAL BATTALION 27th Division, Summary of Operations in the World War, 1; Gas Attack, March 1919, 42–43.

227 "EVERY OFFICER and MAN" and "THE COMPLETE ANNIHILATION" Rutherford Ireland, History of the Twenty Third Regiment N.G.S.N.Y., 295–96.

228 "THIS POSITION WILL BE HELD" New York Times, March 7, 1919.

228 THREE DEEP TRENCHES J. Leslie Kincaid, "The 27th New York's Guard Division," 3; Stars and Stripes, May 9, 1919.

229 THE ALLIED STAFFS O'Ryan, History of the 27th Division, 24.

229 MOVED OUT AT MIDNIGHT and "A PYROTECHNIC DISPLAY" H. G. Rosboro, 1st Lieutenant, 106th Infantry, October 5, 1918, 391 United States Regular Army Mobile Units, 1821–1942, Records of the 106th Infantry Regiment [NM-93] 2133, box 1643, NARA; Ireland, History of the Twenty Third Regiment, 297–298.

230 "A LITTLE OF IT" and THE MOST TERRIFYING Commanding Officer to Commanding General, 27th Division, October 3, 1918, 391 United States Regular Army Mobile Units, 1821–1942, Records of the 106th Infantry Regiment [NM-93] 2133, box 1643, NARA; Ireland, History of the Twenty Third Regiment, 297–98; Mitchell Yockelson, "Brothers-in-Arms," 10; William F. Clarke, Over There with O'Ryan's Roughnecks, 52; History of Company M, 105th Infantry, 120 Records of the A.E.F. (WWI), Records of the 27th Division [NM-91] 1241, box 9, NARA.

230   REFUSED BY THE BRITISH and A HUNDRED YARDS: Operations Report of
       the 27th Division, A.E.F., covering the period September 23 to October
       1, 1918, 120 Records of the A.E.F. (WWI), Records of the 27th Divi-
       sion [NM-91] 1241, box 3, NARA; Summary of the Operations of the
       27th Division, 120 Records of the A.E.F. (WWI), Records of the 27th
       Division [NM-91] 1241, box 2, NARA.

231   TWENTY-FIVE YARDS and A SURPRISE Operations Report of the 27th
       Division, A.E.F., covering the period September 23 to October 1,
       1918, 120 Records of the A.E.F. (WWI), Records of the 27th Division
       [NM-91] 1241, box 3, NARA; Elliott Schoen, History of the 107th
       US Infantry; History of Company M, 105th Infantry, 120 Records of
       the A.E.F. (WWI), Records of the 27th Division [NM-91] 1241, box
       9, NARA.

231   MILLIONS OF MACHINE-GUN and HEAVY CASUALTIES Trench and Camp,
       March 1919; Operations Report of the 27th Division, A.E.F., covering
       the period September 23 to October 1, 1918, 120 Records of the A.E.F.
       (WWI), Records of the 27th Division [NM-91] 1241, box 3, NARA.

231   NINE TANKS and WHO WERE INDEED STILL HOLDING A Short History of
       the 106th Infantry, 4–5; Leslie W. Rowland, The 27th Division Crashes
       Through, 5; Ireland, History of the Twenty Third Regiment,299.

232   MAJOR GILLET Franklin Ward, Between the Big Parades, 140; Ireland,
       History of the Twenty Third Regiment, 298; Operations Report of the
       27th Division, A.E.F., covering the period September 23 to October 1,
       1918, 120 Records of the A.E.F. (WWI), Records of the 27th Division
       [NM-91] 1241, box 3, NARA.

232   GOUGED OUT HIS, "MURDER, HELL-TO-BREAKFAST," and A HUMAN
       CHAIN Ireland, History of the Twenty Third Regiment, 298–99; Ward,
       Between the Big Parades, 136; Stephen L. Harris, Duty, Honor, Priv-
       ilege, 275, 289; Commanding Officer to Commanding General, 27th
       Division, October 3, 1918, 391 United States Regular Army Mobile
       Units, 1821–1942, Records of the 106th Infantry Regiment [NM-93]
       2133, box 1643, NARA; History of Company M, 105th Infantry, 120
       Records of the A.E.F. (WWI), Records of the 27th Division [NM-91]
       1241, box 9, NARA.

232   "THICKER THAN FLIES" and "A SLAUGHTER" Harris, Duty, Honor,
       Privilege, 281; Norman Stone, quoted in Mitchell Yockelson, Bor-
       rowed Soldiers, 172.

233   ORDERS BEFORE THE BATTLE John H. Eggers, 27th Division, 25; Kin-
       caid, "The 27th New York's Guard Division," 4.

233   A LIAISON OFFICER and EVACUATED BY STRETCHER Trench and Camp,
       March 1919; Commanding Officer, 105th Infantry, to Commanding
       General, 27th Division, October 5, 1918, 120 Records of the A.E.F.
       (WWI), Records of the 27th Division [NM-91] 1241, box 3, NARA.

234   THEY WERE FIRED EVERY A Short History of the 106th Infantry, 10.

234   ON HIS HANDS and KNEES, SHEARED FROM HIS BACK, and "THESE INCI-
       DENTS" Lieutenant J. A. Kerrigan, Company G, 106th Infantry, quoted

in Chicago Daily Tribune, December 27, 1920; New York Daily Tribune, April 2, 1919; Trench and Camp, April 8, 1919.

235   "GOT ALL THE HELL," "STILL AS WINE CAVES," and "THE HINDENBURG TUNNEL" A Short History of the 106th Infantry, 11; Trench and Camp, March 1919; Kincaid, "The 27th New York's Guard Division," 4; Eggers, 27th Division, 27.

235   "IN ACTION THROUGHOUT" and THE COOKS, ORDERLIES Lieutenant J. A. Kerrigan, Company G, 106th Infantry, quoted in Chicago Daily Tribune, December 27, 1920; O'Ryan, History of the 27th Division, 39; Trench and Camp, March 1919.

235   "BROKEN IN BODY" Kincaid, "The 27th New York's Guard Division," 4.

19 THE PHANTOM DIVISION

236   "AN ODOR" and "HUMAN VULTURES" Franklin Ward, Between the Big Parades, 148–49.

237   "IT IS FIRST DEPRESSING" John F. O'Ryan, History of the 27th Division: New York's Own, 18.

237   A CRITICAL AUSTRALIAN REPORT Summary of Operations, September 29, 1918, 120 Records of the A.E.F. (WWI), Records of the 27th Division [NM-91] 1241, box 3, NARA; Commanding Officer to Commanding General, 27th Division, October 3, 1918, 391 United States Regular Army Mobile Units, 1821–1942, Records of the 106th Infantry Regiment [NM-93] 2133, box 1643, NARA.

238   "MERE SKELETON" John Bowman letters, AMHI; Rutherford Ireland, History of the Twenty Third Regiment N.G.S.N.Y., 299; Colonel Franklin W. Ward, 106th Infantry, enclosure in Commanding Officer to Statistical Officer, 27th Division, October 12, 1918, 391 United States Regular Army Mobile Units, 1821–1942, Records of the 106th Infantry Regiment [NM-93] 2133, box 1632, NARA.

238   AS A TRIBUTE and CORPORAL PORTER Orders No. 50, 27th Division, August 5, 1918, 120 Records of the A.E.F. (WWI), Records of the 27th Division [NM-91] 1241, box 4, NARA; Missing in Action/Wounded Notices 1918, Brooklyn Standard Union, October–December 1918.

238   DOG TAGS Orders No. 50, 27th Division, August 5, 1918, 120 Records of the A.E.F. (WWI), Records of the 27th Division [NM-91] 1241, box 4, NARA.

239   NO KNOWN GRAVE See the author's Unknown Soldiers for the story of the "unknown dead" of the Great War.

239   BURY ALL SOLDIERS Orders No. 50, 27th Division, August 5, 1918, 120 Records of the A.E.F. (WWI), Records of the 27th Division [NM-91] 1241, box 4, NARA.

239   TINCOURT Ireland, History of the Twenty Third Regiment, 308–9; Gas Attack, March 1919, 42–43.

240   UNBURIED REMAINS and ONE DESTROYED MACHINE-GUN POST Field

Notes, Action of 27th Division Against that Portion of the Line near Bony, 120 Records of the A.E.F. (WWI), Records of the 27th Division [NM-91] 1241, box 2, NARA; Ireland, History of the Twenty Third Regiment, 309–10; Mitchell Yockelson, Borrowed Soldiers, 187.

241　MOVE AT ONCE Field Orders No. 58 and 59, 120 Records of the A.E.F. (WWI), Records of the 27th Division, Historical Files [NM-91] 1241, box 9, NARA; History of Company M, 105th Infantry, 120 Records of the A.E.F. (WWI), Records of the 27th Division [NM-91] 1241, box 9, NARA.

241　NINE HOURS and "SOME SINISTER AGENCY" War Diary of 2nd Battalion, 106th Infantry, October 12, 1918, 120 Records of the A.E.F. (WWI), A.E.F. General Headquarters, War Diaries [NM-91] 26, box 2694, NARA; Trench and Camp, March 1919.

242　TWO TEASPOONSFUL A6/JFG, October 16, 1918, 120 Records of the A.E.F. (WWI), Records of the 27th Division, Historical Files—106th Infantry [NM-91] 1241, box 9, NARA.

242　A HIGH-EXPLOSIVE SHELL History of Company M, 105th Infantry, 120 Records of the A.E.F. (WWI), Records of the 27th Division [NM-91] 1241, box 9, NARA.

242　DEEP HOLES Operations Report of the 27th Division, A.E.F., covering the period September 23 to October 1, 1918, 120 Records of the A.E.F. (WWI), Records of the 27th Division, [NM-91] 1241, box 3, NARA.

242　SERIOUS OBSTACLE History of Company M, 105th Infantry, 120 Records of the A.E.F. (WWI), Records of the 27th Division, [NM-91] 1241, box 9, NARA; Field Notes, Action of 27th Division at and near St. Souplet, 120 Records of the A.E.F. (WWI), Records of the 27th Division [NM-91] 1241, box 2, NARA.

243　COMPASS BEARINGS and JUST WEST War Diary of 2nd Battalion, 106th Infantry, October 17, 1918, 120 Records of the A.E.F. (WWI), A.E.F. General Headquarters, War Diaries, [NM-91] 26, box 2694, NARA; Secret Field Orders No. 18, 120 Records of the A.E.F. (WWI), Records of the 27th Division, Historical Files [NM-91] 1241, box 7, NARA.

243　LOST THEIR WAY and LAY BLOCKING Operations Report of the 27th Division, A.E.F., covering the period September 23 to October 1, 1918, 120 Records of the A.E.F. (WWI), Records of the 27th Division [NM-91] 1241, box 3, NARA; Ireland, History of the Twenty Third Regiment, 318.

243　SLIDING DOWN THE Summary of the Operations of the 27th Division, 120 Records of the A.E.F. (WWI), Records of the 27th Division [NM-91] 1241, box 2, NARA; Ireland, History of the Twenty Third Regiment, 315–17.

243　FORMIDABLE OBSTACLE and MARCHED THEIR CAPTIVES Field
244　Notes, Action of 27th Division at and near St. Souplet, 120 Records of the A.E.F. (WWI), Records of the 27th Division [NM-91] 1241, box 2, NARA; Ireland, History of the Twenty Third Regiment, 317.

244　FULFILLING THE PROPHECY Memorandum for Brigade Commanders,

October 15, 1918, 120 Records of the A.E.F. (WWI), Records of the
27th Division, Historical Files [NM-91] 1241, box 3, NARA.

244   WAS ABOUT TO SHOOT The Evening Telegram, December 30, 1920.

245   UNFORESEEN CIRCUMSTANCES New York Times, December 15, 1918,
March 7, 1919; Memorandum for Brigade Commanders, October 15,
1918, 120 Records of the A.E.F. (WWI), Records of the 27th Division,
Historical Files [NM-91] 1241, box 3, NARA.

245   "ONE OF THOSE UNFORTUNATE" History of Company M, 105th Infantry, 120 Records of the A.E.F. (WWI), Records of the 27th Division
[NM-91] 1241, box 9, NARA.

245   DESPERATELY SEEKING Ibid.

246   NO MORE THAN 850 and AGAIN BEEN HIT Operations Report of the
27th Division, A.E.F., covering the period September 23 to October 1,
1918, 120 Records of the A.E.F. (WWI), Records of the 27th Division
[NM-91] 1241, box 3, NARA; 13721–83, Abstracts of National Guard
Service, box 14, vol. 43.

246   A BITTER ADVANCE ATTACK and "BEGGED TO BE" Ireland, History of
the Twenty Third Regiment, 320–22.

247   "THE PRETTIEST FIGHT" New York Times, March 7, 1919; War Diary
of 2nd Battalion, 106th Infantry, October 19, 1918, 120 Records of the
A.E.F. (WWI), A.E.F. General Headquarters, War Diaries [NM-91] 26,
box 2694, NARA.

20 ALWAYS SHALL WE HONOR THEM

248   "THE COLUMN MOVED" Gas Attack, March 1919, 42–43.

249   "ROADBED and RAILS" Ibid., Rutherford Ireland, History of the
Twenty Third Regiment N.G.S.N.Y., 328–29.

249   BUSSY-LÈS-DAOURS Gas Attack, March 1919, 42–43; War Diary of 2nd
Battalion, 106th Infantry, October 25, 1918, 120 Records of the A.E.F.
(WWI), A.E.F. General Headquarters, War Diaries [NM-91] 26, box
2694, NARA.

249   "FRIDAY'S CASUALTY LIST" Alpine Avalanche (Texas), October 24,
1918.

250   A RECESSION BEGINNING J. P. Morgan, quoted in Howard Zinn,
A People's History of the United States, 353; Sarah Bradford Landau
and Carl W. Condit, Rise of the New York Skyscraper, 279; Howard
Zinn, A People's History of the United States, 341.

250   GASOLINE-POWERED TRACTORS, "WHEATLESS MONDAYS," and "VIC-
251   TORY MENUS" David M. Kennedy, A Freedom from Fear, 17; Elmira
Herald, October 27, November 10, 1917.

251   "WHAT WE NEED TO WIN" http://academic.udayton.edu/health/
syllabi/tobacco/history2.htm#1.

251   "NEVER EMBARKED ON" Gary Mead, The Doughboys, 361.

252   "FORGET THERE EVER" H. C. Peterson and Gilbert C. Fite, Opponents
of War, 11.

252 "WE WILL PRUSSIANIZE" Max Eastman, quoted in Mead, The Dough-boys, 362.

252 SPIRIT OF '76 and FORTY-FIVE MENNONITES Peterson and Fite, Opponents of War, 134.

253 "IT IS SAFE TO SAY" Zinn, A People's History of the United States, 360.

253 27TH DIVISION MEMORIAL REVIEW and "THE HIGHER MILITARY
254 IDEALS" War Diary of 2nd Battalion, 106th Infantry, November 10, 1918, 120 Records of the A.E.F. (WWI), A.E.F. General Headquarters, War Diaries [NM-91] 26, box 2694, NARA; General Orders No. 94, November 5, 1918, 120 Records of the A.E.F. (WWI), Records of the 27th Division, Historical Files [NM-91] 1241, box 6, NARA.

254 "SO SLOW" and WHILE ITS COMMANDER Private William F. Clarke, quoted in James Hallas, Doughboy War, 311; Maurice J. Swetland and Lilli Swetland, These Men, 296.

255 "THE HONOR OF BEING" Gas Attack, March 1919, 42–43.

255 "IT WAS UNDOUBTEDLY" Commanding General to Commanding Officer, 106th Infantry, October 22, 1918, 391 United States Regular Army Mobile Units, 1821–1942, Records of the 106th Infantry Regiment [NM-93] 2133, box 1634, NARA.

255 MONK HAD FOUGHT Abstracts of WWI Military Service, New York State Archives, B0808; New York Daily Tribune, May 9, 1919.

255 THE CITATIONS AMONG See, for example, Headquarters, 106th Infantry, October 6, 1918, 391 United States Regular Army, Mobile Units, 1821–1942, Records of the 106th Infantry [NM-93], box 1634, NARA.

256 "BETWEEN BATTALION HEADQUARTERS" Commanding Officer, 106th Infantry, to Commanding General, 27th Division, January 30, 1919, 391 United States Regular Army Mobile Units, 1821–1942, Records of the 106th Infantry Regiment [NM-93] 2133, box 1636, NARA.

256 27TH DIVISION'S LOSSES Trench and Camp, March 1919; Commemorative plaque erected in Brooklyn by the Brooklyn City Guard Association, 1924; Commanding Officer, 106th Infantry, to Commanding General, 53rd Infantry Brigade, October 27, 1918, 391 United States Regular Army Mobile Units, 1821–1942, Records of the 106th Infantry Regiment [NM-93] 2133, box 1646, NARA; Statistical Section, Headquarters, 27th Division, memorandum to G-3, II Corps, December 15, 1918, 120 Records of the A.E.F. (WWI), Records of the 27th Division, Historical Files—106th Infantry [NM-91] 1241, box 1, NARA.

256 "TERMINATED THE WORLD'S" New York Times, March 7, 1919.

257 WHY HE WASN'T CELEBRATING Mitchell Yockelson, Borrowed Soldiers, 211–12.

257 "I REJOICE TO THINK" Field Marshal Douglas Haig, to the General Commanding Officer and the officers, noncommissioned officers, and enlisted men of the 27th Division, February 12, 1919, 120 Records of the A.E.F. (WWI), Records of the 27th Division [NM-91] 1241, box 1,

NARA.

257 "BEING AMERICANS" John F. O'Ryan, Major General Commanding, to Field Marshal Sir Douglas Haig, February 18, 1919, 120 Records of the A.E.F. (WWI), Records of the 27th Division [NM-91] 1241, box 1, NARA.

257 MOST DOUGHBOYS NEVER Mead, The Doughboys, 74.

258 PREVENT VANDALISM and LE BREIL Bulletin No. 120, 120 Records of the A.E.F. (WWI), Records of the 27th Division, Historical Files [NM-91] 1241, box 1, NARA; War Diary of 2nd Battalion, 106th Infantry, November 28, 29, 1918, 120 Records of the A.E.F. (WWI), A.E.F. General Headquarters, War Diaries [NM-91] 26, box 2694, NARA.

258 CONTINUING TO UNDERGO John Bessette, Lecture at York St. John's University, January 19, 2008; General Orders No. 98, November 11, 1918, 120 Records of the A.E.F. (WWI), Records of the 27th Division, Historical Files [NM-91] 1241, box 6, NARA.

258 ABSENTEEISM and REPORTS THAT ENLISTED Chief of Staff to Commanding General, 27th Division, December 23, 1918, 120 Records of the A.E.F. (WWI), Records of the 27th Division, Historical Files—106th Infantry [NM-91] 1241, box 1, NARA; Adjutant General, A.E.F., to Commanding General, 27th Division, November 21, 1918, 391 United States Regular Army, Mobile Units, 1821–1942, Records of the 106th Infantry [NM-93], box 1638, NARA; General Orders No. 106, December 28, 1918, 391 United States Regular Army, Mobile Units, 1821–1942, Records of the 106th Infantry [NM-93], box 1653, NARA; Orders No. 163, February 19, 1919, 120 Records of the A.E.F. (WWI), Records of the 27th Division, Historical Files [NM-91] 1241, box 1, NARA.

258 "OWING TO CHANGED CONDITIONS" and "NOT ENOUGH ATTEN-
259 TION" Memorandum by command of Brigadier General Pierce, November 15, 1919, 120 Records of the A.E.F. (WWI), Records of the 27th Division, Historical Files [NM-91] 1241, box 1, NARA; Chief of Staff to Commanding General, 27th Division, December 26, 1918, 391 United States Regular Army, Mobile Units, 1821–1942, Records of the 106th Infantry [NM-93], box 1638, NARA.

259 THERE WERE ALSO and EAR CUT OFF Adjutant, 106th U.S. Infantry, to Commandant of the Brigade Gendarmerie of Vibraye, January 26, 1919, 391 United States Regular Army, Mobile Units, 1821–1942, Records of the 106th Infantry [NM-93], box 1638, NARA; Major Scott Button, Major Infantry USA, to the Citizens of Le Breil, 391 United States Regular Army, Mobile Units, 1821–1942, Records of the 106th Infantry [NM-93], box 1646, NARA; Memorandum to all Company Commanders, February 4, 1919, 391 United States Regular Army, Mobile Units, 1821–1942, Records of the 106th Infantry [NM-93], box 1638, NARA.

259 REPLACEMENT UNDERWEAR, ONLY TEN MEN, and "INFATUATION WITH" The Surgeon, 3rd Battalion, 106th Infantry, to Commanding

Officer, 106th Infantry, January 18, 1919, 391 United States Regular Army, Mobile Units, 1821–1942, Records of the 106th Infantry [NM-93], box 1646, NARA; Memorandum to all Company Commanders, 2nd Battalion, January 18, 1919, 391 United States Regular Army Mobile Units, 1821–1942, Records of the 106th Infantry Regiment [NM-93] 2133, box 1636, NARA; Commanding Officer, 106th Infantry, to Commanding General, 27th Division, January 19, 1919, 391 United States Regular Army Mobile Units, 1821–1942, Records of the 106th Infantry Regiment [NM-93] 2133, box 1636, NARA.

259 THE RUMORS FLEW and INSPECTION and REVIEW Gas Attack, March
260 1919, 42–43; Ireland, History of the Twenty Third Regiment, 334.

260 "THREE MILLION ROUNDS OF CANDY" and HIS GRADE OF ARMY
     MECHANIC Brooklyn Daily Eagle, March 24, 1919; Bulletin No. 121, November 19, 1918, 120 Records of the A.E.F. (WWI), Records of the 27th Division, Historical Files [NM-91] 1241, box 1, NARA; Abstracts of WWI Military Service, New York State Archives, B0808.

260 GENERAL O'RYAN HAD ASKED, THE "PURPLE CROSS," and "AMERI-
     CAN HERO" Major General John F. O'Ryan to Colonel F. W. Ward, 106th Infantry, December 16, 1918, 391 United States Regular Army, Mobile Units, 1821–1942, Records of the 106th Infantry [NM-93], box 1638, NARA; CO, Company G, 106th Infantry, to CO, 106th Infantry, December 20, 1918, 391 United States Regular Army, Mobile Units, 1821–1942, Records of the 106th Infantry [NM-93], box 1638, NARA; "Paris Director in League with Purple Cross (?)," in Embalmers' Monthly 33, January 1920; "Rid the Profession of Odium That Has Come to It," in Embalmers' Monthly 33, February 1920; G. Kurt Piehler, Remembering War the American Way, 94.

261 "MRS. ROOSEVELT and I" John W. Graham, unpublished paper, "Quentin Roosevelt and the Gold Star Mothers Pilgrimages," quoted in Lisa M. Budreau, Mourning and the Making of a Nation, 4; Captain H. F. Jaeckel, 106th Infantry, to Commanding Officer, Headquarters Company, 106th Infantry, December 28, 1918, 391 United States Regular Army, Mobile Units, 1821–1942, Records of the 106th Infantry [NM-93], box 1638, NARA.

261 RUMORS THAT THE 27TH and INSPECTED FOR VERMIN Gas Attack, March 1919, 42–43; War Diary of 2nd Battalion, 106th Infantry, October 17, 1918, 120 Records of the A.E.F. (WWI), A.E.F. General Headquarters, War Diaries [NM-91] 26, box 2694, NARA; Trench and Camp, February 1919; Memorandum to Commanding Officers, January 7, 1919, 120 Records of the A.E.F. (WWI), Records of the 27th Division, Historical Files [NM-91] 1241, box 5, NARA.

261 "IT WAS NOTHING" New York Times, February 19, 1919.

262 THEY TOOK THEIR FINAL Gas Attack, March 1919, 42–43; War Diary of 106th Infantry, February 24, 1919, 120 Records of the A.E.F. (WWI), Records of the 27th Division, Historical Files [NM-91] 1241, box 9, NARA.

262   THE *LEVIATHAN* and "TEN HOMING PIGEONS" New York Times, February 16, 1919; Order of Battle of the United States Land Forces in the World War, 508; William F. Clarke, Over There with O'Ryan's Roughnecks, 29; The World, March 27, 1919.

21 THE FIGHTERS THAT THEY WERE

265   A FLYING BOAT and MORE THAN FIFTEEN THOUSAND Trench and Camp,
266   March 1919; New York Times, March 7, 1919.

266   "FROM THE MOMENT" and CONEY ISLAND New York Times, March 7, 1919; Trench and Camp, March 1919.

266   GENERAL O'RYAN STOOD John F. O'Ryan, History of the 27th Division: New York's Own, 6–7; New York Times, March 7, 10, 1919; War Diary of 106th Infantry, March 6, 1919, 120 Records of the A.E.F. (WWI), Records of the 27th Division, Historical Files [NM-91] 1241, box 9, NARA.

267   A LARGE NUMBER OF DOGS, "FIQUE," and FLEMISH ORPHAN BOY The World, March 25, 1919; New York Times, March 7, 1919; New York Sun, March 7, 1919.

267   ELEVEN HUNDRED MEN ON BOARD New York Times, March 7, 1919; O'Ryan, History of the 27th Division, 41.

267   LIQUID SOAP New York Times, March 6, 8, February 23, 1919; War Diary of 106th Infantry, February 24, 1919, 120 Records of the A.E.F. (WWI), Records of the 27th Division, Historical Files [NM-91] 1241, box 9, NARA.

268   EXCLUDING THEIR HAND GRENADES and CARPENTERS OF THE TODD New York Times, March 22, 25, 1919; Brooklyn Daily Eagle, March 24, 1919; The World, March 23, 24, 1919.

268   THE "WILD MEN" New York Times, March 25, 1919.

269   "WITH SET FACES" and "THE STRAIGHT LINES" The World, March 25, 1919; New York Times, March 25, 1919.

269   TWO DOGS and A YOUNG GOAT The World, March 25, 1919; O'Ryan, History of the 27th Division, 71; New York Times, March 25, 1919.

269   "THE SPELL OF THE GRIM" and FOOD FIGHT New York Times,
270   March 25, 1919.

270   "GENERAL JOLLIFICATION" The World, March 25, 1919; Brooklyn Daily Eagle, March 24, 1919; New York Times, March 25, 1919.

270   "THE APPIAN WAY," "A MODERN FAIRY LAND," and "MOST PRETENTIOUS" Trench and Camp, March 1919; The World, March 23, 24, 1919; New York Times, March 25, 26, 1919.

270   PRISTINE WHITE SAND Brooklyn Daily Eagle, March 25, 1919; New York Times, March 26, 1919.

271   "I FEEL HOW WEAK" New York Times, March 26, 1919.

271   "EVEN THE BEST FRIEND" New York Times, March 25, 1919; The World, March 24, 1919.

272   "BLACK FOR IRON" Rutherford Ireland, History of the Twenty Third

Regiment N.G.S.N.Y., 335.

272　AEROBATICS Brooklyn Daily Eagle, March 25, 1919.

272　"THE RESPECT OF THE WORLD" General Orders No. 11, March 15, 1919, 120 Records of the A.E.F. (WWI), Records of the 27th Division, Historical Files [NM-91] 1241, box 6, NARA.

273　REIDAR WALLER The World, March 23, 1919.

273　"MANY PERSONS WIPED" New York Times, March 26, 1919.

273　"YELLS OF 'HELLO MONK,' " "A GOOD PAL," and MORE THAN A PASSING RESEMBLANCE New York Daily Tribune, December 27, 1920; Trench and Camp, April 8, 1919; The World, March 26, 27, 1919.

274　"THOSE WHO BOUGHT" New York Times, March 26, 1919.

274　O'RYAN WAS NEARLY THROWN Ibid.

275　"PARADE AT ATTENTION" General O'Ryan, quoted in New York Times, April 11, 1919.

275　"THE BOYS DIDN'T LET" and "FORGOT THEY WERE WOUNDED" The World, March 26, 1919; New York Times, March 26, 1919.

275　THE SAME MENU New York Times, March 25, 27, 1919.

276　THE HOTEL McALPIN and "THE EAST SIDE DELEGATION" New York Times, March 26, 1919; New York Daily Tribune, December 27, 1920; The World, March 27, 1919.

22 VICTIMLESS CRIMES

277　CAMP UPTON Brooklyn Daily Eagle, March 28, 1919; New York Times, March 27, 1919.

278　MONK'S FORMAL DISCHARGE NYSA 13721–83, Abstracts of National Guard Service, box 14, vol. 43; Trench and Camp, March 1919; Rutherford Ireland, History of the Twenty Third Regiment N.G.S.N.Y., 337; New York Times, April 3, May 2, 1919.

278　TESTIFYING TO New York Times, April 3, 1919.

279　"EASTMAN CAME TO SEE ME" The World, April 9, 1919; New York Times, May 2, 1919.

279　"HIS RECORD," "EXHIBITING GREAT BRAVERY," and "UTMOST COURAGE" New York Daily Tribune, May 9, 1919; The World, April 9, 1919; Albany Times Union, May 8, 1919.

279　"A QUIET, DISCIPLINED" and "SHOULD BE REWARDED" New York Times, May 2, 1919; Albany Times Union, May 8, 1919.

279　MONK EASTMAN WINS New York Daily Tribune, April 3, May 9, 1919; B1201–87 box 3, Clemency Records, file number 7, page 91, New York State Archives; New York Times, May 9, 10, April 3, 1919; Albany Times Union, May 8, 1919.

280　"THE FATHER OF THE MODERN GANGSTER" Herbert Asbury, "Gangland USA," 15.

280　35 PERCENT OF THE WORLD'S and TWO MILLION SOLDIERS Raymond A. Mohl, The Making of Urban America, 97; Order of Battle of the United States Land Forces in the World War, 505.

281 THE FIGHT TO CONTROL BOOTLEGGING Humbert S. Nelli, The Business of Crime, 172.

281 MEDICINAL WITHDRAWAL PERMITS and GARBAGE SCOWS Craig Thompson and Allen Raymond, Gang Rule in New York, 9, 362.

282 NORTH TARRYTOWN and "IN THE HOMES OF THE PEOPLE" Asbury papers, unpublished manuscripts, box 2.

282 "CURBSIDE MARKETS" and "COULDN'T BE ANY FURTHER" Thompson and Raymond, Gang Rule, 9; New York Daily Tribune, December 27, 1920.

283 ON A RAMPAGE and "BOOZE PARTY" New York Daily Tribune, December 27, 1920.

283 THERE WERE RUMORS and "WITH NICKEL PLATE" New York Times, November 11, 1923; Ronald Clarke, In the Reign of Rothstein, 1–2.

283 PROFUSE APOLOGIES and "IT'S A GOOD THING" Virgil W. Peterson, The Mob, 131–32; Thompson and Raymond, Gang Rule, 22.

284 "WITHIN A BISCUIT TOSS," "THE QUIETEST LIFE," and MOST OF THE DAYLIGHT Brooklyn Eagle, December 27, 1920; New York Times, December 27, 1920.

284 A BOUNCER IN A CRAP JOINT and NEW YORK POLICE WENT New York Times, December 27, 1920; Brooklyn Eagle, December 27, 1920.

284 THE COURT CAFE, "THE NORTHERN BOUNDARY," and WILLIE LEWIS Brooklyn Eagle, December 27, 1920; Buffalo Evening News, December 27, 1920; New York Times, December 27, 28, 1920.

284 MEMBERS OF HIS OLD GANG and "DO YOU KNOW WHO" New York
285 Times, December 28, 1920; Brooklyn Daily Eagle, December 28, 1920; New York Daily Tribune, December 28, 29, 1920.

285 "ALWAYS LIKELY TO BE QUARRELSOME" and "HE CRUMPLED UP" New York Times, December 28, 1920; The Sun, January 3, 1921.

285 A FAINT HEARTBEAT and ONE BULLET New York Times, December 27, 28, 1920; New York Daily Tribune, December 27, 1920; New York Death Certificate 33332.

23 DRAPED IN BLACK CLOTH

286 GRAIN ALCOHOL New York World, December 27, 1920.

287 OLD-TIMERS Brooklyn Eagle, December 27, 1920.

287 GOOD SUIT New York Times, December 27, 1920; New York Daily Tribune, December 27, 1920.

287 "THAT FACT, EVEN MORE" Buffalo Evening News, December 27, 1920; The Evening Telegram, December 26, 1920.

287 "A MAN WAS STANDING" and "IF YOU TRY" New York Times, December 28, 1920; Chicago Daily Tribune, December 27, 1920.

287 CHEAP, NICKELED Brooklyn Eagle, December 27, 1920; New York Times, December 27, 1920.

287 "THE MONK WOULDN'T CARRY" The Evening Telegram, December 27, 1920.

288 "THERE IS A NEW KIND OF CRIME" Brooklyn Daily Eagle, December 29, 1920.

288 JOHN EASTMAN New York Times, December 27, 1920.

289 "AS VAGUE" New York Evening Post, December 27, 1920.

289 $144, "WAS UNDERSTOOD TO HAVE," and "TIRED OF WOMEN" New York Times, December 27, 28, 1920; Buffalo Evening News, December 27, 1920; New York Daily Tribune, December 28, 1920.

289 "HE WAS A GOOD GUY" and "YOUNG SQUIRT GUNMEN" The Evening Telegram, December 27, 1920; New York Times, December 28, 27, 1920.

290 "ASSOCIATING WITH PROFESSIONAL" and PROFITS FROM DRUG PEDDLING New York Evening Post, December 28, 1920; Chicago Daily Tribune, December 27, 1920; The World, January 5, 1921; New York Evening Post, December 28, 1920.

290 THE NARCOTICS SQUAD and "I AM NOT MONK" New York Times, December 28, 29, 31, 1920, January 4, 1921; Brooklyn Eagle, December 27, 1920.

290 THE POLICE WERE LATER FORCED New York Times, December 28, 1920, January 4, 1921; Buffalo Evening News, December 28, 1920.

291 "WHIPPED BY DRINK" New York Daily Tribune, December 28, 1920.

291 A SECOND VISIT Buffalo Evening News, December 28, 1920.

291 NO SURPRISE IF New York Times, December 28, 1920; New York Daily Tribune, December 28, 1920.

291 "WOULD NOT DENY" New York Times, December 28, 1920; Buffalo Evening News, December 28, 1920.

291 MORRIS POCKETT and "HE REALLY WASN'T" New York Times, December 28, 1920.

292 "MR. EDWARD EASTMAN" Mara Bovsun, "Gangster, Doughboy, Hero," 36.

292 "I'M SORRY I DIDN'T" New York Times, December 29, 1920; The World, December 27, 1920; The Sun, December 29, 1920.

292 "WHITE ONES FOR DEAD" Betty Smith, A Tree Grows in Brooklyn, 46.

292 OUR LOST PAL and "MERE CURIOSITY-SEEKERS" Brooklyn Daily
293 Eagle, December 29, 30, 1920.

293 A CORPS OF DETECTIVES Brooklyn Daily Eagle, December 30, 1920.

293 "IT IS NOT MY PROVINCE" New York Daily Tribune, December 31, 1920.

293 ONE ESTIMATE PUT The Evening Telegram, December 30, 1920; New York Times, December 31, 1920.

294 ALTHOUGH IT WAS RUMORED and "MOTHERS WITH LINES" The Evening Telegram, December 30, 1920.

295 "THE CHARACTER OF EASTMAN" Ibid.

295 "NO MATTER HOW BAD" New York Daily Tribune, December 31, 1920; The Evening Telegram, December 30, 1920.

296 "A REFORMED GANGSTER WHO" Brooklyn Daily Eagle, December 30, 1920.

296　"DID NOT BELIEVE" New York Times, December 29, 1920.

296　"BOTH LEGITIMATE AND" The Sun, January 1, 1921; New York Times, December 31, 1920.

297　"NOT AN ANGRY WORD" New York Times, December 31, 1920.

297　"WE WANT JERRY BOHAN" New York Daily Tribune, January 1, 1921 (in some accounts, the name was spelled "Bohun").

297　"GOT MUSSY" and GRABBED HIM FROM BEHIND New York Times, January 4, 1921.

298　"THUS THE TWO" New York Times, December 29, 1920, January 4, 1921.

298　"BROODING, WITH HIS HEAD" New York Times, March 20, 27, 1921.

299　IMPRISONED IN THE TOMBS New York Times, March 20, 1921, June 24, 1923.

Epilogue THE WAY THINGS HAVE CHANGED

300　"LOAFERS WITH TURTLE-NECK," "CLUTTER UP THE PREMISES" and "A
301　CANTER IN THE PARK" New York Times, November 10, 1935.

BIBLIOGRAPHY

PRIVATE PAPERS OF HERBERT ASBURY
(COLLECTION OF MRS. EDITH ASBURY)

manuscripts box 1

Asbury, Herbert. Short Story Manuscripts: Chinatown; Prohibition Essays; Sin in New York; That Was New York; The Old Time Saloon; The Whyos Gang.

manuscripts box 2

Asbury, Herbert. The Great Illusion: An Informal History of Prohibition.

research box 2

Asbury, Herbert. Cardboard pictures of liquor establishments of the 1870s; handwritten notes; Prohibition case research: articles, letters, notes, photos, maps, pictures.

miscellaneous box 8

Cook, Fred J., and Gene Gleason. "The Shame of New York" (an independent brochure).

miscellaneous box 9

Asbury, Herbert. Copies of news articles from the late nineteenth century; newspaper; periodical articles.

Asbury, Herbert. World War One sketches, maps, identity card, letters, personal memorabilia on cardboard.

NATIONAL ARCHIVES AND RECORD ADMINISTRATION
(NARA I), WASHINGTON, D.C.

United States of America, Bureau of the Census:

Seventh Census of the United States, 1850, New York Ward 7, District 1, New York, New York, roll M432_539; page 80, image 161

Eighth Census of the United States, 1860, New York Ward 7, District 2, New York, New York, roll M653_792; page 136, image 138

Eighth Census of the United States, 1860, New York Ward 19, District 2,

New York, New York, roll M653_815; page 0, image 600

Ninth Census of the United States, 1870, New York Ward 10, District 1 (2nd Enum), New York, New York, roll M593_1024; page 10, image 20

Ninth Census of the United States, 1870, New York Ward 13, District 3, New York, New York, roll M593_1031; page 70, image 140

Ninth Census of the United States, 1870, New York Ward 19, District 21, New York, New York, roll M593_1005; page 408, image 251

Ninth Census of the United States, 1870, New York Ward 19, District 9 (2nd Enum), New York, New York, roll M593_1042; page 230, image 463

Tenth Census of the United States, 1880, New York (Manhattan), New York City, Greater New York, roll T9_896; Family History film 1254896, page 389.1000, ED 610, image 0781

Tenth Census of the United States, 1880, New York (Manhattan), New York City, Greater New York, roll T9_895; Family History film 1254895, page 542.3000, ED 588, image 0485

Twelfth Census of the United States, 1900, New York (Manhattan), New York City, Greater New York, roll T623_1092; page 5B, ED 240

Twelfth Census of the United States, 1900, Queens Ward 4, Queens, New York, roll T623_1149; pages 19B, 20A, ED677

Thirteenth Census of the United States, 1910, Brooklyn Ward 28, Kings, New York, New York, roll T624_982; page 1B, ED 917, image 495.77

Thirteenth Census of the United States, 1910, Brooklyn Ward 25, Kings, New York, New York, roll T624_973; page 12A, ED 695, image 747

Fourteenth Census of the United States, 1920, Brooklyn Assembly District 4, Kings, New York, New York, roll T625_1150; page 1A, ED 238, image 813

Fifteenth Census of the United States, 1930, Manhattan, New York, New York, roll 1553; page 12B, ED 386, image 474.0

NATIONAL ARCHIVES AND RECORD ADMINISTRATION (NARA II), COLLEGE PARK, MARYLAND

a. Historical Files; Combat Divisions, Records of the 27th Division; Entry [NM-91]1241; Records of the American Expeditionary Force (World War I), Record Group 120

b. Organizational Files; Combat Divisions, Records of the 27th Division; Entry [NM-91]1241; Records of the American Expeditionary Force (World War I), Record Group 120

c. Records of the 53rd Brigade; Entry [NM-91]254; Records of the American Expeditionary Force (World War I), Record Group 120

d. War Diaries; Entry [NM-91]26; American Expeditionary Force, General Headquarters; Records of the American Expeditionary Force (World War I), Record Group 120

e. Headquarters, Decimal Files; Records of the 106th Infantry Regiment; Entry [NM-93]2133; Records of the U.S. Regular Mobile Units, 1821–1942, Record Group 391

f. USS President Lincoln (for USS Leviathan, February 26, incoming), Passenger Lists, 1917–1938, outgoing; Army Transport Service; Records of the Quartermaster General, Record Group 92

g. USS Leviathan (for USS President Lincoln, May 10, outgoing), Passenger Lists, 1917–1938, incoming; Army Transport Service; Records of the Quartermaster General, Record Group 92

Major General John F. O'Ryan, Operations Report, 27th Division, A.E.F., May 29–September 22, 1918, Folder 5, Entry 270, Record Group 120

NEW YORK CITY MUNICIPAL ARCHIVES, NEW YORK CITY

Borough of Manhattan Marriage Certificate 4106: Edward Eastman–Worthy Cecilia Marven
Borough of Manhattan Certificate of Death 33332: Edward Eastman
Borough of Manhattan Certificate of Death 29833: Samuel Eastman
Borough of Manhattan Certificate of Death 6988: Willie Eastman
Court of General Sessions of the Peace, Case Number 45,671: People versus William Delaney, otherwise called Monk Eastman, February 4, 1904
Court of General Sessions Case Number 45,672: People versus William Delaney, otherwise called Monk Eastman, February 4, 1904

NEW YORK STATE LIBRARY AND ARCHIVES, ALBANY

A0412. World War I veterans' service data and photographs, 1917–1938
A0585 Restoration of Citizenship files
A0597 Clemency records
A3167–78B: World War I records, correspondence, unpublished historical articles, etc.
A3354 World War I veterans' service data and photographs, 1917–1938
A3354 Training circular No. 21
B0100 Ab (1) Box 2: Physician's Register, Sing Sing Prison
B0097 Inmate record cards
B0143 Sing Sing Admissions Register, April 23, 1904, page 157, vol. 36, box 14
B0808 Abstracts of WWI military service
B0814 Muster Rolls of N.Y. National Guard units that served in U.S. Army WWI, 1917–1918
B1201–87 Box 3, Clemency records, file number 7, page 91
B1357 NY Bonus Card 235: Eastman, Edward
13721–83, Abstracts of National Guard service, box 14, vol. 43
Kelley, Francis A., Address by Rev. Francis A. Kelley before New York State Senate and Assembly in joint session, February 24, 1919, Albany, N.Y.
Ward, Franklin W. War Struck: The Story of an Albany General Who Served as a Colonel in the 27th Division

NEW YORK STATE MILITARY MUSEUM AND VETERANS RESEARCH CENTER, SARATOGA SPRINGS

(NIC)NYSG792-580-0003 Ireland, Rutherford, History of the Twenty Third Regiment N.G.S.N.Y., Redesignated the One Hundred and Sixth Infantry A.E.F., to which is prefixed a history of the Brooklyn City Guard, the parent organization, New York, c. 1940.

(NIC)NYSG792-580-0003 Officer Service Record cards. Individual service records for New York National Guard, New York Guard, and New York Naval Militia officers, 1910–1965.

JOHN SEALY LIBRARY, JOHN JAY COLLEGE OF CRIMINAL JUSTICE

Trial No. 421, 1904/4/12, reel 73 (421.pdf)

Court of General Sessions of the Peace In and for the County of New York, Part III, People of the State of New York versus William Delaney, alias Monk Eastman. New York, April 12, et seq., 1904.

CENTRAL ARCHIVES FOR THE HISTORY OF THE JEWISH PEOPLE, JERUSALEM

Papers of Abraham H. Shoenfeld, in Archive of Dr. Judah Magnes, P3/1758; P3/1759; P3/1762; P3/1768.

UNPUBLISHED THESES

Bernstein, Rachel. Boarding-House Keepers and Brothel Keepers in New York City, 1880–1910. Ph.D. thesis, Rutgers University, 1984.

Budreau, Lisa M. Mourning and the Making of a Nation: The Gold Star Pilgrimages, 1930–1933. St. Anthony's College Oxford, 2002.

Gandal, Keith. The Spectacle of the Poor: Jacob Riis, Stephen Crane and the Representation of Slum Life. Ph.D. thesis, University of California at Berkeley, 1990.

Thale, Christopher. Civilizing New York: Police Patrol, 1880–1935. Ph.D. thesis, University of Chicago, 1995.

NEW YORK PUBLIC LIBRARY

humanities department

Microforms

Z-BTZS p.v.12, no.3, Official commendations of the 27th American Division, Belgium and France, 1918, Paris, 1918?

periodicals

Albany Times Union
Alpine Avalanche (Texas)
The Argus (Albany)

Bookman
Brooklyn Daily Eagle
Brooklyn Daily Times
Buffalo Evening News
Chicago Daily Tribune
Elmira Herald (New York)
The Evening Telegram
Frank Leslie's Illustrated Newspaper
The Freehold Transcript (New Jersey)
Gas Attack of the New York Division, Camp Wadsworth, Spartanburg, S.C.,
    Camp Wadsworth, Young Men's Christian Association
Harper's Weekly
Jewish Messenger
Kansas City Star
McClure's Magazine
The Monmouth Democrat (New Jersey)
New York Daily News
New York Daily Tribune
New York Evening Post
New York Evening Telegram
New York Herald
The New York Pictorial
New York Post
New York Sun
The New York Times
New York Times Midweek Pictorial War Extra
New York Times Rotogravure section, March 30, 1919: "Complete pictorial
    record of New York's great welcome to her own."
New York World
The New Yorker
Police Gazette
Spartanburg Herald
Stars & Stripes
Tammany Times
Trench and Camp: Edition for Camp Upton, Long Island, N.Y.
Washington Post

ARTICLES

Andrews, Walter Scott. "A Study of the East Side Courts." University
    Settlement Society of New York Annual Report, New York (1899):
    23–29.
Asbury, Herbert. "The Emperor of Gangland." New McClure's Magazine 62,
    no. 2 (February 1929).
———. "Gangland USA," in New McClure's Magazine 62, no. 1 (January
    1929).

Berger, Meyer. "Portrait of a Racketeer (Streamlined)." New York Times, November 10, 1935.

Bingham, Theodore A. "Administration of Criminal Law: Third Degree System." Annals of the American Academy of Political and Social Science 36 (January 1910): 11–15.

———. "The Organized Criminals of New York." McClure's Magazine 34 (November 1909).

Bovie, Verne M. "The Public Dance Halls of the Lower East Side." University Settlement Society of New York Annual Report, New York (1901).

Bovsun, Mara. "Our Lost Pal, Monk Eastman." Jay Maeder, Big Town Biography, New York Daily News, 2000.

"Bowery Amusements." University Settlement Society of New York Annual Report (1899): 14–19.

Brooks, Sydney. "London and New York." Harpers Magazine 104 (January 1902).

Carter, John. "Master of Manhattan: The Life of Richard Croker." The Bookman, April 1931, 203.

Chamberlain, John R. "Gangsters Have Lost Their Last Big Name." New York Times, October 30, 1927.

Conway, Kathleen, Mike McCormack, and Thomas Conway. "Gangs of New York." Social Education 67 (2003).

Czitrom, Daniel. "Underworlds and Underdogs: Big Tim Sullivan and Metropolitan Politics in New York, 1889–1913." Journal of American History 78 (1991): 548–58.

Daniell, F. Raymond. "The Big Business of the Racketeer." New York Times, April 27, 1930.

Davis, Richard Harding. "The Defeat of the Underworld." Collier's 50 (November 9, 1912).

Fagan, Geoffrey, Valerie West, and Jan Holland. "Reciprocal Effects of Crime and Incarceration in New York City Neighborhoods." Fordham Urban Law Journal 30 (2003).

Gilfoyle, Timothy J. "Street-Rats and Gutter-Snipes: Child Pickpockets and Street Culture in New York City, 1850–1900." Journal of Social History 37 (2004).

———. "Strumpets and Misogynists: Brothel 'Riots' and the Transformation of Prostitution in Antebellum New York City." New York History 68 (January 1987): 45–65.

Justice, Benjamin. "Historical Fiction to Historical Fact: Gangs of New York and the Whitewashing of History." in Social Education 67 (2003).

Key, V. O. Jr. "Police Graft." The American Journal of Sociology 40, no. 5 (March 1935): 624–36.

Kincaid, J. Leslie. "The 27th New York's Guard Division That Broke German Line." New York Times Magazine, March 9, 1919.

Levenson, Joseph. "History of the Lower East Side of Manhattan, and Grand Street, Its Leading Thoroughfare." Souvenir Journal of Grand Street Boys, 1921.

Levick, M. B. "Tough Girl of New York Remains Only a Memory." New York Times, June 29, 1924.

Lewis, Alfred Henry. "The Cooking of Crazy Butch." New York Daily Tribune, April 26, 1903.

———. "The Modern Robin Hood." The Cosmopolitan, June 1905.

McClure, S. S. "The Tammanyizing of a Civilization." McClure's Magazine 34 (November 1909): 117–28.

McLean, Frank H. "An Experience in the Street-Cleaning Department." University Settlement Society of New York Annual Report, New York (1899): 20–25.

McShane, Clay, and Joel A. Tarr. "The Centrality of the Horse in the Nineteenth Century," in Raymond A. Mohl (ed.), The Making of Urban America (Lanham, Md.: Rowman and Littlefield, 1997), 105–20.

Mohl, Raymond A. "New Perspectives on American Urban History," in Raymond A. Mohl (ed.), The Making of Urban America (Lanham, Md.: Rowman and Littlefield, 1997), 335–374.

Mustain, Gene. "Good with Electricity." New York Daily News, June 4, 1999.

"New York's 27th, First to Smash the Hindenburg Line, Comes Home," in Literary Digest, March 29, 1919.

Orenic, Liesl. "Murder in New York City." Journal of Social History 36 (2002).

Oskison, John M. "Public Halls of the East Side." University Settlement Society of New York Annual Report, New York (1899): 38–40.

Peiss, Kathy. "Leisure and Labor," in Raymond A. Mohl (ed.), The Making of Urban America (Lanham, Md.: Rowman and Littlefield, 1997), 167–86.

Powers, Madelon. "The 'Poor Man's Friend': Saloonkeepers, Workers and the Code of Reciprocity in U.S. Barrooms, 1870–1920." International Labor and Working Class History 45 (Spring 1994): 1–15.

Pulling, Ezra R. "Report of the Fourth Sanitary Inspection District." Report of the Council of Hygiene and Public Health of the Citizens' Association of New York upon the Sanitary Condition of the City, 1866.

Ralph, Julian. "The Bowery." Century 43 (December 1891): 234.

"A Review of the World." Current Literature 2, no. 5 (May 1911).

Rowland, Leslie W. "The 27th Division Crashes Through." Gas Attack (November 1918): 3–5.

"Sing Sing Prison: The Life of State Prison Convicts—How They Are Treated and Cared For." Frank Leslie's Illustrated Newspaper, February 16, 1878.

Slonim, Joel. "The Jewish Gangster," in Reflex 3 (July 3, 1928).

Soderlund, Gretchen. "Covering Urban Vice: The New York Times, 'White Slavery,' and the Construction of Journalistic Knowledge." Critical Studies in Media Communication, 19, no. 4 (December 2002): 438–60.

Spaulding, Raymond C. "The Saloons of the District." University Settlement Society of New York Annual Report, New York (1899): 34–38.

Steinberg, Alan. "Street Justice: A History of Police Violence in New York

City." Journal of Social History 41 (2007).

Turner, George Kibbe. "The Daughters of the Poor: A Plain Story of the Development of New York City as a Leading Center of the White Slave Trade of the World Under Tammany Hall." McClure's Magazine 34 (November 1909): 45–61.

———. "Tammany's Control of New York by Professional Criminals." McClure's Magazine 33 (June 1909): 117–134.

Yockelson, Mitch. "Brothers-in-Arms: The 27th & 30th American Divisions on the Western Front with the British Army and the Breaking of the Hindenburg Line, 1918." Stand To! 82, Western Front Association, Stockport, U.K., 5–13.

Young, James C. "Crime Gangs Organized as Big Business." New York Times, April 4, 1926.

BOOKS

Albertine, Connell. The Yankee Doughboy. Boston: Branden Press, 1968.

American Battle Monuments Commission. The 27th Division: Summary of Operations in the World War. United States Government Printing Office, 1944.

Anbinder, Tyler. Five Points. New York: Plume, 2002.

Andrews, Walter G. The Story of a Machine Gun Company, 1918–1919. Buffalo, N.Y.: 1924.

Arons, Ron. The Jews of Sing Sing. New York: Barricade Books, 2008.

Asbury, Herbert. All Around the Town. New York: Thunder's Mouth Press, 2003.

———. The Gangs of New York. New York: Arrow, 2002.

———. Sucker's Progress: An Informal History of Gambling in America. New York, 1938.

Astor, Gerald. The New York Cops: An Informal History. New York: Scribner, 1971.

Baker, Kevin. Dreamland. New York: HarperCollins, 1999.

———. Paradise Alley. New York: HarperCollins, 2002.

Barnes, Harry Elmer. The Repression of Crime, Studies in Historical Penology. Montclair, N.J., 1926.

Beer, Thomas. The Mauve Decade. New York, 1926.

Berger, Meyer. The Eight Million. New York, 1936.

———. The Eight Million: Journal of a New York Correspondent. New York: Columbia University Press, 1983.

———. Meyer Berger's New York. New York: Random House, 1960.

Borges, Jorge Luis. Monk Eastman: Purveyor of Iniquities (foreword to Herbert Asbury's The Gangs of New York). New York: Arrow, 2002.

———. A Universal History of Iniquity. New York: Penguin, 2000.

Brailsford, Dennis. Bareknuckles. Cambridge, U.K.: Lutterworth Press, 1988.

Brian, Denis. Sing Sing. Amherst, N.Y.: Prometheus Books, 2005.

Brockway, Zebulon Reed. Fifty Years of Prison Service. Montclair, N.J., 1912.

Brown, Henry Collins. Valentine's Manual of Old New York. New York, 1923.

Burrows, Edwin G. and Mike Wallace. Gotham: A History of New York City to 1898. New York: Oxford University Press, 1999.

Byrnes, Inspector Thomas F. Professional Criminals of America. New York, 1886.

Cahan, Abraham. The Rise of David Levinsky. New York, 1917.

Campbell, Helen, Thomas W. Knox, and Thomas F. Byrnes. Darkness and Daylight: Lights and Shadows of New York Life. Hartford, Conn, 1895.

Casey, Robert. The Cannoneers Have Hairy Ears. New York, 1927.

Champion, Dean J. Corrections in the United States. Upper Saddle River, N.J.: Prentice Hall, 2001.

Christianson, Scott. With Liberty for Some. Boston: Northeastern University Press, 1998.

Clarke, Donald Henderson. In the Reign of Rothstein. New York, 1929.

———. Man of the World: Recollections of an Irreverent Reporter. New York: Vanguard Press, 1950.

Clarke, William F. Over There with O'Ryan's Roughnecks. Seattle: Superior, 1966.

Coffman, Edward M. War to End all Wars: The American Military Experience in World War I. New York: Oxford University Press, 1968.

Cohen, Rich. Tough Jews. New York: Vintage, 1999.

Coleman, Terry. Passage to America. London: Hutchinson, 1972.

Controvich, James T. 27th Infantry Division. Lanham, Md.: Scarecrow Press, 1987.

Crane, Milton (ed.) Sins of New York. New York: Bantam, 1950.

Crane, Stephen. Last Words. London, 1902.

———. The Portable Stephen Crane. New York: Penguin, 1977.

Critchley, David. The Origin of Organized Crime in America. New York: Routledge, 2008.

Dash, Mike. Satan's Circus: Murder, Vice, Police Corruption and New York's Trial of the Century. London: Granta Books, 2008.

Debs, Eugene Victor. Walls and Bars. Montclair, N.J., 1927.

Decker, Scott H., and Barrik Van Winkle. Life in the Gang: Family, Friends & Violence, Cambridge Studies in Criminology. Cambridge, U.K.: Cambridge University Press, 1996.

Doctorow, E. L. Ragtime. New York: Plume, 1996.

———. The Waterworks. New York: Plume, 1997.

Downey, Patrick. Gangster City: The History of the New York Underworld 1900–1935. Fort Lee, N.J.: Barricade Books, 2004.

Dreiser, Theodore. The Color of a Great City. New York, 1923.

Eggers, John Henry. 27th Division: The Story of Its Sacrifices and Achievements. New York, 1919.

Eldridge, Benjamin P., and William B. Watts. Our Rival the Rascal: A Faithful Portrayal of the Conflict Between the Criminals of This Age and the
   Defenders of Society. Boston, 1927.

Ellis, John. Eye Deep in Hell: Trench Warfare in World War I. London: Penguin, 2002.

Epstein, Lawrence J. At the Edge of a Dream: The Story of Jewish Immigrants
   on New York's Lower East Side 1880–1920. San Francisco: Jossey-Bass,
   2007.

Every, Edward van. Sins of New York. New York, 1930.

Ewen, Elizabeth. Immigrant Women in the Land of Dollars: Life and Culture
   on the Lower East Side, 1890–1925. New York: Monthly Review Press,
   1985.

Federal Writers Project. New York City Guide: A Comprehensive Guide to
   the Five Boroughs of the Metropolis Manhattan, Brooklyn, the Bronx,
   Queens, and Richmond. New York, 1939.

Fido, Martin. The Chronicle of Crime. London: Carlton Books, 1993.

Fifth Annual Report of the Inspectors of the State Prisons of the State of New
   York, made to the Legislature. New York, January 6, 1853.

Finney, Jack. Time and Again. New York: Simon & Schuster, 1970.

Flick, Alexander. History of the State of New York (10 vols.). New York,
   1933.

Fox, Stephen. Blood and Power: Organized Crime in Twentieth-Century
   America. New York: Morrow, 1989.

Fried, Albert. The Rise and Fall of the Jewish Gangster in America. New
   York: Columbia University Press, 1980.

Gado, Mark. Stone upon Stone: Sing Sing Prison. www.crimelibrary.com,
   accessed 2009.

Gaffen, Fred. Cross-Border Warriors: Canadians in American Forces, Americans in Canadian Forces, from the Civil War to the Gulf. Toronto: Dun-
   durn Group, 1996.

Gardner, Charles W. The Doctor and the Devil, or, Midnight Adventures of
   Dr. Parkhurst. New York, 1894.

Genthe, Charles V. American War Narratives, 1917–1918: A Study and Bib-
   liography. New York: David Lewis, 1969.

Gibbons, Floyd. And They Thought We Wouldn't Fight. New York, 1918.

Gilfoyle, Timothy. City of Eros: New York City, Prostitution and the Com-
   mercialization of Sex, 1790–1920. New York: Norton, 1992.

————. A Pickpocket's Tale: The Underworld of Nineteenth-Century New
   York. New York: Norton, 2006.

Gold, Michael. Jews Without Money. New York, 1930.

Goren, Arthur. New York Jews and the Quest for Community: The Kebillah
   Experiment, 1908–1922. New York: Columbia University Press, 1970.

Gow, Kenneth. Letters of a Soldier. New York, 1920.

Green, Jonathon. The Directory of Infamy. London: Mills & Boon, 1980.

Hallas, James H. The Doughboy War: The American Expeditionary Force in
   World War I. Boulder, Colo.: Lynne Renner, 2000.

Hamilton, Craig, and Louise Corbin. Echoes from Over There. New York, 1919.

Hapgood, Hutchins. Types from City Streets. New York, 1910.

Harlow, Alvin F. Old Bowery Days. New York, 1931.

Harris, Stephen L. Duty, Honor, Privilege: New York's Silk Stocking Regiment and the Breaking of the Hindenburg Line. Washington, D.C.: Brassey's, 2001.

History of Company "E," 107th Infantry, 54th Brigade, 27th Division, USA. New York, 1920.

Home Again! The 27th Division: The Story of Its Sacrifices and Achievements. New York, 1919.

Hone, Philip. The Diary of Philip Hone (Bayard Tuckerman, ed.), Carlisle, Mass., 1889.

Horan, James D., and Howard Swiggett. The Pinkerton Story. London: Heinemann, 1952.

Ingersoll, Ernest. A Week in New York. New York, 1892.

Jackson, Anthony. A Place Called Home. Cambridge, Mass.: MIT Press, 1976.

Jackson, Kenneth T. (ed.) The Encyclopedia of the City of New York. New Haven: Yale University Press, 1995.

Jacobson, Gerald F. History of the 107th Infantry, USA. New York, 1920.

Janvier, Thomas A. In Old New York. New York, 1922.

Jenkins, Stephen. The Greatest Street in the World: Broadway. New York, 1911.

Johnson, Marilynn S. Street Justice: A History of Police Violence in New York City. Boston, Mass.: Beacon Press, 2003.

Johnson, Ray N. Heaven, Hell or Hoboken. Cleveland, 1919.

Johnston, Alexander. Ten—and Out. New York, 1927.

Joselit, Jenna W. Our Gang: Jewish Crime and the New York Jewish Community, 1900–1940. Bloomington: Indiana University Press, 1983.

Kaplan, Justin. Lincoln Steffens: A Biography. New York: Simon & Schuster, 1974.

Katcher, Leo. The Big Bankroll: The Life and Times of Arnold Rothstein. New York: Harper, 1959.

Kelly, Robert J. Encyclopedia of Organized Crime in the United States: From Capone's Chicago to the New Urban Underworld. Westport, Conn.: Greenwood Press, 2000.

Kennedy, David M. A Freedom from Fear: The American People in Depression and War, 1929–1945. New York: Oxford University Press, 1999.

Kwong, Peter. The New Chinatown. New York: Hill & Wang, 1996.

"Ladies of the Mission": The Old Brewery and the New Mission House at the Five Points. New York, 1854.

Landau, Sarah Bradford, and Carl W. Condit. Rise of the New York Skyscraper. New Haven: Yale University Press, 1996.

Lawes, Lewis E. Twenty Thousand Years in Sing Sing. New York, 1932.

Lederer, Victor. Images of America: Williamsburg. Charleston, S.C.: Arcadia

Publishing, 2005.

Leland, Claude G. From Shell Hole to Chateau with Company I. New York: Published under the auspices of the Society of Ninth Company Veterans, 7th Regiment, N.Y.N.G., 1950

Levinson, Edward. I Break Strikes: The Technique of Pearl L. Bergoff. New York, 1935.

Lewis, Alfred Henry. Nation-Famous New York Murders. New York, 1914.

———. The Boss and How He Came to Rule New York. New York, 1903.

Lightfoot, Frederick S. Nineteenth-Century New York in Rare Photographic Views. New York: Dover Publications, 1981.

Little, Arthur. From Harlem to the Rhine. New York, 1936.

Lord, Eliot, John D. Trenor, and Samuel Barrows. The Italian in America. Freeport, N.Y.: Ayer Publishing, 1970.

Lyon, Peter W. Success Story: The Life and Times of S. S. McClure. New York: Scribner, 1963.

Maeder, Jay. Big Town Biography. New York: New York Daily News, 2000.

Martin, Edward Winslow. The Secrets of the Great City: A Work Descriptive of the Virtues and the Vices, the Mysteries, Miseries and Crimes of New York City. Philadelphia, 1868.

Matsell, George W. Vocabulum; or, The Rogue's Lexicon. New York, 1859.

Maurice, Sir Frederick. The Last Four Months: How the War Was Won. Boston, Mass., 1919.

McAdoo, William. Guarding a Great City. New York, 1906.

McCabe, James Dabney. New York by Sunlight and Gaslight. Philadelphia, 1882.

———. Secrets of the Great City. Philadelphia, 1868.

Mead, Gary. The Doughboys. New York: Overlook Press, 2000.

Miller, Stuart. A Tenement Story: The History of 97 Orchard Street and the Lower East Side Tenement Museum. New York: Lower East Side Tenement Museum, 1999.

Mitchell, Harry T. Company L, 107th Infantry, 54th Infantry Brigade, 27th Division. New York, 1919.

Mitchell, Joseph. The Bottom of the Harbor. New York: Vintage, 2001.

———. McSorley's Wonderful Saloon 1943. New York: Pantheon, 2001.

Monkkonen, Eric H. Murder in New York City. Berkeley: University of California Press, 2001.

Moorhouse, Geoffrey. Imperial City: The Rise and Rise of New York. London: Hodder & Stoughton, 1981.

Morris, Lloyd. Incredible New York: High Life and Low Life of the Last 100 Years. New York: Random House, 1951.

Myers, Gustavus. History of Tammany Hall. New York: Dover Publications, 1971.

Nash, Jay Robert. Bloodletters and Badmen. New York: M. Evans & Co., 1973.

Nelli, Humbert S. The Business of Crime: Italians and Syndicate Crime in the United States. New York: Oxford University Press, 1976.

O'Connor, Richard. Courtroom Warrior: The Combative Career of William Travers Jerome. Boston: Little, Brown, 1963.

Official Commendations of the 27th American Division, Belgium and France, 1918. Paris, 1918(?).

Order of Battle of the United States Land Forces in the World War. Washington, D.C.: Center of Military History, 1987 (facsimile reprint of 1931 edition).

O'Ryan, John F. History of the 27th Division: New York's Own. New York, 1919.

————. Story of the 27th Division. New York, 1921.

Osman, Alfred Henry. Pigeons in the Great War: A Complete History of the Carrier-Pigeon Service During the Great War, 1914–1918. London, 1928.

Parkhurst, Rev. Charles Henry. A Little Lower than the Angels. New York, 1908.

————. My Forty Years in New York. New York, 1923.

————. Our Fight with Tammany. New York, 1895.

Pasley, Fred D. Al Capone; The Biography of a Self-Made Man. Binghamton, N.Y.: Ives Washburn, 1930.

Patterson, Jerry E. The City of New York: A History Illustrated from the Collection of the Museum of the City of New York. New York: Abrams, 1978.

Peterson, H. C. and Gilbert C. Fite. Opponents of War. Seattle: University of Washington Press, 1971.

Peterson, Virgil W. The Mob: 200 Years of Organized Crime in New York. Ottawa, Ill.: Green Hill, 1983.

Peixotto, Ernest. The American Front. New York, 1919.

Piehler, G. Kurt. Remembering War the American Way. Washington, D.C.: Smithsonian, 1995.

Pilat, Oliver, and Jo Ranson. Sodom by the Sea; An Affectionate History of Coney Island. Garden City, N.Y., 1941.

Pizzitola, Louis. Hearst over Hollywood: Power, Passion, and Propaganda in the Movies. New York: Columbia University Press, 2002.

Regier, C. C. The Era of the Muckrakers. Chapel Hill: University of North Carolina Press, 1932.

Reid, Ed. The Shame of New York. London: Gollancz, 1954.

Report of the Council of Hygiene and Public Health of the Citizens' Association of New York upon the Sanitary Condition of the City. New York, 1866.

Report and Proceedings of the Senate Committee Appointed to Investigate the Police Department of the City of New York, volumes 9–13. Albany, N.Y., 1895.

Report of the Special Committee of the Assembly Appointed to Investigate the Public Officers and Departments of the City of New York and of the Counties Therein (Mazet Committee), volumes 1–5. Albany, N.Y., 1900.

Ricks, Christopher, and William L. Vance (eds.). The Faber Book of America. London: Faber and Faber, 1992.

Rider, Fremont (ed.). Rider's New York City. New York, 1924.

Riis, Jacob A. How the Other Half Lives: Studies Among the Tenements of New York. New York: Dover Publications, 1971.

――――. The Battle with the Slum. Mineola, N.Y.: Dover Publications, 1998.

――――. A Ten Years' War: An Account of the Battle with the Slum in New York. Boston, 1900.

Riordan, William L. Plunkitt of Tammany Hall. New York, 1905.

Rockaway, Robert A. But He Was Good to His Mother: The Lives and Crimes of Jewish Gangsters. Jerusalem: Gefen, 2000.

Rosen, Ruth. The Lost Sisterhood: Prostitution in America, 1900–1918. Baltimore: Johns Hopkins University Press, 1982.

Roskolenko, Harry. The Time That Was Then; The Lower East Side, 1900–1914, An Intimate Chronicle. New York: Dial Press, 1971.

Rowan, Richard Wilmer. The Pinkertons: A Detective Dynasty. Boston, Mass., 1931.

Sanders, Ronald. The Lower East Side Jews: An Immigrant Generation. Mineola, N.Y.: Dover Publications, 1999.

――――. The Lower East Side: A Guide to Its Jewish Past. New York: Dover Publications, 1979.

Sante, Luc. Low Life: Lures and Snares of Old New York. London: Granta Books, 1998.

Schmidt, Donald E. The Folly of War: American Foreign Policy, 1898–2005. New York: Algora Publishing, 2005.

Schoen, Elliott. History of the 107th US Infantry, AEF, in the Battle of the Hindenburg Line, September 29, 1918, During World War I. New York: Press Work, 1968.

Schoener, Allon. Portal to America: The Lower East Side, 1870–1925. New York: Holt, Rinehart & Winston, 1967.

A Short History and Illustrated Roster of the 106th Infantry United States, Colonel Frank H. Norton Commanding. Philadelphia, 1918.

Sibley, Frank P. With the Yankee Division in France. Boston, 1919.

Siegel, Larry J. Criminology. Belmont, Calif.: West/Wadsworth Publishing Company, 1998.

Silver, Nathan. Lost New York. Boston: Houghton Mifflin, 1967.

Slang Dictionary of New York, London and Paris. New York, 1881.

Sloat, Warren. A Battle for the Soul of New York: Tammany Hall, Police Corruption, Vice and the Reverend Charles Parkurst's Crusade Against Them, 1892–1895. Lanham, Md.: Cooper Square Press, 2002.

Smith, Matthew Hale. Sunshine and Shadows in New York. Hartford, Conn., 1869.

Smith, Betty. A Tree Grows in Brooklyn. New York, 1943.

Smythe, Donald. Pershing: General of the Armies. Bloomington: Indiana University Press, 1986.

Souvenir of Camp Wadsworth, Spartanburg, S.C. Atlanta, 1917(?).

Spann, Edward K. The New Metropolis. New York: Columbia University Press, 1981.

Squires, Amos O. Sing Sing Doctor. Garden City, N.Y., 1935.

Stallings, Lawrence. The Doughboys. New York: Harper & Row, 1964.

Stallman, Robert Wooster. Stephen Crane: A Biography. New York: George Braziller, 1968.

Starlight, Alexander. Pictorial Record of the 27th Division. New York, 1919.

Steffens, Lincoln. The Autobiography of Lincoln Steffens (2 vols.). New York, 1931.

————. Shame of the Cities. London, 1904.

Strunsky, Simeon. No Mean City. New York, 1944.

Sutliffe, Robert Stewart. Seventy-First New York in the World War. New York, 1922.

Swetland, Maurice J., and Lilli Swetland. These Men: For Conspicuous Bravery Above and Beyond the Call of Duty . . . Harrisburg, Penn., 1940.

Syrett, Harold Coffin. The City of Brooklyn 1865–1898. New York, 1944.

Szucs, Loretto Dennis. Ellis Island: Tracing Your Family History Through America's Gateway. Provo, Utah: Ancestry Publishing, 1986.

Thomas, Lately. The Mayor Who Mastered New York: The Life and Opinions of William J. Gaynor. New York: Willliam Morrow, 1969.

Thomason, John W. Fix Bayonets! New York, 1926.

Thompson, Craig, and Allen Raymond. Gang Rule in New York; The Story of a Lawless Era. New York, 1940.

Thrasher, Frederic Milton. The Gang: A Study of 1,313 Gangs in Chicago. Chicago, 1927.

Tupper, Harmon. To the Great Ocean. London: Secker & Warburg, 1965.

Tyler, Ronnie C. The Big Bend: A History of the Last Texas Frontier. Washington, D.C.: U.S. National Park Service, 1975.

University Settlement Society. University Settlement Society of New York, Annual Reports, 1895–1905. New York, 1895–1901.

Valentine, Lewis J. Night Stick: The Autobiography of Lewis J. Valentine, Former Police Commissioner of New York. New York: Dial Press, 1947.

Vices of a Big City. New York, 1890.

The Volcano Under the City. New York, 1887.

Wakeman, Abram. History of Lower Wall Street and Vicinity. New York, 1914.

Walker, John Otey. Official History of the 120th Infantry. Lynchburg, Tenn., 1919.

Walsh, George. Public Enemies: The Mayor and The Mob and The Crime That Was. New York: Norton, 1980.

Ward, Franklin Wilmer. Between the Big Parades. New York, 1932.

Waterman, Willoughby. Prostitution and Its Repression in New York City, 1900–1931. New York, 1932.

Werner, Morris Robert. Tammany Hall. New York, 1932.

Whitman, Walt. Complete Poetry and Collected Prose. New York: Library of America, 1982.

Willemse, Cornelius. Behind the Green Lights. New York, 1931.

Wodehouse, P. G. Psmith Journalist. New York: Penguin, 1981.

Yockelson, Mitchell A. Borrowed Soldiers: Americans Under British Command, 1918. Norman: University of Oklahoma Press, 2008.

Zieger, Robert H. America's Great War. Lanham, Md.: Rowman & Littlefield, 2000.

Zinn, Howard. A People's History of the United States. London: Longman, 1980.

DIRECTORIES

Lain's Brooklyn City Directory, 1862–1900

R. L. Polk and Co.'s Trow's New York City Directory, 1915–1920

Trow's New York City Directory, 1861–1913

Uppington's General Directory of Brooklyn, New York City, 1902–1920

WEBSITES

http://www.oryansroughnecks.org/index.html

http://www.ls.net/~newriver/ww1/26div.htm

http://www.u-s-history.com/pages/h1086.html

http://www.ossininghistorical.org/

www.worldwar1.com/dbc/meastman.htm

http://www.correctionhistory.org/

http://herbertasbury.com/billthebutcher/eastman.asp

www.immigrantheritagetrail.org/?q=node/1540

http://www.loc.gov/rr/frd/Military_Law/AW-1912-1920.html

http://www.changingthetimes.net/samples/ww1/chosen_few1.htm

http://warandgame.wordpress.com/2007/10/27/the-first-world-war-and-propaganda/

http://academic.udayton.edu/health/syllabi/tobacco/history2.htm#1

INDEX

Page numbers in *italic* refer to maps.

A NOTE ABOUT THE AUTHOR

Neil Hanson's other books include *The Confident Hope of a Miracle* and *Unknown Soldiers*. He lives in the Yorkshire Dales in England.

A NOTE ON THE TYPE

This book was set in a version of the well-known Monotype face Bembo. This letter was cut for the celebrated Venetian printer Aldus Manutius by Francesco Griffo and first used in Pietro Cardinal Bembo's De Aetna of 1495.

The companion italic is an adaptation of the chancery script type designed by the calligrapher and printer Lodovico degli Arrighi.